The Poison Murders
of Jack the Ripper

ALSO BY R. MICHAEL GORDON

The Space Shuttle Program: How NASA Lost Its Way
(McFarland, 2008)

The Thames Torso Murders of Victorian London
(McFarland, 2002)

Alias Jack the Ripper: Beyond the Usual Whitechapel Suspects
(McFarland, 2001)

The Poison Murders of Jack the Ripper

His Final Crimes, Trial and Execution

R. Michael Gordon

McFarland & Company, Inc., Publishers
Jefferson, North Carolina, and London

Material in the Public Record Office is the copyright
of the Metropolitan Police and is reproduced by permission
of the Commissioner of Police of the Metropolis.

LIBRARY OF CONGRESS CATALOGUING-IN-PUBLICATION DATA

Gordon, R. Michael, 1952–
The poison murders of Jack the Ripper : his final crimes, trial and
execution / R. Michael Gordon.
p.   cm.
Includes bibliographical references and index.

ISBN 978-0-7864-3327-8
softcover : 50# alkaline paper ∞

1. Jack, the Ripper.
2. Klosowski, Severino Antoniovich, 1865–1903.
3. Serial murders—United States—History—Case studies.
4. Serial murders—England—London—History—Case studies.
5. Serial murder investigation—History—Case studies.
I. Title.
HV6524.G673   2008   364.152'3092—dc22   2008018622

British Library cataloguing data are available

©2008 R. Michael Gordon. All rights reserved

*No part of this book may be reproduced or transmitted in any form
or by any means, electronic or mechanical, including photocopying
or recording, or by any information storage and retrieval system,
without permission in writing from the publisher.*

Cover photograph ©2008 Shutterstock

Manufactured in the United States of America

*McFarland & Company, Inc., Publishers
Box 611, Jefferson, North Carolina 28640
www.mcfarlandpub.com*

For Mary, Bessie and Maud

Acknowledgments

In 1930 Hargrave Lee Adam edited a work on Severin Klosowski as part of the *Notable British Trials* series. That book was *Trial of George Chapman*, which detailed the poison case which ended with the capital murder trial of Severin Klosowski for the murder of Maud Marsh. It would be this work which would point to Klosowski as a possible candidate for the mantle of Jack the Ripper. Though hard evidence could not be presented, the circumstantial case, even though certain aspects have since been shown to have been in error, was staggering. It is to this work and editor I look as the first to publish in book form the trial of the man who I believe will eventually be proven to have committed the series of crimes known to the world as the "Jack the Ripper" murders.

A thank you to artist Robert DeLaCruz for his graphic contributions and his artistic interpretation of case artwork for this book.

I would also thank Debbie Gosling, who was working full-time as a writer and researcher at a South London newspaper for her continued research and insightful questions into the case of George Chapman. The tiny details she has found certainly have brought much light into the dark world of this Victorian serial killer.

A grateful thank you must also go to the special collections library and computer staff of California State University at Dominguez Hills, as well as a special thanks to my friend John Hearn of the Earth Science Department for his computer and research help. Also a computer thank you goes to Pene Hills, who was kind enough to loan me her computer and time when I needed it most.

Finally, I must thank all of those who have encouraged me to write about the Victorian period and the interesting people who walked those dark and foggy cobble stonestreets so long ago — Teresa C. Eidenbock, Jeanne Cartier, Gene Schwedler, Carole Fraser, Dr. Rudolph Campos, Richard Montagna, Larry and Lee Ann Quigley, Elizabeth Wharry, Mrs. Ruth Victoria Todd, Steve Mateski, and all the hard working folks at "It's A Grind" coffee house in Long Beach, California, who kept the coffee going as I sat for hours in the corner scribbling on my writing pad.

Cheers to all as we continue to pull back the misty Victorian veil of time in search of Jack the Ripper.

R. Michael Gordon
May 2008

Table of Contents

Acknowledgments	vii
Prologue — A Young Man from Poland	1

Section I — A Background of Serial Murder

1. The Ripper and Torso Murders	3
2. The American Murders of Jack the Ripper	37

Section II — The Poison Work of Jack the Ripper

3. A Serial Killer Returns to London	49
4. Mrs. Spink and a Man Called Chapman	57
5. The Slow Death of Bessie Taylor	71
6. A Barmaid Named Maud	81
7. A Death at George's American Bar	89
8. The Arrest of a Serial Killer	100

Section III — The Investigation of a Serial Killer

9. The Investigation Begins: Other Crimes and a Final Torso	109
10. Coroner Waldo's Inquest: The Maud Marsh Matter	115
11. The Police Court Does Its Work: The Case of the Borough Poisoner	133
12. The Police Court Continues: Focus on Mrs. Spink and Bessie Taylor	139

Section IV — The King's Justice

13. The First Day of Trial: The Case of the Borough Poisoner	151
14. The Second Day of Testimony	162
15. Requiem for a Serial Killer	170
16. "You've Got Jack the Ripper at Last"	178

Section V — The Future of Jack the Ripper

17. A Century of Speculation and a Pub called the Crown — 183

Appendix I. A Chronology of the Borough Poisoner — 201
Bibliography — 203
Index — 209

Prologue:
A Young Man from Poland

History would record that Severin Antoniovich Klosowski was a serial killer and, like all serial killers, he held many secrets. Much has become known, however, due to the work of investigators leading up to his 1903 trial for the murder of one woman, but it is not by any means a full and complete record. Over the years this man from Poland would use many aliases and put down many false trails. Indeed, he would seem to be almost constantly on the move as more and more mysterious murders occurred in his deadly wake. His journey began on December 14, 1865, in a small village in Russian-occupied Poland. In the village of Nagornak a child had been born destined to someday carry the mantle of the most infamous serial killer of all time — Jack the Ripper!

There are no records to show whether or not this deceptive killer followed a classic path to serial death, but if he did he would have been responsible for setting fires and torturing small animals. And he would have seemed somehow out of place, but not enough to place any real suspicion upon himself; indeed, at most times he would have appeared to be quite normal and well adjusted. His first teacher, Mr. Merkish, would note that from October 1873 to June 1880 young Severin "completed the full term of studies of the first department, and his conduct throughout his attendance at the school was very good." It is doubtful that history will ever reveal what events transpired to push this "very good student" into becoming a mad killer, but many serial killers point to abuse of a sexual nature at a young age as a key turning point. Betrayal by a trusted family member has been shown to leave a lasting effect and perhaps Severin felt he was betrayed by a woman near to him — most likely his mother. Yet she may not have done anything out of the ordinary to cause this deadly effect. Only the twisted mind of Severin needed to be convinced of such a betrayal to push him to commit unspeakable atrocities.

By age 15, in December of 1880, Severin found himself apprenticed to Senior Surgeon Moshko Rappaport for four and a half years of surgical training. He had found his niche and he would prove to be exceptionally good at cutting up bodies. For Klosowski it would be the first time he was away from his parents and the first time he would feel the power of life and death in his ever more skillful hands. It would be noted by Doctor Moshkovski, a surgeon in Warsaw who employed him for nearly 10 months during 1886, that his new assistant had "performed his surgical functions with a full knowledge of the subject and his conduct was good." History records that Severin had learned to use a knife with great skill, and he was ready to test those skills.

These were the skills that caught the eye of the military in 1886, but 20-year-old Severin was able to obtain a deferment until the next year. It would be the year 1887 that would prove to be a turning point in the life of this future serial killer as the military draft loomed large over his now advancing career and perhaps well-to-do lifestyle. He had his own home at 16 Muranovskaja Street in Warsaw and had applied for the degree of junior surgeon to the dean of the medical faculty of the Imperial University of Warsaw. The reply came with speed: "The Medical Administration hereby testify to the effect that they do not see any reason to oppose his receiving the degree of Junior Surgeon."

On February 28, 1887, Severin paid his hospital fees of 4 rubles for the next month. That receipt would be the last evidence of his life in Poland. Did he run away from military service or did he murder someone and need to leave the country in a great hurry? History is silent on that point. We do, however, know where he fled. He is next found working as a barber in one of the worst ghettos of Europe — the East End of London. And he was ready to kill!

Severin Antoniovich Klosowski, alias George Chapman, from a photograph found by Inspector George Godley at the Crown Public House.

Section I — A Background of Serial Murder

Chapter 1

The Ripper and Torso Murders

Death at the hands of person or persons unknown.
— Coroner's inquest

Victorian London — Late Nineteenth Century

Victorian London has the appeal of being very far away in time and space from our world of the early 21st century so we tend not to see it as it really was. It has become an almost mystical place of gaslights, deep fog, cobblestone streets and proper people going about the work of building a world empire. Indeed, London was thought of as the "World's Metropolis," where an aging queen sat on her gilded throne and all was right with the world. However, as time passes and memories fade we tend to forget that a very large segment of London's population at the time lived in abject poverty a little more than a mile from that throne of Queen Victoria's at Buckingham Palace, held captive to misery in the East End ghettos of London.

The reality of life was harsh for the residents of the East End, once described by American writer Jack London as the "Abyss." It was an overstressed, overcrowded, crime-ridden ghetto and one of the worst in Europe at the time; even today there are areas where it is not safe to walk after dark. It was a place of deep daily despair, widespread poverty and filth in which a child born in that area could expect to have at best a 50/50 chance of seeing a fifth birthday. It was, as London wrote, "A huge man-killing machine." Much of the East End was considered a "throwaway" even though it could brag of the oldest and longest established business in all of London, that of Mears and Stainbanks bell founding, which had been in operation since 1570. Fires were also common in the East End, especially along the docks, which lined the Thames River. Yet, Whitechapel could also lay claim to the location for William Booth's Christian Mission in 1865, situated on Angel Alley. The Christian Mission would become known as the Salvation Army after 1878. Booth himself would report that anywhere from 60,000 to 80,000 women worked, at least part of the time simply to survive, as prostitutes on the streets of London in the 1880s, and he demanded something be done about it.

Onto this less-than-savory scene, barely endured by "outcast London," came an immigrant from war-ravaged Europe whose crimes would so outrage an already hard-pressed population that they would forever link a single square mile of the East End, centered on Whitechapel, to his bloody deeds during that "Autumn of Terror" in 1888. He would become known worldwide as "Jack the Ripper" and no one who lived in the East End at the time would ever know who he really was. Jack, it would seem, knew how to keep a secret or two.

A dark and deadly shadow was about to fall over Whitechapel, but the path of death did not begin in the East End. This serial killer would travel upriver along the Thames before settling in that distant London ghetto. The murders would begin unexpectedly in Rainham in May 1887, with the first of the Thames "Torso" murders discovered fully 15 months before the "Ripper" murders captured the fears and imaginations of not only Victorian London but also the rest of the civilized world. Yet, this first brutal crime would barely register a ripple on the collective consciousness of a London population already struggling to stay alive. One more dead woman meant very little to anyone, especially since she would never be identified. The rest of the world would hear little of this first murder and official London was not paying any attention at all.

RAINHAM, SOUTHEAST OF LONDON — MAY 1887

During the Torso murder series the river Thames would always play a part in the activities of this serial killer, as it would become a favorite location for the disposal of unwanted body parts. And, even when he disposed of the torsos and limbs in other areas, they were always found within short walking distance of the Thames or one of its many canals. Yet, even as the London police added patrols on and off of the river, he continued to drop bits and pieces of his victims, using the river's current to transport those pieces down river. Later, London authorities would do their best to distance this series of murders from those of the Ripper, but they were never able to prove whether or not the same vicious killer was responsible for both sets of crimes, having captured no one responsible for any of the murders, Torso or Ripper. Time and reflection, however, suggest that one man could very well have been responsible for both, as perhaps the reasons for the murders were different.

Two men working near the ferry at Rainham in Essex would be the first to discover that a serial killer had begun his deadly work. A wrapped, coarse canvas bundle was spotted floating past their workplace in the early morning and it was soon brought to shore. To their horror and surprise they discovered, upon opening the bundle, the ripped torso of a young woman whose arms, head and legs had been cut off. Before long the local police began a search of the immediate area in a vain attempt to find more of the unfortunate woman's body. They would be unsuccessful in their searches until the killer deposited more parts in the river. He wanted them around for a while.

The authorities would have to wait until June 8 for the next bundle to float down the river. It contained the missing limbs, which were soon matched to the torso by Dr. Calloway, the local police surgeon who had been called into the case. The final remains would be located by a man walking near the river at Regent's Canal near Chalk Farm. At first, due to the time the package had spent in the water, authorities felt that a new murder of a much older woman had occurred. However, closer examination would reveal that there had not been an additional murder — at least not yet!

On August 13, 1887, an inquest was held in Crowndale Hall in Camden Town by the coroner, Dr. G. Danford Thomas. The victim had not been identified in time for the inquest, which was not unexpected because the victim's head had not been located and, indeed, never would be found. However, the doctors had worked out a general description of the woman. She had been in her twenties, five feet four inches in height, and had never had a child. The doctors had also discovered that an individual with knowledge of anatomy had cut off the arms, head and legs. The disturbing fact was that she had probably been killed by one of their own! Without a suspect, however, it would be "Death at the hands of person or persons unknown." Despite the brutality of this seemingly singular crime, there was very little outrage and by the time of the

Ripper murders the Rainham mystery would be all but forgotten by the people of London. After all, there was much more pressing business at hand.

In December 1887 there was a large gathering held at the Unicorn Tavern in Shoreditch, East End. The occasion was a farewell party for Police Inspector Frederick George Abberline, who had recently completed 14 years of service in the area and was now being transferred to Scotland Yard headquarters. He was presented a gold hunting watch with the inscription: "Presented, together with a purse of gold, to Inspector F. G. Abberline by the inhabitants of Spitalfields, Whitechapel, etc., on his leaving the district after 14 years service, as a mark of their esteem and regard." He would not, however, stay away from "his district" for long, as there was a growing evil nearby and the people of the East End would need one of the best to help put an end to the terror soon to enter their midst in the East End.

It was also noted in local papers that a woman named Margaret Hames had been attacked on December 8 by an unknown man. She was admitted to Whitechapel infirmary with chest and face injuries, possibly inflicted by a knife. She would be released on December 27, 1887. Was this the first attack by Jack the Ripper?

London, East End — 1888

The era of the Ripper murders began with two clumsy attacks on East End prostitutes that could easily have been mistaken simply as background happenings in the everyday brutality of that Victorian ghetto if not for events that would soon quickly unfold. On February 25, 1888, a stranger to Annie Millwood came to the cheap rundown lodging house at 8 White's Row in Spitalfields where she paid for her nightly bed and, without saying a word, took out a clasp knife. Without warning and for no known reason the man stabbed her numerous times in the lower torso and legs as she stood near the front door. Unseen by anyone, her attacker then escaped into the night, leaving Annie bloodied and confused. This attack, as with future Ripper murders, had occurred on a weekend or a holiday.

Annie would survive the attack, but she would die within weeks of an unrelated "sudden effusion into the pericardium from the rupture of the left pulmonary artery through ulceration." She was only 38 years old but death was a common event among the hard-pressed residents of the East End so it was not all that unusual. Her attacker had been very clumsy, and it was far from certain that he even knew his victim. Most likely Annie was simply in the wrong place at the wrong time when the attacker came to that cheap lodging house looking for a target. Later events would show that three years almost to the day, and nine victims later, Jack the Ripper would again choose a victim from that very same building at 8 White's Row. It would become the setting for the final attack under the mantle of Jack the Ripper, but in February of 1888 the series of death had just begun and the killer had yet to acquire his terrifying and unforgettable name.

The next attack nearly caused the killer to be captured, but he would learn a great deal from this second attempt a little more than a month later. On March 28, prostitute Ada Wilson was at home around 12:30 in the morning when a man she had never seen before came to her front door. He soon forced his way into 19 Maidman Street, Mile End, demanding money and telling Ada that "she would not have long to live" if she did not give her money to him. Ada refused, perhaps because she had no money to give, and she was stabbed twice in the throat with a small-bladed knife. It was a clumsy attempt to kill her but it failed as Ada let out a scream that even in the vicious East End caused her neighbors to come running. They were soon hot on the heels of her attacker, but he managed just barely to make his escape into the darkness and coal-choked fog that was nearly always present in Victorian London.

From this attack came the first crude description of "Jack." Ada told the police that he was "a man around 30 years of age with a sun burnt face, fair moustache, standing 5 feet 6 inches in height." It was the description of a man about to become a serial killer. As for Ada, she would spend a month in London Hospital recovering from her ordeal. Her attacker had escaped with two important lessons learned. He would learn to have a hideout close by and to use a sharper, longer-bladed knife. The last thing a serial killer would need would be a living witness to his crimes. He would keep the small-bladed knife for a while longer but he would not make the same mistake again as he struggled to learn his "craft."

For their part, the police were making use of their abilities to communicate and respond to criminal activity as best they could. By 1888 the police had positioned 10 experimental "telephone boxes" around the city, which were accessible by key. None, however, would be located in "Jack's territory" for a very long time. Added to this innovation was the telegraph that most police stations had installed, yet this method would prove to be woefully inadequate for the job ahead.

For a while the detectives on the case were led astray by these and other attacks because some were certainly committed by a gang, possibly the High Rip Gang. As the two women became victims it was first thought that prostitutes were being attacked for not giving up their money for protection. This theory would soon fall by the wayside. There were, however, many gangs in the area, such as the Hoxton High Rips, Limehouse Forty Thieves, Blind Beggar Gang and many others, including gangs made up entirely of young girls.

WHITECHAPEL, EAST END—AUGUST 1888

The killer seems to have moved to Whitechapel just after the unsuccessful attacks on the two women. He now had his lair very close to many prostitute/targets of opportunity and he went nightly (on weekends at least) on the hunt. The first to die would not be found on a cobblestone street, despite the lore of the Ripper. She would come to him and die in the very dwelling he lived in! The first would also be an unintended composite killing, as evidence leads to the conclusion that two men were involved; yet, they probably never saw or even knew each other.

Martha Tabram was a 39-year-old prostitute who spent her last full day of life, August 6, 1888, drinking and finding men to pay for her bed and drinks late into the night. Martha and a friend, Mary Ann Connally, a fellow prostitute, were socializing with a pair of soldiers. Later that evening at around 11:45 P.M. the couples separated to "conduct a bit of business." Mary Ann went into Angel Alley and Martha went with her private into the darkness of George Yard. The Ripper, better known in the area as junior surgeon/barber Severin Antoniovich Klosowski, lived in the George Yard Dwellings on one of the upper floors, only yards from where Martha would be found, and he would be interviewed later by the police. He would not need to look very far for this victim. She came to him.

Cabdriver George Crow also lived in the George Yard Dwellings, and he returned home early that morning from his long day of work to find a woman on the landing. At 3:30 in the morning of August 7, he made his way past the first floor landing to his rooms, spotting this individual whom he thought was sleeping on the floor. This was not unusual for the East End of 1888, so he took no real notice. That individual was later identified as Martha Tabram, and she had been stabbed in the heart by a weapon closely resembling a bayonet. She had been dead for about an hour at that point, but there was no large pool of blood for Mr. Crow to walk through, not yet at least.

By 4:45 that morning Martha's body had again been attacked and mutilated, this time by a frenzied killer who had yet to complete a single known successful murder in the East End. At

Although most of the Ripper murders occurred in a single square mile of the East End of London, all lived in an area no larger than 300 by 150 yards (map by the author).

that time dockside laborer John Saunders Reeves left his upstairs room and walked down to the first floor landing. The lighting was a bit better at the time, but it did not prevent him from slipping on the expanding pool of blood on that first floor landing. What he saw shocked him even for a man who had lived most of his life in the ghettos of the East End. Her clothes "were turned up as far as the center of the body, leaving the lower part of the body exposed...." She had been stabbed 39 times, mostly of a sexual nature. One deadly blow was to the heart (probably by the bayonet) and she was stabbed 38 more times with a much smaller blade — these extra wounds were the blows most likely struck by the Ripper. With this composite murder the Ripper would learn his final lesson — to use a much larger blade, and with that lesson he would never fail to kill again. No one would ever again crawl away from one of his attacks. He was now the master of his craft and he was ready to get back to work!

It would not be long before Inspector Edmond Reid, local head of CID, was placed in charge of the case. He was one of the first to later state that this was the first murder in the Ripper series, which he believed to total nine.

The newspapers were quick to form their own theories. The *East London Advertiser* reported on August 18, 1888: "The police seem to be as far from solving the mystery as they were on the morning the crime was committed. The police state that they should not be at all surprised to find that the murder was not entirely the work of soldiers or that soldiers had a hand in the crime at all. Old bayonets, they assert, can at any time be bought in Petticoat Lane, and at the old iron stalls there, for about a penny each...."

It had been a vicious crime that shocked the East End as even the inquest jury was reminded: "This was one of the most horrible crimes that had been committed for certainly some time past. [The victim was] foully and brutally murdered."

On August 31, the Ripper would strike again along a dark and dirty cobblestone street named Buck's Row. Polly Nichols was a 43-year-old prostitute who was so ill that she would not have lived long even without her visit to Buck's Row. On that dark night she was drunk, staggering and barely able to move, which is just the way the Ripper, a true coward to be sure, liked his victims. It would be an easy kill as he first strangled Polly and then drew his very sharp blade across her throat twice — deeply. Unconscious in seconds, she would have died in less than a minute. Jack never wasted any time.

At around 3:30 in the morning as constables patrolled the nearby streets the Ripper began to open up Polly's still warm and steaming body. He attacked the abdomen in an apparent attempt to remove some of the organs, but it was very dark in Buck's Row so he would fail in the attempt. He wanted whole organs, not just bits and pieces. If this was the true reason for the murder then he had failed once again to accomplish his task. He would, however, try again!

Polly would soon be found by two men coming from one direction and, soon after, as they searched for a constable, she would also be discovered by an officer on patrol. It looked to the men like a piece of tarpaulin at first, but, upon closer inspection, they found it to be a body lying next to the gutter. Neither man noticed in the dim light that she had been ripped open or that her eyes were open, staring straight up at them.

PC John Neil discovers the body of Polly Nichols in Buck's Row (*Illustrated Police News*, September 1888).

Before long the police surgeon was at the site to declare death, and the blood would be washed away. Only later would Dr. Llewellyn find that she had literally been gutted. "I have seen many terrible cases, but never such a brutal affair as this." As for the killer, there was at the time no description of the man, who had quietly walked away only to fade into the morning traffic on Whitechapel Road and a new dawn in the "Abyss."

It did not take long for the hard-pressed residents of the East End to take measures into their own hands. Vigilance committees made up of local men began conducting patrols in and around the areas of Whitechapel, Spitalfields and Mile End. As might be expected, some of the groups were not overly concerned about the condition of the "suspects" they brought to the local police stations. The police themselves more than doubled their patrols pulling men from other areas of the great city in an attempt to capture the mad Whitechapel killer. One of the better known groups was one made of businessmen, who formed the Mile End Vigilance Committee. It would be this group under the guidance of builder/contractor Mr. George Lusk who would come into direct contact through the mails, and perhaps a bit more, with the killer.

IMPORTANT NOTICE

To the tradesmen, Ratepayers, and Inhabitants Generally of Whitechapel and District.—Finding that in spite of Murders being committed in our midst, and that the Murderer or Murderers are still at large, we the undersigned have formed ourselves into a Committee, and intend offering a substantial REWARD to anyone, Citizen, or otherwise, who shall give such information that will bring the Murderer or Murderers to Justice. A Committee of Gentlemen has already been formed to carry out the above object, and will meet every evening at nine o'clock, at Mr. J. Aaron's the "Crown," 74 Mile End Road, corner of Jubilee Street, and will be pleased to receive the assistance of the residents of the District....

As for the investigation into Polly's death, even though the police canvassed the common lodging houses in the area and interviewed local residents and prostitutes, no hard evidence was ever found which could point to her killer's identity. The spot where Polly had met her death soon became an area of curiosity as groups of visitors from around London, and eventually the world, came to see where the killer had struck. In fact, so many came that one man set up a piano organ and entertained anyone who cared to listen to his rendition of *Men of Harlech*. The East End was always a grand mix of despair, death and bizarre episodes of normalcy.

SPITALFIELDS, EAST END—SEPTEMBER 1888

As fears began to grow that a serial killer (not a term used at the time) was stalking the back streets and allies of the East End of London, local papers and, very soon, the world press began daily and sensational front-page coverage. At times local papers put out several editions in one day, as reporters swarmed into the ghetto. The press could not keep up with the demand as the government began to worry about possible riots breaking out. They would soon have more to be concerned about as the killer quickened his pace.

It had been a long cold night for Annie Chapman as she searched the streets for one last customer. It would be just before dawn when she met a man in front of 29 Hanbury Street who would "invite" her into the building's small backyard. As she said "yes," a friend of hers named Elizabeth Long walked slowly past. It was 5:30 A.M. September 8, and Annie had less than 15 minutes to live. Later, Long would give the first detailed description, albeit from a back view, of the man all of London would soon be looking for.

At 5:45 that morning car man John Davis, who lived at 29 Hanbury Street along with 16 other residents, made his way to the small backyard to use the outhouse. Before he could even enter the yard by the old back door he spotted Chapman's body in the early morning light. She was obviously dead. Just as obviously she had been savagely mutilated. Before long detectives and police surgeons would arrive to investigate this latest murder, as large crowds formed around Hanbury Street.

The yard itself was no more than a few flat stones with sections of dirt showing through. Looking closely at the wooden fence, Inspector Chandler, the first detective on the scene, was able to see that there were no signs of anyone having climbed over to escape the small yard. The killer had come and gone through a fully occupied tenement building and escaped without being seen by anyone in the building.

It was soon discovered that Chapman had been subdued by strangulation before having her throat deeply ripped open. Her abdomen had been opened and her intestines had been taken out and placed on her shoulder. Her uterus, upper vagina and two-thirds of her bladder had been cut away and removed. The taking of body parts had begun in earnest. The Ripper had found a place and time hidden from general view yet well enough lit to allow his "surgical work" to go on. Later, he would show the world how "good" he really was by working in the dark of night and cutting out several organs at the same time.

Once again the killer would simply walk away and fade into the din of an early Whitechapel morning. Later the corpse of Annie Chapman would be removed in the same old mortuary shell which had so recently held the remains of Polly Nichols.

It would not take long for news of this latest murder to be flashed around London and, soon after, the world. Reports focused on a leather apron found in a basin in the yard as posters began to be seen around the East End calling for the capture of a man known as "Leather Apron." A local thug and part-time butcher named John Pizer, well known for harassing local prostitutes, soon became the prime suspect. It would not be long, however, before Pizer was captured and soon released as he was clearly not the "Whitechapel Killer."

For some the news in the local papers was so disturbing that they simply could not handle reading about these deaths. One such individual was Mrs. Mary Burridge, a resident of 132 Blackfriars Road in the heart of the killing ground, who passed out reading the *Star* newspaper. She regained consciousness; however, two days later, on September 12, she was found dead.

The *Star* was living up to its first editorial in January. "The *Star* will be a radical journal. It will judge all policy—domestic, foreign, social—from the radical standpoint. Londoners are ruled by one of the worst and most corrupt oligarchies that ever disgraced and robbed [a] city...." It would not be untrue to report that the radical press, led by the *Star*, were more than happy to take full advantage of the situation in order to advance their political agenda. The first London County Council elections were coming soon and it was possible for the radicals to take control of the East End.

It would be a long cold "Autumn of Terror" for the official forces of Her Majesty's government. As for the murder site at 29 Hanbury Street—one may now visit the area and stay at a hotel which has been built on the site. It is a hotel which is said to play host to not only Annie Chapman's ghost but to the ghost of Jack the Ripper as well!

There had also been a less-publicized attack on a 64-year-old woman named Susan Ward. She had survived so the press were not really interested. Ward was described in reports as "a drunk married prostitute" once again working the East End off of Commercial Street on September 15. Instead of a paying client she had run into a man who pulled a knife; but Susan, despite her age and drunken condition, was not about to go down easy. She fought off her attacker sustaining a deep cut on her upper arm, requiring her to seek treatment at London Hospital. Her screams and spirited defense of her life had scared off her attacker, who may have been Jack the Ripper. Her attack had also come on a weekend.

The names "Whitechapel Killer" and "Leather Apron" had been used by the local population and were soon picked up by the press. But these would not be used for long, as a new twist to the bizarre story was about to unfold. The killer was about to acquire a new name and it would be one which would keep this series of murders in the public's mind for well over a century—"Jack the Ripper." The new name would come from a letter sent to a local news agency. It was the later to be famous "Dear Boss" letter.

Dear Boss, 25. Sept. 1888

    I keep on hearing the police have caught me but they won't fix me just yet. I have laughed when they look so clever and talk about being on the right track. That joke about Leather Apron gave me real fits. I am down on whores and I shan't quit ripping them till I do get buckled. Grand work the last job was. I gave the lady no time to squeal. How can they catch me now? I love my work and want to start again. You will soon hear of me with my funny little games. I saved some of the proper red stuff in a ginger beer bottle over the last job to write down with but it went thick like glue and I can't use it. Red ink is fit enough I hope ha ha. The next job I do I shall clip the ladys ears off and send them to the police officers just for jolly wouldn't you. Keep this letter back till I do a bit more work, then give it out straight. My knife's so nice and sharp I want to get to work right away if I get a chance. Good luck.

                                        Yours Truly
                                        Jack the Ripper

Dont mind me giving the trade name

    In the second postscript written on a 90-degree angle from the letter in red crayon he wrote:

Wasn't good enough to post this before I got all the red ink off my hands curse it.
No luck yet. They say I'm a doctor now ha ha

On October 1, a postcard written in red crayon was received at the *Central News Agency* written by the same hand. It was postmarked "London, E., Oct. 1."

    It read:

> I was not codding
> dear old Boss when
> I gave you the tip.
> you'll hear about
> Saucy Jackey's work
> tomorrow double
> event this time
> number one squealed
> a bit couldn't
> finish straight off.
> had not time
> to get ears for
> police. thanks for
> keeping last letter
> back till I got
> to work again.
> Jack the Ripper

    Investigators would later speculate that the original Ripper letter and postcard had been sent by one of the local reporters to keep the business alive. Generally Tom Bulling of the *Central News Agency* gets the credit. Indeed, it is generally viewed that none of the letters signed "Jack the Ripper" came from the killer. However, although the letter, written in red ink as was a subsequent postcard, did not come from the actual killer, the effect was electrifying. News reports of the letter, which wrote of murders to come, sold newspapers by the millions. To say the least the press agencies were quite pleased with the results. The killer, however, was not so amused. Someone was taking credit for his work and that would not be allowed to stand. The next time he killed he would send his own letter directly to the men who were searching for him — along with a small sample of his work!

Even today the so-called Ripper letters seem to have a grip on the imagination, so much so that individuals have sought to obtain DNA and fingerprints from some of them in an attempt to prove authorship. Nevertheless, since the killer wrote none of the letters signed Jack the Ripper, authorship would prove to be little more than an interesting exercise in exposing crude Victorian practical jokers. It would be of little historical value, and of no value whatsoever toward uncovering the true identity of the killer. And the letters from "Jack" would not stop there. Hundreds would be sent but none were ever linked to the killer. They would continue to be sent to the police well into the mid 20th century.

By this time Scotland Yard had assigned one of its best investigators to oversee the growing case at the street level. Inspector Frederick George Abberline was called back to the East End, which he knew so well. Abberline, described as 45 years old, a bit overweight and standing at a full 5 feet, 9½ inches tall with dark brown hair and thick moustache, would have his hands full with this case. He would become one of the best known investigators to look into the Whitechapel murders. Working closely under Abberline from H Division would be Inspectors Moore, Nearn and Reid as well as Detective Sergeants Godley, McCarthy, Pearce and Thicke.

As Abberline came onboard the police were finally able to field a crude description of the man all London was searching for. The probable killer had been spotted, albeit from behind, speaking to Chapman only minutes before she was murdered, in front of 29 Hanbury Street.

Official Police Notice

Description of a man who entered a passage of the house at which the murder was committed of a prostitute at 2 A.M. on the 8th — Age 37; height, 5ft. 7 in; rather dark beard and moustache. Dress-shirt, dark vest and trousers, black scarf, and black felt hat. Spoke with a foreign accent.

There was great uneasiness in the district as word began to spread that the killer was a foreigner and perhaps Jewish. The *Jewish Chronicle* would report, "There may soon be murders from panic to add to murders from lust of blood. A touch would fire the whole district in the mood in which it is now."

On September 14, Eliza Annie Chapman was buried at Manor Park, City of London Cemetery. On the same day Edward McKenna was arrested on suspicion of being her killer. McKenna was an itinerant peddler who seemed to match the description of a man seen carrying knives on Flower and Dean Street, near the murder site, but he was soon released after witnesses failed to pick him out of a lineup.

On September 18 the police felt they had possibly captured the Whitechapel killer in the person of German hairdresser Charles Ludwig, alias Charles Ludwig Wetzel. Ludwig had immigrated to England from Hamburg in 1887 or early 1888, making his home in London. He worked as a hairdresser for a Mr. C. A. Partridge in The Minories and was living in a nearby hotel in Finsbury.

The early morning hours of September 18 found Mr. Ludwig in the company of an East End prostitute named Elizabeth Burns. She had accompanied him to Three Kings Court, Minories, to conduct a bit of business near some railway arches. For some reason business was not well arranged and negotiations came to an end when Ludwig pulled out a large-bladed knife and waved it menacingly at her. Burns then began to yell "Murder," which immediately attracted the attention of Police Constable John Johnson on nearby beat duty. Johnson investigated and came to the conclusion that it was a dispute between customer and client and dismissed the heated Mr. Ludwig.

As Ludwig moved into the darkness of the London morning PC Johnson escorted Elizabeth away from the general area to the end of his beat. At this point the still frightened woman told PC Johnson, "Dear me, he frightened me very much when he pulled a big knife out." Johnson could not believe his ears and he demanded to know why she had not reported this information to him when he still had Ludwig in the area. Burns explained that even with the police officer there she was too afraid to make a complaint while Ludwig was still present.

Constable Johnson then began a search of the area but it was too late. Even as he alerted other officers in the area Ludwig was long gone and could not be located. He would not escape for long. By 3 A.M. Ludwig had made his way to a small coffee stall on Whitechapel High Street. Standing nearby was Alexander Freinberg, who casually looked toward Ludwig. Greatly offended by this glance Ludwig demanded to know what Freinberg was looking at, at which point the now confused Mr. Freinberg apologized for whatever was the problem. The apology, however, was not accepted and a now aggravated Charles Ludwig pulled out his knife. Freinberg, seeing the better part of valor, and the large knife, backed away while throwing a dish from the coffee stand at Ludwig's head. Freinberg then quickly located Police Constable John Gallagher, 221H, for help. Before long Charles Ludwig was under arrest.

Later that morning he was brought before the Thames Magistrates Court and was charged with being drunk and disorderly, with the added charge of threatening to stab someone. It was not a charge which could be expected to cause a great deal of concern in the East End in what passed for "normal times" but these were not normal times in London. Ludwig was remanded for a week. However, when the police learned that he also carried a razor and was not afraid to show them to prospective opponents he was held much longer. Police were also able to locate witnesses who reported that they had seen blood on his hands on the day Annie Chapman was murdered. It was starting to look like the authorities had finally captured the Ripper, but the elation, if that was what it was, soon faded. On the night of the next two Ripper murders Mr. Charles Ludwig was safely behind bars and therefore could not have been the Ripper.

History would show that the police had the correct occupation of the killer but they did not have the right man.

WHITECHAPEL, EAST END AND ALDGATE, LONDON— SEPTEMBER 1888

The next bit of work has become known as the night of the "double event," conducted during the early morning hours of September 29–30, as two East End prostitutes met their deaths at the practiced hands of "Jack." The first to die that night was Elizabeth Stride, known locally as "Long Liz." Stride had been born in Sweden, but she was a longtime resident of the Whitechapel area and a well-known prostitute. She may well have been the only victim in the series who can best be described as a "hit." The earlier murder of Annie Chapman had produced a witness, Elizabeth Long. And, even though she saw the killer only from behind, she may very well have been able to point him out in a court of law. He may not have wanted to take the chance. The killer may have mistaken the well-known prostitute "Long Liz" for eyewitness Elizabeth (Liz) Long, as both were prostitutes.

On her last night of life Elizabeth Stride seemed to be searching for someone, or at least waiting to meet a particular individual. She had been with several men that evening for drinks but for some reason "conducted none of her usual business." By 12:45 A.M. on September 30, Stride had made her way to 40 Berner Street outside of the International Working Men's Educational Club. The area was then mostly inhabited by Germans and Poles occupied in making cigarettes, shoes and the tailor trade. (Jack was a Russian-Pole who spoke at least a few words of German.)

Soon she was seen arguing with a man a bit shorter than herself. In a back office in the rear of the yard was Jacob Rombro, who had been working on the club's weekly paper since 9 P.M. He had heard nothing about the murder until he was informed at 1 P.M. He had been only a few feet from the Ripper and his victim, but he could only hear singing coming from the club as he had closed both his windows and the door to his office.

Before long Stride was thrown to the ground in the very dark walkway leading into a side yard known as "Dutfield's Yard." Without a sound the killer drew his very sharp blade across her throat twice—very deeply. Death came very quickly to the tall Swedish prostitute, but in this case there would be no attempt to remove any organs. In point of fact, there were no other wounds at all on her body. Dr. Frederick William Blackwell arrived to examine the body and would later report, "I removed the cachous from the left hand of the deceased, which was nearly open. The packet was lodged between the thumb and the first finger, and partially hidden from view. It was I who spilt them in removing them from the hand. My impression is that the hand gradually relaxed while the woman was dying in a fainting condition from the loss of blood."

This would be the third victim of the Whitechapel killer to have her throat cut while lying on the ground and the cut had once again been from left to right. A hit? Did he think he was killing Elizabeth Long? Perhaps. What is known is that the killer soon left the area moving west toward the edge of the City of London proper and toward his second victim of the night. This time he would once again be in search of body parts.

It has been reported that club member Joseph Lave informed the police that a stranger had come to the club earlier in the evening. He described the man as being possibly Polish or Russian, working as a barber and living in George Yard. This would have been a very good description of Severin Klosowski. Was he at the club? The police seem to have never followed up on this clue! This was possibly the greatest error in the investigation.

Catherine Eddowes was a prostitute and, in the early morning of September 30, she was still feeling the effects of too much drink. She had been in police custody earlier and had passed out in a cell at one of the local stations. When she was well enough to walk, just barely, she was released. If she had walked north toward her room at a cheap lodging house she would have lived past that night; instead, Catherine turned south toward Mitre Square and into the arms of Jack the Ripper. Earlier, she had been warned about the Ripper by a friend who asked her to be careful. She replied, "Don't you fear for me. I'll take care of myself and I shan't fall into his hands."

The square itself had only three entrances, two of which were overseen by either detectives on watch for the Ripper or firemen standing by for duty. That left only the southern entrance as a possible escape route for the killer. Witnesses would later describe a woman matching the description and clothing worn by Eddowes with a man as they entered the square from the north/east through St. James Place. In fact, no fewer than five individuals saw the victim with her killer only minutes before she was murdered in the darkest corner of the badly lit square. Catherine must have known that people were very close as she was being murdered yet she would not be able to call to them, and none would realize at the time that the Ripper was "working" very close by.

With only a few minutes available, due to the patrolling officer's route directly through the square, the Ripper began his purposeful work of the night. After cutting deeply into Catherine's throat from ear to ear he lifted her clothes above the waist and began to remove her organs. Several were cut out including a very difficult removal of the left kidney. It would be this removal, done under great pressure and in very dismal lighting conditions that would spark a debate, which continues to this day. It took a great deal of skill to cleanly remove that organ from that particular front angle, an act which points directly to a man who had surgical skills and training. The killer was certainly not your average East End criminal. He was a professional in some kind of medical field, and he was very skilled with a knife.

After the organs were removed the killer continued to mutilate the victim as he cut part of her ear and face and nearly removed her nose. He also further damaged and ripped the abdomen for no purpose other than the enjoyment he must have felt. Rage was beginning to show in the murders of Jack the Ripper, but he may have made the extra cuts simply to cover up his skills. And he was perhaps not finished for the night as he left a little reminder of his presence. Several minutes after he murdered Eddowes in Mitre Square detectives would find a message chalked on a dark wall a few blocks away. Incredibly, the killer seems to have either gone to his rooms and returned to the general area of the second murder or stayed in the area while dozens of men searched for him. Whichever the case, he reportedly wrote a message on the wall and left a cut and bloodied section of Eddowes's apron next to it to prove that the message was from him.

> The Juwes are
> The men That
>   Will not
> be Blamed
>   for nothing

Speculation as to the reason for the "needed" apron piece has been that it was used as a wraparound rag for an accidentally self-wounded Ripper! The speculation — and that is all it amounts to at this late date — suggests that in the heat of destroying Eddowes's body the killer cut himself on one of his hands as he rushed to finish his work in the darkness of Mitre Square. After he wrapped his hand he is said to have finished the job, took out his anger on his victims face and then moved to a safer spot to tend to his wound. Since the Ripper never took any other pieces of clothing from any of his victims and eventually tossed aside this small piece of cloth, it is a bit of speculation which should not be easily dismissed. Two types of blood on the cloth could have confirmed this speculation — but alas! Was this the reason why it took weeks for the killer to kill again? Was he recovering from a knife wound?

The message was an attempt to blame the Jews in the mostly Jewish section of London, centered on Whitechapel. However, history would show that the Ripper was not Jewish — he was Roman Catholic. The authorities moved to prevent riots against the Jews, soon washing the message away before it could be photographed. Later, both Sir Robert Anderson and Chief Inspector Moore would state that they believed the chalk message was undoubtedly left by the murderer and thus a vital clue had been lost by the very men searching for the killer. This action would be greatly criticized. However, the police could not prevent the population of the East End ghetto from discovering that the cold-blooded killer they had been hunting had taken two in a single night, despite the massive increase in patrols. The East End erupted with masses of people flooding onto the streets demanding action — and soon. This was becoming more than a murder case, this was becoming a political problem, and that fact caught the attention of those in government as no other murder case would.

Charles Warren soon afterward wrote a letter explaining his reasons for removing the message.

Confidential

4 Whitehall Place, S.W.   6th November 1888
The Under Secretary of State
The Home Office
Sir,

In reply to your letter of the 5th instant, I enclose a report of the circumstances of the Mitre Square Murder so far as they have come under the notice of the Metropolitan Police, and I now give an account regarding the erasing the writing on the wall in Goulston Street which I have already partially explained to Mr. Matthews verbally.

On the 30th September on hearing of the Berner Street murder, after visiting Commercial Street Station I arrived at Leman Street Station shortly before 5 am and ascertained from the Superintendent Arnold all that was known there relative to the two murders.

The most pressing question at that moment was some writing on the wall in Goulston Street evidently written with the intention of inflaming the public mind against the Jews, and which Mr. Arnold with a view to prevent serious disorder proposed to obliterate, and had sent down an Inspector with a sponge for that purpose, telling him to await his arrival.

I considered it desirable that I should decide the matter myself, as it was one involving so great a responsibility whether any action was taken or not.

I accordingly went down to Goulston Street at once before going to the scene of the murder: it was just getting light, the public would be in the streets in a few minutes, in a neighborhood very much crowded on Sunday mornings by Jewish vendors and Christian purchasers from all parts of London.

There were several Police around the spot when I arrived, both Metropolitan and City.

The writing was on the jamb of the open arch way or doorway visible in the street and could not be covered up without danger of the covering being torn off at once.

A discussion took place whether the writing could be left covered up or otherwise or whether any portion of it could be left for an hour until it could be photographed; but after taking into consideration the excited state of the population in London generally at the time, the strong feeling which had been excited against the Jews, and the fact that in a short time there would be a large concourse of the people in the streets, and having before me the Report that if it was left there the house was likely to be wrecked (in which from my own observation I entirely concurred) I considered it desirable to obliterate the writing at once, having taken a copy of which I enclose a duplicate.

After having been to the scene of the murder, I went on to the City Police Office and informed the Chief Superintendent of the reason why the writing had been obliterated.

I may mention that so great was the feeling with regard to the Jews that on the 13th ultimo, the Acting Chief Rabbi wrote to me on the subject of the spelling of the word "Jewes" on account of a newspaper asserting that this was Jewish spelling in the Yiddish dialect. He added "in the present state of excitement it is dangerous to the safety of the poor Jews in the East (End) to allow such an assertion to remain uncontradicted. My community keenly appreciates your humane and vigilant action during this critical time."

It may be realized therefore if the safety of the Jews in Whitechapel could be considered to be jeopardized 13 days after the murder by the question of the spelling of the word Jews, what might have happened to the Jews in that quarter had that writing been left intact.

I do not hesitate myself to say that if that writing had been left there would have been an onslaught upon the Jews, property would have been wrecked, and lives would probably have been lost; and I was much gratified with the promptitude with which Superintendent Arnold was prepared to act in the matter if I had not been there.

I have no doubt myself whatever that one of the principal objects of the Reward offered by Mr. Montagu was to show to the world that the Jews were desirous of having the Hanbury Street Murder cleared up, and thus to divert from them the very strong feeling which was then growing up.

I am, Sir,
Your most obedient Servant
(signed) C. Warren

Three weeks after the message was erased, and after a great deal of pressure, mostly unrelated to the Ripper case, Sir Charles Warren resigned.

Understandably frustrations were felt by both the police investigators and the ever-present reporters trying to cover the ever-expanding story. Police secrecy did not help, nor did the inflammatory headlines in many of the local papers. The persistent presence of the press came to the attention of Home Secretary Henry Matthews during a meeting held by his secretary, Sir Evelyn Ruggles-Brise, and Sir Charles Warren. Ruggles-Brise sent a note to Matthues.

Sir Charles came to see me both yesterday and today about the Whitechapel murders.... He remarked to me very strongly upon the great hindrance which is caused to the efforts of the police, by the activity of agents of press associations and newspapers. These "Touts" follow the detectives where ever they go in search of clues, and then having interviewed persons, with whom the police have had conversation and from whom inquires have been made, compile the paragraphs which fill the papers. This practice impedes the usefulness of detectives' investigations and moreover keeps alive the excitement in the district & elsewhere.

HO 144/221/A49301C/8

Many high-ranking officers were called upon that night, including Lt. Col. Henry Smith, the assistant commissioner for the city police. He had been spending the night at Clock Lane Police Station near Southwark Bridge attempting to get some rest when word came in about the Mitre Square murder. Within three minutes he was fully dressed and on his way to the site by Hansom cab. He would later say of his ride, "This invention of the devil claims to be safe. It is neither safe nor pleasant. In winter you are frozen; in summer you are broiled. When the glass is let down your hat is generally smashed, your fingers caught between the doors, or half your front teeth loosened. Licensed to carry two, it did not take me long to discover that a fifteen stone (210 pounds) Superintendent inside with me, and three detectives hanging on behind, added neither to its comfort nor to its safety. Although we rolled like a 'seventy-four' in a gale, we got to our destination — Mitre Square — without an upset, where I found a small group of my men standing round the mutilated remains of a woman."

The *Star* would report the next day that an unidentified witness had seen a man cleaning himself up after the second murder. But was it Jack? "From two different sources we have the story that a man, when passing through Church [passage at Mitre Square] at about half past one, saw a man sitting on a doorstep and wiping his hands. As everyone is on the lookout for the murderer the man looked at the stranger with a certain amount of suspicion, where-upon he tried to conceal his face. He is described as a man who wore a short jacket and a sailor's hat." Was he wiping his hands with the piece of cloth cut from the body of Catherine Eddowes?

The Jewish issue would surface once again during Chapman's investigation in 1903. London papers would report: "*The Jewish Chronicle* has made inquires into the allegation that Chapman is of the Jewish faith, and is enabled to state authoritatively, as the result of personal investigation made by the Rev. Francis L. Cohen at Brixton Prison, where Chapman is detained under remand, that Chapman is not a Jew, but a Roman Catholic."

POLICE NOTICE.
TO THE OCCUPIER

On the mornings of Friday, 31st August, Saturday 8th, and Sunday, 30th September, 1888 Women were murdered in or near Whitechapel, supposed by some one residing in the immediate neighborhood. Should you know of any person to whom suspicion is attached, you are earnestly requested to communicate at once with the nearest Police Station.

Metropolitan Police Office, 30th September, 1888

Commenting on the filthy conditions in the East End and the lack of solutions to them by the so-called enlightened individuals, George Bernard Shaw would write, "Whilst we conventional Social Democrats were wasting our time on education, agitation and organization, some independent genius has taken the matter in hand...." He was writing about Jack the Ripper.

In Victoria Park, London, a meeting was held which attracted around 1,000 people, who passed a resolution calling for the resignation of Home Secretary Matthews and Sir Charles Warren, the police commissioner. Four other meetings were held around the East End with generally the same results. The Ripper, it would seem, was beginning to set political policy. But did the police notice that both Eddowes and Stride, killed on the same night, also lived on the same street — Flower and Dean Street? Did the police also realize that there was a barbershop exactly opposite where both had lived? There is little doubt that floating Whitechapel barber/surgeon Klosowski would have made the connection!

City of London — October 1888

On October 4, the inquest into the murder of Catharine Eddowes began. Joseph Lawende was one of the three men who saw the victim with her killer just before they entered Mitre Square. They were only yards away as "Jack" went to work.

> I was at the Imperial Club with Mr. Joseph Levy and Mr. Harry Harris. We could not get home because it was raining. At half past one we left to go out, and left the house about five minutes later. I walked a little further from the others. We saw a man and a woman at the corner of Church Passage in Duke Street, which leads into Mitre Square.
>
> CORONER LANGHAM — Were they talking at the time?
>
> JOSEPH LAWENDE — She was standing with her face towards the man. I only saw her back. She had her hand on his chest.
>
> Q — What sort of woman was she?
> A — I could not see her face, but the man was taller than she was.
> Q — Did you notice how she was dressed?
> A — I noticed she had a black jacket and black bonnet. I have seen the articles at the police station and I recognize them as the sort of dress worn by that woman.
> Q — Can you tell us what sort of man this was?
> A — He had a cloth cap on, with a peak of the same material.
>
> MR. CRAWFORD THE POLICE SOLICITOR — Unless the jury particularly wish it, I have special reason for not giving details as to the appearance of this man.
>
> Q — You have given a special description of this man to the police?
> A — Yes.
> Q — Do you think you would know him again?
> A — I doubt it, sir.
> Q — Did you hear anything said?
> A — No, not a word.
> Q — Did either of them appear in an angry mood?
> A — No.
> Q — Was there anything about them or their movements that attracted your attention?
> A — No, except that Mr. Levy said the court ought to be watched, and I took particular notice of a man and a woman talking there.

October 4 would also bring a strange event to Vigilance Committee chairman George Lusk. The event was reported in *The News of the World*, in the Sunday edition of October 7. On the 4th a man described as 5 feet, 9 inches tall, 30 to 40 years of age with florid complexion, bushy brown beard, whiskers and moustache went to Mr. Lusk's home on Alderney Street to inquire for Mr. Lusk. He was not home but the man was told he could find Mr. Lusk at his son's tavern nearby. Arriving at the pub the stranger soon located the chairman and "after asking all sorts of questions relative to the beats taken by members of the committee, attempted to induce Mr. Lusk to enter a private room with him."

George Lusk was not about to go into a room alone with this strange man he felt was "repulsive and forbidding," but he did agree to have a quiet conversation with him in the bar parlor. During the conversation the man took a pencil from his pocket, dropped it over the table they were sitting at and said "Pick that up." Mr. Lusk looked away to see where the pencil had gone but while he did he "noticed the stranger make a swift though silent movement of his right hand towards his side pocket." The stranger saw that Lusk was on to him and nonchalantly asked directions to the nearest coffee room. As the man left the tavern, Lusk directed him to a coffee house on Mile End Road. However, Lusk was so disturbed by the man's questions and strange actions he decided to follow him to the coffee house. Upon arrival the individual was nowhere to be seen. He had disappeared into one of the many allies which crisscrossed most of the East End.

Was this a meeting with Jack the Ripper? We shall never really know, but very soon George Lusk would indeed receive a "gift" from the man all of London was searching for.

In New York City the readers of the *New York Times* could read of "Dismay in Whitechapel" and the *Los Angeles Times* heralded "The Whitechapel Fiend Again at Work." "Two more Unfortunate Women Butchered in One Night." Closer to home, London residents took in page after page reporting on "London's Awful Mystery." Official London was starting to worry about riots in the streets, which could, if taken to extremes, bring down a government. Something would need to be done if law and order were going to prevail, albeit on a reduced scale familiar to the East End population. Before the authorities could act, however, the Thames Torso Killer would strike again.

He killed his second victim around August 20 — suggestively not on the same day as a Ripper murder — but her torso, sans head, arms and legs, would not be discovered until October 2. And it was discovered in a most unexpected place. She had been dumped in the deepest vault area on the construction site of the new Metropolitan Police Headquarters at New Scotland Yard!

The large bundle had been carried down to a very dark and inaccessible location. In fact, only someone very familiar with the worksite could have safely negotiated the many twists, turns and dangerous open places required to make it to the dumpsite. After the discovery it was found that the torso matched an arm, which had been discovered near the Thames River a few days earlier. The arm itself did not make much in the way of copy for the local newspapers, as it ordinarily should have, because at the time most of the attention was on the East End and Jack. The arm had been found in South London well outside of the Ripper's patch. And, although the authorities would not place this victim in the Ripper's column, neither were they ever able to provide any evidence that the same killer had not committed the murder. The hard-pressed police forces did not want the people of London to believe that Jack had expanded his killing grounds. In the end, the headless torso would never be identified as the inquest jury delivered a remarkable verdict of "Found dead," end of case.

On October 5 the *Central News Agency* received yet another letter from "Jack," which was surely not written by the killer. However, this letter not only boasted of more Ripper murders to come, it also conveyed the writer's supposed horror at the Torso Murder recently uncovered at New Scotland Yard. Once again the press had a field day.

5 Oct. 1888

Dear Friend

In the name of God hear me I swear I did not kill the female whose body was found at Whitehall. If she was an honest woman I will hunt down and destroy her murderer. If she was a whore God will bless the hand that slew her, for the women of Moab and Midian shall die and their blood shall mingle with dust. I never harm any others or the Divine power that protects and helps me in my grand work would quit for ever. Do as I do and the light of glory shall shine upon you. I must get to work tomorrow treble event this time yes yes three must be ripped. Will send you a bit of face by post I promise this dear old Boss. The police now reckon my work a practical joke well Jacky's a very practical joker ha ha ha keep this back till three are wiped out and you can show the cold meat.

yours truly
Jack the Ripper

As the police, under the watchful eye of Sir Charles Warren, began an unprecedented and detailed house-to-house search for the killer in central Whitechapel, the killer seemed to have taken a bit of a rest. For six weeks he did not kill. Indeed, he may very well have been moving from the "grand search area" to much safer quarters only a few blocks outside that area. He did, however, take time out to send a little message to the men who had been searching so hard for him. He also sent the one thing only the real killer could have possessed — a portion of a body part taken from one of his victims. It was the one way he had of saying that he was the one and only, that his message was real.

Coroner's inquest into the murder of Elizabeth Stride (*Illustrated Police News*, October 1888).

The small brown package arrived on the evening of October 16, at the home of 49-year-old building contractor George Akin Lusk. Lusk had formed the Mile End Vigilance Committee along with other businessmen in order to help the police in any way they could and he was about to become fully involved. The package contained a single page note and half a kidney, which had been "prasarved" in spirits. It had not decayed, as it would have had it come from a victim housed in the morgue nor had it been preserved in a way which would suggest it had come from a medical training hospital. This kidney had been removed fresh from a newly killed individual and quickly placed in some kind of red wine.

> From hell
> Mr Lusk
> Sor
> I send you half the
> Kidne I took from one woman
> prasarved it for you t other piece I
> fried and ate it was very nise I
> may send you the bloody knif that
> took it out if you only wate a whil
> longer
> Signed Catch me when
> you can
> Mishter Lusk

The killer never used the name Jack the Ripper, and despite the note and body part there is still debate as to whether or not the killer actually sent the note. But if he did not send the letter to "Mishter Lusk," then the question remains: just how many women in the East End of London, or for that matter all of London, had a "Kidne" ripped out of their bodies that cold and wet month of October 1888? One would hope that it was only one, and certainly one was more than enough.

And what of the great search for the killer of these women? The police found nothing for three days, but at least the very hard-pressed people of the East End could point to a grand effort done on their behalf. And in the end that may have been the main point of the whole exercise as, understandably, police relations with the people of the East End were at the time at an all-time low. The cooperation of the residents themselves to opening their houses to police searches was noted by many in government as being truly remarkable.

In view of the community's cooperation with the police search, Sir Charles Warren was moved to thank all of those involved with a letter to the London press on October 18.

THE EAST-END MURDERS

We are requested to publish the following:—
Sir Charles Warren wishes to say that the marked desire evinced by the inhabitants of the Whitechapel district to aid the police in the pursuit of the author of the recent crimes has enabled him to direct that, subject to the consent of occupiers, a through house-to-house search should be made within a defined area.

The "Letter from Hell" sent to building contractor and head of the Mile End Vigilance Committee, George Akins Lusk. It is the only known example of the killer's handwriting.

With few exceptions the inhabitants of all classes and creeds have freely fallen in with the proposal, and have materially assisted the officers engaged in carrying it out.

Sir Charles Warren feels that some acknowledgement is due on all sides for the cordial cooperation of the inhabitants and he is much gratified that the police officers have carried out so delicate a duty with the marked good will of all those with whom they have come in contact.

The next day, Chief Inspector Donald Swanson, the desk officer in charge of the Ripper case, reported that "the movements of over 300 individuals had been investigated and around 80 other people had been 'detained' at local police stations for questioning into the case. There are now 994 dockets besides police reports." It had indeed been a grand effort to catch a most elusive serial killer.

In the meantime, Reverend Samuel Augustus Barrett, rector of St. Judes, Whitechapel, expressed his opinions about the area: "Rows, fights and thefts had been allowed to go unchecked in these rookeries of crime so long as the main thoroughfares were safe. The back streets were gloomy and dirty and encouraged crime." He was also much concerned about the habit of local women who, when fighting in the streets, would often strip down to the waist. "The murders were, it may almost be said, bound to come; generation could not follow generation in lawless intercourse, children could not be familiarized with scenes of degradation, community in crime could not be the bond of society and the end of all be peace."

October 19, 1888

The Police Gazette

At 12:35 A.M., 30th September, with Elizabeth Stride, found murdered at 1 A.M., same date, in Berner — street — A MAN, age 28, height 5 ft 8 in., complexion dark, small dark moustache; dress, black diagonal coat, hard felt hat, collar and tie; respectable appearance. Carried a parcel wrapped up in newspaper.

At 12:45 A.M., 30th, with same woman, in Berner—street—A MAN, age about 30, height 5 ft 5 in., complexion fair, hair dark, small brown moustache, full face, broad shoulders; dress, dark jacket and trousers, black cap with peak.

At 1:35 A.M., 30th September, with Catherine Eddowes, in Church—passage, leading to Mitre—square, where she was found murdered at 1:45 A.M., same date—A MAN, age 30, height 5 ft 7 or 8 in., complexion fair, moustache fair, medium build; dress, pepper-and-salt colour loose jacket, gray cloth cap with peak of same material, reddish neckerchief tied in knot; appearance of a sailor.

Information to be forwarded to the Metropolitan Police Office, Great Scotland—yard, London, S.W.

SPITALFIELDS, EAST END—NOVEMBER 1888

Very few people in London thought the killer had ended his killing, even though it had been six weeks since he had used his blade. One of the local prostitutes who was still terrified was Mary Jane Kelly. She had followed the news reports daily by asking a friend to read to her many of the accounts of the Ripper. She would confide to a friend: "This Jack the Ripper business is getting on my nerves. I have made up my mind to go home to my mother." Mary Kelly had less than one day to live. To Caroline Maxwell, who lived on Dorset Street and across the street from Miller's Court, Mary was "a pleasant little woman, rather stout, fair complexion, and rather pale. She spoke with a kind of impediment."

Like many of the local residents of Whitechapel and Spitalfields, Mary had spent her day drinking at local pubs. The *Britannia* was a particular favorite located on the corner of Dorset and Commercial Streets. It was only a few steps from her small and dirty room at 13 Miller's Court. It was no more than the backroom of number 26 Dorset Street, but it was warm and it was out of the rain, a better abode than thousands of people living in the ghetto could claim.

That last evening and early morning found Mary as always in need of money, as she was several weeks behind in her rent. At around 2 A.M. on November 9, she was seen talking to a well-dressed man who carried a small parcel in his left hand. She laughed at something he said and both soon made their way to her room. Keeping an eye on these events was a local man named George Hutchinson, who knew Mary quite well and could very well have been one of her regular customers. He followed the pair back to her small room and waited outside. He waited for about 45 minutes for the man to leave but when he did not come out Hutchinson decided that he had waited long enough in the cold and drizzle of the night. He left Mary alone with her "customer" and did not hear anything suspicious coming from the room. For a brief time the Ripper had been trapped in that small room and had not known it as he began to cut Mary Jane Kelly to pieces. After Hutchinson left, the killer had all the time he would need to do whatever he wanted to the still warm corpse of Mary Kelly.

Mary's body would not be discovered until 10:45 in the morning. Thomas Bowyer's job that morning was to collect the rents due from the few people who lived in Miller's Court and he needed to make a call on Mary. He knocked on the dirty door twice but received no answer. Walking around to the side he pushed aside a curtain covering a broken window to a sight he would never forget. "All those lumps of flesh lying on the table—it was more the work of a devil than of a man." All of the color drained from his face as he staggered away for help. He could hardly talk.

The people of London received the news like an electric shock, and it did not take long for the streets to fill with people. So many had come to Dorset Street that the police could barely move to the murder site. When it came time to remove the body the crowds pressed even closer

1. The Ripper and Torso Murders

DAILY TELEGRAPH, SATURDAY, NOVEMBER 10, 1888.

LOCALITY OF THE SEVEN UNDISCOVERED MURDERS.

The above chart represents the locality within which, since April last, seven women of the unfortunate class have been murdered. The precise spot where each crime was committed is indicated by a dagger and a numeral.

1. April 3.—Emma Elizabeth Smith, forty-five, had a stake or iron instrument thrust through her body, near Osborn-street, Whitechapel.
2. Aug. 7.—Martha Tabram, thirty-five, stabbed in thirty-nine places, at George-yard-buildings, Commercial-street, Spitalfields.
3. Aug. 31.—Mary Ann Nicholls, forty-seven, had her throat cut and body mutilated, in Buck's-row, Whitechapel.
4. Sept. 8.—Annie Chapman, forty-seven, her throat cut and body mutilated, in Hanbury-street, Spitalfields.
5. Sept. 30.—A woman, supposed to be Elizabeth Stride, but not yet identified, discovered with her throat cut, in Berner-street, Whitechapel.
6. Sept 30.—A woman, unknown, found with her throat cut and body mutilated, in Mitre-square, Aldgate.

Figure 7 (encircled) marks the spot in Goulston-street where a portion of an apron belonging to the woman murdered in Mitre-square was picked up by a Metropolitan police-constable.

Figure 8. Nov. 9.—Mary Jane Kelly, 24, her throat cut and body terribly mutilated, in Miller's-court, Dorset-street.

Daily Telegraph from November 10, 1888, showing the locations of the Whitechapel murders to that date.

to the small van, which was used to move the body to the morgue. As the old shell was removed containing the mutilated remains of Mary and placed in the van the noisy crowd became silent as "Ragged caps were doffed and slatternly looking women shed tears as the shell, covered with a ragged looking cloth, was placed in the van." The event constituted a body blow to the East End of London.

At this point in the investigation the police were truly at a loss as to how to proceed. They had pulled out all of the stops and still the killer was able to continue his murderous series. They had no real suspects and leads were very thin. Hundreds of fresh men from other areas of London had been called in; vigilance committees were on patrol, rewards and a massive house-to-house and room-to-room search had failed to find any trace of the killer. In an almost desperate move, Charles Warren, commissioner of police, signed a murder pardon for anyone who had helped the killer. But that too would fail as no one took him up on it. The police did not seem to realize that they were dealing with a lone killer who needed no assistance during his one-man murder spree.

MURDER — PARDON — Whereas on November 8 or 9, in Miller's Court, Dorset Street, Spitalfields, Mary Janet (sic) Kelly was murdered by some person or persons unknown: the Secretary of State will advise the grant of Her Majesty's gracious pardon to any accomplice, not being a person who contrived or actually committed the murder, who shall give such information and evidence as shall lead to the discovery and conviction of the person or persons who committed the murder.

CHARLES WARREN, the Commissioner of Police
of the Metropolis
Metropolitan Police Office, 4 Whitehall Place,
S. W., Nov. 10, 1888

Only days later a traveling salesman who dealt with hairdressing equipment would be accused of being the killer. Wolff Levisohn, who knew Klosowski personally, was accosted by two prostitutes in Whitechapel on November 15, 1888. They felt he was the killer because he "carried a black bag like the Ripper." Although he was held only briefly, mostly for his own protection, history would show that he would learn much about serial killer Klosowski and would testify at his trial in 1903. Did he know much more?

Needless to say, the local businessmen were not happy at the bad press and the increased crime in the area. The East End was indeed becoming lawless as Samuel Montagu wrote to the home secretary representing some 200 local businessmen demanding action.

> The traders in Whitechapel have for some years past been painfully aware that the protection afforded by the police has not kept pace with the increase of population in Whitechapel. Acts of violence and of robbery have been committed in this neighborhood almost with impunity, owing to the existing police regulations and the insufficiency of the number of officers. The universal feeling prevalent in our midst is that the government no longer ensures the security of life and property in East London and that, in consequence, respectable people fear to go out shopping, thus depriving us of our means of livelihood.

Mary's funeral took place on Monday afternoon, November 19. Just as the church bell began to toll its noon message thousands of East End residents gathered in front of St. Leonard's Church, Shoreditch. Soon four men bore the casket through the gate to the open car as the crowd massed forward to touch it. The emotion of the gathered crowd was unconstrained and spontaneous as many had tears on their faces. The polished oak and elm coffin had on it a plate reading: Marie Jeannette Kelly, died 9th Nov. 1888, aged 25 years.

The cortege moved with great difficulty as thousands of people blocked the streets for a view of the procession. It finally made its way to St. Patrick's Roman Catholic Cemetery at Leytonstone. The sky had been dark and cloudy all day, as it was when her remains were lowered into the ground. In attendance were those who had been acquainted with Mary, but few who knew her well. Joseph Barnett was there to see her off, but no members of her family attended the funeral. And if his behavior was typical of those who move in the dark abyss within the tormented mind of a serial killer, so was Jack the Ripper!

In a letter to Robert Anderson, then head of the CID, Dr. Thomas Bond reported on his thoughts concerning the ongoing Whitechapel murders on November 10. He had just finished his postmortem on Mary Jane Kelly.

7 The Sanctuary,
Westminster Abbey
November 10th '88

Dear Sir,

Whitechapel Murders
I beg to report that I have read the notes of the four Whitechapel Murders viz-:

      1. Buck's Row
      2. Hanbury Street
      3. Berners Street
      4. Mitre Square

I have also made a Post Mortem Examination of the mutilated remains of a woman found yesterday in a small room in Dorset Street —:

1. All five murders were no doubt committed by the same hand. In the first four the throats appear to have been cut from left to right, in the last case owing to the extensive mutilation it is

impossible to say in what direction the fatal cut was made, but arterial blood was found on the wall in splashes close to where the woman's head must have been lying.

2. All the circumstances surrounding the murders lead me to form the opinion that the women must have been lying down when murdered and in every case the throat was first cut.

3. In the four murders of which I have seen the notes only, I cannot form a very definite opinion as to the time that had elapsed between the murder and the discovery of the body. In one case, that of Berners Street the discovery appears to have been immediately after the deed. In Buck's Row, Hanbury St., and Mitre Square three or four hours only could have elapsed. In the Dorset Street case the body was lying on the bed at the time of my visit two o'clock quite naked and mutilated as in the annexed report. Rigor Mortis had set in but increased during the progress of the examination. From this it is difficult to say with any degree of certainty the exact time that had elapsed since death as the period varies from six to twelve hours before rigidity sets in. The body was comparatively cold at two o'clock and the remains of a recently taken meal were found in the stomach and scattered about over the intestines. It is therefore, pretty certain that the woman must have been dead about twelve hours and the partly digested food would indicate that death took place about three or four hours after food was taken, so one or two o'clock in the morning would be the probable time of the murder.

4. In all the cases there appears to be no evidence of struggling and the attacks were probably so sudden and made in such a position that the women could neither resist nor cry out. In the Dorset St. case the corner of the sheet to the right of the woman's head was much cut and saturated with blood, indicating that the face may have been covered with the sheet at the time of the attack.

5. In the first four cases the murderer must have attacked from the right side of the victim. In the Dorset Street case, he must have attacked from in from the left, as there would be no room for him between the wall and the part of the bed on which the woman was lying. Again the blood had flowed down on the right side of the woman and spurted on to the wall.

6. The murderer would not necessarily be splashed or deluged with blood, but his hands and arms must have been covered and parts of his clothing must certainly have been smeared with blood.

7. The mutilations in each case excepting the Berners Street one were all of the same character and showed clearly that in all the murders the object was mutilation.

8. In each case the mutilation was inflicted by a person who had no scientific nor anatomical knowledge. In my opinion he does not even possess the technical knowledge of a butcher or horse slaughterer or any person accustomed to cut up dead animals.

9. The instrument must have had been a strong knife at least six inches long, very sharp, pointed at the top and about an inch in width. It may have been a clasp knife, a butcher's knife or a surgeon's knife; I think it was no doubt a straight knife.

10. The murderer must have been a man of physical strength and of great coolness and daring. There is no evidence that he had an accomplice. He must in my opinion be a man subject to periodical attacks of Homicidal and erotic mania. The character of the mutilations indicate that the man may be in a condition sexually, that may be called Satyriasis. It is of course possible that the Homicidal impulse may have developed from a revengeful or brooding condition of the mind, or that religious mania may have been the original disease but I do not think either hypothesis is likely. The murderer in external appearance is quite likely to be a quiet inoffensive looking man probably middle-aged and neatly and respectably dressed. I think he must be in the habit of wearing a cloak or overcoat or he could hardly have escaped notice in the streets if the blood on his hands or clothes were visible.

11. Assuming the murderer to be such a person as I have just described, he would be solitary and eccentric in his habits, also he is most likely to be a man without regular occupation, but with some small income or pension. He is possibly living among respectable persons who have some knowledge of his character and habits and who may have grounds for suspicion that he isn't quite right in his mind at times. Such persons would probably be unwilling to communicate suspicions to the Police for fear of trouble or notoriety, whereas if there were prospect of reward it might overcome their scruples.

Dr. Thomas Bond

Poplar, East End — December 1888

The police patrols in other so-called non Ripper areas of London were stretched even thinner as more men joined the search for the elusive killer. Whitechapel and Spitalfields were becoming saturated with police and others searching for Jack. It would have been foolhardy for the killer to continue to murder women on the streets of that small area, and Jack was no fool. Indeed, Mary Kelly's murder showed that the Ripper was adapting to an ever-changing situation. He would adapt once again with his next killing, committed fully two miles east of his central killing ground. It would be committed in Poplar, East End, an area he had lived in for around five months less than a year earlier. The still warm body would be found only a few blocks from his old rooms. No other supposed suspect ever lived in this area of London. Time and space were clearly marking who the killer was.

Prostitute Rose Mylett had a few aliases, but the most telling was what her friends called her—"Drunken Lizzie Davis." She was well known in Whitechapel, but she used different names in different areas. At the time of her death she lived in the central Ripper killing ground but for some reason had made her way to Poplar on the evening of December 19. She had been spotted several times in the Poplar area, mostly near or in the pubs and cheap eating establishments. She did not, however, seem to be picking up any men, as would usually do. She seemed to be searching for one particular individual, similar to Elizabeth Stride. It is not known if she found him, but the Ripper certainly found her.

At 4:15 A.M. on December 20, Police Constable Robert Goulding could be found walking his beat along Poplar High Street. His patrol had been extended due to the recent murders so he did not pass his familiar areas as often as he normally would have. His pass by Clarke's Yard, however, nearly caused him to run into the Ripper as he discovered the still warm body of Rose Mylett lying on her side in the yard, which was normally used to store building materials.

Mylett had been strangled but had not been ripped, and this murder led the forces of government to begin a debate on whether or not she had been killed by the Ripper or was just another background death out of the ghettos of the Victorian East End. In the end the coroner's inquest would rule that it was a murder and that, if it had been by the Ripper, he may have been interrupted as he took her life. Or he may not have been properly prepared for mutilating the body. Official London, however, would not investigate any further as police authorities called it an accidental death! Whatever the police really believed, the Rose Mylett murder file did find its way into the folder marked "Ripper Victims." Perhaps official London simply decided not to investigate in order to continue the myth that the Ripper was no longer "working." It would seem to have been a case of look the other way and hope for the best. Jack, however, had other ideas in mind as he began to expand his killing grounds.

On January 2, 1889, a little noticed article appeared in the *County of Middlesex Independent* reporting on a body found in the Thames. Under the banner "FOUND IN THE RIVER," the paper reported: "The body of a well-dressed man was discovered on Monday [December 31, 1888] in the river off Thorneycroft's Torpedo Works, by a watchman and the deceased was conveyed to the mortuary. The body, which is that of a man about 40 years of age, has been in the water about a month. From certain papers found on the body friends at Bournemouth have been telegraphed to. An inquest will be held today."

It was the body of Montague John Druitt, whose death would be used by the police to propagandize that Jack the Ripper had possibly killed himself in the Thames. However, there were two problems with that. First, the police had no evidence whatsoever to show that he was the killer, and "possibly" does not close a murder case. Second, the real Ripper had yet to finish his bloody work. Simply said, Druitt was not Jack the Ripper.

Dr. Thomas Bramah Diplock, coroner for the western division of the County of London and West Middlesex, held an inquest into Druitt's death. The jury came to the conclusion that Druitt had drowned himself in the Thames River after writing a suicide note. They did not find that he had any involvement with the Ripper murders.

London, East End—June 1889

For a few years after the murders of 1888 official London worked hard to place any additional unsolved murders committed in the East End into any column other than the Rippers. By doing so they sparked a debate, which continues to this day. The reason was simple enough. The authorities had failed to capture the killer, despite numerous claims by the police that he was either dead or in an insane asylum. The either/or part, in and of itself, would show that they simply did not know who, or where, he was. If the public believed that he was still alive, still active and expanding his killing range, the authorities could very well have lost their tenuous control over the expanding and hard to control ghetto population. Riots in the streets of London were a very real possibility the authorities would do just about anything to suppress, including lying and covering up the facts. After all, the cry of the well to do in the West End of London was: "She was just a prostitute."

On June 4, 1889, the first of a new set of body parts was discovered on the banks of the Thames River near St. Georges's Stair at Horselydown. The Thames Torso Killer had struck again, but this time the victim would be identified. Elizabeth Jackson's body parts, minus her head, would be found for the better part of the month in or near the river. It was clear from the locations and the number of individual discoveries that the killer had kept many of the pieces for a time before disposing of them. And, because not all of her body was ever located, it is quite possible that some pieces of it were collected and held by the killer. He was a collector as was the Ripper!

Before long Doctor Bond would have enough parts to declare that the woman had been "from 24 to 25 years of age and of fair complexion." She had also been pregnant when she was killed, which could point to a possible motive in the Torso series. It is possible that most, if not all, of the Torso victims had been failed abortions committed by a back alley surgeon who had failed to save the life of his "patient." If they were indeed unplanned deaths then the killer had an extra body to deal with without a plan to dispose of the remains. Cutting up the body into easy-to-carry pieces for disposal would seem the best plan. And if he or others knew the woman, her identification would have been a problem to say the least.

The authorities were very quick to state that this victim had not fallen under the blade of the Ripper. In fact, they reached that conclusion just a bit too quickly. It would not be so easy to dismiss the next cases, however. The record would show that the next two murders would be committed right in the heart of his killing ground. Also, the police did not know that Jack had been trained in the art of surgery and could very well have been working in the general area under another alias in one of the local clinics. Indeed, several of the prostitutes killed by the Ripper had visited these clinics shortly before their deaths. It was a connection the police do not seem to have fully explored at the time.

Whitechapel, East End—July 1889

Alice "Clay pipe" McKenzie lived in a Spitalfields lodging house only three blocks from where Mary Jane Kelly had been murdered. She would die in a dark alley two blocks from the murder site of Martha Tabram in Whitechapel, where serial killer Severin Klosowski had lived at the time of Tabram's death. And even though the victim and method of attack matched that of the Ripper, the police would work very hard to convince the ghetto residents of London that Jack had not taken this victim, another well-known prostitute. Everything about the murder, however, pointed to the Whitechapel killer.

At 8:30 P.M., July 16, Alice was more or less drunk as she left her lodging house. She would be seen again and again as she hurried about the area seemingly searching for someone or getting her business completed so she could meet someone. The last confirmed sighting of "Clay pipe" was at 11:40 P.M. on Flower and Dean Street. As she hurried past some friends seated in front of the hairdresser's shop she said "All right. I can't stop now." She had a little more than one hour to live as she rushed off to the south of town.

It began to rain at around 12:45 A.M. as Constable Walter Andrews finished his talk with Sergeant Badham. Andrews had last walked through the dark passage known as Castle Alley some 27 minutes earlier and had seen nothing. It was 12:50 A.M. as he moved passed the streetlight heading into the narrow passage. A few feet into the alley he discovered the still warm body of Alice McKenzie. She was lying on the wet ground with her feet toward the wall. With his lamp Constable Andrews was able to see the two four-inch jagged stabs, which had penetrated her throat. She was still bleeding from the wounds, which had just killed her. The killer had to be very close even as he was on point duty!

The attack had clearly been murder, not an assault to obtain any monies the victim may have had. The killer simply wanted to take a life, but almost immediately there was disagreement as to who had killed her. The police and government officials had already spread the lie that the killer was in custody or had died so they could not change that piece of propaganda. Now they would need to grab hold of any fact they could, any argument they could make to differentiate the case from other Ripper murders. It would be left to old Dr. Phillips to raise official medical doubts. The public failed to understand that if any doubt existed, then the police did not know who the killer was. Dr. Phillips stated: "After careful and long deliberation, I cannot satisfy myself, on purely anatomical and professional grounds that the perpetrator of all the 'Wh Ch. Murders' is our man. I am on the contrary impelled to a contrary conclusion in this noting the mode of procedure and the character of the mutilations and judging of motive in connection with the latter."

Dr. Thomas Bond, who had also worked on the case, saw the murder in a different light. He affirmed: "I see in this murder evidence of similar design to the former Whitechapel murders viz. Sudden onslaught on the prostrate woman, the throat skillfully and resolutely cut with subsequent mutilation, each mutilation indicating sexual thoughts and a desire to mutilate the abdomen and sexual organs. I am of opinion that the murder was performed by the same person who committed the former series of Whitechapel murders."

After the better part of a year spent searching for a single killer the police had gotten nowhere. Jack was still out there and, although he had slowed his deadly pace and had changed some of his methods, he was still in the murder business. McKenzie's case file would also be kept in the "Ripper Victims" folder.

On July 25 another letter was sent to Scotland Yard signed "Jack the Ripper."

> Dear Boss
>
> Have not caught me yet you see, with all your cunning, with all your "Lees" with all your blue bottles. I have made two narrow squeaks this week, but still though disturbed I got clear before I could get to work — I will give the foreigners a turn now I think — for a change — Germans especially if I can — I was conversing with two or three of your men last night — their eyes of course were shut and thus they did not see my bag. Ask any of your men who were on duty last night in Piccadilly (Circus End) if they saw a gentleman put 2 dragoon guard sergeants into a hansom. I was close by and heard him talk about shedding blood in Egypt I will soon shed more in England. I hope you read mark and learn all that you can if you do so you may and may not catch
>
> > Jack the Ripper

WHITECHAPEL, EAST END—SEPTEMBER 1889

It would be only days after Coroner Wynne Baxter declared, during McKenzie's inquest, that she had indeed been murdered, that once again a woman's body would be discovered in the East End. And, once again it would be dumped in Whitechapel as the Torso Killer claimed number four in his series. The torso had been disposed of only a few blocks south of where Ripper victim Elizabeth Stride had met her death and only two days from the first anniversary of Annie Chapman's murder. These facts were not lost on the detectives who had charge of the case. And the boys of the press were not about to let them forget either.

On September 10, 1889, at 5:15 in the morning Constable William Pennett, on regular beat duty, first smelled, and then saw, the decomposing torso of a woman under the railroad arch on Pinchin Street. The head and legs had been cut off and the abdomen had been slashed open with a 15-inch gash. Pennett's first thought was "Ripper!" He knew that the killer had to be close, very close. He would never know how correct he really was as Jack's home was almost directly in sight of the officer. Across the railroad tracks and just to the south ran Cable Street, where Severin Klosowski—alias Jack the Ripper—had moved, possibly just before the great search. His new barbershop was just outside of the search area and within view of, and easy walking distance to, Pinchin Street.

Constable Pennett could see no blood on the ground and it quickly became apparent that the murder had occurred elsewhere. As he looked around he noticed that the Pinchin and Johnson Paint Company had put up a fence. That fence effectively blocked anyone from coming to the arch area from the north and so the killer must have come from the south, possibly from Cable Street.

As the police gathered strength to mount a new search, three men were found to be sleeping in two of the other railroad arches. All three were taken into custody but they had all been drunk the night before and had simply used the cover of the railroad arches to find a bit of rest. They knew nothing of the murder but were held just in case. The killer must have been within a few yards of three possible witnesses as he dropped off his grisly cargo and yet he seemed not to have seen them. It can only be imagined what he must have thought when he read of his latest kill in the papers. And make no mistake—he did keep track of news reports and at times seemed to adjust his efforts accordingly.

It did not take long for the police to fan out, mostly to the south and, if reports can be taken at face value, all residents in the area of Pinchin and Cable Streets were questioned and their homes searched, including the home and business of Klosowski and his new wife. Once again police investigators had come face to face with serial killer Klosowski and they had not known it. They were also unaware that his wife, who had come to London from Poland (his first and legal wife), was missing from his home. She had lived with him and his new wife Lucy for a time (reportedly with his Polish wife's two children) and had simply disappeared. Klosowski did not bother to report her as missing and there are no known reports of his wife after this period. This is proof that Klosowski could face a police interview without giving any sign of concern or guilt.

> Found at 5:40 this morning, the trunk of a woman under railway arches in Pinchin Street, Whitechapel. Age about 40; height, 5 ft. 3 in.; hair, dark brown; no clothing, except chemise, which is much torn and bloodstained; both elbows discoloured as from habitually leaning on them. Post-mortem marks apparently of a rope having been tied round the waist.

Once again despite similar a method of disposal and a similar pattern of mutilation police officials reported to the public and the press that this was not a Ripper murder. Internal reports, (some of which remained closed until 1990), tell a much different story. "If this is a fresh outrage by the Whitechapel murderer known by the horribly familiar nickname of Jack the Ripper the answer would not be difficult.... [This] murder, committed in the murderer's house [is] a new departure from the system hitherto pursued by this ruffian." Once again Scotland Yard, despite public reports, could not rule out the Ripper as the killer of the woman found on Pinchin Street, and they wanted that fact covered up for over 100 years!

It would be up to James Monro to submit a detailed report to J. S. Sanders on this latest crime. Sanders was the private secretary to Home Secretary Henry Matthews, who had asked to be kept up to date on these matters. It would be this eight-page report, marked closed until 1990, which would show conclusively that police and government officials did not know who Jack the Ripper was. Moreover, it was proof that when the police had stated that the Ripper was either dead or in an asylum they had clearly lied. It was held in Home Office File — HO 144/221/A49301 K.

Dated 11 September 1889   Closed until *1990*
                                                            A 0144/221/A49301 K

Subject: The Whitechapel Murder (Pinchin Street)
Mr. Sanders.

I communicated to you yesterday the finding of the trunk of a female, minus head & legs in one of the railway arches in Pinchin Street.

This street is close to Berner Street, which was the scene of one of the previous Whitechapel murders. It is not a very narrow street, but is lonely at night, and is patrolled every half-hour by a constable on beat. The arch where the body was found abuts on the pavement.

The constable discovered the body somewhat after 20 minutes past five on the morning of Tuesday. He was in consequence of the pressure for men in Whitechapel just now, working part of two beats in addition to his own, but even so he passed and re-passed the spot every half-hour. He is positive that when he passed the spot about five the body was not there. I am inclined to accept his statement thoroughly, for from another circumstance, which has come to my knowledge he evidently was on the alert that night. It may therefore be assumed that the body was placed where it was found sometime between 5 and 5:30 A.M. of Tuesday the 11th.

Although the body was placed in the arch on Tuesday morning the murder, (and although there is not as yet before me proof of the cause of death, I assume that there has been a murder) was not committed there nor then. There was almost no blood in the arch, and the state of the body itself showed that death took place about 36 hours or more previously. This then enables me to say that the woman was made away with probably on Sunday night, the 8th September. This was the date on which one of the previous Whitechapel murders was committed.

The body then must have been concealed, where the murder was committed during Sunday night, Monday, and Tuesday up till dawn. This leads to the inference that it was so concealed in some place to which the murderer had access, over which he had control, and from which he was anxious to remove the corpse. We may say then that the murder was committed probably in the house or lodging of the murderer, and that he conveyed the portion found to Pinchin Street to get rid of it from his lodging where the odor of decomposition would soon betray him.

Why did he take the trunk to Whitechapel and what does the finding of the body there show? Is this a fresh outrage of the Whitechapel murderer known by the horribly familiar nickname of Jack the Ripper? The answer would not be difficult although this murder, *committed in the murderer's house* would be a new departure from the system hitherto pursued by this ruffian. I am however, inclined to believe that this case is not the work of the Ripper. What has characterized the previous cases has been a/. death caused by cutting the throat — b/. mutilation. c/. evisceration d/. removal of certain parts of the body. e/. murder committed in the street, except in one instance in Dorset Street — In this last case there were distinct traces of furious mania. The murderer having plenty of time at his disposal slashed and cut the body in all directions, evidently under the influence of frenzy.

In the present case, so far as the medical evidence goes there is a/. nothing to show that death was caused by cutting the throat — b/. There is no mutilation as in previous cases, although there is dismemberment. c/. There is no evisceration — d/. there is no removal of any portion of the organs of generation or intestines. e/. The murder was undoubtedly committed neither in the street, nor in the victim's house, but probably in the lodging of the murderer. Here, where there was as in the previous case of murder in a house, plenty of time at the disposal of the murderer, there is no sign of frenzied mutilation of the body, but of deliberate and skillful dismemberment with a view to removal. These are all striking departures from the practice of the Whitechapel murderer, and if the body had been found <u>elsewhere than in Whitechapel</u> the supposition that death had been caused by the Ripper would probably not have been entertained.

But the body <u>has been found in Whitechapel</u> and there is a gash on the front part extending downwards to the organs of generation — and we have to account for these facts. I place little importance on the gash; it seems to me not to have been inflicted as in the previous cases. The inner coating of the bowel is hardly touched, and the termination of the cut towards the vagina looks almost as if the knife had slipped, and that as if this portion of the wound had been accidental. The whole of the wound looks as if the murderer had intended to make a cut predatory to removing the intestines in the process of dismemberment, but then changed his mind. Had this been the work of the previous frenzied murderer we may be tolerably sure that he would have continued his hideous work in the way, which he previously adopted. It may also be that the gash was inflicted to give rise to the impression that this case was the work of the Whitechapel murderer and direct attention from the real assassin.

As to how the body got to Whitechapel this is a great difficulty unless it be supposed that it was removed in some conveyance and placed where it was found, unless it be supposed that the murderer, being other than the "Ripper," had good knowledge of the locality. I may get some light on this point as the case goes on. Meanwhile I am inclined to the belief that, taking one thing with another, this is not the work of the Whitechapel murderer but of the hand which was concerned in the murders which are known as the Rainham mystery — the new Police buildings case — and the recent case in which portions of a female body (afterwards identified) were found in the Thames.

        Sept 11 89
        Monro

Thank Mr Monro for
This report
  H.M.
12 Sept./ 89.

(The underscores were made by the author of the report)

It is interesting to note at this point that the Ripper Suspects file — MEPO 3/141 32-135 — is missing since the mid 1970s. And although the few officials who had reportedly viewed the file before it was "lost" would tell us that there was not much of interest in that file we are left with little but their words to denote its importance. The bottom line is that it did not walk off by itself. Someone has that file. Was it a government employee?

WHITECHAPEL, EAST END—FEBRUARY 1891

There is no documentation to explain why the serial killer responsible for the Ripper or Torso murders would wait so long to kill again, but a long break did occur. For 16 months not a single attack occurred which can be attributed to "Jack." Was he in prison for some other minor offense or was he perhaps in some other part of the country experimenting with other forms of murder? Perhaps he simply had too many other mundane things on his mind such as a new wife, child or business. The record for the present stands silent on that question but this serial killer had to be doing something and the odds are that it would have been of a criminal nature.

It was business as usual in the East End as the population tried to put the Ripper murders behind them and there was very little talk of the Torso Killer. Even the residents who felt that the killer was still out there somewhere preferred to believe that he had stopped killing of his own accord. He had not, and the East End was about to relive the "Autumn of Terror" for one last time.

Frances Coles was a 25-year-old alcoholic and a prostitute who spent the last three days of her life going from one bar to another mostly with a 53-year-old merchant seaman named James Thomas Sadler. Before the final night was over Sadler would lose his money and get into several fights, leaving him badly bleeding but alive. Frances, however, would be dead. Between 9 and 11 P.M. on February 12, the couple broke up due to some kind of argument. Frances made her way back to her familiar lodging house at 8 White's Row for a bit of rest. It was the same lodging house in which Annie Millwood had lived when she was attacked nearly three years earlier on February 25, 1888. Frances Coles would become the tenth and final victim in the Ripper series, which began and ended with women from the same building. That fact has never been explained and only the killer could explain why.

Frances woke up from a drunken stupor that early morning of February 13, 1891, at around 12:30 A.M., having rested her head on a kitchen table. From the lodging house she made her way to Shuttleworth's Eatery on Wentworth Street. She was later seen on Commercial Street at 1:45 A.M. where she met a fellow prostitute named Ellen Callagher. She then walked off with a man whom Ellen had just told her was very violent and with whom she should not get involved. Frances ignored her concerned friend's advice and, in doing so, had less than 30 minutes to live.

Just to the south, Constable Ernest Thompson was on his first night of beat duty patrolling on his own. He had been on the force for less than two months. He would nearly be responsible for the capture of Jack the Ripper. At 2:15 A.M. the young constable was walking toward the west along Chamber Street. It was very foggy and as he patrolled he could hear, but not see, a man slowly walking away from him. As he turned into a covered passage known as Swallow Gardens he almost tripped over the body of Frances Coles.

As he aimed his lantern on her face he could see that her throat was fearfully cut. In a flash he connected the woman he saw on the wet ground with the footsteps he could still hear, but they were becoming fainter. He said one word "Ripper." As he turned to give what he knew would be the chase and battle of his life he suddenly saw that, unexpectedly, Frances opened one eye. She was still alive! It took every nerve in his body but he knew where his duty lay; he had to stay with the mortally wounded Frances and allow the man he knew in his mind was Jack the Ripper to slowly walk away into the deepening fog. He had followed his orders to the letter, but he would regret his decision for the rest of his life. The Ripper series was over and the killer who had completely bested London's finest simply walked away into the fog of British history.

Constable Frederick P. Wensley, who would become chief constable of CID, was a friend of Thompson and later wrote, "I fancy that the lost opportunity preyed on Thompson's mind, for I heard him refer to it in despondent terms more than once, and he seemed to regard the incident as presaging some evil fate for himself." Indeed, in 1900 Constable Thompson would be killed by a knife wound as he attempted to arrest a suspect who was causing a disturbance at a coffee stand.

The "Ripper Victims" folder still has individual case files marked:

A contemporary sketch of Frances Coles, the Ripper's last victim in London.

EMMA ELIZABETH SMITH, aged 45, murdered on 3rd April 1888.
MARTHA TABRAM alias TURNER, aged 35 to 40, murdered on 7th August 1888.
MARY ANN NICHOLLS, murdered on 31st August 1888.
ANNIE SIFFEY alias CHAPMAN, murdered on 8th September 1888.
ELIZABETH STRIDE, murdered on 29th September 1888.
CATHERINE EDDOWES, murdered on 29th September 1888.
MARIE JEANETTE KELLY, murdered on 9th November 1888.
ROSE MYLETT alias LIZZIE DAVIS, murdered on 20th December 1888.
ALICE McKENZIE, murdered on 17th July 1889.
TRUNK OF A FEMALE, found on 10th September 1889.
FRANCES COLES, murdered on 13th February 1891.

To answer those who felt that the Ripper murders had ended in 1888 with the death of Mary Kelly, Detective Inspector Edmond Reid would write in 1903 for the *Police Review*: "I was not aware that the last horror was committed in Miller's Court (Kelly in 1888). I was always under the impression that the last of the so-called 'Ripper Murders' was committed in Swallow Gardens; it was there that the late Police Constable Thompson heard footsteps receding, but did not see anyone about the spot where he found the body of Frances Coles, on the morning of the 13th February, 1891."

As time passed memories faded and buildings were torn down or lost to war. Indeed, a good majority of the city police files on the Ripper case were lost in the Nazi bombing of London during World War II. However, from time to time a piece of the lost puzzle does indeed resurface. Perhaps in the future we will be able to look at that one piece of evidence, now hidden, which will once and for all put to rest the mysterious murders of Jack the Ripper.

THE ESCAPE TO AMERICA — APRIL 1891

In early 1891, London police were not exactly hot on the trail of Jack the Ripper, but they may have been a great deal closer than conventional wisdom would lead one to believe. No fewer than three top serving officers, Henry Smith, the assistant police commissioner; Sir Robert Anderson, the police commissioner; and Chief Constable Melville Macnaghten, would later write that the Ripper's identity was known to the police by that time, but there was not enough evidence to charge him. Further, the story persists that after the last murder the killer was captured and confronted by a witness who identified him at once, but who would not testify against him for religious reasons.

Two other officers closely connected to the case, Chief Inspector Frederick George Abberline, who had charge of the Ripper investigation at the street level, and Police Superintendent Arthur Neil, who investigated the same man for three other murders years later, would both write that the man they believed was behind the Ripper murders was none other than Severin Antoniovich Klosowski, better known as George Chapman the "Borough Poisoner." Adding to these officer's comments comes notes written in Anderson's book by Chief Inspector Donald Swanson, desk officer for the Ripper murders and, in effect, Abberline's boss. It was through Swanson that all reports passed so he would know as much about the investigation as anyone. Swanson confirms that "a" suspect was taken to a police location known as the Seaside Home and was identified by a witness. However, Swanson writes in his private notes not meant for publication that the witness "refused to give evidence against him because the suspect was also a Jew and also because his evidence would convict the suspect, and witness would be the means of murderer being hanged, which he did not wish to be left on his mind."

These men also agreed that no further Ripper murders occurred in England after the suspect was confronted. The London series had ended but Chief Inspector Abberline would, in a later interview, state, "there is a coincidence also in the fact that the murders ceased in London when Chapman [Klosowski] went to America, while similar murders began to be perpetrated in America after [he] landed there."

Many authors and researchers writing later point to Abberline's comment about other murders in America and ridicule his opinion, stating that only one (as if one was not enough) Ripper-style murder occurred in America after the London series. And would Jack only kill one? These researchers point to the murder of Carrie Brown in a seedy dockside hotel in lower Manhattan as the only possible victim. However, a closer view reveals no fewer than four possible murders—all unsolved—in the New York/New Jersey area, all committed while a serial killer named Klosowski was, as they say, in town! Klosowski is the only "suspect" in the Ripper murders known to have been in the area during the entire American murder series. The researchers and conventional wisdom were wrong; Inspector Abberline, however, was right. A series of mysterious unsolved murders occurred in America from 1891 to 1892. Before Jack turned to poison upon his return to England in mid–1892 he had a bit of business to conduct across the pond in the United States of America.

> That Chapman's career coincides exactly with the movements and operations of Jack the Ripper must appeal strongly to all who endeavor to throw light upon the shadows of the latter's obscurity.
> — Hargrave L. Adam, *Trial of George Chapman*, 1930

The Torso and Ripper Victims*

Date	Victim	Description
c. May 1887	Unknown (Torso)	First torso murder, body parts found near river Thames at Rainham.
February 25, 1888	Annie Millwood (1850–1888)	Stab wounds on legs and lower torso with a clasp knife (Survived the attack, died later)
March 28, 1888	Ada Wilson (1849–)	At home when attacked by an unknown man. Stabbed twice in the throat. (Survived the attack.)
August 7, 1888	Martha Tabram (1849–1888)	39 stab wounds; 5 in left lung, 2 in right lung, 1 in heart, 5 in liver, 2 in spleen, 6 in stomach. Possible composite murder.
August 31, 1888	Mary Ann Nichols (1845–1888)	Throat cut down to the vertebrae, cut abdomen several times, no parts taken.
September 8, 1888	Annie Chapman (1841–1888)	Strangled? Throat cut deeply, abdomen laid open; uterus, upper vagina and posterior ⅔rds of bladder taken.
September 30, 1888	Elizabeth Stride (1843–1888)	Throat cut deeply, not mutilated. Could have been an assassination.
September 30, 1888	Catharine Eddowes (1842–1888)	Throat cut deeply, face mutilated, body opened from breast bone to pubes, liver stabbed, kidney and womb taken.
c. August 20, 1888	Unknown (Torso)	Headless torso dumped at building site of New Scotland Yard. 2nd torso murder.
November 9, 1888	Mary Jane Kelly (1863–1888)	Attacked inside. Throat cut deeply, body and face greatly mutilated, parts removed, heart taken, most mutilated victim of Jack.
December 20, 1888	Rose Mylett (1863–1888)	Strangled by cord, and no knife wounds.
c. May 31, 1889	Elizabeth Jackson (–1889) (Torso)	Headless torso, parts of her body were found in the Thames River from May 31–June 25, 1889. Only torso victim identified.

1. The Ripper and Torso Murders

July 17, 1889	Alice McKenzie (1849–1889)	Stabbed twice in throat, cut on chest from left breast to navel.
c. September 8, 1889	Unknown (Torso)	Headless torso found on Pinchin Street. Abdomen mutilated, missing womb found in Ripper territory.
February 13, 1891	Frances Coles (1865–1891)	Throat cut. Alive when found, but died on stretcher. Ripper almost caught by police.
c. June 1902	Unknown (Torso)	Chopped up body parts of a woman found just south of the river Thames in single pile. Final torso murder.

*Original chart data adapted from *Alias Jack the Ripper: Beyond the Usual Whitechapel Suspects*

Descriptions of Jack the Ripper

Witness (England)	Description
Ada Wilson	He was a man of around 30 years of age with a sun burnt face, fair mustache, standing 5'6" in height.
Elizabeth Long	Dark complexion, and was wearing a brown deerstalker hat. He was a man over forty, (from behind) as far as I can tell. He seemed a little taller than the deceased. He looked to me like a foreigner as well as I could make out. He looked what I should call shabby genteel.
Joseph Lawende	30 years old, 5'7" in height, fair complexion and mustache, medium build, wearing a salt and pepper colored jacket fitting loosely, gray cloth cap with a peak of the same color. Reddish handkerchief knotted around his neck.
Matthew Parker	Age 25 to 30 years old, 5'7" tall. Long black coat buttoned up, soft felt hawker hat, broad shoulders.
P.C. William Smith	5'7" tall, hard dark felt deerstalker hat, dark clothes. Carried newspaper package 18" × 7", 28 years old, dark complexion, small dark mustache.
James Brown	5'5" tall, age 30, dark complexion, small mustache, black diagonal coat, hard felt hat, collar and tie.
Israel Shwartz	Age 30, 5'5" tall, dark haired, fair complexion, small brown mustache, full face, broad shoulders, dark jacket and trousers, black cap with peak.
George Hutchinson	Age 34–35, 5'6". Pale complexion, dark hair, slight mustached curled at each end, long dark coat, collar cuffs of astrakhan, dark jacket underneath. Light waistcoat, thick gold chain with a red stone seal, dark trousers and button boots, gaiters, white buttons. White shirt, black tie fastened with a horseshoe pin. Dark hat, turned down in the middle. Red kerchief. Jewish and respectable in appearance.
Witness (United States)	Description
Mary Miniter	Around 32 years old, 5'8" tall, slim build, long sharp nose, heavy mustache of light

"Is he the murderer?" A noted resemblance to the 2006 Scotland Yard composite is remarkable (artwork re-created by Robert DeLaCruz, from an illustration originally published in the *Illustrated Police News* from Saturday, November 24, 1888).

Witness (United States)	Description
	color, foreign in appearance, possibly German. *Dark brown cutaway coat, black trousers, old black derby hat with dented crown.* Speaks broken English.
Mr. Kelly	About five feet nine inches in height, light complexion, long nose and light mustache, wore a *shabby cutaway coat and a shabby old derby hat*. He was smeared with blood. Pronounced German accent.
George A. Arsten	A man dressed in light-colored clothes who *wore a derby hat* to match. Rapidly driving a close carriage, with the blinds drawn down.
William Martin	Could be German. He is about five feet eight inches, of rather sturdy build, and had a good *suit of dark clothing and a derby hat*.

*Original chart data adapted from *Alias Jack the Ripper: Beyond the Usual Whitechapel Suspects* and *The American Murders of Jack the Ripper.*

Chapter 2

The American Murders of Jack the Ripper

... attempted, in such a cold-blooded manner, to murder his first wife with a knife in New Jersey.
— Inspector Frederick George Abberline, 1903

A WHOLE NEW WORLD

In 1888, as London reeled from the murders of Jack the Ripper, Chief Inspector Thomas Byrnes, highest ranking police officer in New York City at the time, commented in his very comfortable office that if the killer ever came to his city he would be "in the jug within 36 hours." That theory was about to be put to the test in 1891. Severin Klosowski was on his way to America on a small passenger ship called the *Waesland* and a series of mysterious murders was about to begin in New York City in an area not unlike the ghettos of the East End of London. He "needed" to begin as soon as he could and he would arrive just hours before, and only a few blocks away from, the murder site of Carrie Brown. "Jack" was ready to go back to "work" in a whole new world. Severin arrived in the early afternoon of April 23, 1891.

LOWER MANHATTAN, NEW YORK CITY—APRIL 1891

Carrie Brown was a 60-year-old prostitute and well known in the crowded slum areas of the New York City docks within easy sight of the Brooklyn Bridge. She had once been an actress but that was a long time ago. The only remnant of her former life was her nickname "Old Shakespeare." It seems Carrie still liked to quote the Bard whenever she was drunk, and she quoted him a great deal.

On her last night alive she could be seen working the waterfront bars as usual looking for drinks. By 9 P.M. on April 23, 1891, she had made her way to the familiar and very run down East River Hotel. Carrie was with a fellow prostitute named Mary Healey, both swapping stories and drinks at the local hangout. Both would soon leave for different locations looking for men to pay for their beds.

Carrie returned to the East River Hotel around 10:45 or 11 P.M., still very much intoxicated, but she was not alone. She was with a much younger man who did his very best to stay in the

Carrie Brown, aka "Old Shakespeare" (New York City Municipal Archives).

background. He would later be described as "apparently about 32-years-old, five feet eight inches in height; of slim build, with a long, sharp nose and a heavy mustache of light color. He wore an old black derby hat, the crown of which was much dented." He was thought by Mrs. Mary Minter, the housekeeper at the hotel, to be German, but Polish would do just as well. (Just before his murder trial in 1903 it would be reported that Klosowski "speaks with a foreign accent, and has been heard to converse in German.") This odd couple was then assigned to room number 31. It would be the last time anyone saw Carrie Brown alive — save her killer.

After Carrie's brutal and disturbing Ripper-style murder the killer made his escape. At first he walked down the hallway, but even though it was around 2 A.M. people were still hanging around the lower floors and the bar area. Turning around he saw the ladder used to access the roof and his escape route was readily apparent. He was soon on the street moving away from the cheap lodging hotel, but he did not go far. For whatever reason he seemed confused (did he not know the area?) and walked for only five minutes before stopping at the Glenmore Hotel.

The clerk at once saw that the man had blood smeared on his hands and clothing as he walked toward the desk. He was later described as "about five feet nine inches in height, light complexion, long nose and light mustache." There would be no doubt that this was the man who had gone with "Old Shakespeare" into room 31.

The night clerk, in an interview with the *New York Times* published on April 26, would state, "The man was very nervous and agitated. 'His hat was pulled down over his eyes,' Kelly explained, 'and he acted queer. He asked me in broken English if I could give him a room for

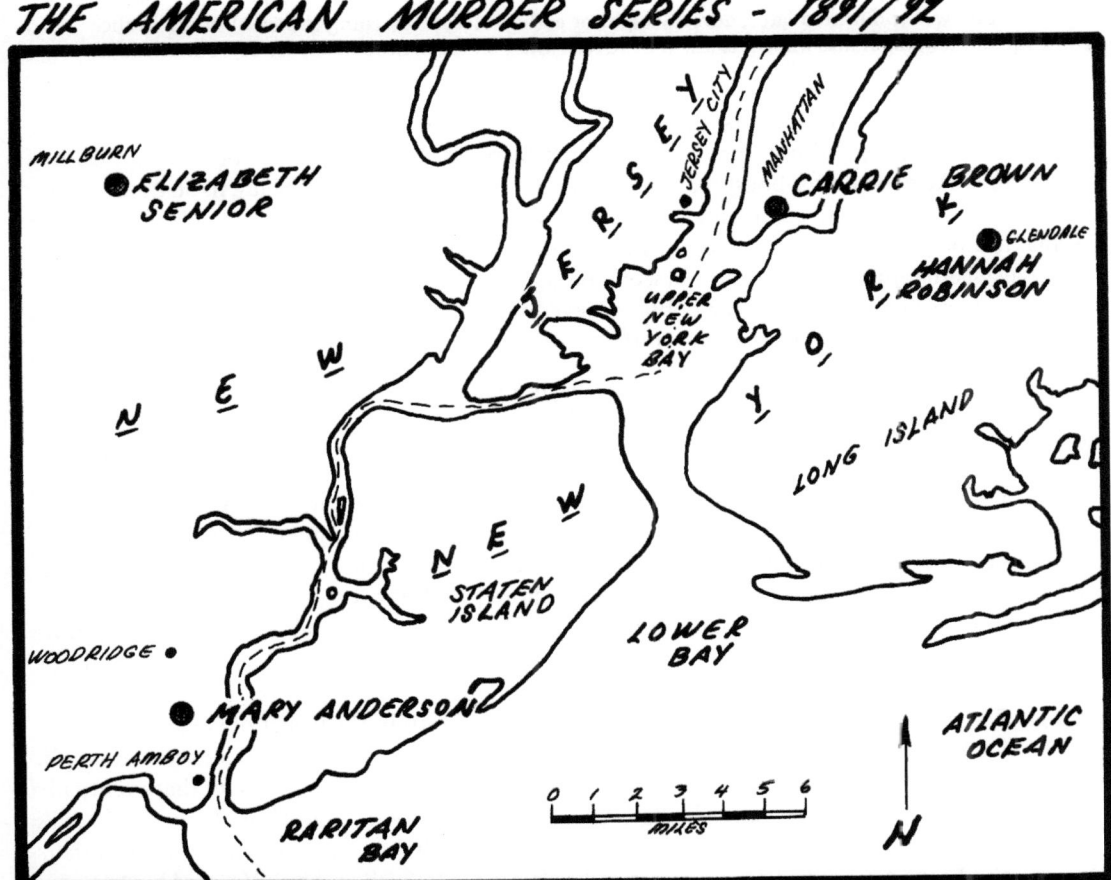

During the American murder series there would be no combined investigation into the four murders. Only later would Inspector Frederick George Abberline, who was in charge of the Ripper investigation at the street level, state that the same man responsible for the London murders could very well have been responsible for three or four murders in America (map by author).

the night. At the time his right hand rested on my desk and I noticed it was all bloody. I noticed it looked as though he had tried to wipe the blood off, but it was smeared all over. There were also two blotches of blood on his right cheek, as though he had put the bloody hand to his face. There was also blood on his right coat sleeve and it was spattered on his collar. Altogether the fellow looked very bad. I asked him what price room he wanted. He answered nervously that he wanted me to give him a room, as he did not have a cent. I told him that I could not give him a room, as the house was full. He turned to go away, but instead of going down the stairs to the street he started for the washroom. I came out from behind my desk and told him we only allowed the guests of the house the use of that room. He turned then without a word and went down into the street. As he did so I turned to Tiernman, our night watchman, who was in the office at the time, and said: 'That man looks as though he had murdered somebody!"

New York Times— April 25, 1891
CHOKED, THEN MUTILATED
A murder like one of "Jack the Ripper's" deeds
Whitechapel's Horrors Repeated In an East Side Lodging House
— An Aged Woman the Victim — Several Arrests on Suspicion

A murder which in many of its details recalls the crimes with which "Jack the Ripper" horrified London was committed late Thursday night or early yesterday morning in a small room in the squalid lodging house known as the East River Hotel, on the southeast corner of Catherine and Water Streets.

It would not take long for the New York police to announce that they "had a clue" even though they really had nothing to go on. Chief Inspector Byrnes was now on the political hot seat to make good on his boast that he would soon have the killer "in the jug in 36 hours." One mistake during public comments that Byrnes would not make, however, would be to declare that the man who had killed Carrie Brown was the real Jack the Ripper. "Inspector Byrnes refuses to say whether in his opinion the old woman was killed by the genuine 'Jack the Ripper' or not." He could not afford to fail if the public believed that "Jack" was in town, and the panic would have been immediate, not to mention the increased costs of investigating the murder.

General Alarm!— Arrest a man 5 feet 9 inches high, about thirty-one years old, light hair and mustache; speaks broken English. Wanted for murder.

THOMAS BYRNES, Acting Superintendent.

Before long Byrnes had a suspect, albeit not a very good one. But the man had been in the hotel that night taking a room on the same floor, and he was a foreigner. His name was Ameer Ben Ali, Alias "Frenchy," but he did not fit the description of the man seen in the hotel with Carrie or the bloody man seen later at the Glenmore Hotel. Press reports described Ali as "[A] typical Algerian Arab, with a dark, sallow skin, coal-black hair and eyes, and a thin, aquiline nose." He was simply not Carrie Brown's killer, but the police had "a" man — that would be good enough for the New York police at the time.

The trial began on June 24, 1891, before Recorder Smith in the Court of General Sessions. District Attorney Nicoll would take the floor himself to present the bloody evidence against Ali. It would be the bloody evidence found on the suspect's clothes and in his room that eventually convicted the Arab. It was later shown however, that the blood "found" by the police in Ali's room, number 31, and on his clothes had been "accidentally" placed there by police or others who had been at the crime scene. In other words Ameer Ben Ali had been framed by someone in authority for the murder of Carrie Brown in order to effect a quick conviction in a very bloody murder case. As in the London murders, the real killer had not been found, but the public was not to be trusted with the truth.

Even through the Arab had been convicted, Byrnes did not completely have his way. The

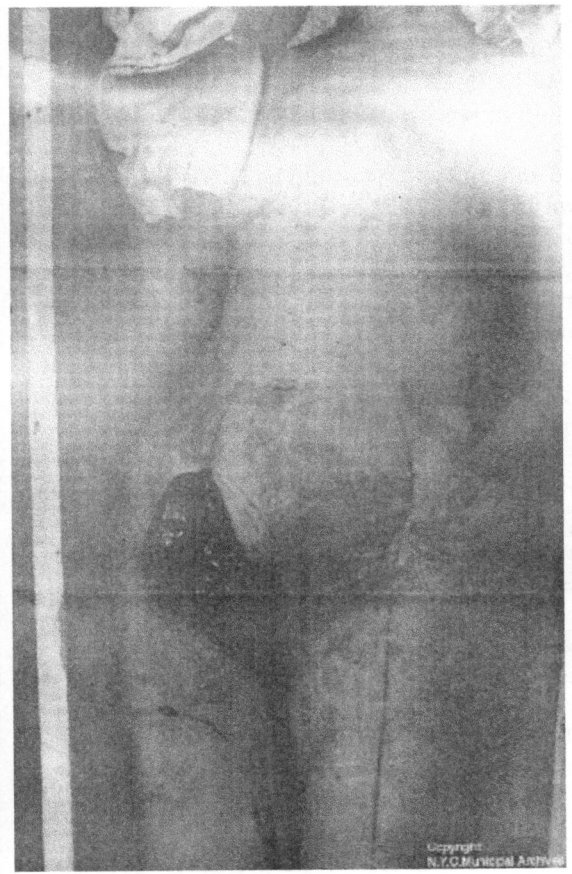
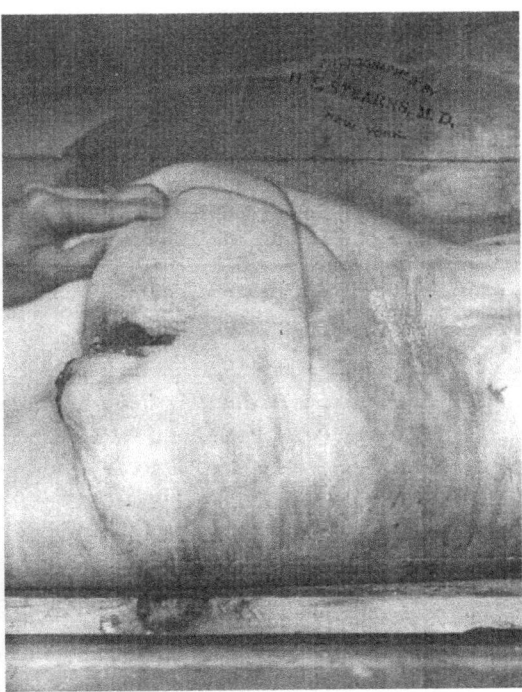

Left and above: Mortuary photographs of Carrie Brown (New York City Municipal Archives).

acting police superintendent had wanted the death penalty imposed, which would have ended any future problems had the case been overturned with "real" evidence. Instead, the less than fully convinced jury voted for a second-degree murder conviction, which gave Ali a life sentence and a possibility of a future release. Inspector Byrnes would give no comment to the press about Ali's future.

Ameer Ben Ali would spend 11 years of his life behind bars, at first in the notorious Sing Sing prison and then at the Mattewan State Hospital for Insane Criminals. He would finally be freed due to the continuing work of journalists Jacob Riis, Charles Russell and others who continued to unearth the truth of Ali's erroneous conviction. On April 17, 1902, Governor Benjamin Odell pardoned Ali because of "grave doubts of the prisoner's guilt.... To refuse under such circumstances would be plainly a denial of justice, and after a very careful consideration of all the facts, I have reached the conclusion that it is clearly my duty to order the prisoner's release."

With the governor's pardon Ali was free to return home to Algiers. As for Carrie Brown's killer, he was also free and would continue to hunt women for the next 12 years beginning with his next victim in Long Island, New York.

Near Glendale, Long Island—August 1891

She was a 25-year-old native of Sunderland, England, who had immigrated to the United States five years earlier. Her name was Hannah Robinson and she may have added to her meager income with occasional prostitution. When her body was discovered on August 2, next to a factory building site, Severin Klosowski had been in America for a little more than three months and he was preparing to move across the river to Jersey City with his wife. Once again it was a weekend as Klosowski hunted for a woman to kill. Once again a mysterious murder would occur while this serial killer was living nearby.

At first the woman remained unidentified and, in fact, she would be falsely identified by a tramp that tried to claim her body as his own relative. (What he wanted her body for is best left unsaid.) According to the August 3 edition of the *New York Times*, "the woman was apparently about twenty years of age. Her features were regular, and she had dark hair and eyes and a well-developed form, although below the medium height. She wore a black cashmere dress, a red flannel embroidered petticoat, white underclothing, black stockings, French kid gaiter shoes with patent-leather tips, and a black flat-shaped straw hat trimmed with black ribbon and yellow flowers. On the right hand there was a black silk glove, and there were two gold rings on the fingers of the left hand. One had a garnet stone and the other a Rhine stone."

The victim was first thought to have been one of the many women who worked in H. W. Meyer's cigar factory just down the road near the town of Glendale. Indeed, the building next to where her body had been found was being built as a home for the new foreman of the factory. However, a check of the female workforce soon showed that no one was missing from the factory. The victim had come from outside the local area and her body had been dumped by the edge of the railroad tracks on the site.

She had been strangled to death, witnessed by the "five abrasions of the skin on the left side of the throat while fingernails had cut deep into the flesh." There was a great deal of personal rage in this murder, but it is not known whether or not Hannah knew her killer. Perhaps she had simply been picked up by a stranger. Due to a rainstorm, which had passed that night, it was surmised that she would have been placed on the site some time after 10:30 P.M. as her clothes were not soaked through.

Police would later discover a possible witness to the movement of the body. A man named George Arsten of Greenport was drinking at the bar in Kreuscher's Hotel. The hotel was located at a quiet corner in Ridgewood on Myrtle and Cypress Avenues. Mr. Arsten's attention was called to a fast-moving closed carriage, with its blinds drawn, going up Myrtle Avenue toward Glendale. He said: "Upon the box sat a man dressed in light-colored clothes who wore a *derby hat* to match." It was 12:30 A.M. on that early Sunday morning. This was an unusual event for that time of night and it gave the police a general description of the man they were looking for. "Jack" had a carriage!

New York Times— August 3, 1891
A LONG ISLAND MYSTERY
THE BODY OF A STRANGLED WOMAN
FOUND NEAR GLENDALE

The body of a young woman was found yesterday near Glendale, L. I., half a mile from the Brooklyn city line, by a man who had been blackberrying. It was lying under the walls of a new building. The girl had been strangled to death.
There is a by-path from the factory across the fields to the partially-erected house and a road which runs from Fresh Pond passes it. The supposition is that the girl and her murderer came by the path, as some of the red sand of the latter was found on her shoes.

It would take days for the authorities to finally discover the identity of the mysterious murdered woman. But just as the New York police began to trace Hannah Robinson's background and movements, news came on the wire from London of yet one more East End murder. Once again a woman had been taken into a dark alley in Whitechapel, her throat cut. It did not take long for the newspapers to plaster the name of Jack the Ripper all over London, as London's best detectives took up the chase. They would later settle on the theory that it had been a copycat murder of a much older woman who was not a prostitute. What they could not know was that the real Ripper had already made a new home in New York City — and he was still very active with his knife.

A picture of the identity of Hannah Robinson was quickly painted by New York detectives, who had become frustrated by all of the dead ends they had run into. They were soon able to trace her movements from when she came to America to work as a servant in 1886 until just before her death. One interesting fact about her clothes and income did emerge. She seemed to have a great deal more clothes than would be expected for a poor servant girl, and they were of good quality. The detectives also discovered that she kept with her at most times a good deal of money — at least hundreds of dollars in a large roll plus another set in her purse. It was a significant sum at the time. And, although the authorities never stated it outright, it was suggested that Hannah might have been earning some extra money outside of her regular servant's duties.

On the night/early morning of her death as she visited the "Big City" she had her roll of bills with her. When her body was discovered the roll was gone and so was her purse. With this information now in the hands of the police, robbery became the prime focus of the investigation. At the same time the police discovered a name to go on. It was Mortimer Phillips. Phillips had been an earlier love of Hannah's and had sent her letters, which were discovered by the police in a trunk. Using these new clues, the police would search for Mortimer Phillips, while the real killer made plans for a move from New York to New Jersey. He was never one to stay in one place for very long.

It was soon discovered that at the time of Hannah's murder young Phillips had been with friends in New Jersey. After he was picked up by the police and interrogated, detectives quickly discovered that he was not their man. His story was "corroborated by a telegram from Detective Smith, whom the District Attorney had sent to New Jersey to investigate." Not skipping a beat, however, the police then shifted their investigation to another old flame of Hannah's named Martin.

At one point a few years earlier, Martin and Hannah had been engaged, but, for reasons not fully clear, the marriage never occurred. In fact, when the case was finally put on the back burner do to a lack of leads it would end with that loose end undiscovered. The police would never find Martin nor discover his last name, but he was never a solid suspect in the case.

When Hannah was buried on August 8, 1891, in Mount Olivet Cemetery in Maspeth, press coverage of her murder guaranteed a good crowd. In fact, so many had come to see her off that the building was soon filled to capacity, with hundreds forced to wait outside. It would be a short service as few who had come had known the victim, but that would not stop the town officers of nearby Newtown from offering a $500 reward for her killer's capture. The small town had adopted Hannah as their own and the residents were going to give her a good send-off.

The final police investigation into Hannah's murder would come in September 1892, some 13 months after her death. This time the police focused on a local small-time criminal named Clarence Almy. Almy had been reported to have been in the general area at the time of the murder. When he was taken into custody in New York City he had a newspaper report of Hannah's murder as well as a lock of hair. The newspaper article reportedly stated, "Clarence Almy was suspected of murdering Hannah Robinson."

Almy was held in jail as he recovered from typhoid but was never charged. He was described by the *New York Times* as a "bull-headed, ill-looking fellow." And even though it was reported that the authorities "have obtained damaging evidence against Almy," the bull-headed Almy would never go to trial. He would eventually be released due to a lack of evidence. In fact, the police had no real evidence to place anyone under arrest for Hannah's murder. The case would go unsolved. As for Jack, by the time police forces were focusing on Clarence Almy, Klosowski had already returned to the slums of the East End of London. Before he sailed back to London, however, he had a bit more business to conduct in America — this time it would be in New Jersey!

MILBURN, NEW JERSEY—JANUARY 1892

Serial killer Klosowski had by this time spent a few months in the Jersey City area working in or running a barbershop. It was not reported if he was happy in his work, but his wife, Lucy, six months pregnant with their second child, most certainly was not. (Their first child had died at age five months just before they had left London for America.) Klosowski was once again staying out late at night, and we are led to believe in the company of other women. He had even gone to the extreme of attacking his wife in what could have been a bloody assault with a large knife had a customer not come into the front of the shop at that exact moment. Business seemed to come before murder. Klosowski later coldly informed his wife that he planned to murder her and "cut off her head." Lucy then said: "But the neighbors would have asked where I had gone to." Not missing a step Klosowski stated, "Oh, I should simply have told them that you had gone back to New York!" That was enough for Lucy Klosowski. She left America — and out of the clutches of Klosowski — arriving back in the East End of London in early February 1892. Severin Klosowski had lost control of a woman and he needed to gain control once again — and soon!

For 40 years Joseph and Elizabeth Senior lived in their small but tidy two-story home on Springfield Avenue in Milburn. The neat and well-kept house stood across the street from the Milburn schoolhouse. Seventy-year-old Joseph worked as a watch repairman and local taxidermist but he supplemented his modest income by working as the night watchman at Mr. Fouratt's hat shop. Seventy-three-year-old Elizabeth kept the house in good order while her husband was at work as the town seemed to grow up around them.

It was not too difficult for the killer to enter the house as very few if any residents of Milburn bothered to lock their doors. Violent crime was not a part of the day-to-day concerns of the villagers. Indeed, some had even forgotten where they had last placed their house keys. After January 31 the keys would be held close and the doors would most assuredly be locked.

Joseph Senior had finished watching the shop as it opened for business that morning. It did not take him long to walk home, as everything was nearby in the small village. As he went into his home he was surprised not to see Elizabeth in their bedroom. As reported in the *New York Times* of February 2, "Going to the stove he found in front of it the body of his wife, who had been brutally murdered during the night. The body lay at full length on the floor. The throat was cut, there were eleven stab wounds in the breast, and both arms were frightfully gashed."

Her killer had chosen a defenseless old woman to vent his murderous sexual rage and yet he had not chosen well. Elizabeth Senior did not go down easily. Later investigation would show blood splattered all over the murder scene; silent evidence that Mrs. Senior had fought hard for her life. She may have been surprised by her killer at first, but the many deep gashes on her hands and arms showed that she soon recovered and could very well have injured her cowardly attacker. Before long, however, her killer found her throat and then out of rage he stabbed her breast again and again. Once she was dead and control was established her killer simply washed off his hands and carefully searched the house for any money he could find. For his efforts he was rewarded with a mere $45. It was the price of a life for a serial killer who was low on funds.

After he found his dead wife on the floor Joseph Senior ran out of his home to find the local constable. And even though there were no witnesses to the brutal crime, the authorities soon announced that they had a suspect. Before the detectives finished their investigations at the home, the telegraph wires came alive with news of an arrest warrant.

Arrest for murder August Lyntz, German, Thirty-three, 5 feet 7 inches, dark hair and mustache, dark complexion, small brown eyes, dark suit, brown overcoat, old-style derby hat, with a wide brim and high crown; clothes must have some blood on them; working shoes, with strap and buckle.

Information to the District Attorney of Newark.

There was never any evidence to show that August Lyntz had anything to do with the murder of Elizabeth Senior. He did know the couple who lived on Springfield Avenue, but so did everyone else in town. He had worked in Fouratt's Hat Shop as an engineer before losing his job for drinking while at work. He was also seen in town near the Senior home that night but so were two other men—both strangers—and it was not a very large town. For their part, the police would attempt to overstate their case by calling Lyntz a "dissolute character," but what of the other two men? They would never be found and no one would ever come forward to state that they had been one of the two strangers in town that night. Which one was Jack?

New York Times— February 4, 1892
THE MURDER OF MRS. SENIOR
NEWARK POLICE BELIEVE THAT THE
PRISONER LENTZ IS THE CRIMINAL

Newark, Feb. 3.— The police of this city have evidence which they claim establishes beyond doubt that in the person of August Lentz they have the murderer of old Mrs. Senior, at Milburn last Sunday.

The police are trying to hunt down two other suspicious characters; but the general belief is that Lentz is the man they want.

Before long August Lyntz was in custody; after all, he had not been hiding, and may not have even known of the murder until he was arrested. He had gone to a lodging house at 5 New Chambers Street in New York City very near where Carrie Brown had been murdered. When he was picked up he still had his brown overcoat with him as he told the officer: "All right; I supposed you were after me." What the police could not find was blood on any of his clothing even though his clothes were removed and gone over very closely. The murder weapon, which had not been left at the murder scene, was not found with Lyntz either. The fact that the murder weapon was not found was evidence, however, that the killer intended to murder Mrs. Senior, not just rob her.

On February 17, an inquest was held into the murder of Elizabeth Senior at Bonnell's Hall in Milburn. It would take less than a full afternoon and would feature only 12 witnesses. The police did not produce any real evidence against August Lyntz. It was an easy and swift verdict of "death at the hands of person or persons unknown." August Lyntz was free to go and once again the real killer had escaped the hands of justice. In fact, he was not even suspected.

BETWEEN WOODBRIDGE AND PERTH AMBOY, NEW JERSEY—JUNE 1892

Severin was running out of money and it had been months since his wife had "escaped" his brutal control. Once again he would be on the move as he decided to go back to London and look her up. After all, he had a new daughter he had yet to see and there were those body parts he had left in London that he had worked so hard to "harvest." He could not leave them just sitting around forever. Just before he left America, however, there would be one last mysterious murder committed in New Jersey. It would be the last of Jack's murders in the United States.

Herta Mary Anderson was not a prostitute as far as anyone would discover. The 28-year-old woman worked as a servant at Maurer's Hotel near Rahway, New Jersey. On June 8, she had begun her last day early, walking to Perth Amboy to do a day's shopping. At 2 P.M. she was seen leaving town with her purchases as she made her way along the old railroad tracks back to the hotel. It was a route used by many of the locals, and there were many areas in which an individual could easily hide in thick woods along the tracks that twisted north and south. In fact, as Herta made her way home there was a man walking in front of her and another man walking not too far behind. Neither one would see her on the track, hear anything or even see the face of her killer. He would come from the darkness of the woods and he probably returned by the same path.

It was later estimated that Herta was attacked sometime between 5:15 and 5:25 P.M. on the track between Woodbridge and Perth Amboy. She was less than a mile from Maurer's Hotel. Herta never had a chance and may never have even seen her cowardly killer. She was shot in the back with a 32-caliber pistol, the round entering her heart, killing her instantly. It was a new "American twist" for the series, but old habits die hard as her killer then slit her throat from ear to ear with a sharp, but small-bladed knife. The job done, the killer then grabbed Herta by the right arm and dragged her lifeless body across the tracks and into the dense woods. It took only seconds and no one heard or saw anything. As for the pistol, the New Jersey police would never recover the weapon. However, when Klosowski was arrested in 1902 a fully loaded American pistol would be recovered in his room. In London that would be a rare find, but whatever happened to the weapon?

Before long the rail walkers found the first of Herta's packages from her shopping trip. Looking around, the murdered woman was soon discovered dumped in the brush close to the tracks. The knife used to cut her throat was later located where it had been thrown only 24 feet from her body. Investigators soon concluded that this was not a robbery gone very wrong, but that this was murder for murder's sake. None of her packages had been opened or even appeared to have been moved from where they had been dropped. This would prove to be strong evidence that the killer intended murder and nothing else.

New York Times—June 9, 1892
FOUND WITH HER THROAT CUT
THE DEAD BODY OF A HOTEL SERVANT IN A SWAMP

Rahway, N. J., June 8.— Mary Anderson, a servant employed at Maurer's Hotel, was found dead, with her throat cut, in the swamp between Woodbridge and Perth Amboy.... This short cut ... leaves the railroad and leads through a piece of dense woods. It is used by laborers in factories in the neighborhood on their way to and from work ... the motive is yet a mystery.

At first the police focused on any strangers in the woods at the time. Soon at least two tramps were discovered to have been seen in the area of the murder that very afternoon. Near the time of the murder two men had jumped out of the woods and frightened two young boys, who soon told their story to detectives working on the murder case. It did not take long for the Jersey Central Railroad police to check the local rail yards. Before long two men were found hiding in one of the cars and were immediately arrested. Soon a third was located nearby and he was taken into custody as well. The men were identified as John Lynch, John Smith and Michael Casey, all tramps. They were ordered held for 10 days in jail while the police attempted to sort out who, if anyone, may have been involved in the murder. It did not take long, however, for the "Murdering Tramp Theory" to fall apart, as the police were unable to tie any of the men to the crime.

As Herta's funeral was being conducted on June 12, focus shifted to a former boyfriend named Axel Peterson. Some 5,000 people attended her services, the largest funeral ever held in Perth Amboy at the time, as Acting Chief of Police Burke put detectives on the trail of young Peterson. It did not take long for conflicting stories to come to light. Peterson's mother informed the police that her son had been in Chicago at the time of the murder while his sister pegged his location "somewhere in the Dakota Territory." In fact, Axel had been in Perth Amboy at the time and had seen his old girlfriend Herta just days before her death. And testimony would show that there had been an argument.

It would not be long before the murdering boyfriend theory also fell apart. Peterson could easily prove that he was not in the area of the murder at the time. His family need not have supplied stories to cover his possible involvement. However, another young man who also knew Herta soon replaced Peterson as the prime and, as time would show, the last suspect to come to the attention of the authorities.

New York Times—June 14, 1892
PETERSON'S FRIEND ARRESTED
MARY ANDERSON HAD NURSED HIM—
SEEN NEAR THE PLACE OF MURDER

Perth Amboy, N.J., June 13.— Acting Chief of Police Burke, together with Detective Oliver and Marshal Burke, arrested Harry Schlipf, a Pennsylvania Dutchman, in the Lehigh Valley coal yards this morning upon suspicion of being the murderer of Mary Anderson.

Night Watchman Schutlz positively identified Schlipf as being the man he met upon the edge of the woods about 200 yards from the scene of the murder, and about 10 minutes after the crime had been committed.

Chief Burke had his detectives searching for Harry Schlipf since the murder, but they could not locate their suspect. Yet Harry had not left the area in a hurry and he had not tried to cover his movements. In fact, he had been at the funeral and was decidedly not in hiding. For Acting Chief of Police Burke it was a closed case but it would soon fall apart. No fewer than 16 affidavits were filed with the District Attorney's office stating that at the time of the murder young Schlipf was working at the local railroad yard, where he was employed until 6 P.M. that night. Much to the dismay of Chief Burke, Schlipf could not have committed the crime. It would prove to be yet another dead end.

Schlipf would be the last suspect the police would arrest in connection with the mysterious murder of Herta Mary Anderson. With her murder the series ended, and yet no police force ever investigated these four American murders as a series possibly committed by a single killer. Local and state police forces instead focused on separate individuals, including the conviction of an innocent man in New York, and no one ever thought to link these murders.

And what of serial killer Severin Klosowski? He would leave the New York/New Jersey area for a whole new set of murders in and around London. There were no more Ripper-style murders in America after he left town because Jack had gone home to his old killing grounds and for a short reunion with his family. There would, however, be one last torso murder in England, but that lay a few years in the future and only after Klosowski had moved back to London, just south of the river Thames. Once again murders would seem to follow the ever-moving Klosowski.

The American Victims*

1.	April 24, 1891	Carrie Brown (c.1831–1891)	First American murder, strangled and attacked with a sharp knife in bed. Very similar attack to the Ripper murder of Mary Jane Kelly with throat possibly cut. Not as a brutal by far with less damage. Wrong man convicted of the murder.
2.	August 2, 1891	Hannah Robinson (1866–1891)	Strangled to death and dumped near a railroad line. Similar situation to Ripper victim Rose Mylett. No one was ever brought to trial in this case.
3.	January 31, 1892	Elizabeth Senior (1819–1892)	At home when attacked by an unknown man. Stabbed many times, cut throat. Similar to Ripper victim Martha Tabrum. Wrong man was arrested. No trial.

4. June 8, 1892	Herta Mary Anderson (1864–1892)		Shot, cut throat and dragged away from tracks to woods. Wrong man arrested. First use of a gun. No trial.

*Original chart data adapted from *The American Murders of Jack the Ripper*

Events in Klosowski's life coincidental with the American murders:

- Klosowski and wife move from London, England, to New York City—first murder.
- Klosowski and wife move from New York City to Jersey City, New Jersey—second murder.
- Lucy Klosowski leaves her husband and returns to London—third murder.
- Klosowski moves from America back to London for a short stay in Whitechapel—fourth murder.

Section II — The Poison Work of Jack the Ripper

Chapter 3

A Serial Killer Returns to London

Always the same — same la-di-da, 'igh' 'at and umbrella. Two wives he had while at Tottenham — one English, one foreign.
— Wolff Levisohn, 1902

LATE NINETEENTH CENTURY

Lucy Klosowski had left her husband Severin in New Jersey after he threatened to kill her with a very large knife around the end of January 1892. She knew he was fully capable of carrying out that threat. It was a move which could be described as an escape from an individual she knew to be very violent. Yet, only five months later, conventional wisdom places Severin Klosowski living with his wife at her sister's home at 26 Scarborough Street, in the heart of Whitechapel. The Ripper had returned to his home ground, and his wife had taken him in.

At this point the evidence becomes somewhat clouded and much of it has been lost through time. It is true, thanks to trial testimony in 1903, that Severin did return to his wife. Most later sources report that the reunion lasted only a month and that Klosowski left the home never to see his wife or his newborn daughter again, except for a brief meeting, for identification purposes only, with his wife in 1903 during the investigation of his three suspected murders. However, the short visit to Whitechapel may very well have been much longer than earlier suggested. Further trial testimony from Lucy's sister, Mrs. Stanislaus Rauch, suggests that the couple planned to make a go of it once again. "When the child was about a fortnight old (two weeks c. June 1892) [Klosowski] came back from America, and I left my sister, as they were going to live together. I left them together in the same lodgings. That was the last I saw of him." (This testimony also suggests that they had left her home and had a new place of their own.)

We find further statements (from 1903 testimony) of a possible longer reunion from Stanislaus Baderski, Lucy's brother and the man who had introduced Lucy to barber/hairdresser Klosowski in 1889. "Saw them in City Road about 10 years ago [c. December 1892/January 1893]. Lucy left (Klosowski), and after that I did not know what became of him."

In 1894, when Klosowski was living with a woman named Annie Chapman, he brought another woman home to live with them. From Annie Chapman's testimony at his trial we learn that the new woman was none other than Lucy Klosowski — his wife! Annie Chapman was asked "Do you recognize that woman?" (Pointing to Lucy Klosowski in court.) Annie replied: "Yes, he brought her to the shop where I was living with him. He said she was his wife." So for at least a few weeks in 1894 Lucy and Severin were living together along with Annie Chapman. Annie, however, did not mention Lucy's then two-year-old little daughter who may have been elsewhere at the time.

A Return to England—June 1892

On February 7, 1892, Chief Inspector Frederick George Abberline retired from a long and mostly successful career as an officer of the law on a yearly pension of £206 13s 4d. He had been the prime investigator at the street level in the "Jack the Ripper" murders before moving on to the Cleveland Street scandal in 1889, which had involved Albert Victor, better known as Queen Victoria's grandson. Even though another officer had been assigned to the Ripper case, with little or nothing to go on, the case was for all intents and purposes closed without a satisfactory conclusion. Abberline would later note: "Theories! We were almost lost in theories; there were so many of them." It is interesting to note that no photos of Inspector Abberline have ever been discovered.

There were no suspects of any note to investigate so the killer was free to move about and continue his murderous work, just so long as he did not draw too much attention to his "new" series. The way for a killer to continue to take innocent lives in a very personal manner was to put down the knife and find a new method. That was exactly what serial killer Severin Antoniovich Klosowski was about to do when he returned to London from America and the series of death he left behind in the United States.

When Klosowski returned to London in June 1892, he knew he had been successful during the Ripper series. No one was looking for him and he could take his time collecting his hard-earned body parts. He was also within easy walking distance of Buck's Row, Mitre Square, and all the rest of the Ripper murder sites. Klosowski was still in the habit of roaming around the neighborhood in the dead of night and must have smiled to himself as he retraced the steps of Jack the Ripper! He could relive each and every murder. He may have even carried a body part or two or his knife with him as he visited the sites. It would not have been out of character.

There is no known record or testimony to document the date when Lucy once again left Severin in 1892, so his movements become lost in the shadows until he resurfaces in late 1893. After he was arrested in 1902 officers would locate an interesting clue concerning that period of time. It is interesting to note that the suspicious and always wary Klosowski would keep that small piece of paper for ten years. Why he did has never been fully explained. It began with "Came from America in 1893...."

This was clearly not the truth. More than a few individuals came forward to state that Klosowski was in London in 1892. Yet, why would Klosowski attempt to mislead anyone who may have been looking at his activities in 1892? Klosowski certainly possessed no real documents recording his activity from mid 1892 to the end of 1893, so we may never know. Perhaps a series of crimes in and around London were committed that were never solved in which Klosowski was never suspected, yet for which he was responsible. Was he being held somewhere? It has been reported that Klosowski may have been busy running a small hairdresser's shop at 209 Pentonville Road in Isllington around the end of 1892 into 1893. Word of this comes from a report on the Ripper Web site "Casebook" in which Neal Shelden reports that an 1893 post office directory gives that address for Klosowski. An even more interesting possibility could be that he went back to America after visiting London, killed once again in America and then returned to England for a third and final time. Could the note be true? One thing is probably true; he must have been moving around a lot—he always did that.

Klosowski's story continues toward the end of 1893 when he found work in Mr. Haddin's hairdresser's shop at 5 West Green Road, South Tottenham. He had by then separated from Lucy, most likely she left him for the final time, and he was using an alias of "Schloski." This was at least the second time he would use an alias but it would not be the last. Alfred Wicken serves as the source of this information — he worked with Klosowski at Haddin's on a daily basis. "Never heard him called by any other name other than Schloski," he said. By this time Klosowski claimed to be an American but he clearly did not look the part. No one seems to have pressed him on the point, but speaking broken English and looking like an Eastern European did not help his cover story. They may have suspected that he was German. He was heard to speak some German, which would be later published in news reports. (German spoken in New York City?)

Wicken would later report that "He (Klosowski) worked there (Haddin's) for about nine or twelve months with me after which he took a shop in High Road Tottenham, which had formerly belonged to Mr. Haddin. I left the neighborhood before the accused." It would be at the High Road hairdresser's that Klosowski would come in contact with a young woman named Annie Chapman. On the stand years later Annie would recall the first meeting with this serial killer. She stated: "I first became acquainted with the accused Chapman towards the end of 1893, when he was going under the name Klosowski. He was employed as an assistant at Mr. Haddin's Hairdresser's shop, West Green Road. I went there one day and saw the accused there and made his acquaintance. After that I went out with him for awhile. I think he said he was either single or widower. He was living at Haddin's and he proposed I should go as his housekeeper, and after a time I did so." Eight years later Miss Chapman was still in Tottenham at 9 Hartington Road, living with friends.

Annie Chapman is perhaps the best link to Klosowski's past as the Ripper. Although it has yet to be proven, the Annie Chapman who moved in with Klosowski could very well have been the daughter of Ripper victim Annie Chapman. Chapman was killed by "Jack" on September 8, 1888, in the backyard of 29 Hanbury Street and her daughter's name was Annie Georgina Chapman. If this is the same woman, than Klosowski would have been playing a very dangerous game. Any police follow-up to the Ripper murders would have brought investigators to Annie's place of employment and they could have easily run into Klosowski. (He had been questioned at least twice during the Ripper and Torso investigations and the officer may have recalled the connection.) It would have been a calculated risk but one that serial killer Klosowski would have thoroughly enjoyed.

Before long the "happy couple" could be found living together as Mr. and Mrs. Klosowski. The arrangement would last from November 1893 until December 1894, beginning in some rooms in Haddin's. But working for someone else was not what Klosowski was looking for. Besides, there would be far too many people around his living quarters to suit him. For the work ahead he needed a place of his own.

A detail of that period of Klosowski's life can be taken from a statement made by William Lemain Bray, the managing clerk to Mr. Braund, a solicitor who had an office at Grey's Inn Square. He lived at 52 Park Lane, in Tottenham, at the time, and he affirmed, "very near the shop in question. I know a Mr. Pincott; he is a personal friend of mine. In 1895 he was the owner of the shop at 518 High Road Tottenham. About December, 1894, I was consulted by him with reference to the getting of that shop. The man who proposed to take it came alone to see me on several occasions, and he gave his name as Severin Klosowski. After giving me some references an agreement was drawn up, which he signed in my presence." The agreement was signed on January 7, 1895, and Klosowski became the operator of his own business, but he could not make a go of it and he was in business only for two months.

Bray would also remember the woman who had been with Klosowski: "I remember a young woman coming to me on several occasions. I have no doubt she gave me her name, but I do not remember it now. It may have been Annie Chapman." In reference to Klosowski's movements, Bray was examined in Police Court in 1902 by Klosowski's attorney Mr. Sydney. He had pointed out Klosowski as the man he had met in 1894, in saying, "that is the man." When Mr. Sydney asked how long ago that was, he replied, "that was eight years ago, yes." "And since that time you have had no reason to think about the man?" "Oh, yes, I have. I have thought of him many times." "Why was that?" "Because it was alleged that he got a young girl into trouble, and she came to me about it several times." "At what date was that?" "In March or April 1895."

This was a very busy time for Klosowski. He had purchased a home on High Road in Tottenham and was trying to put together a threesome with Annie and his wife Lucy. It was not the first time Klosowski would try to acquire two women at the same time. In November 1889, as the Ripper series was slowing down, Lucy and Severin were living at 123 Cable Street, St. George in the East. He had moved there from the central killing zone just to the north (which was also the central search area for the Ripper) to Cable Street — just outside of the "Grand Search Area." Around October or November 1889 Klosowski's "real" wife and perhaps two children newly arrived from his home country of Poland stepped into the picture. There is no record of what Lucy must have thought about her new husband's Polish wife, but the record does show that the Polish wife did not stay with the newly wed couple for long. She "disappeared" around the same time as a headless torso was discovered just across the tracks from Klosowski's business/home on Pinchin Street. The timing is crucial, and the question that arises is whether Lucy knows what happened to his first Polish wife, or did she simply not care?

This time however, his "manly charms" seemed to have failed him as the pregnant Annie Chapman moved out of Klosowski's home and away from his "old wife." How long the three lived together is a matter of conjecture but it was long enough to capture the attention of Wolff Levisohn, who seemed to have a window at times into the comings and goings of fellow barber/surgeon Klosowski. Levisohn had lost track of Klosowski when he went to America, but they met again when Klosowski was an assistant barber at the South Tottenham shop. At Klosowski's hearing in 1903, Levisohn spotted Klosowski and stated: "There he sits! That is his description. He has not altered from the day he came to England; he has not even a gray hair. Always the same — same la-di-da, 'igh 'at and umbrella. Two wives he had while at Tottenham — one English, one foreign." (The English one would have been Annie and the foreign one would have been Lucy.) Interestingly, both Annie and Lucy would be able to walk away from Klosowski and live out their lives, which was a rare event to be sure. Both would also give birth to children who would become the legacy of Jack the Ripper — one Klosowski and one Chapman! One wonders if there are any decedents walking around old London today? And what of the Polish children? More to the point, are any of them active serial killers?

Levisohn would also report: "Later on he sold the shop and went away for several months, when he came back to a shop opposite Bruce Grove Railway Station. I called upon him there." Klosowski seemed to be well aware of Levisohn being able to, as it were, track him down. It would not do for a serial killer to be known for two long by one individual who could place him in many different areas. Levisohn also knew that Klosowski had changed his name at least twice. "I knew him as Ludwig Zagowski," he said. This next move and name change seemed to put an end to Levisohn's knowledge of Klosowski's movements. He would not see the barber/surgeon from Tottenham again until his arrest for murder in 1902. But was Klosowski the only man with deep criminal secrets, or did Levisohn leave a body or two himself? Perhaps! So far history is silent on this matter. What we do know is that a new name and job seems to have put Levisohn off the trail for at least 6 or 7 years.

The house with the extra rooms would not be required, however. Annie might not be living with Klosowski, but she would need his help. She would visit Klosowski in early 1895 to inform him of her "trouble." "I went there one evening in January or February, 1895, and asked him to help me in my trouble; I was going to have a baby," she recounted. Annie needed Klosowski's acknowledgment for the record but Klosowski was finished with Annie and would have none of it from her. "When I told him I was going to have a baby he did not take much notice," she related.

She would later confirm that Klosowski was the father of her child. After her final encounter with Klosowski, at least on the streets, she felt that he had gone back to Whitechapel. She said: "I heard he had gone to Whitechapel. He also had a shop opposite Bruce Grove Railway Station." The question is: Is that where he went with Lucy and did his wife know many more secrets than she would ever tell? As for Annie Chapman, she would see Klosowski one last time in the dock under a new alias, fighting for his life on the second day of his trial on March 17, 1903. Annie's child, who would bear the legacy of Jack the Ripper, would never meet her infamous father. The most interesting questions about the child would be: Are there any descendants walking the dark allies of Whitechapel and Warsaw today? And do they have any idea to whom they are related?

Wolff Levisohn — (artwork re-created by Robert DeLaCruz, from an original March 1903 set of Severin Klosowski trial sketches presently held in Scotland Yard's Black Museum file on George Chapman).

In February 1895, the police in Spitalfields, East End, London, arrested William Grant Grainger for stabbing a local woman. The ship's fireman was immediately considered a possible Ripper suspect, but the police were unable to prove he was in London in 1888, the critical Ripper time period, let alone in Whitechapel. And, although he was certainly not the Ripper, the arrest and intense newspaper coverage confirmed that the police were still very much interested in the capture of that serial killer. The case remained an open wound that Scotland Yard would love to have closed with the killer's arrest. They were still looking for "Jack," and Jack was most certainly back in town with new plans of his own!

It was at this point that a major transformation occurred in Klosowski's life, which has never been fully explained. Klosowski needed to keep on the move and a name change would be critical if he was to stay out of investigators' sights, even though they had no idea who he was or what murders he had committed. With Annie Chapman now gone from his life and his wife Lucy soon to depart as well (the theory being that he would not have changed his name while she was still in the area), he could become a new man and none would be the wiser. At least that was the plan. He would still be able to use Annie, however, since all he needed was a name. And if she was Ripper victim Annie Chapman's daughter, Annie Georgina Chapman, then few changes would be necessary. All that was required would be to remove the female portions of the name and Polish junior surgeon Severin Antoniovich Klosowski became ~~Annie Georgina~~ Chapman — (George Chapman) American. Klosowski was, after all, very good at removing female parts!

Now Klosowski had a name, which he hoped would mask his past, even though in his mind it served as a constant reminder and a direct link to the bloody murders committed in Whitechapel only a few years earlier. Anyone addressing him as George Chapman would instantly remind him of his past and of the fact that he had bested London's finest. In the years to come he would never again admit to being Severin Klosowski or that he had come from Poland. Not even a sentence of death by hanging would lead him to admit to being Klosowski. He was the American barber from Jersey City and he needed a woman. (Some writers have suggested that he became an American citizen during his short stay in the United States, but there would have been little time for that change of citizenship and no record to such effect has ever been located.) But not just any woman would do. He needed someone who was weak and easily controlled — he needed his next victim. He would find her in the guise of Mary Isabella Spink.

A Confidential Report— February 23, 1894

Ripper letter received in 1888 and rereleased to the public in 2001. Originally sent to Dr. Thomas Openshaw, London Hospital.

On February 23, 1894, Chief Constable Melville Macnaghten wrote a controversial report on the Ripper case in which he detailed his prime suspects. Even though he was not employed by Scotland Yard during the Ripper murders, his "memoranda" has been used as a source of information and conjecture for over 110 years.

Confidential

The case referred to in the sensational story told in "The Sun" in its issue of 13th, & following dates, is that of Thomas Cutbush who was arraigned at the London County Sessions in April 1891, on a charge of maliciously wounding Florence Grace Johnson, and attempting to wound Isabella Fraser Anderson in Kennington. He was found to be insane, and sentenced to be detained during Her Majesty's Pleasure.

This Cutbush, who lived with his mother and aunt at 14 Albert Street, Kennington, escaped from the Lambeth Infirmary, (after he had been detained only a few hours, as a lunatic) at noon on 5th March 1891— He was rearrested on 9th idem. A few weeks before this, several cases of stabbing, or jabbing, girls behind had occurred in the vicinity, and a man named Colicott was arrested, but subsequently discharged owing to faulty identification. The cuts in the girl's dresses made by Colicott were quite different to the cut(s) made by Cutbush (when he wounded Miss Johnson) who was no doubt influenced by a wild desire of morbid imitation. Cutbush's antecedents were enquired into by Ch. Inspr. (now Supt.) Chris ( ), by Inspr. Race, and by P.S. McCarthy C.I.D.—(the last named officer had been specially employed in Whitechapel at the time of the murders there,)— and it was ascertained that he was born, and had lived, in Kennington all his life. His father died when he was quite young, and he was always a "spoilt" child. He had been employed as a clerk and traveler in the Tea trade at the Minories, & subsequently canvassed for a Directory in the East End, during which time he bore a good character. He apparently contracted syphilis about 1888, and, — since that time, — led an idle and useless life. His brain seems to have become affected, and he believed that people were trying to poison him. He wrote to Lord Grimthorpe, and others, — & also to the Treasury, — complaining of Dr. Brooks, of Westminster Bridge Road, whom he threatened to shoot for having supplied him with bad medicines. He is said to have studied medical books by day, & to have rambled about at night, returning frequently with his clothes covered with mud; but little reliance could be placed on the statements made by his mother or his aunt, who both appear to have been of a very excitable disposition. It was found impossible to ascertain his movements on the nights of the Whitechapel murders. The knife found on him was bought in Houndsditch about a week before he was detained in the Infirmary. Cutbush was the nephew of the late Supt. Executive.

Now the Whitechapel murderer had 5 victims — & 5 victims only, — his murders were

(i) 31st Aug. '88. Mary Ann Nichols — Buck's Row — who was found with her throat cut — & with (slight) stomach mutilation.
(ii) 8th Sept. '88. Annie Chapman — Hanbury Street: — throat cut — stomach & private parts badly mutilated & some of the entrails placed round the neck.
(iii) 30th Sept. '88. Elizabeth Stride — Berner's Street — throat cut, but nothing in shape of mutilation attempted, & on same date
(iiii) Catherine Eddowes, Mitre Square, throat cut, & very bad mutilation, both of face and stomach.
(iiiii) 9th November. Mary Jane Kelly — Miller's Court, throat cut, and the whole of the body mutilated in the most ghastly manner.

The last murder is the only one that took place in a room, and the murderer must have been at least 2 hours engaged. A photo was taken of the woman, as she was found lying on the bed, without seeing which it is impossible to imagine the awful mutilation.

With regard to the double murder which took place on 30th September, there is no doubt but that the man was disturbed by some Jews who drove up to a Club, (close to which the body of Elizabeth Stride was found) and that he then, "mordum satiatus," went in search of a further victim who he found at Mitre Square.

It will be noted that the fury of the mutilations increased in each case, and, seemingly, the appetite only became sharpened by indulgence. It seems, then highly improbable that the murderer would have suddenly stopped in November '88, and been content to recommence operations by merely prodding a girl behind some 2 years and 4 months afterwards. A much more rational theory is that the murderer's brain gave way altogether after his awful glut in Miller's Court, and that he immediately committed suicide, or, as a possible alternative, was found to be so hopelessly mad by his relations, that he was by them confined in some asylum.

No one ever saw the Whitechapel murderer; many homicidal maniacs were suspected, but no shadow of proof could be thrown on anyone. I may mention the cases of 3 men, any one of whom would have been more likely than Cutbush to have committed this series of murders:

(1) A Mr. M. J. Druitt, said to be a doctor & of good family — who disappeared at the time of the Miller's Court murder, & whose body (which was said to have been upwards of a month in the water) was found in the Thames on 31st Dec. — or about 7 weeks after that murder. He was sexually insane and from private information I have little doubt but that his own family believed him to have been the murderer.

(2) (Kosminski) — a Polish Jew, & resident in Whitechapel. This man became insane owing to many

Chief Inspector Frederick George Abberline, prime investigator of the London Ripper murders at the street level (Robert DeLaCruz).

years indulgence in solitary vices. He had a great hatred of women, specially of the prostitute class, & had strong homicidal tendencies; he was removed to a lunatic asylum about March 1889. There were many circumstances connected with this man which made him a strong "suspect."

(3) Michael Ostrog, a Russian doctor, and a convict, who was subsequently detained in a lunatic asylum as a homicidal maniac. This man's antecedents were of the worst possible type, and his whereabouts at the time of the murders could never be ascertained.

And now with regard to a few of the other inaccuracies and misleading statements made by the "Sun." In its issue of 14th February, it is stated that the writer has in his possession a facsimile of the knife with which the murders were committed. This knife (which for some unexplained reason has, for the last 3 years, been kept by Inspector Race, instead of being sent to Prisoner's Property Store) was traced, and it was found to have been purchased in Houndsditch in February '91 or 2 years & 3 months after the Whitechapel murders ceased!

The statement, too, that Cutbush "spent a portion of the day in making rough drawings of the bodies of women, & of their mutilations" is based solely on the fact that 2 scribble drawings of women in indecent postures were found torn up in Cutbush's room. The head & body of one of these had been cut from some fashion plate, and legs were added to show a woman's naked thighs & pink stockings.

In the issue of 15th inst. it is said that a light overcoat was among the things found in Cutbush's house, and that a man in a light overcoat was seen talking to a woman at Backchurch Lane whose body with arms attached was found in Pinchin Street. This is hopelessly incorrect! On 10th Sept. '89 the naked body, with arms, of a woman was found wrapped in some sacking under a Railway arch in Pinchin Street: the head & legs were never found nor was the woman ever identified. She had been killed at least 24 hours before the remains, (which had seemingly been brought from a distance), were discovered. The stomach was split up by a cut, and the head and legs had been severed in a manner identical with that of the woman whose remains were discovered in the Thames, in Battersea Park, & on the Chelsea Embankment on the 4th June of the same year; and these murders had no connection whatever with the Whitechapel horrors. The Rainham mystery in 1887, & the Whitehall mystery (when portions of a woman's body were found under what is now New Scotland Yard) in 1888, were of a similar type to the Thames & Pinchin Street crimes.

It is perfectly untrue to say that Cutbush stabbed 6 girls behind — this is confounding his case with that of Colicott. The theory that the Whitechapel murderer was left-handed, or, at any rate, "ambidexter," had its origin in the remark by a doctor who examined the corpse of one of the earliest victims; other doctors did not agree with him.

With regard to the 4 additional murders ascribed by the writer in the "Sun" to the Whitechapel fiend:

(1) The body of Martha Tabram, a prostitute, was found on a common staircase in George Yard buildings on 7th August 1888; the body had been repeatedly pierced, probably with a bayonet. This woman had, with a fellow prostitute, been in company of 2 soldiers in the early part of the evening. These men were arrested, but the second prostitute failed, or refused, to identify, and the soldiers were accordingly discharged.

(2) Alice McKenzie was found with her throat cut (or rather stabbed) in Castle Alley on 17th July 1889; no evidence was forthcoming, and no arrests were made in connection with this case. The stab in the throat was of the same nature as in the case of the murder of

(3) Frances Coles, in Swallow Gardens, on 13th February 1891—for which Thomas Sadler, a fireman, was arrested, & after several remands, discharged. It was ascertained at the time that Sadler had sailed for the Baltic on 19th July '89 & was in Whitechapel on the night of 17th idem. He was a man of ungovernable temper & entirely addicted to drink, & the company of the lowest prostitutes.

(4) The case of the unidentified woman whose trunk was found in Pinchin Street: on 10th September 1889 — which has already been dealt with.

M.S. Macnaghten
23rd February 1894

Chapter 4

Mrs. Spink and a Man Called Chapman

Dose, ¹⁄₁₆th grain to ¼. To be taken with caution.
— W.H. Davidson, chemist

LEYTONSTONE, ENGLAND—1895

Klosowski, now Chapman, got, as it is said, out of town, but he would not be on the road for long. After all, he did not have much money and he would need to find employment and a place to stay. He soon found a new home and a new job in the town of Leytonstone. There he could rest, save some money, develop his new identity and find a new wife. It would seem that he needed to take a killing break before he was ready to go at it again. It would seem that he had put away his knife for a while and he did not yet have the needed connections to obtain the poison he would later use to dispatch his wives.

In the spring of 1895 the newly minted "Mr. Chapman" could be found in rooms at the Renton home in Leytonstone. He had told the Renton's that he was "single and had come from Tottenham." It must be assumed that he did not expect anyone to check his story, as no one would have known him as Chapman in Tottenham. Nevertheless, he had a place to stay while he looked for work. As for a new wife, he would not need to look very far to locate his target of opportunity.

Her name was Mrs. Mary Isabella Spink, wife of Great Eastern Railway Company porter Shadrack Spink. She was the former Mary Isabella Renton. By the time Chapman moved into nearby rooms her husband had departed. It seems, although reports are far from complete, that Shadrack had grown tired of Mary's drinking and had left her at the Renton family home. He had also taken their first son with him. At the time Mary was pregnant again and about to give birth to her second son, to be named William or Willie for short.

Mary, it would seem from reports, did not have a great deal of self-respect or self-control. Those who knew her described her as "short and plump with short blonde hair, and not overly intelligent." She was possibly an alcoholic and thus would have been the perfect victim for a serial killer who had decided to kill with studied slowness. She could, it would seem, be easily manipulated with only a few suggestions wrapped around a few drinks. And she had the required low self-esteem. Mary Spink had fallen right into Chapman's hands and he fully intended to take advantage of the situation. After all, Mary had a nice sum of money, which at the time was something that Chapman had very little of, and he would, of course, kill to get more.

As for her drinking, questions arise as to whether or not she was indeed as heavy a drinker as had been suggested by Chapman and possibly others. When Mrs. Spink's body was examined by Doctor Thomas Stevenson in December 1902, he could find no evidence of alcohol abuse. He reported: "There was nothing to indicate that the woman had been a confirmed drunkard. If she had drunk it had not produced any serious injury to the kidneys or liver. The inflammation which I found in the stomach was not attributable to alcohol." It is possible that Mary's supposed drinking problem was simply a cover story provided by her killer to direct any suspicions as her health slowly declined due to the poisons flowing through her body.

Chapman soon found work as a barber in Leytonstone. William Wenzel had advertised for an assistant barber for his established shop on 7 Church Lane and it was soon answered. "I knew him as George Chapman, and he told me he had come from Tottenham," Wenzel said. From all indications the new assistant did his job well, but Chapman was not a man to allow the grass to grow around his feet. He stayed at his position for only 6 or 7 months. By then he had "come into some money."

As was his habit Chapman again changed his lodgings and moved out of his rooms at the Renton home sometime around October 1895. He found new quarters in a small lodging house on Forest Road owned by Mr. and Mrs. John Ward. He seemed, however, to have made a small tactical mistake at this point. Chapman was supposed to be an expatriate American, but John Ward remembered it just a bit differently. "He said he was a Polish Jew," Ward recounted. Granted, he was not Jewish but rather Roman Catholic, which made his statement to Ward a lie, but he seems to have forgotten that he was supposed to be an American Jew, or some such. Perhaps he was starting to get his lies a bit mixed up. At any rate, no one was doing a background check — not yet at least.

Before he left the Renton home Chapman began an affair with Mrs. Spink. Perhaps that was why he decided to move to other, perhaps more private quarters. Before long the pair could be seen about town with Mrs. Spink visiting Chapman at his shop on Church Lane. As for Chapman, he was none too discreet about his supposed "affection" for Mrs. Spink. It would not take long for the proper Mr. Ward to comment to Chapman on his actions. He confronted Chapman in the lodging house and tried to lay down some rules. He told him, "My wife has seen you kissing Mrs. Spink. We cannot allow that sort of thing to go on in the house." Chapman, never one to be caught off guard was fast with a response. He said, "It's all right Mr. Ward. We are going to get married about Sunday week."

On October 27, 1895, Chapman made an entry in his diary, which he seemed to be keeping to create a phony background for himself in case anyone ever checked. The entry read: "Oct 27, 1895 — Married Mary Isabella Spink." It was a lie. Chapman and Mrs. Spink did make a show of going away to be married, but all they really did was ride around town for a while. Chapman had told the Wards that they were going to be married in Whitechapel but both were already married and neither of them had gone to the bother of getting a divorce. It would seem that a real wedding might have caught the attention of the authorities. (It is interesting to note that Whitechapel seemed to be on Chapman's mind at the time. Perhaps they visited the local Whitechapel murder sites together?)

When the couple returned to Mr. Ward's lodgings later that evening both were ready to play the part. With the new "Mrs. Chapman" in tow, Chapman declared, "Allow me to present you my wife." For some reason, however, Chapman was never able to completely fool John Ward or his wife. Mrs. Ward would later ask to see the marriage certificate but Chapman simply dismissed her by saying, "Oh, our laws are different to your laws." It would not be long before this serial killer would decide that it was time to move on. The Wards were becoming just a bit too interested in his business and that was not a good thing for a serial killer. Chapman needed to be on the move.

The tissue of lies and the phony wedding date did seem to be good enough, however, to fool Mrs. Spink's relations, but why none of them asked about her obtaining a divorce from Shadrack is an open question. Surely they kept in contact with him and the older Spink boy? One cousin, Joseph Smith Renton, seemed not to have had a clue as to what was really going on when he later commented, "I noticed my cousin was keeping company with the accused, whom I knew as Chapman, and who was employed at Wenzel's. About March of 1896, my cousin left Leytonstone. I was given to understand she was married to Chapman, as she passed as Mrs. Chapman." Spink's family seemed to have been completely fooled by "Mr. Chapman." They would not be the last. Their failure to make inquiries would be an opportunity lost to involve the police in the activities of a serial killer, and it would cost three lives! The people whom Mrs. Spink would meet and inquire about her real husband she would simply answer by telling them that her porter husband Shadrack "had been killed on the railway."

Before long alias George Chapman tired of his work at Wenzel's shop. As the "husband" to Mary he had suddenly come into a good amount of cash, and his fortunes at least were starting to look better. Mrs. Spink at one point must have told him about a nice little trust fund her grandfather had left her at his passing in the amount of £600, which must have been a very big draw on Chapman's mind. It can only be guessed how long after he found out about the money before he popped the question to the so-called former Mrs. Spink.

Before he could acquire the funds, however, it seems that Chapman decided to go into business for himself. Early in 1896, Chapman quit his job at Wenzel's shop and took out a lease in Hastings on a small store. It seems however, that he did not choose his area very well. Perhaps he did not have enough money or enough credit at the time to afford a better place. Whatever the reason, his shop soon failed due to a lack of business.

With what must have been financial help from Mary, he soon moved to George Street in Old Hastings. It would be there in March of 1896 that he would establish his new hairdressing business. It was a much better location, a site just behind the Albion Public House in Albion Mansions, Hastings. In that more affluent section of town the new hairdresser and his so-called alcoholic wife would do quite well indeed. The coastal town of Hastings is well known in Europe as the site of the Battle of Hastings in 1066, which became a turning point in British history. (We young students all had to learn about the battle of the Normans and the English as we sat in our small wooden desks with the old and well-used ink wells.)

So as not to lose track of his wife's assets, Chapman contacted the Hastings lawyer of Mrs. Spink in May 1896. By then he had decided that he needed more funding. On June 11 of that year, Messer's. Langham, Son & Douglas Lawyers paid £195 to "Mr. & Mrs. Chapman." It is doubtful that his wife saw any of the money. Two years later the final trust fund payment would be paid just about the same time his wife would become deathly ill! In January 1903 the readers of the *Southwark and Bermonsey Recorder and South London Gazette* would be able to read about some of the many transactions initiated by "George Chapman and wife" that allowed Chapman to control his wife's estate.

MRS. SPINK'S FORTUNE

Mr. Henry Dacre, a solicitor practicing at Ottley, who acted as trustee of a voluntary settlement under which Mary Isabella Renton, afterwards Mrs. Spink was entitled to a sum of £600, was called, and stated that from time to time he made her advances, and received a great many letters from her. In one of these he noticed that her name had been changed from "Spink" to "Chapman." In 1896 Messrs. Langham, Son and Douglas, of Hastings, wrote witness on her behalf, and as a result he sent them a sum of £195, and received a release in the name of "Mary Isabella Chapman." After that he had £300 in hand, and in 1897, after correspondence with Messrs. Davenport, Jones and Glenister, also of Hastings, witness paid over to that firm the balance of the money, of which he had been the trustee. The sum paid over was £298 7s. 11d.

Frederick George Langham, member of the firm of solicitors in Hastings, identified the accused

[George Chapman] as one of the persons who consulted him in May 1896 with reference to some trust fund to which Mrs. Chapman was entitled. Money was wanted to enable her to go into business as a hairdresser in George Street, Hastings. As a result of the proceedings £191 17s. was paid over by cheque to Mrs. Chapman.

In the meantime, writers—possibly newspaper men trying to keep the story going—still found time to send letters to the authorities signed "Jack the Ripper." On October 14, 1896, the police at the Commercial Street Police Station, in the very heart of Jack's old killing ground, received one such letter. The letter, like all of the Ripper letters, was not from the killer. It was written in red ink and became the last serious lead investigated by the authorities into the Jack the Ripper murders. By then the trail of this most elusive of serial killers had grown very cold.

> Dear Boss,
> You will be surprised to find that this comes from yours as of old Jack-the Ripper. Ha. Ha If my old friend Mr. Warren is dead you can read it. you might remember me if you try and think a little Ha Ha. The last job was a bad one and no mistake nearly buckled, and meant it to be best of the lot & what curse it, Ha Ha Im alive yet and you 'll soon find it out. I mean to go on again when I get the chance wont it be nice dear old Boss to have the good old times once again. you never caught me and you never will. Ha Ha
> You police are a smart lot, the lot of you could nt catch one man Where have I been Dear Boss you d like to know. abroad, if you would like to know, and just come back. ready to go on with my work and stop when you catch me. Well good bye Boss wish me luck. Winters coming "The Jewes are people that are blamed for nothing" Ha Ha have you heard this before
>
> Yours truly
> Jack the Ripper

When this latest bit of fiction was investigated by Chief Inspector Henry Moore he found it to be somewhat less than authentic. He reported to Melville Macnaughton: "I beg to report having carefully perused all old 'Jack the Ripper' letters and fail to find any similarity of handwriting in any of them, with the exception of the two well remembered communications which were sent to the 'Central News' office; one letter, dated 25th September 1888, and the other a postcard, bearing the postmark 1st October 1888. In conclusion I beg to observe that I do not attach any importance to this communication."

Despite the fact that the killer known as Jack the Ripper did not write this, or any other letter signed as the Ripper, it does show conclusively that the police did not know the whereabouts of the Whitechapel killer in 1896. Moreover, the letter shows that the writer of the letter and postcard, which gave the name to one of the most infamous serial killers of all time, was still in the habit of writing out warnings and playing games with the authorities. Was this writer still a member of the press and did his bosses know that he was still writing some of the most infamous threatening letters of all time? Those in the know kept silent on that point.

Hastings, South England — 1896–97

With his business growing it would not be long before "Mr. and Mrs. Chapman" were able to move offsite from his barbershop. The couple moved to their new rooms at 10 Hill Street in Hastings, not far from the shop. At the time little Willie was still living with them but Chapman was not pleased to have him around. Also in residence was Mrs. Anna Helsdown, who would take note of the new family who moved in down the hall and the effects on Chapman's new wife. She later testified: "After they had been there some time the accused [Chapman] opened a barbershop in George Street. That was in 1896. I left them there in 1897."

Even though Mrs. Spink had never met Mrs. Helsdown before, she soon confided in her that things were not going all that well with the "marriage." In fact, Mrs. Spink would not need to say anything as Mrs. Helsdown could easily see the bruises on her face and, more ominously, her throat. Later, Mrs. Helsdown would report that she could hear Mrs. Spink cry out in the night as Chapman abused her. However, it never seemed to have crossed her mind to call the police so as to put an end to these attacks by this vicious and cowardly thug. It must also be noted that neither did the reportedly alcoholic Mrs. Spink ever call the police nor did she simply walk away from Chapman to save her own life. Much later, after the deaths of three woman, Mrs. Helsdown's report would be heard during an open police court investigation in 1903:

> Previous to 1897 she lived at 10 Hill Street, Hastings, and for the last nine months the prisoner [Chapman/Klosowski] lived in the same house with his wife (Mrs. Spink) and little boy. The family passed in the name of Chapman. The prisoner opened a barber's shop at George Street, Hastings, and the woman and child went there for meals. The witness remembered hearing the woman cry out once or twice at Hill Street, and being shown marks on her face and throat, which were said to have been inflicted by the prisoner. The woman's health was very sadly at times, and she complained of violent sickness and pain in the stomach. This went on for a period of three months before the witness left. No doctor was called in. She never spoke to Chapman with regard to the woman's illness. She only entered Chapman's rooms once or twice, and never spoke to him, except to say 'good morning.

Life was not much better for little Willie. Chapman had little or no use for the young boy, who was a little younger than Chapman's son would have been had he lived. Willie was dispatched to live in the filthy basement of the barbershop, which was reported to have also been the home of some not so well fed rats. Willie eventually moved into the lodgings on Hill Street, but it could not have been easy or safe living in the same house as Chapman.

It was also during Chapman's time at his Hastings's barbershop that he would once again run into George Sherman. At the time, Sherman was working as a barbershop traveling salesman and had first come across Chapman when Chapman was doing his barbering at the White Hart Public House on High Street in Whitechapel in 1890. Sherman, who would later run his own barbershop on Nile Street in Horton, recalled at Chapman's police court hearings that Chapman "also had a shop, and was assisted in the business by a short dark woman." It did not seem to strike Sherman as strange that the man he knew as Klosowski in 1890 was Chapman in 1897! Of course, he reported none of this to the authorities in 1897. He did not seem to know that the "short dark woman" was acting as Chapman's wife nor that Lucy Klosowski, Chapman's real wife, was no where to be seen.

Despite the many problems, life went on at the shop and very few customers were aware that all was not right with the new family who had moved into town. Perhaps the men receiving close shaves from the good Mr. Chapman would have been less than amused to learn that the man who had worked on them for a price had also cut the throats of at least eight women in the East End of London. At the time, however, the thoughts may have centered on the work of Chapman's wife. It was a rare thing at their time to find a female barber in England, but more to the point some of the customers were fully aware that Mrs. Chapman was, as one would state, not "in full control of her faculties." It would not be long before the business began to slow down, and that was something the 'Mr.' would not allow.

In order to drum up new business Chapman came up with the idea of renting a piano and having his wife play while the very practiced ex-junior surgeon played the necks of his well-lathered guests. It was a very successful idea and the Chapmans' musical shaves soon became quite popular with the locals. Before long the business was prospering and Chapman made a point to show off a bit.

With the newfound cash Chapman decided to enjoy some of his prosperity and he purchased a small boat. Hastings, located on the south coast, had a good selection of small sail boats to choose from. The boat he purchased could hold no more than four persons, but christened by him the *Mosquito*, it would serve his needs just as well.

One afternoon, Chapman attired in nautical wear, set out for a sail up and down the coast with Mrs. Chapman. And if it was a normal day the "Mrs." was probably much the worse for drink. Before long the always reckless and quite unskilled Chapman managed to capsize the little boat, tossing both into the water. Depending on the point of view, it was either good or bad positioning as they were not near enough to the shore to swim back. Chapman could swim and, if reports are correct, swim quite well, but it may not have been that easy for his wife. And with a serial killer that may very well have been the plan. However, plan or not, Chapman would not become a widower that day as some nearby fishermen soon came to the rescue. The fishermen thought them both on the point of drawing when they were pulled from the sea, but Chapman was a good actor so his condition may have been overstated, by himself of course. As for his alcoholic wife, the end of her life would come soon enough after other methods were investigated by this clever and very practical serial killer.

Before long Chapman was on the move again. He was continuing his practice of never staying in one place too long and if the so-called accident with the small boat had been something else, then he needed to find another place to stay and plan a new killing strategy. With much to occupy his mind, Mr. and Mrs. Chapman moved to the boarding house at 1 Coburg Place still in the town of Hastings in February of 1897.

At the new boarding house the couple would meet Harriet Greenway. Mrs. Greenway had lived in the house for some time and would soon be moving to other quarters (Chapman seemed to do that to people), but Chapman had made enough of an impression at the time for Mrs. Greenway to recall some details years later when she was interviewed about the new people at the house in Hastings. Her statement would show that once again Chapman/Klosowski forgot parts of his not so well fabricated cover story about being an American. She recalled, "Up to 22 March, 1897, I lived at 1 Coburg Place. A family named Chapman came to live [in] the same house about a month before I left. There was a man, a woman and a child. He went to a hairdresser's shop in George Street. He said he was a Russian Pole, and that he had been in America. He once wrote down a name and said it was his name in Russian. I had some volumes of *Cassell's Family Physician* which I gave to Mrs. Chapman to keep for a time. I never got them back." She would later see those very same books presented to her at his trial. Chapman, after all, was still a collector. Greenway's servant, Mrs. Edith Simmonds, would also later identify Chapman as the man she saw borrowing the books from her employer.

Despite the short time the Chapman's lived in the same house as Mrs. Greenway it seems that Mrs. Chapman confided in her about some possible dark secrets. One such secret focused on a little black bag. Mrs. Greenway stated: "Once Mrs. Chapman showed me a black bag, secretly. Prisoner [Chapman] used to keep the bag." It is noted that neither Greenway nor Mary Spink seemed bold enough to actually open the secret bag, at least neither would admit to doing so. But what was in the 'secret black bag?' No one could or perhaps dare to say. Mrs. Greenway would also remember one other item not normally part of the average British home. "Chapman had a revolver." (The final American murder weapon?)

Inspector George Godley would later report that George Chapman did indeed have a bag during the period he spent in Whitechapel. Some reports also suggest that the Ripper did so as well. Yet if Chapman carried, and seemingly protected, his "secret black bag" from at least 1888 through 1897, where did the bag end up? He must have carried it from England to America and back again, yet when he was arrested in 1902 there was no report of any black bag being discovered at Chapman's home/business. Chapman would not have thrown that bag away if it had anything to do with the Ripper murders. The building at 213 Borough High Street is reported to be still standing, at least the fronting is still in place. Is there a small space between the walls or a patched-up section of the basement where the old and now rotting bag might still be found? And, more to the point, does it still contain Chapman's secrets, which would once and for all prove beyond a shadow of a doubt that Severin Klosowski was once known as Jack the Ripper? And would the detectives at Scotland Yard still be interested in finding this out at this late date? Perhaps, since detectives from the Metropolitan Police did indeed conduct a search of that very building in late 2002. Did they find anything related to the Ripper murders?

That question has yet to be answered because the Metropolitan Police have yet to answer this writer's inquiries. What is known is that shortly after Mrs. Greenway departed the lodging house, George Chapman began his deadly work again. Did he discover that his wife had fallen upon his deadly secrets? If she had it would only be a matter of time, and a short time at that, before Mary Spink, alias Mrs. Chapman, became the late wife of Mr. George Chapman, American barber. The very next week Chapman acquired his poison. As always he was working very fast.

Some Fine Powder from Schedule I—April 3, 1897

When George Chapman first saw a young domestic servant by the name of Alice Penfold go by his shop he decided that he must have her. It was early in 1897 and Mr. Chapman made his plans to meet Miss Penfold. Chapman had noted that the young lady enjoyed taking walks around Hastings on Sunday evenings, so he arranged to be out one Sunday in order to "bump" into Miss Penfold. After the "accidental" meeting Chapman introduced himself as a single man who worked as the manager of a local piano shop in Hastings. He seems to have forgotten about Mary Spink waiting at home as his wife, but that oversight could be taken care of at a later date.

Chapman would manage to meet Miss Penfold several more times and it is suspected that he tried to get the young lady to stay with him or work for him at his "piano shop." It would seem, however, that Miss Penfold was just a bit smarter or a bit more circumspect than Chapman had hoped for. His charms failed this time. Miss Penfold turned him down. Miss Penfold would live to tell the tale of the amorous Mr. Chapman. As for Chapman, he still had a little problem named Mary Spink to deal with and he would soon be more than ready to deal with her.

Local chemist William Henry Davidson ran a small shop located at 66 High Street in Hastings. His chemist's shop was not far away from the new town barber so he visited the latter for a few musical shaves. It would be during those shaves that Davidson would discover that barber Chapman possessed a great deal of knowledge about medical matters. Chapman may have even showed Davidson his documents in Russian and Polish to impress his customer. Davidson would later recall, "I was at Hastings for about 18 years, and while there I used frequently to go to a barber's shop to get shaved. The accused (Chapman) was employed there, and he shaved me on many occasions. [He] was an intelligent man to talk to."

From Davidson's viewpoint, the conversations were no more than an interesting way to pass the time while he was in the chair. For Chapman there was a much more sinister reason to catch the ear of the local chemist. For Chapman it was a golden opportunity to impress on Davidson that he had the required medical education and background to qualify him to purchase a few needed grams of powder from Schedule I — poison! Antimony!

It would not take long for Chapman to put his plan into action. He found his way to the chemist's shop on April 3, 1897. Chapman had been denied the required powder in early 1888 just before the Ripper murders commenced in the East End of London. This time, however, he had planned well and he would be successful. On that day Davidson agreed to sell to his barber a small bottle of fine-grained white powder with its deep red label. Chapman would keep that small label hidden away for the rest of his short life. He was still a serial killer who collected trophies of the kill!

> W. H. Davidson, dispensing chemist.
> Poison, Tartar-emetic.
> Dose, $\frac{1}{16}$th grain to $\frac{1}{4}$.
> To be taken with caution.
> 66 High Street, Hastings.

Davidson would also remember that day: "One day he bought several things from me, and asked me to let him have a particular poison. I think he did have some other poisons, but they did not come under Schedule I. I also sold the accused two or three old editions of medical books." Of course Chapman was required by law to sign for his ounce of death and so he dutifully signed "G. Chapman." For Chapman it did not matter since, in reality, he was Severin Klosowski — what did it matter one more lie. Chapman was also required to write down the purpose of the poison, so he wrote out a word that looked like "take" but no one could be certain — that was his plan. When shown the entry Davidson would state: "I cannot make out what is written here; it is in the accused's handwriting. It looks like 'take' or 'teke.' He wrote that in my presence after he signed 'G. Chapman.'"

Davidson would recall that he knew Chapman "was not practicing as a medical man," but he sold him the deadly poison anyway. He said, "No doubt he gave me a cogent reason why he wanted it, although I cannot say what it was now (1903)." It would seem that memories can at times fail greatly. Did Davidson know what the ounce of white powder that would really be used for? He would never really answer that question and, after a few more questions at Chapman's trial, he would simply walk away and fade into history.

As for barber George Chapman, he put down his very sharp knife, at least for the time being, to begin his new "work" as the "Borough Poisoner." There was much to do and Mary Spink was not getting any younger. It would be later reported that "Mrs. Martin, widow, of Queen's Road, Hastings, said she was housekeeper at Albion Mansions, George Street. The Prisoner (Chapman) had a barber's shop there, which he gave up in September. The witness remembered seeing Mrs. Chapman ill several times in May."

THE POISON WORK BEGINS—FALL 1897

Chapman now had his poison and so he began the next phase in his series of murders, but he had not yet given up on Alice Penfold. It is certain that he still expected Alice to replace the reportedly often drunk Mrs. Spink (Mrs. Chapman I). For a while Alice seemed to play along because from time to time she would go out with "George." On one of their outings Alice complained of not feeling well and she told Chapman that she had a cold. It was at that point that Chapman told her of his medical background and how he could fix her something to take for her symptoms. Her new caring friend said he would send it right along.

Before long Chapman sent some of his powders to Alice at her home, but, being a cautious person, Miss Penfold decided she would rather keep the cold and dispose of the so-called cure. Alice may very well have been Chapman's first test subject to see how much damage he could do with a pinch of his newly acquired poison. We will never know for sure but it is a pretty safe bet since Alice was fast moving away from the amorous Mr. Chapman. Chapman never did enjoy being rejected by any woman. For Chapman that was a deadly sin. Perhaps if she had taken the "cure" and became ill she may have been able to put two and two together and turn in Chapman to the police — if only!

As a final attempt to win Alice over Chapman took her to a pub at St. Leonards. He wanted her to know that he intended to lease the pub and set himself up in business. And Chapman, always the good businessman, would need a hearty bar maid to help out with the customers. It would be their last outing together. Alice seemed to be aware that something was not quite right with all that Chapman was saying. Even after their last meeting, however, he would not stop his attempts. He wrote to her several times asking her to join him in his pub. The problem was, he had yet to sign any lease for any pub! Alice read Chapman just right, and in the reading probably saved her own life.

Years later Alice would come forward to be interviewed at a police court hearing into the background of the man she knew as George Chapman. Her remarks would be made available to the readers of the *Southwark and Bermondsey Recorder and South London Gazette* on Saturday, January 17, 1903.

> Alice Penfold, who resides in Devonshire Road, Hastings, said that six years since she was employed by a Mrs. Field in that town. One Sunday evening when she was out for a walk she met Chapman, who spoke to her and introduced himself as the manager of a pianoforte shop. She "walked out" with him two or three times, and he told her he had studied medicine, and would send her something for a cold. He sent some powders, which she put on the fire. (A laugh.) He took her to see a public house at St. Leonard's, which he said he thought of having, but after that she did not see him again. He wrote her two letters, however, as well as a note with the powders. She saw him after receiving the powders, and told him she had not taken them. The letters came from London; one was signed "Chapman" and the other "Smith." She destroyed them. It was about four years ago. One letter was dated from the Prince of Wales, St. Luke's, and asked her to go up there. She did not go, and received no other communication.
>
> Cross-examined; Altogether she received 'about' four letters from Chapman. She did not want to meet him, but he used to follow her about, and once called at her mistress's house. She did not like that, and complained to her mistress. She did not meet him afterwards.
>
> Re-examined: She answered none of his letters. She asked once if he was married, and he said he was not.

After only a few months in business at his Hastings barbershop Chapman decided to sell out. In September 1897 he sold his business to a local furniture businessman named Robinson. It was time to move again and this time he would return to London with his new "wife," a new business and his little bottle of white powder. He knew he had to move out of the vicinity of where he had purchased the poison. To begin his new career as a publican, 31-year-old George Chapman, along with his "wife," leased the old, well-established pub in Bartholomew Square in the fall of 1897. The Prince of Wales beer house was only a short ride from the killing fields of Jack the Ripper, just a bit off of City Road. Continuing his cover as an expatriate American, Chapman decorated the bar in American colors and artifacts, including an upside down American flag on the wall overlooking the bar. Chapman was now back in business and the locals would remember the place as "George's American Bar." Just a few years later the locals would have a new reason to remember the not-so-American bar owner, but for the time being the American flavor of the local bar would do just fine.

> "Transfer of the license of the 'Prince of Wales'
> from Andrews to Chapman—
> September 27, 1897—£56."

At about the same time Chapman was beginning his publican career, he began a new hobby—photography. In fact, he did so well at it that he not only took a good many photos but he also learned to develop the film and make his own prints. Many of his photos would later be found in a search of his business by the police. These photos showed Chapman at his bars and on his small boat and each and every one of his last three wives—and—poison victims. The police would discover a series of photos showing the slow decline of each of the three women. It should be noted that his photo collection of victims mirrors the same type of collecting the Ripper did when he collected body parts, albeit a little less bloody. Through each collection the killer could return to the murder event and once again relive the emotions he felt at the time of the murder. The photos gave Chapman less of a problem with storage. They were cleaner but certainly no less deadly, and they were readily available any time he "needed" them.

One of the traits of some serial killers is their almost universal ability to fit in or fade into the background and therefore divert any suspicions from coming their way. For the most part it is unintentional, but there are times when a serial killer will direct his (or very rarely her) actions in the hope of fitting in. Such was the case in the fall of 1897 when alias "George Chapman" joined a local cycling club sponsored by the police department. It was good cover for this man who seemed for all the world to be a married businessman with one child. Married life is always very good cover for a serial killer, especially when he is slowly poisoning the woman he is living with. Who would suspect the caring and ever-so-attentive husband of foul play?

Perhaps as a safety measure Mrs. Spink did not seem to show any signs of illness until the 'happy couple' arrived in London. The amounts of poison must have been very small indeed at that time. By that time Mrs. Spink (read that as intercepted by Chapman) had received her final monies from the trustees of her grandfather's will. After that last check had been cashed the alcoholic Mrs. Spink became just one more object to be disposed of, and Chapman by then was well on his way toward that goal.

Mr. and Mrs. Chapman's banking

May 31, 1897	Deposit £250	Lloyd's Bank, Hastings	open
July 18, 1897	Deposit £50	Lloyd's Bank, Hastings	
August 12, 1897	Deposit £305	Lloyd's Bank, Hastings	
August 23, 1897	Withdraw £369 6s1p	Lloyd's Bank, Hastings	
September 8, 1897	Withdraw £250	Lloyd's Bank, Hastings	closed
September 28, 1897	Deposit £230	Midland Back, London	open
September 30, 1897	Deposit £55	Midland Bank, London	

Before long Mrs. Spink began to complain of severe abdominal pain and she began to experience severe vomiting. It would not be long before the normally robust woman, despite her supposed drinking problem, was too weak to move about and became confined to her bed. Chapman's colorless, odorless and tasteless powders were working their magic when mixed with juices and other drinks. Chapman was making sure that his wife took in a good deal of liquids. However, Chapman was using old medical books and may not have realized that the poison he selected could now be detected. That is of course if anyone bothered to look for it, and it would be a few years in the future before anyone investigated.

Chapman knew that poisoning someone with antimony involved a long and difficult job. Too little at a time and the victim develops a form of immunity, allowing the victim to hold on for a long time; too much poison and the victim will vomit the dose and would not die. It would take an expert in death to administer the correct amount over a long period (months) of time in order for the effects to properly occur and in such a manner that it would appear death came from natural causes. Serial killer Chapman planned to enjoy every single moment of the death agony as closely as he could — he recorded on film every stage of life slipping away.

Things were going so well for Chapman at the time that he was able to hire a staff to work at his beer house. Of course, this meant that there would be more than enough witnesses to his abusive relationship with the, by then, slowly dying Mrs. Spink. Although the locals who visited the bar could not read about the abuse, and many may perhaps not have even noticed it at the time, the readers of the *Southwark and Bermonsey Recorder and South London Gazette* in 1903 would indeed have the opportunity to read about events leading up to the death of Mrs. Mary Spink, alias Mrs. George Chapman.

> Susan Paget, of Coventry Street, Bethoral Green, said, she and her husband worked at the "Prince of Wales" five years ago, when Mrs. Chapman came there. Mrs. Chapman had a fresh color, but complained of her head, and was ill at times. When she came into the bar prisoner [Chapman] said, "Get out of it: you can't get drunk here." The witness, however, never saw her in drink. The first day the witness asked the prisoner where Mrs. Chapman was, he replied, "Get about your business; she will soon be in the bar again getting drunk." That night she saw Mrs. Chapman, who was very ill. She told Chapman that unless he fetched a doctor she would get the parish medical officer. Chapman said his wife was delirious; subsequently he sent for Dr. Rogers, and after the doctor had gone Chapman said his wife was only suffering from delirium tremens. That same night the witness looked into a glass, which seemed to contain cold water, but heard from Mrs. Chapman that he had put a red powder in it. She told Chapman so, and he said she was to take no notice of what Mrs. Chapman said, because she was delirious. The witness replied, "Delirious or not, I moved in quick, and I can move out quick," and thereupon she and her husband went back to their lodgings. Before leaving the witness's husband said to Chapman, "If you have no respect for your wife, and want to kill her, I have respect for my wife, and you can't kill her."

It never seemed to dawn on Paget to report Chapman to the local authorities. Perhaps he felt that they would not really do anything about the situation. Paget would become just one in a long string of people who would observe, yet never report, any abuses committed by Chapman's on his victims.

Despite verbal abuse of his wife, Chapman knew that appearances needed to be kept up. With that in mind, he hired a neighbor named Mrs. Martha Doubleday to help in Mary's expected recovery — expected, that is, by everyone other than George Chapman. Mrs. Doubleday would later relate how she had met the Borough Poisoner and his dying wife: "I have known the Prince of Wales beer house in Bartholomew Square for many years. In the autumn of 1897 the accused became a tenant there. I knew him as Chapman. Her name had been Mary Isabella Spink. She was a nice little-built person, with a fresh color. I became friendly with her. After they had been in the house about twelve months I noticed that she was white, and she got very thin. She said she had pains all over her, and she seemed to be getting worse."

Later, Mrs. Doubleday realized that her care would not be enough as Mary was sinking fast. Mrs. Doubleday asked, "If I could fetch a doctor." Chapman asked who was the closest, and the cheapest, and Mrs. Doubleday replied that Dr. Rogers was the nearest to the pub. Chapman was reluctant to call anyone, but the doctor was old and he must have felt secure enough in his murder method to allow the doctor a visit. Before long the doctor was prescribing medications for an illness that had nothing to do with the poisons being introduced into Mary's body by her attentive husband. Chapman even took it upon himself to administer the medicines he knew would do no good as a cover for his murderous work. As always Chapman was in full control of the situation and enjoying every minute of it. Doctor Rogers would do just fine!

After the doctor's visit Mrs. Doubleday took over the care once again. She recalled, "I stayed with Mrs. Chapman every night. She was in bed in the front room on the second floor. The accused lay on the couch. I was locked in. Mrs. Chapman was in bed all the time I was there. She was suffering very much. She vomited, and had pains all over her. She vomited frequently, and it was dark brown. I gave her nothing at all during the night. After the doctor came the accused gave her brandy and medicine. He brought the brandy up with him at night and put it on the table. After she had the brandy she vomited. I was only there at night. I saw Mrs. Mumford there during the day. Mrs. Chapman had diarrhea very badly. I had to get her out of bed. Dr. Rogers asked me to go and get Mrs. Waymark to nurse her, as I could not do it any longer. I did not find out what was the matter with Mrs. Chapman. I did not ask the accused what was the matter with her."

It would later be reported: "She saw medicine bottles, but did not herself administer anything to the deceased. Chapman always gave her the medicine, as well as the brandy, night and day. The vomiting continued, with frequent diarrhea. A day nurse was employed, who administered nourishment from a feeding cup ordered by the doctor. (All the better it would seem to have qualified witnesses in case of unforeseen problems.) Chapman and the doctor used to discuss the case in the bar. The deceased looked like a skeleton. She (Mrs. Chapman) took the meat extract which the doctor ordered, and was not sick after that. Chapman used to order [Mrs. Doubleday] out of the room when he gave the medicine."

Mary Spink's slow death was also witnessed by Mrs. Jane Mumford who had "known the family who ran the local pub." She said,

> I knew the Chapman's when they came to the Prince of Wales. Mrs. Chapman seemed very well indeed at first. In the autumn I saw her in bed and I relieved Mrs. Doubleday in the night nursing. The accused was in the room during the night — locked in. I did not see Mrs. Chapman have any nourishment at night. She had some medicine given to her by the accused, but I cannot say what it was. She always complained of thirst, but I do not know what she had when she was thirsty; the accused would never let me see it. She asked for a "pony" of stout, and accused went down and got it. She suffered from sickness and diarrhea very much. The accused gave her something in a wineglass, but I could not see the color of it. I suppose he got it from the medicine bottle that was kept on the sideboard. After she drank what he gave her she was generally sick.
> The accused said that Mrs. Chapman was suffering from "delirium tremens" through drink. I saw him reading books in the bar. He said they were doctor's books, and that he was giving her stuff to cure her of "delirium tremeno." I said, "She seems very bad," and he said, "Oh, she will get better when she gets on." He said he had been a bit of a doctor. I did not know what he meant. I had very little to say to him. I was not present when Mrs. Chapman died. I attended her until some three or four days before her death.

It was also reported, "The patient complained of her husband. The door of the bedroom was kept locked. Chapman always gave the patient what she wanted, but whether it was medicine or not the witness (Mrs. Mumford) did not know. She supposed it was medicine. Witness did not see patient have any other nourishment, but she had brandy in a bottle under the pillow, which Chapman gave her. The patient always vomited after what Chapman gave her, and also had dreadful diarrhea. She always vomited after the prisoner had given her anything to drink. The last time she got out of bed she was so weak that she vomited on the floor. He (Chapman) said he had been a kind of doctor on board ship. There was no fire in the room. The patient complained that the brandy made her sick."

It would appear, however, that Mrs. Mumford never bothered to taste or even check the brandy which had so obviously given Mrs. Spink her fits of vomiting and diarrhea. It would never occur to Mrs. Mumford to discuss the matter with a doctor or anyone in authority. Chapman had indeed chosen his women very well.

Mrs. Spink was at death's door and in a great deal of pain as Chapman continued to oversee her "care and feeding." She may have even begun to suspect what was really going on at the last by what Mrs. Doubleday heard her tell Chapman. "Pray God, go away from me." She spoke as Chapman leaned over her to again check how well the murder was coming along. Mrs. Doubleday would also recall that at the time she could not understand why his wife would say such a thing with all the attention he was paying to his now clearly dying wife. She would understand later.

Christmas, Prince of Wales Public House — 1897

For a few days as Mrs. Spink wavered in and out of consciousness everyone knew that the end was very near. She was wasting away and just before Christmas her condition was pronounced hopeless by the doctor. Chapman was ready to deliver the final dose of poison. On Christmas day, 41-year-old Mary Isabella Spink, alias Mrs. Chapman, died. There could have been no greater gift to the Borough Poisoner than her death. All of his hard work and long planning had finally paid off and he was now free to seek other victims.

The events leading up to her death were also witnessed by Mrs. Elizabeth Waymark, the neighbor who had nursed Mary during her final struggle. She would long remember the death and the coldness displayed by Chapman, who showed more concern for his business. She testified:

> Towards the end of 1897 [Dr. Rogers] sent me to the Prince of Wales to nurse Mrs. Chapman for about a fortnight (two weeks) before her death. I saw the accused and made arrangements with him for the nursing. He said she was wasting away, but he did not say what was the matter with her. I saw her in bed. She complained of diarrhea and vomiting, and violent pains in her stomach. I very often saw her vomit. It was slimy and green, (a sign of metallic poison) and as she vomited she was purged; she had diarrhea. She did not take much food, only a little beef tea, brandy, milk and soda, and water. The accused generally gave them to her. After she had had the drink she was sick, and then she used to go off in a stupor. She gradually grew worse. When the accused came into the room he would go to the bedside and feel her pulse. I told him that she was very bad, and I asked him what was the matter, but he did not make any answer. He said he knew. I was with her when she died. Just before the end she had a severe flooding. (An indication that Chapman had introduced a massive dose of poison.)

Mrs. Waymark would later recall: "The prisoner (Chapman) did not treat Mrs. Spink like one would expect a man to behave to his wife. When she asked him to kiss her he did not do so. He frequently visited the sick room, and always felt the patients pulse. She was really dying when I went there."

As Mary began to sink Mrs. Waymark called down to Chapman as he began to open the pub for Christmas day business, which he had expected would be substantial. She said, "At first he did not come up, and when he did she said to him, 'Do kiss me.' She put up her arms out for him to bend over to kiss her but he did not do so. The last time I sent for him before she died he did not come up in time. I prepared the body for burial. It was a mere skeleton."

Mrs. Doubleday would also be at Mary's side when the end came. It was almost as if Chapman was determined to display his deadly skills in front of other women when he could just as easily have had no witnesses at all. Mrs. Doubleday would call to him, "Chapman, come up quickly. Your wife is dying!" She would later recall, "On Christmas morning she got much worse and became unconscious. She had been vomiting very much. A severe flooding came on. I called out for the accused, but he did not come up for some time afterwards. (Business in the bar was going to be very good and he had much to do. After all, he was about to lose his "wife" and he would have to do her job as well!) When he did come he only leant over the bed and went into the next room. Before she died I called him again, and he leant over her and said, 'Polly, Polly, speak! She had just died then."

Mrs. Doubleday was quite certain that he had called out "Polly"! But just who was Polly? No one ever reported that Mary Spink was ever called "Polly" by anyone. Or was it that Chapman was playing just one more game. Was he calling out the name of Ripper victim Mary Ann "Polly" Nichols? It is no more than mere speculation, but it is interesting nevertheless. Chapman then went into the next room to shed a few well-calculated tears (of joy) before going downstairs to continue his work at the bar. After all, he had a business to run, and death was just business as usual.

It would be Mrs. Doubleday who would express her utter shock at Chapman's next move. She remembered: "He went down and opened the house. She died at one o'clock. I said, 'You are never going to open the house today?' He said, 'Yes, I am.' I saw Mrs. Chapman's body after she was dead. It was in a very shocking condition; it was very much bruised." For Chapman the corpse upstairs in the front room was now no more than a throwaway, but not to Mrs. Doubleday. "There were signs of flooding; it looked as if it was wrapped up in a sheet. The boy (little Willie) was in the next room when she died. I never ascertained what the deceased died of. Dr. Rogers, who is now dead, gave the certificate."

Chapman had chosen his doctor well as the aged doctor ascribed the death to natural causes. Her death certificate would list the cause to be phthisis, but the bruises should have spoken volumes to the doctor. The condition of the body, however, did not seem to overly impress Dr. Rogers despite the bruises and the emaciated condition of the corpse. Chapman was certainly able to "chat him up" very well.

Chapman now began to work with great speed as he wanted the corpse removed as fast as possible. The *Southwark and Bermonsey Recorder and South London Gazette* would inform their readers on January 17, 1903, about the speed of removal. "Henry Edward Pierce, who conducted the funeral of Mary Isabella Spink, known as Mrs. Chapman, said the prisoner (George Chapman) was the man who sent for him to the Prince of Wales beerhouse, in Bartholomew Square, to bury his wife. He wanted the coffin in the same night, and the burial as soon as possible. There was a veil over the face of the dead woman, and the yellow color of the flesh struck him as unusual." Cremation never seems to have crossed his mind.

On December 30, 1897, Henry Pierce buried the first victim of the Borough Poisoner in the form of Mary Spink in a common grave. It would be a short and sparsely attended funeral held at St. Patrick's Cemetery, Leytonstone, Essex. Six more bodies would later be buried on top of Mary, all of whom of course would need to be removed in less than five years. For now, however, Chapman had gotten away with murder once again, and he would shortly need a replacement — not only to tend his bar business but also to fill his murderous requirements.

As for little Willie, he was certainly no longer needed (as if he ever was) and would be sent away as soon as possible from his home and his mother's killer. It should be noted that Chapman could just as easily have murdered Willie, but the young boy was not a female. George Chapman's murderous rage was reserved almost exclusively for women. On January 30, 1898, Chapman took Willie Spink to Dr. Barnard's Home, where he dumped the boy. It did not work, however, as a fast check of the so-called facts supplied by Chapman to the home's officers soon proved to be completely false. Willie returned home for a while longer; just long enough to become acquainted with the next victim of the "Borough Poisoner of Southwark."

Chapter 5

The Slow Death of Bessie Taylor

I understand she had been married.
— Elizabeth Ann Painter

PRINCE OF WALES PUB, BARTHOLOMEW SQUARE, LONDON — 1898

After the death of his "wife" George Chapman decided that it would be best for him to play the part of the grieving husband, for a while at least. He knew that people would be naturally interested in his welfare and that of the young boy Willie. He also decided that he would stay at the Prince of Wales pub since he was not suspected of any crimes and business was doing well. The death of Mary Spink (Mrs. Chapman I) made the pub better known and he could, at least for a while, take full advantage of the situation, after all there was money to be made.

One bit of unfinished business did need to be taken care of, however—that of 8-year-old Willie. He was no relation to Chapman, not that it would have mattered much. But he could not simply kill the boy as another sudden death would certainly have aroused a great deal of unwanted attention, and that was the last thing a serial killer needed. With this in mind Chapman went to Dr. Barnardo's Home on January 13, 1898. John Klaiber, applications clerk at the home, would remember the visit: "A man who gave the name of George Chapman came to me with reference to a little boy named Willie Spink, aged eight, and his application was handed over to William Henry Stringer, an inquiry officer." Chapman told Mr. Klaiber that "he wished to get the boy into (the home)." Chapman made sure to emphasize that "the child was that of Mrs. Spink, and has no relations whatever." Chapman was unsuccessful on this first attempt because the information he had supplied had been false. Willie would spend one more year living in the pub with Chapman. It can only be imagined how badly he was abused for that period of time living with the man who had murdered his mother. And why not send him to Mrs. Spink's family?

It would not take long, however, for the ever amorous Chapman to decide that he needed a woman to use and abuse. Within months of Mary's death Chapman placed ads in local papers for a new barmaid. After all, the local people would surely understand that he had a growing business to attend to and of course he was a single man with "certain needs." From a long list

Bessie Taylor and Severin Klosowski, alias George Chapman. Photograph found by Inspector Godley at the Crown Public House.

of women who applied only a few made the short list for a personal interview with the proprietor of the Prince of Wales, and only one would meet Chapman's special requirements. It was Easter week of 1898 and Bessie Taylor had gotten her last job at the local pub.

Elizabeth "Bessie" Taylor was a former domestic servant who had gotten into the restaurant business. Some sources, however, placed her in the position of housekeeper at a Peckham restaurant, which was a mix of the two. Bessie was the daughter of Thomas Parsonage Taylor from Warrinfton. Her father was a simple but well-respected farmer and cattle dealer. Bessie herself had very little real experience behind the bar and would have been better suited working the family farm. Nevertheless, she was exactly what Chapman was looking for. Chapman needed a woman he could manipulate and use, but not as a barmaid.

At first the job consisted of actually working in the bar, but the new live-in barmaid soon gave in to the attentions Chapman paid her. And his methods had not changed — she was soon accepting gifts from her new boss. Before long Chapman asked Bessie to enter into a fully bogus marriage. Soon the friends at the pub would see the happy couple drive out on a Sunday morning for a reported marriage. It was alleged to have occurred at St. George's Cathedral in Southwark, but no marriage actually occurred. Detective Arthur Neil would later testify that "I have searched the records of Somerset House between January 1898, and March 1900, and I can find no record of a marriage between George Chapman and Bessie Taylor, or Severin Klosowski and Bessie Taylor."

After the "marriage" the couple returned to the still open pub to business as usual. There would be no time for a honeymoon as Mr. Chapman felt he had to acquire as much money as possible. Perhaps he felt that if he needed to get out of town in a hurry, cash would be needed. As for the new "Mrs. Chapman"— she had a little less than three years to live with serial killer Severin Klosowski, alias George Chapman!

Hargrave Adam would make note of one of Chapman's cover operations in writing: "He was always careful to cultivate the good opinions of the police, and, while licenses of the Prince of Wales, it was his custom to cycle with members of the local police cycling club on their outings. At that time he was the author of at least one murder — that of Mrs. Spink. The subsequent revelation of this must have made the policemen wonder at the novelty of their own experience."

After Chapman had "acquired" his next victim he decided to give up the lease on the Prince of Wales. In August 1898, he moved with "the missus" to Bishops, Stortford, where he took up a new lease on the old Grapes Public House.

"Transfer of the license of the 'Prince of Wales'
from Chapman to Newson —
August 10, 1898 — £80."

BISHOPS, STORTFORD—FALL 1898

Once again Chapman was on the move, never staying in one place too long. Indeed, because of his frequent moves no one could state that they really knew the man, which was exactly what Chapman wanted. The move to Stortford also had a practical purpose. There would have been too many deaths under strange circumstances in one place. He would later move again, this time to 8 Haberdasher Street, Shoreditch, with Bessie Taylor (Mrs. Chapman II) and 9-year-old Willie Spink. Willie for the most part stayed in the cellar. Even with the rats it was safer there.

Just before Christmas 1898, Bessie's friend, Elizabeth Ann Painter, paid a visit to her now "married" friend at the Grapes. They had met during Bessie's days as a domestic servant and she stayed for two weeks over the holiday. She recalled, "I was acquainted with Bessie Taylor for many years. I remember her being in a situation at Peckham. About Easter time, 1898, she left there and went to live at the Prince of Wales. I understood that she had been married. I visited there and saw the accused (Chapman). They were living as Mr. & Mrs. Chapman."

The boldness of Chapman is apparent in the advances he made on Elizabeth Painter even though he had never met her before her Christmas visit. Painter would later report that "He kissed me once or twice." Possibly Chapman was trying to have two women living with him at the same time as he had done at least twice before. Painter, however, would not go for it and would only stay for the planned two weeks. She did stay long enough, however, to glimpse a portion of the real Chapman. She would later recall that he often yelled at Bessie and even threw things at her. It was a very strange way to act in front of Painter if he was trying to get her to stay on, but that was the way he treated women. For Chapman it was business as usual and the way he acted when dealing with women. And yet it must be asked: why did so many women seem to be drawn to this killer? What hold did he have on them?

Chapman was also a very reckless man, even with the revolver he had acquired in the United States. Chapman was so reckless with the weapon that he even brandished it about while Painter was visiting. Painter would later tell investigators that Chapman was "very unkind to her (Bessie) when she came back; he carried on at her all the afternoon, and in the evening he frightened her with a revolver, because she had been telling the customers that she was going into the hospital. She was not strong when she came out of the hospital, but she was better." (Was this the same weapon used to murder Mary Anderson in New Jersey some six years earlier? The police would never look into that possibility.)

It did not take long for Chapman to begin trying out his slow poison method on Bessie. Even during Elizabeth Painter's first visit to her old friend she noticed something wrong with her normally healthy friend. Bessie was losing weight and she had "lumps in her face, caused by her teeth." She could not keep food down. Not long after the Christmas visit, Bessie went to the hospital for a small operation. The doctors could not really say what was wrong with her but, away from Chapman, her general condition did seem to improve. No one was feeding her poison at the hospital. Painter said: "She came out of the hospital in about a week and returned to the *Grapes*."

Elizabeth would remember that when her friend "went into hospital at Bishop's Stortford, for abscesses on the gums, and was there a week. She underwent an operation, and when she came out she seemed very ill, and was unable to take solid food." It would later be reported that while Bessie was in the hospital Elizabeth Painter had stayed alone with Chapman at the Grapes. It is possible that Chapman felt he could "capture" Painter even as he was slowly murdering her friend Bessie.

Coming back from the hospital, it was not an easy homecoming. One would expect a "husband" to give a bit of care to his returning "wife," but just the opposite occurred. Chapman's treatment of Bessie went from bad to worse. It was a sure sign that he was getting close to finishing off his victim when his brutality increased. Chapman did not want any interference from "those fool doctors,' and he was very angry that Bessie had been helped, if not been cured, by her absence from him. His resentment of the surgeons and what they had done, compounded by the fact that he was not a respected surgeon in England, could very well have helped trigger his renewed attacks on Bessie.

Yet, with these ever-increasing verbal and physical attacks on Bessie, one must ask why she would stay with Chapman? Surely she saw the worst of the man. Chapman had indeed picked the correct victim, probably convincing her that she was nothing without him and that she should stay to serve him no matter what. He employed a psychological tactic — pulling an individual down as far as you can take them until they are completely at their attacker's will.

Cults and many religious groups use this method of physical and psychological abuse and control.

A Return to London's Killing Grounds — Spring 1899

It was time to try once again to "remove" little Willie from his home before he took care of Bessie. Willie was a witness to his mother's death and could very well have noticed similarities in Mrs. Spink's death and the slow decline and eventual death of Bessie. It is not good serial killer policy to keep an eyewitness around. On March 20, 1899, Willie Spink was finally accepted into a home for orphans. It was a workhouse called St. Leonards in Shoreditch and it was right out of a Dickens novel. Willie would, however, escape from the place on March 22, and he would never see George Chapman again. The relieving officer for the parish of St. Leonard, Ernest John Sibley, remembered his conversation with Chapman. He said "Chapman applied, and gave the name of Isabella Spink as that of the mother. One of the references given was Bessie Taylor, described as a housekeeper of the same address." As for Bessie, she had only 11 months to live. It should be noted at this point that there was never any evidence that misogynist Chapman ever attacked a man. And even though young Willie was not fully grown he did represent the male side of the equation and was thus, as the record would show, never attacked by Chapman. If anything Chapman was a complete coward.

With Willie now out of the picture, Chapman was free to move about once again. In March or May 1899, depending on the source, Chapman and Bessie left the Grapes behind and returned to London to make a new start. There he contacted the Bridge House Estates Committee with the intention to lease the Monument Tavern on Union Street, Southwark. The tavern was only one mile south of the Thames River and the heart of Ripper territory in Whitechapel. He was also free to continue the slow poisoning of Bessie Taylor.

Before long the once strong constitution of Bessie began to weaken as Chapman slowly introduced the antimony poison into her body. It would be a very slow and very controlled process and one in which he planned to enjoy as closely as possible. As Bessie became progressively weaker Chapman's abuse became more and more pronounced, but not in front of Bessie's family. In fact, Bessie's father would later compliment Chapman for his treatment of his daughter saying that "he had never seen a better husband." Neither of Bessie's parents, who kept in close contact with her, would ever suspect anything was going on. They would both die before Chapman was ever charged with murder, and they believed to the end that Chapman had done all he could to save their daughter. They would also never discover that the money they had sent their daughter, in the form of £50, was being intercepted by Chapman and held in his own accounts. Chapman, it would seem, was a very good actor when he had to be — he always seemed to keep his eye on the prize.

Southwark, London — Fall 1900

Chapman made sure to always behave like a proper gentleman when he was out on the town with his "wife." It was a psychological cover he developed to push aside any complaints made in case anyone investigated his wife's deaths. After all, if no one actually saw him abuse his wife then the matter would be simply one of his word against hers. At the time, Bessie was still able to visit her family and in September 1900 she visited her brother William. Although she was sick at the time and was not eating well she still looked generally the same as she had always had. Her brother would remember her visit and recall how quickly her health had deteriorated only three months later. The poisons in her system were starting to take a heavy toll on Bessie.

As Bessie became sicker her friends would visit her at the tavern, including her longtime friend, Elizabeth Painter. Painter would ask Chapman how her friend was doing and more than once Chapman would show his true disregard by telling Elizabeth that "Your friend is dead." Each time, however, Elizabeth would go upstairs to find her friend gravely ill but very much alive in her bed. She recalled:

> He was not kind to her there; he was always carrying on at her. She seemed to be fading very much. She complained of pains all over her, and her head was bad. She got very thin. Towards the end of 1900, I visited her every evening. She always felt sick, and it always came on after she had had anything to eat or drink. She was in bed, and had pains in her stomach. I do not know if she had diarrhea. When [Chapman] came into her room he felt her pulse with his watch in his hand. After a time I saw medicine bottles in the room. [Chapman] would shake them and then look up to the light through them. I asked him what was the matter with her, and he said it was a complication of diseases. Chapman always prepared her food downstairs, but sometimes I carried it up to the bedroom. My visits were always in the evening.

The newspapers would later report on Painter's comments about how Chapman treated Bessie before she was confined to her death bed. On March 24, 1903, the *Pall Mall Gazette* reported that "the 'carrying on' was generally after the house (tavern) was closed, before they went to bed, and on Sunday afternoon. Sometimes they went out, and then they did not carry on in the street. The witness (Painter) never interfered, nor complained to anyone about Chapman's conduct; but she talked of it after Chapman was arrested. The witness used to tell them they ought to be happy as anyone together. Mrs. Chapman was very fond of the prisoner (Chapman). He used to be angry if the money was not right. She did not answer him back, but cried very much."

It did not bring Chapman any pleasure to find that, no matter what he did, Bessie was still able to meet with her many friends. In fact, her many new friends on Union Street would remember Bessie not only for her kindness to the local poor but also for her small hand-made gifts she gave out to customers at the pub during Christmas, even though she was very ill at the time. She could also be seen visiting the neighborhood after the Monument was closed for the evening, riding her bike up and down the streets of South London. Chapman, it was reported, never came along for a ride as he had other business to tend to.

During the latter part of December 1900, Bessie's brother William Taylor made a final trip to the tavern to visit his ill sister. At the time Chapman put on an act of caring, playing the part of the dutiful husband so well that the entire Taylor family believed that he was doing everything in his power to help Bessie regain her once good health. In reality, of course, Chapman was doing his very best to kill Bessie as slowly as he possibly could in front of as many visitors as would fit into the small bedroom. It was one of the best examples of just how cold-blooded this serial killer really was. For her part, Bessie did not tell her brother about not really being married to Chapman and would hold on to that little secret even near death.

William Taylor would later tell a hushed and packed courtroom about his sister's decline as he and their mother visited Bessie at the tavern, which would soon become her death house. He recounted: "In December, 1900, I heard that she was ill, and my mother came up from Cheshire. I saw my mother, and after some conversation with her I went to see my sister at the Monument. I had not seen her for about three months, when she had called on me. When I saw her at the Monument she appeared to be very ill and shrunken; she had gone like a little old woman. She said she had violent pains in her inside, and that she had been very sick. The next I heard was a message from my mother that she had died." Bessie was only 36 years old.

As more doctors were called in it became evident to Chapman that he could easily get away with the poison murder of his "wife." None of the doctors suspected or even looked for poison as a possible cause of Bessie's illness. Even accidental poisoning never seems to have crossed any of the doctors' minds. This was why Chapman could later state that 50 doctors could not cure her. In this case he knew what he was talking about.

Bessie's last full-time physician was Dr. James Maurice Stoker, who had an office nearby at 221 New Kent Road and lived near the tavern at 81 Borough Road. He had been called into the case by a nurse named Mrs. Martha Stevens. Mrs. Stevens had been caring for Bessie herself, but she felt that a doctor was needed if Bessie had any chance of recovery. Bessie had also been cared for by two sisters from All Hallow's Mission Church around the corner on Pepper Street as well as several members of the church. It is a testimony to how beloved Bessie was in her local community as well as a testimony to how many people were fooled by the cover of kindness Chapman displayed as he slowly murdered Bessie right in front of them.

Sister Martha Elizabeth Ibbs would later be called in to testify at the police hearing into Bessie's death. She seemed to feel that Chapman had done all he could. The records state: "The case was perplexing, and the cause of death was inexplicable to the witness, who had much experience of illness. She remembered seeing Mrs. Taylor one day visiting her daughter. The patients exhaustion increased visibly towards the end, and she was often drowsy. The witness usually spoke to Chapman, who appeared to be very kind and attentive to the patient. The doctor came regularly, and there appeared to be a proper supply of medicine and food. As the patient got worse Chapman seemed very anxious. The witness thought from his manner and behavior that he was desirous of doing the best he could for Mrs. Chapman."

Two years after the events, nurse Stevens would tell investigators about Bessie's decline and slow yet unexpected death.

> I used to live at Union Street, Borough. Two or three months before Christmas, 1900, I got to know [Chapman] and Bessie Taylor at the Monument. When I first knew Bessie she seemed pretty well in health. Later on she complained to me of being fatigued, languid, and having pains in her stomach. I suggested that she should go to the doctor. She made a complaint to me, and I mentioned Dr. Stoker's name. I went with her to his surgery more than once. He gave her some medicine. She seemed to rally, but not for long. (Perhaps because Chapman became concerned that the doctor may have suspected poison. When he did not, Chapman was free to continue his "work.") I went to the Monument and nursed her about a week or ten days before Christmas. She engaged me herself. At first I only stayed during the day. She had vomiting and diarrhea, and great pain. She complained a little about her throat burning, and it was very red. After a time I stayed there during the night as well as the day.

The South London news reports would further detail what Mrs. Stevens had seen during Bessie's last days.

> The patient rallied a little, and then got worse, and was laid up, whereupon the witness nursed her until she died. The illness lasted about two months. The symptoms were great weakness, nausea, and purging, severe pains, and a burning sensation in the throat. The vomits and excreta were slimy. As she was complaining greatly of thirst the patient was given ice, iced water, brandy, milk, and sometimes champagne. Chapman would bring things to the door or the witness would fetch them.

Doctor Stoker later discussed his efforts to find out what was causing the "illness." He brought in other medical men to assist in the work. None of them, despite her violent symptoms, even considered slow death by antimony poison to be a possible cause. It is an interesting observation considering the fact that poison was not exactly an unknown method of wife removal at the time. One could read reports of such cases in the local newspapers. Chapman's acting skills must have been extraordinary to fool so many doctors for so long. Doctor Stoker related:

> I was called to the Monument on 1st January, 1901. I first saw [Chapman] about a fortnight (two weeks) before that, when he came to my surgery. Previous to that Bessie Taylor had called on me and asked for some medicine. I then attended her. Mrs. Stevens was there. I visited Mrs. Chapman almost

daily from 1st January to 13th February, when she died. When I first called she was in bed; she had been vomiting and diarrhea, and pains in the stomach, and the stomach was very tender. The vomit was green. I cannot recollect if I saw her vomiting. I prescribed for her. She used to get better and then go back again. (Chapman was playing perhaps?) I suggested another doctor being called in. I had three separate consultations with three other doctors. One was Dr. Sunderland, who is a specialist in the diseases of women. He only saw her once. I was under the impression that Mrs. Chapman was suffering from some womb trouble. I do not recollect if Dr. Sunderland suggested any alteration in the treatment.

She did not make any improvement, and I then suggested another doctor. Somebody in the house suggested Dr. Thorpe of Southwark Bridge Road. He and I examined Mrs. Chapman together. He said he thought she was suffering from a severe form of hysteria. I then got Dr. Cotter, and we examined the patient together. He thought she was suffering from some cancerous disease of the stomach or intestine. In consequence I sent a portion of her vomit to the Clinical Research Association, with directions to see if there was any trace of cancer. That would be a microscopical examination. They found no trace. The constant vomiting and diarrhea continued more or less during the whole time that I was there.

Not one of the doctors seems to have felt that Bessie Taylor should have been sent to the hospital. Is it any wonder that her killer felt so safe in his murderous adventure? It is interesting to note that when samples were sent to the Clinical Research Association after the next Chapman wife died under nearly identical circumstances doctors would ask for a different analysis—they would ask for poison to be checked and they would finally discover the cause of these mysterious deaths. That investigation, however, would have to wait nearly two more years and after the death of one more Chapman "wife."

A few days before Bessie finally succumbed to Chapman's slow, relentless poisoning she seemed to make a dramatic turnaround and it seemed that she would finally be on the road to recovery. Indeed, Dr. Stoker arrived one day to find Bessie downstairs playing the piano. When the totally clueless doctor saw what Bessie was doing, and that she was in such good spirits, he rubbed his hands together and told Mrs. Stevens: "Capital." Was this the same piano that Mrs. Spink had played for the famous musical shaves before she died? History is silent on that interesting point.

Mrs. Stevens also recalled the incident as well as Chapman's attempts to show his "great concern" for his wife: "One Sunday in January Mrs. Chapman felt so well that she got up and played the piano. Mr. Chapman got everything I asked for on behalf of the patient. Nothing was spared, and he did everything so far as I knew, to make the patient happy and cured. She was always anxious to see him, and he was very fond of her, so far as I could tell. Had there been anything wrong I would not have noticed it, because they seemed so fond of each other. He was very pleased when she got up and played the piano, and they sat down to dinner together, but she could not eat it."

The delighted doctor made a quick examination and pronounced Bessie better and on her way to recovery. On February 7, 1901, he sent Mrs. Painter home because she would no longer be needed to care for Bessie Taylor. It can only be guessed what went through Chapman's mind as he recalled all of the efforts he had gone to, only to have Bessie make what appeared to be a dramatic turn for the better. This determined serial killer then set about to finish off his work and within two days Bessie was on her deathbed, never to rise again.

When Doctor Stoker returned on February 10, he was shocked to see his patient in such a bad state. He immediately called Mrs. Stevens back to the Monument to care for his now clearly dying patient. At that point Dr. Stoker gave up trying to cure Bessie and simply attempted to ease her pains as she moved in and out of consciousness. In the early morning hours of February 13, surrounded by friends, nurses, a doctor and one serial killer, Bessie Taylor died of antimony poison. Only the serial killer knew the exact cause of her death and it was time for him to put on his show. "On the early morning of February 13, about half past one, Mrs. Stevens noticed a change, and called Chapman. The patient was just dead as he entered the room."

Chapman, who checked Bessie's pulse and condition just to be sure the "job" had been done raised up and said "Ah, she's gone." Nurse Stevens would later recall that Chapman put on a show for the gathered few as he "cried bitterly." It was a show worthy of the stage and it was successful enough to cause the then greatly disappointed Dr. Stoker to immediately fill out a death certificate. The certificate would state that Bessie had died due to "exhaustion from vomiting and diarrhea," but he failed to state the actual cause of death of his formally healthy patient. What had brought on the vomiting and diarrhea in the first place? Only later would that question even come to his mind and only after the death of another woman. Stoker was not a very good doctor by any standard.

The day after Bessie's death found her friend, Elizabeth Painter, visiting the Monument. She found the tavern open for business as usual and Chapman tending the bar. As she had done before, she asked Chapman how Bessie was doing. He replied that she was "much about the same." Bessie's corpse had yet to be removed so perhaps for serial killer Chapman things were about the same. For Chapman, Bessie Taylor was simply a throwaway, and death was, after all, business as usual!

Mrs. Stevens met Elizabeth and brought her upstairs. "The nurse took me upstairs and told me something, and I found she was dead." It was at that point that Elizabeth realized that the tavern was not only open but that Chapman seemed to be doing a brisk business. The contrast between what she found in the pub and what she knew had just happened was disconcerting. When she went downstairs to speak to the "widower," Chapman tried to kiss her. Mrs. Painter was startled by the advance but Chapman was never one to miss an opportunity even with the cold body of his wife upstairs being prepared for a coffin. Elizabeth simply put it off, reasoning that the stress of the whole situation caused Chapman to act that way.

Handling the removal of Bessie's body for a very fast funeral would be William Tull, manager of Mr. Smith's undertaking shop at 122 Southwark Bridge Road. (Mr. Smith's undertaking firm is still in business in Southwark, and is ready to take care of all your funeral needs.) On February 13, he was called to the Monument by Chapman ready with a fresh coffin. He had been there earlier in the day to make arrangements for the pickup of the corpse, and he had gone upstairs where he "saw a woman's body." Chapman told him "Bessie Chapman" was her name and he "confined the body, and early on 15th February it was conveyed to St. Pancras Station." It is certain that the good Mr. Tull felt that he had seen the last of the premises of the unfortunate Bessie Taylor — Mrs. Chapman II. However, he would be on hand less than two years later when he would help with the removal and identification of another coffin and nameplate, which he had personally engraved.

As for nurse Stevens, she would stay on at the tavern for a week after the funeral. It was long enough for her to see the now happy widower begin his advertisement for further assistance at his tavern. After all, he now had an opening to fill and business was up. Many people came by to have a pint and console the "widower."

It would not be long before both Bessie's mother and father followed their daughter into the grave. Later, at the inquest, both would need to be removed in order to allow access to Bessie's coffin, which would also be removed and brought to a side shed for a closer examination at the end of 1902. But that was in the near future. For the time being Chapman would play the part of the grieving husband as he thanked those around him who had cared for his wife. He was especially thankful to the incompetent Dr. Stoker.

Bessie's final — for a few months at least — resting place was only five miles from the village where she had been born and grew up in Cheshire. Her brother William Taylor would remember that "On 15th February I met [Chapman] at St. Pancras Station, and with him and other members of the family I went to Lymm Churchyard, in Cheshire, where my sister was buried."

In a last final assault on Bessie, Chapman wrote out a final lie on a mourning card to be placed on her grave. It read:

> *In Loving memory of Bessie Chapman,*
> *wife of George Chapman, and daughter of*
> *Thomas P. and Betsy Taylor,*
> *who died February 13, 1901,*
> *aged 36 years, and was interred at*
> *Lymm, February 15th.*
>
> *Farewell my friends, fond and dear,*
> *Weep not for me one single tear,*
> *For all that was or could be done,*
> *You plainly see my time was come.*
>   G. Chapman

Chapman was finished with Bessie Taylor but he was not finished with murder. Before long he would seek out and find his last victim in a series of deaths that had gone on for at least 15 years. Very soon the Thames Torso Killer would be back at work as well, but not before Chapman once again moved his lodgings.

Later that year Sir Robert Anderson, former assistant commissioner for crime at the time of the 1888 Ripper murders, retired from public service. His retirement was noted in the *Pall Mall Gazette* as once again the name "Ripper" came to mind. "The mystery surrounding those crimes has never been solved (at least in the public light), though the police have an explanation which they believe satisfactory." Were they looking once again for Chapman? Perhaps, but as far as official investigations would go, the case was closed with no real leads to follow. As for the police having an "explanation which they believe satisfactory"? At the time that was highly unlikely. The only things they knew for certain was that "Jack" was not killing the same way he had in the past, and they had failed to capture him. Anderson would further note that most of London never needed to fear the Ripper. "No amount of silly hysterias could alter the fact that these crimes were a cause of danger only to a particular section of a small and definite class of woman, in a limited district of the East End...."

Also in early 1901 the case against Ameer Ben Ali began to unravel. He had been improperly convicted of the murder of "Old Shakespeare" in New York City in 1891, but reporters who had covered the original investigation were finding disturbing problems with the evidence. Ameer was not out of prison yet, but things were starting to look a lot better for the French Algerian who was known as "Frenchy."

Chapter 6

A Barmaid Named Maud

I will try dear George and get better so as to come home and help you.
— Maud Marsh

MONUMENT TAVERN, SOUTHWARK—AUGUST 1901

Bessie Taylor had been very popular in the neighborhood around the Monument and her death had been a surprise to everyone, except of course her "grieving" husband. With the burden of Bessie now removed, community attention was turned to the widower whom they all knew as George Chapman. Chapman once again found that a death in the family could be turned into very good business at the tavern. Chapman easily enjoyed the new profits but too much attention to his welfare meant he would need to wait a few months before looking for a live-in replacement for Taylor. He had barmaids but none who fitted his real needs, so he had to wait. It would later be reported that "During the remainder of Chapman's tenancy of the Monument several barmaids are said to have been engaged." After all, this was Victorian London and proper appearances needed to be kept up at least for a while. So for six months, as far as the local neighborhood was concerned, Chapman was without female companionship at the pub, but it was now time to change that situation. Chapman "needed" to kill and for that need to be fulfilled a victim was required.

In August 1901, eighteen-year-old Maud Elizabeth Marsh could be found living with her parents at 14 Longfellow Road in West Croydon. Maud had recently held a position at the Duke of York public house on Canterbury Road in West Croydon. She had enjoyed the work, which included helping out at the bar and taking care of the owner's children. Maud is described as being "a fresh-looking country girl, smart and attentive to her business." After a short break of some two months she was once again ready to go back to the work that she had enjoyed so much. With that in mind young Maud began to advertise for a position as barmaid. She would never learn that one of the men who would see her ad was a serial killer who had once graced the front pages of the same paper she advertised in under the mantle of Jack the Ripper. With her ad he had located his final victim in a series that had crossed oceans and continents lasting at least 15 years using several methods for his murders. Yet, he was free to continue as no law enforcement agency in the world was looking for him. He was a simple publican working behind a bar in South London just a mile or two south of the central killing grounds of the Ripper.

Never one to waste a letter when a postcard would do, Chapman sent a card to Maud asking for an interview:

Maud Marsh and Severin Klosowski, alias George Chapman. Photograph found by Inspector Godley at the Crown Public House.

*Call at the Monument ASAP,
fare paid engaged or not.
G. Chapman*

It is interesting to note that Maud would later burn all of Chapman's letters to her as well as that first postcard. Was this on orders from Chapman? History is silent on that question, but it does seem a strange thing to do.

Maud had received ten replies to her ad but for whatever reason she chose to answer the one from the Monument. She could have worked closer to her home in West Croydon, but the big city of London was too much of an attraction and seemed to be the best bet. It was time for her to be on her own. Before she could accept any offer of work from Chapman, however, her parents decided that it would be best to see for themselves the conditions Maud might be asked to work under. Mr. Marsh had to work but Mrs. Marsh, who would later describe her daughter as "healthy but hysterical," went with young Maud to the Monument Public House. They took the morning train to London and before long got off at the famous, but often misidentified, London Bridge, which is one of the many bridges which connects north and south London across the Thames River. From there mother and daughter took the short walk south on Borough High Street to Union Street and the Monument.

Chapman, who explained to Mrs. Marsh that he was a bachelor, stated that he needed Maud to do housework as well as tending the bar. But not to worry as the "rough work was done by someone else." When Mrs. Marsh wondered if Maud was expected to live at the tavern with an unmarried man, Chapman was quick to point out that the upper floors of the

Monument were occupied by a very respectable family who happen to not be in at that very moment. It was, of course, one of the many lies and half truths he told Mrs. Marsh in an effort to capture Maud. In the end, Maud's mother would tentatively accept the words of Chapman even though she was never really comfortable with the situation. She would later recall, "My daughter had been out of a situation for two months before she became barmaid to the accused. I, as a mother, made all the inquires I could to satisfy myself that the place was respectable. From the very first the accused was attentive. My daughter was ill at the Monument for three days, but not sufficiently to keep her in bed."

After the interview Maud and her mother sat down for a bit of conversation and "a pint of bitter" at the Monument before going home to West Croydon. It would not be long before Chapman offered the position to Maud, but not before he had time to check the Duke of York pub for a reference. Maud was soon moving into a small room upstairs at the Monument to begin work. One of her first discoveries would be that there was no respectable family living in the upstairs quarters of the tavern. Her next discovery would be that her new boss wanted her *very* much.

Despite the little lies Chapman had told her, Maud liked the work very much and told her father that she enjoyed being at the tavern. She also informed her father that "the mister" had told her that she was doing her work very well.

Before long her new boss began "paying her attentions." In fact, it had taken only one week for Chapman to begin making his moves on the young woman. After the first week Chapman presented his new barmaid with a gold watch and chain. It was clear what his intentions were and he was pressing hard for Maud to be just a little more than the hired help. The speed of his advances must have surprised even Maud as she informed her mother of the gift from her new boss. Giving gifts freely to women he wished to "own" was nothing new to Chapman, however. He knew that upon their deaths all such gifts would naturally fall back into his bloody hands. "Lots of presents from Chapman" meant nothing. It was all part of the temporary cost of the murder business.

The gifts meant something to Maud's father though. When Robert Marsh heard about the gift he told his wife: "It seems funny he gave her that so soon. Go up and see her." Chapman had also given Maud three or four rings, one of which was said by a friend, Mrs. Toon, who would later care for Maud, as being "thick and too big for her." Had he taken these rings from other victims? And, were these victims to be placed in the Ripper or Torso column? As far as the records show, that possibility was never looked into by the police even after they felt he may have been the Ripper. The coroner's report on (Ripper victim) Annie Chapman's death at the hands of the Ripper states: "The stiffness was more noticeable on the left side, especially in the fingers, which were partly closed. There was an abrasion over the ring finger, with distinct markings of a ring or rings." Annie Chapman's rings would never be found as they were never pawned by her killer, who kept them as a reminder of the murder. Both Jack the Ripper and the Borough Poisoner were "collectors."

Monument Tavern, Southwark—September 1901

One week after Maud received her gold watch she told her father that "Mr. Chapman has asked me how I would like to be called Mrs. Chapman." Mr. Marsh was not amused and he told Maud to wait because he felt it was far too soon and after all she "did not really know the man." Indeed, Chapman had proposed to Maud on several occasions and his "attentions" were starting to concern Maud's parents a great deal. It was at this point in the very new relationship that Maud sent a letter to Mrs. Marsh. The letter was sent in secret and the message was very clear that Chapman had designs on Maud and she did not quite know how to handle the situation.

Sept. 11, 1901
Monument, Borough, S.E.

Dear Mother,

Just a line to say on the QT. Mr. Chapman has gone out, so I write this to you to say George says if I do not let him have what he wants he will give me £35 and send me home. What shall I do? He does worry me so; but still I am engaged, so it will not matter much, and if he does not marry me I can have a breach of promise, can't I? I must close, with love.

Write soon. I remain your loving daughter,

Maud

P.S. I have sent this without him knowing it. Love to all.
Let me know how Papa is.

The fact that she was engaged was shock enough but the pressure Chapman was putting on Maud for sexual favors was more than Mrs. Marsh could tolerate. Mrs. Marsh wrote to her daughter by the next day's post as she fully understood that Chapman was about to have his way with her young daughter. She advised Maud to leave London as soon as possible and return home.

Before long Maud would again write to her mother, now very worried as was her very ill father. The new quite upbeat letter sent by Maud seemed to be a complete change from the first as if Maud had someone looking over her shoulder. Chapman it would appear was not aware of the first letter before it was sent, but by the tone of the second letter he was most certainly aware of the second. Maud's hand may have penned the words but the control was fully Chapman's. He knew that he had possibly moved too swiftly. New more measured steps would need to be taken if he was to successfully capture the young Maud Marsh. He would need to meet the parents in their town and show his "concerns" for Maud. Care needed to be taken with this one.

Sept 12th 1901

Dear Mother,

Your letter at hand this morning. I am very pleased to say there is nothing between us as far as only friendship. I was silly enough to write that letter to you yesterday and hardly knew what I was doing. I had not been very well and he tried to do the best for me and I thought he was going to take advantage of me. Dear Mother there is no need to worry about me as I am alright here and was sorry I wrote the letter to you as I see different this morning of him. I had to show

Top: Robert Marsh, father of Maud Marsh. *Right:* Mrs. Marsh, mother of Maud Marsh. (Both drawings re-created by Robert DeLaCruz, from an original March 1903 set of Severin Klosowski trial sketches presently held in Scotland Yard's Black Museum file George Chapman).

the letter from you to Mr. Chapman and was surprised at my own folly after receiving such a nice letter from you last night. Mr. Chapman said he will come down on Sunday if he does not have a different understanding between us, I am quite comfortable and am getting on all right. We must take things from a different light from this but will tell you more when I come down to see you. Hoping to hear from you again before Sunday. Must close with love and best respects from Mr. Chapman and myself.

I remain
Your loving daughter Maud
Xxxx

Hoping all is well and Papa is better.

Mrs. Marsh would later state: "I then wrote and said I was glad she was all right, and should be pleased to see them down on the following Sunday. They came down on the following Sunday."

Monument Tavern, Southwark—Fall 1901

In the months to come both Maud and Chapman would visit her parents, often on a Sunday. They usually traveled to West Croydon on their bikes. It would be on this first trip, however, that Chapman would declare his wish to marry Maud. Chapman knew it would be a very tough sell so to speed the process along he produced a worthless document in Maud's favor, or so it seemed. Dated December 13, 1901, the document was a "will," which bequeathed £400 to "my wife in the event of my death." The "will" was witnessed by Maud's brother Alfred and her mother but it was worthless. It was signed by "George Chapman," a fictitious name, and left money to "my wife," which Maud would never become!

It is not known whether or not this little fraud helped convince the Marsh's of Chapman's good intentions, but it is very doubtful. It did, however, insure the continued presence of Maud at the Monument Tavern, and for serial killer Chapman that was good enough for the time being. As it was, only a few weeks would pass before Maud's father decided to visit the Monument to check on the situation firsthand. The visit, probably a complete surprise to Chapman, did not go very well for the "widowed publican." It showed Robert Marsh that he could not trust the man and he told Maud "not to do anything secretive or underhanded." However, despite his mistrust Marsh did not attempt to bring Maud home. It was not recorded if he even asked her to leave the pub. It would be a fatal mistake on his part, but at this point there was still time.

Not long after Mr. Marsh's impromptu visit he once again became ill and had to be hospitalized. It would be during his brief stay at the hospital during the latter part of October 1901 that Maud would visit. It did not take long for Marsh to see that his young daughter was wearing a new ring on her finger. When questioned Maud informed her ill father that she had married George Chapman in the "Roman Catholic Room in Bishopsgate Street." It is interesting to note that the Marsh family was not Catholic. Nevertheless, Chapman had convinced his third intended victim to enter into a fictional marriage. None of his three "wives" would ever tell anyone that the marriages had been nothing more than games played on their families and friends.

On October 13, 1901, Maud and Chapman informed those gathered at the Monument Tavern that the "happy couple" were going out to be married and would soon return to celebrate. So a carriage was called to whisk the couple off, except there would be no marriage. The two conspirators simply stayed away for an appropriate amount of time and then drove back to the tavern. With the fiction now complete the "married couple" presented themselves to the friends and customers at the tavern, who showered them with confetti and many congratulations. The drinks, of course, were not on the house. This was still business!

Maud had earlier sent a letter to her mother asking her "to call at the Monument." Mrs. Marsh went by train to London to visit Maud and "took a little girl with her, Jenny Field," as a travel companion. When she arrived at the tavern she saw confetti outside and as she went inside Maud informed her for the first time that she had just married George Chapman. Despite her surprise and great concern for her young daughter Mrs. Marsh agreed to go that day on a trip on the electric railway and the "Tuppeny Tube" with Chapman, Maud, Jenny Field and Maud's sister Helen. Nothing Chapman could do or say, however, could convince Mrs. Marsh that Chapman was anything other than some sort of confidence man, and she would never be on friendly terms with the "Borough Poisoner."

Maud's 14-year-old sister, Daisy Harriet Helen Marsh, would remember that day in testimony before the court during Klosowski's murder trial. She was, as they say, 'in the thick of things!' "I remember Maud going as a barmaid to the Monument. I went and stayed with her there. The accused was living there. One Sunday they went out together between 10 and 11 A.M. and returned just before 1 P.M., and Maud showed me a wedding ring on her left hand. The accused was present. Maud said she was married. She did not say anything as to where the marriage had taken place, but I understood that they had been married that morning. Later that day my mother came to the house and dined there. I cannot fix the date. I stayed in the house for about two months after that. I only went to the Crown twice with my father."

Maud's parents would never fully accept the marriage, having not been told in advance that a ceremony had been planned. In fact, they were suspicious from the very beginning and their grave doubts would eventually cause the downfall of Chapman. Informed of the marriage while still in the hospital, Mr. Marsh wanted proof of the union. Maud, of course, had no proof to give as she had no marriage certificate to show. She could only say that her new "husband" had the document, and that it was locked up for safe keeping. She also said that she had not informed her father of the marriage in advance because Chapman "did not want to make a fuss about it." For Robert Marsh, Maud's reluctance to provide proof signaled to him that his daughter and Chapman were involved in some sort of fraud, yet he would never demand that she remove herself from the grip of Klosowski, alias George Chapman. But Chapman's grip on his luck was fast running out.

The first the family would hear of abuse would not come from Maud but from her sister Louisa Sarah Morris. Maud's married sister had visited Maud at the Monument and the pair had taken a day trip to Streatham and were on the way home by train when Maud suddenly burst into tears. The sisters did not arrive back at the pub at a time when Maud had told Chapman they would. Louisa, and eventually the whole Marsh family, would learn that Maud was living in fear of Chapman's beatings. No one in the family *ever* called the police or tried to interfere with these attacks!

MAUD—Look at the time, how late.
LOUISA—There's no good crying.
MAUD—You don't know what he is.
LOUISA—Well, has he hit you then?
MAUD—Yes, more than once.
LOUISA—How did he hit you?
MAUD—He held my hair and banged my head.
LOUISA—Didn't you pay him back?
MAUD—Yes, I kicked him.

Indeed, Chapman would become well known for his continuing abuses of the women he would call his wives. Yet, once again the Marsh family did nothing to protect or remove Maud from Chapman's control and abuse. And, despite living in complete fear of Chapman, there is a very good possibility that not only did Maud conceal a fictional marriage but she also may well have known of Chapman's aliases and helped to conceal them. Maud's sister Louisa would later reveal to a silent court that "My sister told me he was an American. I never had any idea that [Chapman] was not his real name." Now that he had his victim it was time to leave the Monument.

A Fire at the Monument—October 25, 1901

It is not really understood why Chapman would attempt to burn down the Monument Tavern other than for the insurance money. But that could not have been the only reason because he did not own the building, he held only the lease. He did have considerable liquid assets, however, but with a very good business it makes much greater sense to just stay at that location and continue to make money. It may have been his constant need to be on the run or the very real possibility that he may not have been able to renew his lease that pushed him on. Others were looking the place over and the owners did not necessarily like their lease holder. So early in the morning of October 25, 1901, that master murderer George Chapman tried his bloody hand at a bit of arson. As it turned out his skills at murder would not transfer to the fine art of arson for insurance fraud.

After the close of business, proprietor Chapman closed the doors to the tavern and cleaned out most of the money from the tills. Just to make it look good, however, he did leave a few coin of the realm. He had taken the time to remove most of the furnishings as well. It would later be revealed by Maud's sister Daisy that Chapman had moved his and Maud's clothing to her parent's home in Croydon just before the fire. He had also deposited some boxes at London Bridge Cloakroom. Were these *the* boxes, which held his hardwon collection of body parts? Perhaps, but there are no reports about what the boxes held nor what the Marsh family thought of the clothing being stored at their home at that most opportune time. Apparently the authorities never questioned the Marsh's about the fire. The fire brigade and insurance company did not know about the transfer. Maud Marsh did, and she helped cover up Chapman's arson!

The men of the South London Fire Brigade arrived at the pub in the early morning as thick smoke but very little fire could be seen coming from the Monument. As they arrived and prepared to smash down the front door they were surprised to find the tavern doors wide open with no one in the building. Even more surprising, and of great concern, the well-established beer hall had very few furnishings about the place. The fire fighters soon fought their way to the smoky basement, making hard work of this not so mysterious fire. It had clearly been a case of arson, pure and simple, and it had not been a very well planned one either. It took a good deal of effort on the part of the brigade, but the fire was finally brought under control with mostly only smoke and water damage beyond the basement. For the most part, the fire had been held to the almost empty basement. Had Chapman set the fire in the upper floors of the wood-and-brick building it could very well have destroyed the entire structure and perhaps a great deal more than that.

That day the story of the Monument fire ran in the *Morning Advertiser*, the same paper that had run Maud's ad. The paper reported the facts as they were known at the time. And the facts enlisted from the men who had fought the blaze spoke clearly of arson. As a reader of the *Morning Advertiser*, Chapman was outraged to see his false name linked to the fire and he was quick to "issue a writ for libel" against the paper. The paper, however, was on very firm ground in its reporting, and the editors had the backing of not only the police investigation but also the insurance companies own investigation. When confronted with the overwhelming evidence that the fire had been intentionally set, Chapman quickly backed away from his libel writ.

The local papers would later report: "Considerable damage was done to the lower part of the house. Chapman never returned to the premises, and they remained closed ever since, the windows being boarded up, and a board announcing that 'This eligible site' is for sale."

For Chapman, however, the work of insurance fraud was not yet complete. After he knew the police and other investigators discovered the fire had been set, and most probably set by Chapman, he still had the audacity to file an insurance claim. It can only be imagined what the insurance company thought of his boldness, but the claim was easily dismissed and his policy was cancelled. Most interesting and a bit confusing at this point, the police entertained no further actions or investigations into the case and Chapman was never charged with a crime. In fact, the investigation ended without any result. Had it continued, Chapman would surely have been arrested and perhaps Maud Marsh's life would have been spared. As it happened, the police again became interested in the fire only after Maud's death while Chapman was in jail awaiting his trial on multiple murder charges. The prosecution wanted the arson charge held in case Chapman somehow evaded the hangman for the three murders. Note that one year later, to the day, on October 25, 1902, Chapman would be arrested for murder!

For the moment Chapman was free, but he and Maud had no where else to go. Even after the fire Chapman and Maud continued to live at the Monument for some weeks before he was able to move into his next pub. For three days during this time period, as later recalled by Mrs. Marsh, Maud would suddenly become ill. Perhaps Chapman understood that Maud now knew far too much about the type of man he really was and that could be very dangerous. One thing she must have known was that he set the Monument fire, and, not being his wife, she could be forced to testify against him in a court of law. Once again, it was time for a new "wife," but this time his plans would not quite go as expected. Perhaps he was becoming tired of the game. No matter what the reason was, Chapman had decided that Maud had to go, and soon, before she could talk!

Chapter 7

A Death at George's American Bar

I remain your ever true and loving wife.
— Maud Marsh

THE CROWN PUBLIC HOUSE—LATE 1901–1902

The arson plan had failed and Chapman was very lucky to remain a free man. Nevertheless, he had not gotten out of the pub business. Despite the fraud attempt on the insurance company, he did not find it difficult at all to obtain a new lease on another pub. In fact, the new concern was just around the corner from the now ruined Monument. Just before Christmas 1901 George Chapman became the new proprietor of the local, well-known Crown Public House. Owned by Watney's Brewery, it had operated at 213 Borough High Street since at least 1841.

The pub is located south of the river Thames a little more than a mile from Whitechapel crossing the world famous London Bridge (the one now located in the state of Arizona). Appropriately enough, the Crown is located on the site of the old Marshalsea Jail (or county gaol), one of three in the general area established in the early 1500s. In 1750 the two other facilities were moved and made into prisons while their occupants were all transferred to Marshalsea. Later, the jail was used as a debtors' prison and was made famous in Charles Dickens' work *Little Dorrit*. It released its last debtor in late 1840, and was then torn down to make way for the Crown Public House, a pub with a very old stone floor and always thirsty customers.

The new bar, also known locally as George's American Bar, would be the last business Chapman would ever operate. As for the Crown, it would continue to serve its many customers "a pint of Bitters" long after Chapman "gave up his lease." It would end its run as a pub in 1975, but it continued to serve the community, first as a postal office and then as a private business office. It still stands today, awaiting a final close-up inspection of its old stone basement and Victorian walls for any remaining evidence that it was once occupied by Jack the Ripper. Scotland Yard—take note.

As one would expect, when entering "George's American Bar" one could see an American flag displayed, but just to keep his mostly local British customers happy he also displayed a British banner. A photo of these two flags would be later found at the Crown by detectives investigating a series of deaths. The British flag turned out to be an upside down British naval flag known as the "White Duster." Neither flag was kept in very good shape judging by the photos.

Across the Atlantic ocean readers of the *New York Times* would learn that the man wrongly convicted of the Carrie Brown murder in 1891 had been pardoned.

> Gov. Odell today pardoned Amer Ben Ali, better known as "Frenchy," who has been serving a life sentence in the Matteawan State Hospital for Insane Criminals for the murder of a woman called "Old Shakespeare" in New York City in 1891. The pardon was granted by the Governor because he believes there are grave doubts of the prisoner's guilt.
>
> About twelve years ago the world was astir over atrocious murders committed by a "Jack the Ripper" in London. The press at that time printed interviews with police chiefs and famous detectives on the possibilities of such a crime being committed in this country. Superintendent Thomas Byrnes, in an interview, said that a crime of that sort being committed in this city was out of the question. A few days after the [final] Whitechapel murder in London, however, a woman, known as "Old Shakespeare," was found murdered in the Forth Ward Hotel at Catharine and Water Streets. Immediately the question became prevalent in the public mind that New York had a "Jack the Ripper."

What the New York readers could not know was that the real killer of "Old Shakespeare" had returned to London and was well into his work on dispatching the final victim of his murder spree.

The background to Chapman's criminal activity was his slow and methodical poisoning of Maud Marsh. From the beginning of 1902 Maud suffered for the most part continuously from cramps, diarrhea and vomiting. It took far too long for her to decide to seek outside help but on July 28, 1902, she finally made her way to the Queen Victoria Ward at Guy's Hospital. In fact, Maud did not really want to go, fearing Chapman's reaction, but when her sister Alice found her very ill during a visit to the Crown, she insisted that Maud go to the hospital at once. Alice made certain by going to Guy's with her and staying until she was admitted. Alice would later testify that Chapman was "cross with her for doing so."

In point of fact, Maud was near death at the time. For the first two weeks Maud could not be fully examined due to the intense abdominal pain and tenderness in her stomach. She was given opiates for the pain, which seemed to help, as she registered an average temperature of 103. She also had a very rapid pulse induced by her system attempting to work the poison out. Nevertheless, she was able to write a short note to "Dearest George."

> July 31st 1902
> 17 Queen Victoria Ward
>
> Dearest George
>
> A line as promised. I had a good nights sleep last night and feel very much better this morning. The Doctor said when he saw me I had not got a very good prospect which meant I was not going on as well as he would like me to, I think this is all this time so with fond love.
>
> I remain
> Yours forever,
> Maud
>
> My temperature is still getting higher.

The doctors at Guy's Hospital could not seem to pinpoint the cause of Maud's medical problems. The team, lead by obstetrics surgeon Dr. James Henry Targett, never considered any type of poisoning as a possible cause of her slow and obvious deterioration. Yet Maud had been a healthy young woman until she met "Mr. Chapman." The team diagnosed her as having internal rheumatism, cancer and then acute dyspepsia. One of the doctors even began with a diagnosis of peritonitis before deciding on tuberculosis as the cause, but only because the symptoms were more in line with TB. None of the medical team really had any clue as to the real cause was as Maud's temperature topped out at 104.6 before she began a slow recovery. It would be a recovery which had no chance of continuing as long as Maud remained with Chapman.

Even during the worst of her pain Maud seemed to be under Chapman's control as she wrote to him again through her pain from her hospital bed. He had written to Maud telling her to come back to work as soon as possible because he had no one to rub his sore back! Ever the collector, he would keep her letters as souvenirs of the hunt.

> 17 Queen Victoria Ward
>
> My dear husband
>
> Just a line to let you know I am better. I had no sleep last night, was in pain all night long and have not been much better today. I come over queer in the night and of course that made matters worse.
>
> I will try dear George and get better so as to come home and help you. I am sorry to hear your back is so bad but I will rub it when I came home, my own darling husband. I think this is all this time.
>
> So with love
> I remain
> Your ever true and loving wife
> Maud.

At the time Maud could very well have been on her death bed had it not been for her sister's insistence that she enter the hospital. Despite the complete inability of her doctors to find the cause of her ailment, she began to show signs of recovery. No one in the hospital or any member of her family seemed to understand that her short recovery was due solely to her separation from the man she called her "dear husband."

By August 11, Maud was eating again, not a lot, but she was able to keep food down, no doubt because her hospital food, bad as it may have been, was not laced with poison. She was doing so well in fact that she would soon be on her way back to the Crown and the waiting arms of her husband, bad back and all. The doctors knew, of course, that Maud was still in a great deal of pain as her still weak body struggled to purge itself of the antimony. With this in mind, the medical men prescribed strong opiates to help with the pain to be taken with light foods and a bit of brandy. By August 20 Maud was back at the Crown.

Maud's mother, however, had a slightly different view as to why Maud left the hospital even though she was still in pain. Mrs. Marsh would relate that it was Chapman who "fetched her away from the hospital because she was going to be examined" in detail. She affirmed, "Because he strongly objected to it. She (Maud) said, George said she was not to have an examination. When she wrote telling him she would have to be examined he took her away in a cab." Yet, Mrs. Marsh failed to act even though her daughter was in obvious danger in Chapman's care. Certainly the Marsh family did not trust Chapman so when Maud returned to the Crown one would have expected that they would have interfered in some manner. Sadly for Maud, the family neither complained to the hospital, reported any suspicions to the local police nor brought in an outside doctor. Only later, hours before Maud's death, would any action be taken by the family.

It was not long after Maud returned to her

Mrs. Stanislaus Rauch, sister of Maud Marsh — (artwork re-created by Robert DeLaCruz from an original March 1903 set of Severin Klosowski trial sketches presently held in Scotland Yard's Black Museum file on George Chapman).

home above the Crown that her illness would again force her to her bed. In fact, Chapman began to introduce poisons into her body as soon as she returned. He was not about to give up, and, with full control now back in his bloody hands, there would not be any loose talk of any return to the hospital. He could not of course keep doctors away from Maud, but he knew to whom he should call. He had fooled old Dr. James Stoker before and there was no reason to believe that he would not be able to fool him again.

Chapman certainly knew how to pick doctors and Stoker was a very good choice for a serial killer. Before long the doctor was attending Maud and prescribing medications which did nothing at all. He did seem to understand that this so-called Mrs. Chapman was suffering the same illness which had killed the last Mrs. Chapman, but he was unable to link the two sick women to any actions by Chapman. He continued to see Maud as she became sicker and sicker while her "husband" continued to see to it that Maud took all of her prescriptions—along with a bit of his special white powder.

Throughout the summer and fall of 1902 Maud continued her slow decline into death. It was a show only Chapman could be witness to as he presented for several concerned friends and family his very skilled and practiced abilities as a master poisoner. But he was soon to make some critical errors. He began to ever so slightly brag about his abilities to Maud's family members. It would seem that he had been at it for so long that he failed to realize that bragging about murder can put a noose around one's neck. It would not be a case of live and learn.

A New Barmaid, June 1902

Never one to allow a "sickness" in the family to interfere with business, Chapman decided in June of 1902 that he needed a new barmaid for the Crown. Maud would soon be on the way to the hospital and so it is possible that Chapman expected her to be dead and a new woman would be required for his special needs. With this possibly in mind the proprietor of the Crown Public House began a search for a new barmaid. It would be very short search because he knew exactly the woman he wanted to take Maud's place. Her name was Florence Rayner. This time, however, the "Borough Poisoner" would not succeed.

Miss Rayner lived at 2 Cerise Road in Peckham and she worked near the Crown as a domestic servant and dressmaker for a local company. At times during her busy work week she would make her way to the local pub for a simple dinner before going home. It was during these dinners on the first floor of the Crown that she met Mr. and Mrs. Chapman. It did not take long for George Chapman to decide that young Florence would become Mrs. Chapman IV. He put his plans together to end his relationship with Mrs. Chapman III.

Chapman had for some time been stashing away funds at the Crown, preparing for his inevitable next move. In fact, he was planning on leaving England for a second trip to the United States and his "wife" Maud was not to be on the passenger list. Her place would be in the grave as Chapman went on his merry way with his new "wife." For a while, however, he would once again have at least two women in his household. He would be courting one while he slowly murdered a second, enjoying every single moment.

It would not take long for Florence to accept Mr. Chapman's offer of a job. It was after all less work than she had been doing, and she would have a place to stay, plenty of food and drink, and would be making 5s. a week. Room and board were hard to come by in crowded south London and she really did like the pub and the local area. It would also not take her long to change her mind about the arrangement.

As always, Chapman moved with great speed when he found something or someone he wished to "own." Later, Florence explained how she managed to escape the situation and just

Crown Public House, located at 213 Borough High Street, Southwark, London. Jack the Ripper's last residence and business.

how aggressive Chapman could be. She said, "After I had been there about a fortnight (two weeks) the accused kissed me and asked me to be his sweetheart and go to America with him. I used to take my meals with him alone. When he asked me to go to America with him I said, 'You have got your wife downstairs; you don't want me!' He said, 'If I gave her that (snapping his fingers) she would be no more Mrs. Chapman.' I left because the accused came upstairs into my bedroom in the afternoon during my rest. He kissed me constantly when we were at meals together."

Although Florence felt it was improper for Chapman to enter her bedroom, she did not protest when he kissed her. In fact, she might very well have taken Chapman up on his offer of a move to America if he had not moved with such speed. But Chapman's huge sexual appetite was something he could never control. Florence would later testify that Chapman told her to leave when he could not get his way. He had found a woman who would not submit to his many demands and a strong woman was one who would not be welcome in Chapman's household. He was afraid of most men and of any strong woman.

Before long Florence gathered up her belongings and, in July, after only a few weeks at the Crown, she left for a new, and one may say, safer job. She accepted the barmaid position at the Forester's Tavern in Peckham. She had known about the old tavern for a while and it was closer to her home. She had not however, seen the last of serial killer George Chapman. Never one to give up easily and truly hating to be bested by a "mere woman," Chapman traveled to Peckham and stopped in at the Forester's Tavern for a pint of bitters.

Chapman had decided to give it one more try. He told Florence about his travel plans. He told her he could send her to America and that he would follow her. It was an offer that Florence, despite her knowledge of Chapman's temper and callus talk, may very well have accepted. At the time however, in late July of 1902, Florence knew that the very sick wife of the publican was still very much alive. And, although we are not able to read the thoughts of serial killer Chapman, it is a very safe bet that had Florence finally accepted Chapman's offer of a trip to America she probably would have become the first murder victim in a second series of killings on Chapman's second trip "across the pond." This one, however, was destined to get away. Interestingly, Miss Rayner, according to police reports, was arrested two days after she left Chapman's employ for being drunk outside the Crown! This may have been the reason why Chapman felt he still had a chance of getting to Florence. Drunk and vulnerable women were just his cup of tea. For the moment, however, he had other things on his mind. He still had a bit of "work" to do concerning his still very much alive "wife."

Biggs & Company 8th September, 1902

We regret having been unable to find a customer for the Crown lease and in order to push matter forward we suggest advertisements being inserted in the daily papers, which would no doubt effect a sale.

NO MORE MRS. CHAPMAN—OCTOBER 1902

Chapman knew that he needed to play the part of the dutiful husband if he had any hope of killing Maud on schedule. Too many people were now investigating the situation for him to be too openly hostile toward her and he could not risk a second trip to the hospital. As he slowly inched Maud toward her death he kept up the act, going so far as to hire a domestic servant named Beatrice Cole to "care for his aiding wife." Cole would stay on until just after Maud's death. For a time this woman hater had no fewer than three women living with him, which must be considered a bit unusual for a misogynist serial killer. And when Maud's mother and sisters visited he was certainly surrounded by women, yet he was still able to maintain control of the poisoning, although just barely.

Any act of kindness on Chapman's part, however, was not about to impress Maud's mother. She certainly was not going to be kept from coming to the Crown and caring for her young daughter even through she lived in West Croydon. She would see for herself that Maud's condition continued to deteriorate despite all she and the others had done. Nevertheless, Mrs. Marsh would not press the issue and demand Maud's admission to the hospital. That part of Chapman's plan at least would surely work. It is possible that her first trip to the hospital was enough to convince those in attendance that a second visit would be of little use. Not even the doctors would argue for a hospital return. Of course, no one was looking at Chapman as the source of the ills afflicting his "wife." That would come too late.

On October 10, Chapman returned to Dr. James Stoker's office for a visit. The doctor, who had seen Bessie Taylor before she died, was informed by Chapman that he wanted some medicine for Maud. He was able to impress on the aging doctor that he had a medical background and as such would be able to minister to Maud's needs with the help of the medicines. It was also during this visit that Chapman made an unexpected admission. He informed Dr. Stoker that he was not really married to Maud but that both had "passed as man and wife." The doctor's reaction to the admission remains unknown, but he never informed the authorities so he could not have been too shocked. Chapman, however, was showing signs of losing the control he desperately needed. He was starting to talk and he was about to talk to the wrong people.

Not long after, a frustrated Chapman had a conversation with Maud's sister, Mrs. Louisa Sarah Morris, who was visiting her sister and spending time at the Crown. Chapman's frustration was most likely due to the protracted time and effort he expended in slowly murdering Maud, and he made a point of illustrating his abuse of his "wife" to her sister.

While Louisa was visiting Maud in her bedroom she picked up a green ball syringe and asked her very ill sister what Chapman did with it. Maud told her that she "was a fortnight over her time," and George had used injections on her! Louisa was shocked. She picked up a small bottle and asked Maud what it was. Maud told Louisa "that's some of the stuff." At that point Louisa noticed a strong smell of carbolic coming from the bottle, which contained some type of "frozen crystals." When Chapman entered the room to make one of his many inspections of his wife Maud whispered to Louisa to "put it down, he's coming."

After Chapman's check on how well the slow murder was coming along he left the room. When he had gone Maud told her sister that the syringe "had brought on flooding and it was then used again to stop the flooding." Chapman would continue to use his syringes during his "work" on Maud. The green syringes can now be found proudly, yet surprisingly, secretly displayed at Scotland Yard's Black Museum. In point of fact, the men who watch over these relics of death do not always admit that they are in the museum at all. Some visitors are allowed to view them and some are not.

Before Louisa left Maud's room her dying sister told Louisa "George does not want any children yet, but after we get enough to live privately I could have as many as I like then." After saying her goodbyes, Louisa kissed her sister, then went downstairs to confront Chapman. Chapman was about to make a critical error and he was not prepared to be confronted by a "mere woman."

LOUISA—Don't you think it is funny that Maud is like this?
CHAPMAN—It is constipation.
LOUISA—That is funny, because I saw her a short time before and she had diarrhea.
CHAPMAN—She should have done what I told her, taken the medicine I gave her.
LOUISA—Maud would never take medicine.
CHAPMAN—If she comes out of this lot, she will do as I tell her.
LOUISA—It seems very funny that the doctors cannot find out what is the matter with her.
CHAPMAN—I could give her a bit like that (snapping his fingers) and fifty doctors could not find out.
LOUISA—What do you mean?

Chapman did not answer. He knew that he had said too much. He had bragged about the slow murder of Maud and he had placed his own life at grave risk. Yet, when Louisa reported the conversation to the rest of her family no one came forward to challenge Chapman's statement nor his obvious control over Maud. Maud's family had completely failed her.

As Maud continued to weaken, Chapman added one more person to the audience of women he had assembled for the final act of Maud's life. Mrs. Jessie Toon of 23 Eltham Street, Borough, was asked by Chapman to help care for his "wife." She had been a regular customer at the Crown, but she was not a nurse by training. Nevertheless, Chapman insisted that she "attend his wife." When Mrs. Toon first saw Maud on her deathbed she was greatly shocked. By that time Maud had "stiff arms, a port wine color and black around her mouth." It was October 17 and nothing seemed to be working as Maud had less than a week to live. The cure of course would have been to remove Maud anywhere away from Chapman. No one, it would seem, was prepared to do that.

Chapman continued to direct this little play insisting that he and he alone should prepare the meals and drinks given to Maud. In fact, he would not allow Mrs. Toon or anyone else to give Maud water from the tap unless he first had control of it and could inspect the liquid. He may have thought that this showed proof of his caring; however, it would be easy to prove in a court of law that if only one person was feeding Maud only one person could have fed her poison. But then again Chapman never thought in his wildest dreams that anyone would ever suspect what game he was really playing.

It would be up to Inspector Godley to later report: "I may add that from inquires I found that [Chapman] was the only person who used to feed her, and would not allow any other person in the kitchen while he made the food. He has had three deaths in five years—two Mrs. Chapmans and Marsh."

Was Chapman overconfident, reckless or just getting tired of the game he had been playing for years? He was, after all, killing a young woman in full view of at least half a dozen witnesses, who would soon include two doctors. It is quite possible that this serial killer really began to believe that no matter what he did no one was going to ever catch him. Perhaps Hargrave Adam expressed it best writing in *Trial of George Chapman*. He affirms: "It has been proved many times that multiple murderers become more daring and reckless with each successful crime, until at length they fail to observe even very ordinary precautions." It would appear that even Jack the Ripper got a bit careless in the end.

Interestingly, Chapman told Mrs. Toon to ask Mrs. Marsh if she "suspected any fowl play." Mrs. Toon reported back to Chapman that indeed Maud's mother suspected that her daughter had been poisoned. Chapman did not like the news from Mrs. Toon and told her to "watch her mouth." Yet, even with those suspicions neither Mrs. Toon nor Mrs. Marsh said anything to the police. It is no wonder that serial killer George Chapman felt that he could do anything he wanted and not get caught. No one was prepared to challenge him.

As the last painful days came for Maud any food or drink she tried to take gave her a violent reaction. She vomited a green liquid. She was only able to ingest very small amounts of liquid during periods of consciousness, but only with great difficulty. Louisa Cole would later state that she saw Chapman "pouring something from a bottle into a tumbler" while he prepared a drink for Maud in the kitchen, but she had no way of knowing what the colorless liquid had been. It is noteworthy that she did not think to ask.

However, there was one incident that shows that Chapman was becoming careless with his poisoning, which, considering all that had already occurred, should have sent members of Maud's family running to the police. It began with Chapman doing his best to show that he cared for Maud by preparing for her one of his "special" brandy and sodas. According to Mrs. Marsh, "Chapman kept giving [Maud] brandy-and-soda. The soda was kept on the landing in ice. The nurse, [Mrs. Toon], kept giving Maud pieces of ice to suck. She was given injections, which put her in more pain. Chapman injected her food via the back passage."

Maud was unable to drink very much of the brandy, but Chapman insisted that she try to drink as much as she could. Soon, however, the glass was set aside and forgotten. Only later in the day, as Mrs. Marsh and Mrs. Toon were cleaning up and caring for Maud, did they remember the drink and both women took some from the glass on the desk. Before long both women became very ill with both vomiting and bouts of diarrhea. Surely one would think that these two women now knew the source, if not the direct cause, of Maud's illness, yet sadly that simply was not the case.

Mrs. Marsh would later tell a shocked and hushed courtroom, "I put a little iced water with it and drank it myself. I was taken very sick. About two hours, I was taken with sickness and diarrhea very bad. I had to leave my daughter, and while I was away the accused (Chapman) was with her." Mrs. Toon had taken less of the drink and was therefore affected a bit less, but she did display the same symptoms as Mrs. Marsh and, for that matter, Maud. Mrs. Toon would recover soon enough to ask Chapman if Maud was any better. She had not known at the time about Mrs. Marsh. Chapman was more than happy to inform her that Maud was about the same as well as her mother. "No," he replied, "Her mother is bad now. You had better go upstairs and tell her to get to bed out of the way, the old bat." Even when Dr. Stoker was informed of the incident, incredibly, he was unable to link it to the condition of his patient. He continued to treat Maud for a number of unknown illnesses.

It was not long after the brandy incident that Mr. Marsh again visited the Crown. On October 18, he arrived with Maud's sister Alice May to help care for Maud and both were surprised to see the pub still open, attended by a very happy Chapman. For this serial killer the Marsh's arrival simply allowed him to perform before a larger audience with no fewer than seven individuals closely watching Maud's slow but certain decline. He was fully into his element, wearing an outward expression of deep concern as he slowly went about his careful end game with Maud It was almost time to finish her off and what an opportunity it would be to kill in front of so many people.

Robert Marsh visited his now gravely ill daughter as she lay on her deathbed at the Crown and tried to speak to her. He wanted to be alone with her but Chapman kept coming in "on more than one occasion bringing her water. She drank a little but brought it up immediately. The fluid she brought up was discolored but of no particular color." Chapman was demonstrating to Robert Marsh that he could continue to slowly poison his daughter right in front of his eyes. Only later would Marsh realize what had happened on that day. Chapman seemed to know that he could do almost anything he wanted and no one, including Maud's weak father, was going to do anything at all — at least until it was far too late to help Maud.

It was also during this time that Alice would find one of the green ball syringes that Chapman was using to give injections to Maud. As Chapman returned once again to Maud's room, Maud touched Alice's arm and told her to put it down because "George is coming." There seemed to be, according to Alice, a great deal of fear in Maud's words. George it would seem was always coming in. He wanted to see how well the murder was going and to see if anyone had yet caught on to his little game.

Mrs. Toon remembered his attentions as well: "On Sunday before she died she said her mouth and throat burned, and that they seemed to be on fire. On 20th October the accused brought a stethoscope into the room. (Confirming that he still had his medical kit if not his black bag but did he still have his surgical knives?) He first felt the pulse of the girl Marsh, then pulled her eyelids up and examined her eyes, afterwards putting the stethoscope to her heart and listening for two minutes. I have never seen him use the stethoscope before, or examine her eyes." Chapman was not about to miss out on any aspect of this slow torture, no matter who was watching.

It was all becoming too much for Mrs. Marsh as she saw that her daughter was failing fast. Aside from Chapman she went to Dr. Stoker for any medical treatment he could think of but he did not have a clue. Stoker told Mrs. Marsh, "I am at my wits end to know what to do with her; my means are exhausted." He did not recommend sending Maud to the hospital and away from Chapman. By then, however, it may have already been too late to save Maud.

With no help expected from Dr. Stoker, Mrs. Marsh finally began to believe that Maud's so-called mysterious illness was being caused by Chapman. When she spoke to her husband Robert about her suspicions they both decided to bring their own local family doctor into the case. Dr. Francis Gasper Grapel was a very practical man who practiced out of 282 London Road and, from the very start of his examination of Maud, he knew something was very wrong with her medical care. When Dr. Grapel arrived he found Maud in a semi-comatose condition with a jaundiced appearance and sallow skin. He also found that she had a very rapid pulse. He knew that Maud's body was trying to purge itself of some type of irritant and he would not be looking for any natural causes for her condition. From the start he suspected foul play and would say as much to her family. Even Grapel failed to send Maud to the hospital!

Dr. Grapel's approach gave him a distinct advantage over the other medical men who had been called into the case. And his entry into the situation would cause George Chapman great concern — control was being lost and he knew it. It was also evident to Dr. Grapel that Chapman resented his arrival the moment he met him. Robert Marsh was the first to confront Chapman about the new doctor, to which Chapman gave his now classic and deeply felt opinion of any doctor looking into his murder plans. "If one doctor cannot cure her, fifty cannot." Robert Marsh, however, finally stood his ground, faced up to serial killer Chapman and replied, "It is no good making a bother; I wished the doctor to come." Chapman had been faced down and knew that he was about to lose control of the situation. He said nothing and simply walked back to the bar to serve his customers.

It did not take long for Doctor Grapel to come to the correct conclusion, one that had escaped the eyes of several other doctors who had examined the three women Chapman had lived with over the years. Maud was being slowly poisoned. After he completed his initial examination early on October 22 he took Maud's father aside to tell him the results. "Your daughter is very ill and I do not see why she should not get better if the sickness would stop. My opinion is your daughter has been poisoned by arsenic but how she got it I could not tell." He was the first medical man to suspect that one of Chapman's so-called wives was being slowly murdered and it was a logical, short step to suspect that Chapman was the one who was administering the poison. But could he risk accusing anyone of this crime without placing his own reputation, property and possibly freedom at risk?

Edward Carson, the solicitor-general, would later recognize the predicament Doctor Grapel found himself in. "It is a most serious thing for a doctor to throw suspicion upon a household," he said. Perhaps, but unlike the aging Dr. Stoker, Dr. Grapel would move with great speed in an attempt to prove his suspicions and possibly save Maud Marsh's life. Dr. Grapel's only problem was that he did not yet know how the poison was being administered or for how long. He did feel, however, that Maud could still be saved. As Dr. Grapel returned to his home he decided he had to act, risk or not, and so he immediately telegraphed Dr. Stoker, who was still attending Maud. Dr. Grapel advised Stoker that, in his opinion, arsenic was the agent of poison and that he needed to look for the cause immediately.

The day before, Mr. Marsh saw his daughter for the final time at the Crown. Marsh told Chapman, "Maud is very bad." To which Chapman replied in a superior tone, "Yes, she is." Confident that the new doctor would help his daughter he told Chapman, "I think my daughter will pull through now, George." Chapman had by then decided to finish Maud off before anyone could find the cause of her illness. He coldly told Robert Marsh, "She will never get up no more." Maud's fate was sealed. She was in the back room on the second floor and Maud had been vomiting the entire time her father had been there. He would later testify that despite her obvious distress, he did not feel "she was about to die."

At 12:30 P.M. on October 22, 1902, Maud Marsh died. She would be the final victim of serial killer Severin Antoniovich Klosowski, alias George Chapman, in a series which had begun in 1888 and possibly sooner. To the end Maud never suspected that "George" was the one who was slowly killing her. Maud's last words would be to her killer: "I am going." Enjoying each precious moment of his crime, a cold Chapman, now devoid of any human emotion, replied: "Where are you going?" Maud could only reply, "Good-bye, George."

Mrs. Marsh would later recall the same last moments in Maud's life. She said, "Just before my daughter died she threw all the clothes off her, and said, 'Take them away. I am going. Good-bye George.' Those were her last words. Soon afterwards she passed away."

Chapter 8

The Arrest of a Serial Killer

Can I have bail?
— Alias: George Chapman

THE CROWN PUBLIC HOUSE—OCTOBER 23, 1902

For the first time in his murderous career, Chapman, ever the stone-faced cold-blooded killer, panicked. He could have insisted that Maud be taken immediately to the hospital and then gone back to the Crown to destroy the overwhelming evidence of his guilt. Perhaps he could have even directed the officer to someone else while he collected his money for a fast escape to the United States. Instead, Chapman, serial killer and collector of murderous souvenirs, did what he knew best — he killed. Chapman administered a massive final dose of antimony to Maud even as several individuals stood watch. The Borough Poisoner could not allow himself to let this one go after all he had done to bring on her slow death. Even if he risked what he cherished most — his own life.

According to Mrs. Marsh, who was in her daughter's room when she died, Chapman put on quite a show. After Maud's death Chapman "came out to the landing and cried." But who was he crying for? Certainly not for Maud, for her struggle was over. But for the man all in the neighborhood knew as George Chapman, his struggle and courtroom fight for his life was just about to begin.

The death had taken old Doctor Stoker by surprise even though he had been briefed by Dr. Grapel that foul play was involved. Stoker would be quoted by the press: "I heard that the deceased had died at 12:30. When I went there the Crown was open for business; there was nothing to indicate there had been a death there. When I saw her on Tuesday (she died the next day) I had no reason to anticipate she would die so soon." Stoker still seemed to not have any clue as to what was going on. In his case at least, Chapman had chosen very well the man to oversee his deadly acts of murder.

However, Stoker was armed with Dr. Grapel's telegraph when he last visited the Crown, and the death of Maud had finally brought him to his senses. He had arrived to inform a now very relaxed George Chapman that he would not issue a death certificate, which was much more than Chapman would have expected of the old man. Chapman began to lose control as the doctor stood his ground during a fact-to-face encounter with the killer. Chapman had lost control and he knew it. He had killed one too many and he had been careless. The doctor told "the grieving husband" that he did not know what had caused the diarrhea and vomiting and that he would conduct a private postmortem.

CHAPMAN—I do not see the good of it.
STOKER—I shall have a post-mortem. I cannot give a death certificate.
CHAPMAN—Why?
STOKER—I cannot find what is the cause of death.
CHAPMAN—It was exhaustion caused by inflammation of the bowels.
STOKER—What caused the inflammation?
CHAPMAN—Continual vomiting and diarrhea.
STOKER—And what caused the vomiting and diarrhea?

Of course Chapman could not give an answer to the final question. He could only and very reluctantly agree to allow the examination of Maud's body still held at the Crown. Without an agreement Chapman knew the old doctor would go directly to the police and Chapman needed time. He understood that Dr. Stoker knew he would have no standing with Maud since Stoker knew they had never been married. Chapman was being backed into a corner and he was running out of time.

It was very lucky that his thinking was not up to par for, if it had, Chapman could have easily removed all evidence of his crimes by simply setting the Crown on fire as he had at the Monument. But was there something at the Crown so important so critical that it could not be destroyed at any cost? And even more interesting to think about today—is it still there? What secrets were so important to Severin Klosowski, alias George Chapman, that they could not be destroyed, no matter what?

Stoker now moved with a speed he should have shown while Maud was alive, obtaining permission from the clerk at the Old Vestry Hall to remove the body for a private postmortem. Located in the hall, the Southwark Borough Council Medical Department was responsible for such matters. As soon as he had permission, Dr. Stoker had the body picked up and moved to the small local "mortuary" located in the back of St. George's Church in the Borough. It would seem, however, that Stoker forgot to notify the local coroner until the medical examination was complete.

Interestingly enough, Chapman did not raise many objections to the postmortem. He seemed to have confidence that the old doctor would not find any cause of death. He would be proven wrong. Dead wrong!

The mortuary itself was Alf Smith's Mortuary, which still stands at the same location and is still doing business—one would hope not investigating possible murders. The attending undertaker for Maud's workup was none other than Alf Smith himself, who lived on nearby Southwark Bridge Road. He was assisted by morgue attendant Frank L. Gilbert who had rooms at 9 Kings Place, a short walk from the mortuary.

When the coroner, Dr. Ludwig Freyberger, had a chance to view the body at the mortuary he was shocked. He could not understand why Maud's doctors had waited so long and felt that she should have been taken to the hospital long before she died. He would later testify that she was "5'-3" tall and wasted."

While the examination was being conducted Chapman did a bit of cleanup at the Crown, but he made no preparations to run. His old confidence had returned and he moved to put Maud's "unfortunate" death behind him. His first task was to remove Maud's old things, including her clothes. Mrs. Toon was still at the Crown helping out and she recommended to Chapman that he "ought to have the clothes and dirty things washed the day after she died, because they smell nasty." Chapman had already taken care of those "throwaways." He informed Mrs. Toon "I have destroyed them." He did, however, keep his photo collection of snaps he had taken of Maud showing her slow decline and death.

Doctor Stoker was taking no chances with the postmortem. He called in several other medical men to aid in the examination. Doctor P. G. Cotter of 57 Caledonian Road assisted along with Doctors Poycott and French. Despite the work of those four men none of them could find a medical reason why Maud had fallen ill, let alone died. They could, however, rule out any known natural cause. The men at that point knew that some kind of foul play was involved and poison was the most probable cause. On that supposition, the men removed Maud's stomach and other internal organs for closer chemical analysis. Placed into separate containers the organs were taken to the nearby Clinical Research Association at 1 Southwark Street. The facility, as fate would have it, was very near the Crown and, to be sure, association members probably drew a pint or two at the local pub.

Doctor Stoker would later testify, in answer to a question, that he "did not examine the uterus as she was not pregnant. There were no suspicious marks about the uterus and parts." For the most part Chapman would beat Maud on other parts of her body.

Even though there was a very good chance that the doctors would uncover evidence of a crime, Chapman seemed to once again slip into his old and arrogant misogynist ways. On October 23, the day after his "work" on Maud had been completed, Mrs. Marsh and Maud's sister, Alice May, visited the "grieving husband" at the Crown. The unlikely group went out for tea and an opportunity to recollect good times with Maud. Chapman did not allow the opportunity to pass; he turned it into an attempt to capture another female. He invited Alice May to live with him at the Crown, saying, "There is a chance for you as barmaid now. Will you come?" It had been little more than 24 hours since her sister had died and Alice May could hardly believe her ears. She could say very little and would later recall: "I said, no thanks, London does not suit me."

Alice May would testify at Chapman's trial that "The accused had asked me [before] to go and live with him and my sister." Time and time again this hater of women would attempt to live with more than one at a time. It was one sign that he not only hated women but also that his self-hate was always so much deeper.

A later statement furnished to the investigators by the funeral director would once again show the cold-hearted nature of Chapman. Chapman had told the director to hold the funeral at 9 A.M. so that he would be able to open the pub on time for a full day's business!

By then the stress on Chapman was starting to show. A few days before he finished off Maud he had an encounter with a 37-year-old woman who sold flowers on the streets in the area. Mary Reed, who lived on nearby Tabard Street, had gone into the Crown for a pint and probably tried to sell some flowers to customers at the bar. Before long she came face to face with Chapman and words were exchanged. The local paper reported the incident.

> Mary Reed ... was charged with unlawfully breaking a pane of glass valued at 15s at the Crown Public House, Borough High Street.

Chapman would explain that "he had to eject her from the premises because of her obscene language. She was very violent and threatened to break every pane of glass in the house." Mary would later explain that "Chapman smacked her face and nearly shook the life out of her." She would soon find herself sentenced to 21 days hard labor by Mr. Paul Taylor, who, interestingly enough, would face George Chapman in a few days on a much more serious charge of willful murder. The report of Mary Reed's window breaking with a hard beetroot would appear in the *Southwark and Bermondsey Recorder and South London Gazette* on the same day that Chapman was arrested. There was no record of what Mary Reed might have thought but one can guess that she would have been quite pleased indeed. Perhaps she did not have to finish her 21 days. As for Chapman, he was never able to fix that window at the Crown. Events were moving ahead with great speed. It would have to be repaired by the next pub owner.

The Results of the Tests

It would take only a day for the chemical results to come in from the Clinical Research Association. Dr. Richard Bodmer, a fellow of the Institute of Chemistry, had completed his work on Maud's stomach. Dr. Bodmer had been assisted by Joseph Henry Marks, who worked at the association. The men had discovered conclusive evidence of arsenic and antimony poisoning. It was now quite clear that Maud Marsh had died through ingestion of massive amounts of antimony with trace amounts of arsenic. She had surely been murdered. The only questions now were: how and by whom?

Dr. Stoker now had all the information he needed to inform the authorities and complete his death certificate. He informed Dr. F. J. Waldo, the South London area coroner for the Borough of Southwark, of the results of the private postmortem. Dr. Waldo was angered that he had not been called in earlier and later voiced his concerns: "I lunched with the judge in the case at the Old Bailey, and he agreed with me that the post-mortem carried out by the medical attendant on Maud Marsh might have ended in the contents, etc. of the stomach being lost...."

Chapman's luck had finally run out and the evidence of his crimes would not be lost. It was Saturday morning, October 25, 1902, and Severin Klosowski, alias George Chapman, was about to be arrested on a single murder charge. An investigation, however, would soon show that a great deal more than that had happened. The people of London would begin to read about the case of the Borough Poisoner.

In Custody at Long Last

It may have taken a long time for the doctors to act on what was surely strange circumstances in the deaths of Chapman's three wives. It would not, however, take long for Inspector Godley and Sergeant Kemp to make their way to the Crown Public House once they suspected a murder had taken place. Just after midnight on October 25 Dr. Stoker telegraphed police to inform them of a poisoning and his suspicions that a murder had been committed. As the forces of law gathered for the upcoming inquiry, a telegram was sent to the coroner, Dr. Waldo, at 4:19 A.M. By 10 A.M. the police and staff from the coroner's office were meeting and they arrived at the conclusion that a murder had indeed been committed. It was time to act.

Assuming that nothing untoward was underfoot, Chapman had all of his money in his possession and tried to raise even more by attempting to sell his lease on the Crown. Chapman was about to skip town and he also had his eye on a new woman, who was not displeased at the attention given to her by the man she knew as George Chapman. He was making some fast plans to return to America. Inspector George Godley and Detective Sergeant William Kemp of A Division would get decidedly in the way of those plans, and it would be just in time.

Godley would later recall, "At noon I went to the Crown and saw the accused. I said, 'Are you Mr. Chapman?' He said, 'Yes.' I said, I wish to speak to you quietly." Godley had not yet informed Chapman that he was from the police but it would have been difficult for Chapman not to have suspected that the game was up. Inspector Godley reported that the parlor on the ground floor was empty as a calm Chapman asked the men to go in there for the interview. It was there, in a small and, one would expect, escape resistant area, that the officers informed the publican of the reason for their midday visit.

Chapman was told: "I am inspector of police for this district; Maud Marsh, who has been living with you as your wife, has been poisoned with arsenic, and from the surrounding circumstances I shall take you to the police station while I make inquires." Chapman, still quite calm, did not lose a step in the conversation. He said, "I know nothing about it; I do not know how she got the poison; she has been in Guy's Hospital for the same sort of sickness."

"Same sort of sickness?" Was Chapman giving the officers a clue when he admitted that Maud's illness was similar to poison and that he, Chapman, could tell that it was? Perhaps, but if Inspector Godley clued in to Chapman's words, the good inspector did not give any hint to Chapman. He simply continued the examination and moved on to the next order of business. He would not, however, forget Chapman's words. Godley said: "Before we go to the police station I am going to examine the bedroom where she died."

Chapman did not say anything to the officers as he led them to Maud's room in the 60-year-old building. She had died in the small second-floor back room, which had a small sink of its own and a fireplace. Chapman had closed and locked the door after Maud's body had been removed and he took the keys from his pocket to open the door. For the most part the room had not been touched and it would prove to be a treasure trove of incriminating evidence against Chapman.

Inspector Godley soon found three medicine bottles on the floor by the fireplace. These were the bottles labeled "Dr. Stoker." Not taken aback at all by the easy discovery, Chapman himself reached down to pick up the three bottles to hand to the inspector. Godley said: "I am going to take possession of all medicine bottles." It was clear that Chapman was not going to do or intentionally say anything which would throw any suspicion on himself. He had been getting away with murder for years—fooling doctors and escaping police dragnets—and there was no reason to believe at this point that he would not get away with killing Maud either.

As Godley and Sergeant Kemp continued their systematic search for clues to what they thought was the death of a single woman they found a small safe. The safe was broken and not used by Chapman, however, he did have keys to a small drawer he used to safeguard his money.

Detective-Inspector George Godley, the officer who headed up the Borough Poisoner investigation.

Godley told Chapman: "If you have any money in that safe you had better count it." Chapman replied: "The safe is broken," and he went for a second set of keys. Godley would later report that Chapman "produced a bunch of keys from his pocket and unlocked one of the small drawers in the chest of drawers, and took from it in coin and notes £268 10s." It was a princely sum indeed, and it was all the cash Chapman had on hand. The readily available money was proof that Chapman was ready to leave town at a moment's notice. Chapman counted out £143 10s in gold, £15 in silver, three £10 notes, and sixteen £5 notes.

During an interview with reporters from the *Washington Post*, on October 26, 1913, retired inspector Kemp reflected on the search for evidence at the Crown:

> You of course remember the Borough poisoning case, where a man named Klosowski or Chapman, as he chose to call himself, was convicted of the murder by poison of a number of women. Well, I was engaged on the case, which I remember with a certain degree of satisfaction, for it enabled me to procure the release of a wrongfully convicted man who was then in prison. Some time before the murders were discovered the man Chapman had accused another

man of robbing him. The man was innocent, but he was convicted in the face of the sworn testimony of Chapman and the very woman, Maud Marsh, who, among other women, he was afterward convicted of murdering.

Chapman wanted this man removed, and this was his way of doing it. Among the money supposed to have been stolen were bank notes bearing certain numbers. I and a mate of mine arrested him at the public house which he kept in the borough. It was on the day of the coronation procession, and the public house was decorated with flags and bunting. After his removal from the house in custody I made a search of the place, and in a drawer upstairs I found a bundle of bank notes. When I came to look at the numbers I noticed that several of the notes bore precisely the same numbers as those which Chapman had sworn he had been robbed of. I promptly embodied this discovery in a report, and soon after I had the satisfaction of knowing that the man had been released.

On hand to witness the arrest of Chapman was Mrs. Marsh. She would later recall asking a question of her daughter's "husband." "I stayed in the house a day or two after the death. I remember the police coming on the Saturday. In the presence of Inspector Godley I asked the accused if he really had been married to Maud, and he said, 'No.' Godley had told me something before I asked that question."

It was at that point that Inspector Godley locked the door to Maud's room and, with the keys in his pocket, took charge of suspect George Chapman. He was taken to the station locally known as "Stones End." Police Sergeant Leck was left to guard the murder room upstairs at the Crown. It would be the last time Chapman would ever see 213 Borough High Street and the Crown Public House. The Crown and "George's American Bar" were closed for the day as the coronation procession of Edward VII moved past the old pub and the crowds cheered the new king of England.

The police had acted with such speed after the death of Maud Marsh that Chapman did not have a chance to remove any evidence. Godley left Sgt. Kemp in charge of the Crown, which would be closed for business for a few days as the police investigated the case the press would soon label the Borough Poisoner. Alone now with his prisoner, Inspector Godley placed Chapman in the charge room. On hand at the Southwark Police Station to meet the officers and Chapman was police forensic medical examiner Dr. Jaquet. He would advise the officers and serve as a witness to Chapman's indictment. Chapman was later formally arrested, upon written statement, by Detective Sergeant Kemp.

Inspector Godley returned to the Crown at around 4 P.M. to find Sergeant Kemp still guarding the crime scene. Both men went back upstairs for a more complete search. Godley would later describe his detailed searched of the pub and what he found. "I went into the room and took possession of the bottles and some other articles. I went into the box room on the other side of the passage. I found several boxes and other articles there." He also found a box marked "B. T." Inside was a photo of Bessie Taylor as well as her death certificate. (Chapman was still a collector.) The press would report that: "A further search of the premises has been made, and the police have seized a number of books, papers and *newspaper reports of crimes.*" Jack?

From the Police Court Proceedings we learn: "Among the papers found by the police at the Crown were a memorial card to Bessie Chapman, the undertaker's account for the funeral, certain letters from Mr. Taylor to the accused, a draft letter in reply, a telegram from Mrs. Taylor relating to the funeral arrangements, and documents in reference to the purchase, and later the sale, of the Grapes Public House, Bishops Stortford."

Inspector Godley continued his search of the room. He later stated:

In the bedroom I found three powders, which were produced yesterday (at court), and some medical books. The pocket book I found in the office downstairs with a Pharmacopoeia (a directory of medical drugs with directions for use). I found one of the syringes and [Sgt] Kemp found the other, which he handed to me. I also found the little book in Polish, the papers in Russian, the will, an American revolver in a case, fully loaded (Was it a 32 caliber pistol like the one which was used to kill Mary Anderson in New Jersey?), a number of photographic chemicals, and bottles of various kinds (about 20); also a number of papers and documents, amongst them the photograph of Bessie Taylor. Some of the papers related to the change from the Prince of Wales to the Grapes, from the Grapes to the Monument, and from the Monument to the Crown; also a typewritten letter from Biggs & Co., dated 8th September, 1902, to "Mr. G. Chapman," at the Crown. I also found bills relating to the funeral of Mrs. Spink and Bessie Taylor. In the pocket book there is an entry, "13th February, 1901, Wednesday. Bessie Taylor dead, at 1:30 A.M., with great sorrow," and on 28th October, 1901, "Sunday, 27th, to Mabele Spink married." I gave certain bottles and powders to [Sgt] Kemp, with certain instructions. I made a complete search all through the house, and dealt with everything that I considered relevant to this charge. I took everything that was there.

There was no indication, however, that the inspector ventured into the basement. Perhaps he felt that he had found so much evidence upstairs that a visit to the dark and damp basement would have been a waste of time. Perhaps! What we do know is that such a search was never mentioned in any court documents or any interviews of the officers, and no evidence was ever reported to have been found there. The police did not search the small backyard garden. The question must be asked: Is there some evidence of other murders still buried in the back of the pub, and would such evidence point to Jack the Ripper?

Both officers returned to the police station at around 7 P.M. Inspector Godley, after checking in, went to the charge room for a little chat with the suspect. Chapman had only one thing on his mind.

CHAPMAN—Can I have bail?
INSPECTOR GODLEY—No. I have not finished my inquiries yet. It is a very serious case of poisoning.
CHAPMAN—She did not die suddenly; if she had been poisoned she would have done.

Godley did not address the issue of how long it would have taken to poison someone. Clearly Chapman was attempting to deflect the investigation away from the possibility and away from himself—the only suspect. Yet, with the inspector telling him it was a case of poison, he had to have known that his little game was up. The inspector then showed his charge the three bismuth powders that had been found in Maud's bedroom.

GODLEY—I found these powders on the drawers in your bedroom.
CHAPMAN—The doctor sent them.
GODLEY—I am going to see the doctor and finish my inquires.

With that Inspector Godley made his way to Dr. Stevenson. He recounted: "I left [Chapman], and again saw him at 10:15 [P.M.]" Sergeant Kemp was left to keep an eye on the prisoner. Just after Godley left, Chapman called to the sergeant to ask a question.

CHAPMAN—Can I speak to you a minute?
SGT. KEMP—Yes.
CHAPMAN—Your Inspector brought some white powder in just now, which he said he had found on the drawers in the bedroom. Has the doctor examined them yet?
KEMP—I do not know at present.

Sergeant Kemp would later relate that Chapman then lowered his head and began to speak in a low tone. It was all an act.

CHAPMAN—I would not hurt her for the world. I have had a lot of trouble with my barmaids, but I took a great fancy to this one. There was some jealousy lately. She said to me, "I have been with you now twelve or thirteen months, and have not had a baby yet; if I do not have one, you won't have me with you long." Her sister would bring her baby with her sometimes, and after she had gone Maud would sit and cry for a long time.

Just after 10 P.M. that evening Inspector Godley returned to the station having completed his preliminary researches into the death of Maud Marsh. With the information given to him by Dr. Stevenson he went directly to the charge room. By 10:15 P.M. George Chapman was given the news he did not expect. The inspector told him, "It is now my duty to charge you with the willful murder of Maud Marsh by poisoning her with arsenic." (Small amounts of arsenic were found in the antimony and it was detected before the true poison was discovered to be mostly antimony.)

Chapman may at that point have felt trapped for the first time in his life as he tried once again to secure his freedom. He said: "I am innocent; can I have bail? My brewers will bail me." Godley's answer was quick, short and to the point. "No!" For the time being he would be "held on remand" at Southwark Police Station.

Chapman would never stop asking for bail and he would never succeed in acquiring it. This serial killer was not about to slip out of the hands of the authorities. When Chapman was told that the charge was murder, he replied to Inspector Godley, "By what means, stabbing, shooting, or what?" This was a major slip of the tongue by Chapman. He had killed by three methods, including poison, but both he and Godley knew Maud had been poisoned and he did not mention that method in his statement. For the veteran detective, this must have raised an eyebrow or two. Chapman was starting to lose more self-control and he was less circumspect in what he said. Chapman knew he was trapped!

In later testimony during Chapman's trial, Inspector Godley would expound on what he found as he searched the Crown. He related: "I found a number of documents, amongst them being a book of prescriptions which I found in the box room (next to the bedroom). On the front and back of that book is written 'S. Klosowski.' I also found a photograph and a number of documents in the Polish language in a drawer in the accused's bedroom. I found a diary for 1893 in which there appears the following entry: 'Hairdresser wanted, indoors, 300., to W. Holton, Clifton Baths Market.' In the same book there are some newspaper cuttings pasted in, such as 'Hair brushing machinery, send for prices to manufacturers, complete sets; easy payments arranged; new patterns.' In the pocket of the book there is a sheet of notepaper on which is written: 'Came from America in 1893, independent;' also, 'Deposits £100, when from America I had £1000.'"

Godley had also found several interesting books related to medical subjects, such as how to treat poison cases and *The Family Physician*. The most interesting book found was a rare copy of Mr. James "Hangman" Berry's book detailing his career as a government hangman. When Berry read in his local paper that his book had been found, he wrote to Inspector Godley asking that his name be kept out of the case if possible. "Hangman" Berry had gone to great lengths to destroy as many copies of his own book as he could and he did not want any publicity. As it turned out, Berry's book would not need to be used because the case against Chapman was airtight, needing no extra items for the jury of twelve.

It is an interesting historical note that Berry had been approached by Scotland Yard detectives some years earlier while the Ripper investigation was in full swing. He was about to dispatch wife killer William Bury and detectives hoped that "Hangman" Berry could coach a confession out of Bury in regards to the Ripper murders. All William Bury would say about the matter was, "I suppose you think you are clever to hang me?" Some of the detectives and perhaps Berry felt he was confessing, but Bury would not elaborate. James Berry finished his hanging work on April 24, 1889, as he dropped William Bury the required distance to snap his neck cleanly at the end of his brand new rope. As for that old copy of *My Experience as an Executioner*, it is said to now be in a place of honor in the Black Museum.

Godley continued, "Some of the things I found in a chest of drawers and others in a back room, but the pocket book I found in the small office off the bar. I had no difficulty in getting the documents; I received them on the same day as I arrested the accused. I locked all the things up, took the accused to the station, and then went back to the house." Godley would also locate a small red label from Chapman's poison purchase. This label, which had fallen out of one of the medical books, would be later marked "exhibit 7Rv Chapman," and would conclusively prove that Inspector Godley's suspect was indeed a serial killer.

A list of documents and other evidence may now be found in the file of the case.

- Book of prescriptions: "S. Klosowski"
- Photograph & documents in bedroom drawer
- Diary for 1893 — Sheet of paper "Came to America in 1893..." (rough)
- Pocket Book — Note death of Bessie Taylor, Marry to Mabele Spink
- 4 bottles
- Undertaker's bill for Mary Spink
- Certificate of death for Mary S. Dec. 25, 1897
- £268 10s in funds
- Found several boxes and other articles
- Medical books—*Family Physician*, *A Practice of Physics* (5 in all)
- Three Powders (Bismuth)
- *Pharmacopoeia* (book)
- 2 Syringes — Green
- A little book in Polish
- Papers in Russian
- A Will
- An American Revolver in a case, fully loaded
- A number of photographic chemicals
- Photograph of Bessie Taylor (Found in box marked B.T.)
- Papers showing changes from Prince of Wales to *The Grapes* to *Monument* to the *Crown*
- Typewritten letter from *Biggs & Co.* date 8th Sept. 1902
- Funeral bills for Bessie Taylor
- Book —*Aristotle's Works*
- Book — By James Berry
- Poison label
- Book —*Five Hundred Prescriptions for Diseases and Complaints*
- Memorial card to Bessie Chapman
- Letters from Bessie Taylor to Chapman

Inspector Godley would continue to press Chapman in trying to get him to admit to his true identity, which the authorities had learned very early in the investigation. When Godley called him Klosowski, Chapman denied he was that man. Godley would remember his talk with his prisoner at the police station: "He said, 'Who is the other fellow?' I said, that is you; we call you Severin Klosowski, otherwise George Chapman. He said, 'I do not know anything about that other name.'" Klosowski would never admit to being himself and the police were never able to learn why he was so determined to be known as George Chapman. Perhaps somewhere in the back of his evil and twisted mind he felt that Severin Klosowski and Jack the Ripper could be tied together. As George Chapman he at least had a chance, albeit a very small one; as Jack the Ripper he would have no chance at all! Was it a lie that was stupid and easy to prove or was Chapman's mind so twisted that he actually believed that he was George Chapman from Jersey City? History is silent on that point.

November 1, 1902
Southwark and Bermondsey Record and South London Gazette

Mr. Sydney states that his attention has been called to a variety of statements in the newspapers concerning his client, and he asked that in fairness to the accused man no ex parte statements will be inserted during the progress of the inquiry.

Section III — The Investigation of a Serial Killer

Chapter 9

The Investigation Begins: Other Crimes and a Final Torso

In Memoriam, From a devoted friend, G.C.
Southwark, London — October 25, 1902

    Among the many within the desperately poor and hungry crowds who watched the grand spectacle of the coronation of Edward VII on October 25, 1902, stood American writer Jack London. London wore the rags of an East End laborer and he was soaked to the bone as he moved among the crowd, taking notes for his ground-breaking work *People of the Abyss*. London wanted to be sure that he did not stand out in any way from the people of the area he was writing about. It was more than just cover, however; it provided a bit of safety from the always dangerous conditions to be found in the ghettos of London. One danger, however, had been removed with the arrest of Severin Antoniovich Klosowski, alias George Chapman. It was now time for the men of Scotland Yard to begin investigation into the background of a man they, at the time, suspected of killing only one barmaid. In the end they would find much more, leaving many to wonder if they would ever really know how many had fallen to this Victorian serial killer. The question was: Could they find hard evidence that he was Jack the Ripper?

    It is interesting to note that a report on Chapman's arrest written by Inspector Godley can be found in the May 15, 1908, edition of *The Police Review and Parade Gossip*. The good inspector had by then recently retired from 30 years service in the metropolitan police when this fully fictional account was written.

> Directly the officers asked for him, Chapman, who was in the bar, dashed down a trap-door into the cellar. The officers quickly followed, only to find that for the moment their quarry had eluded them. A slight beam of light from behind a door led them to break it down, and they found Chapman standing behind some barrels, a loaded revolver in each hand. He threatened both officers, but a quick and plucky dash made him their prisoner.

    A quick reading of the rest of the article shows that the authors were equally unable to come up with the facts in the Ripper case. It is not recorded how Inspector Godley reacted to this little piece of fiction, but he was probably not in favor of it.

    The evidence found at the Crown would prove to be a bonanza for the prosecution. Godley had located Chapman's files full of documents in Russian and Polish as well as the undertakers bills for Mary Spink and Bessie Taylor, a prescription book and memorial cards. Because Chapman was a collector of memorabilia surrounding his crimes, as many serial killers seem to be, the authorities would have no trouble locating his poison victim's graves. The police also located the series of photos Chapman had taken of Maud Marsh, which had documented her slow decline and death. Godley also located Chapman's diary written in Polish, which clearly established him as Severin Klosowski and not the expatriate American known as George Chapman. However, despite growing evidence that he was indeed Klosowski, the prisoner would never admit, even under pain of death, who he really was. Whatever he was hiding it was something so important that he wanted no one to know it. Was he Jack the Ripper?

It would not take long for the police to locate people in and around London who had known Klosowski by his real name. With all of the available documentation Detective-Sergeant Arthur Neil was soon able to track down Klosowski's real wife, Lucy Klosowski. (At least she was the real wife in England. The authorities did not seem to know about any woman who may have married Klosowski in Poland. They were also unaware at the time that she had gone missing!) She had been living very close to "Chapman" in Southwark. Klosowski did not seem to know this at the time of his arrest. Did Lucy ever visit him at the Crown?

It was quite easy for Lucy to pick her husband out of a police lineup. There was no doubt as to who he was, but he still insisted on the now ridiculous lie that he was George Chapman. Confronted by Inspector Godley and Sergeant Neil with Lucy Klosowski, Chapman would only retort, "I don't know this woman." Lucy was not prepared for his response and she replied, "Oh, Severin, don't say that. You remember the time you nearly killed me in Jersey City!"

This was the first time the police had heard of his attack on his wife and they would explore that episode in later interviews with Lucy. For the time being the police were more interested in establishing his identity than looking into his background in the United States and so a second lineup was conducted for William Davidson. Davidson was the now retired chemist who had sold Klosowski the poison. The identification was also an easy one but Davidson knew the prisoner only as George Chapman. It was a direct link from the purchase of the poison to the prisoner and the little red label found during the police search of the Crown. It would seem to have been a good time to start admitting to being Severin Klosowski, someone who did not purchase poison. However, even the positive identification of Klosowski by Mrs. Rauch and by Lucy's sister and brother did not induce the prisoner to abandon his claim of American identity.

OTHER CRIMES—OTHER TIMES

The search of Chapman's pub would yield more than a bonanza for the prosecution, it would prove the innocence of a man whom Chapman had accused of fraud. In May 1902 Chapman had accused 28-year-old Matilda Gilmor, whose real last name was Oxenford, and 32-year-old Alfred Clark of defrauding him of £700. Some reports name him as Arthur Clark, "a Traveler." In court Chapman declared that he had given the couple the £700 in two payments for a series of mining certificates. The certificates were, of course, worthless but, more to the point, Chapman had not paid the stated sum for the documents so his charges were perjured.

The certificates themselves were not the property of Oxenford and Clark, however. They had been stolen from her employer and bore the name of Mrs. Gilmor, a widow who lived in Liverpool. Oxenford had been working as a domestic servant when she took the Caledonian Gold Mining Company stock expecting to make a great deal of money. The mining company had dissolved on June 20, 1900, and was no longer in business. When they found them to be mostly worthless, the luckless pair went from pub to pub searching for a buyer and ended up at the Crown downing a "pint of bitter" with George Chapman.

It is not clear what happened at the bar but for some reason Chapman smelled a rat and no monies were passed other than a few pounds. Perhaps the fact that Chapman, as a long-term criminal, was sensitive to other con men kept him from being conned. It is not clear what Chapman expected to gain from this fully fraudulent claim. Certainly Oxenford and Clark had little or no money so it could not have been a monetary gain. And if Chapman felt he could remove Mr. Clark and gain Miss Oxenford he was not really thinking clearly since she was the one who had stolen the certificates.

During the fraud trial Chapman was asked by defense council to provide the banknote numbers he had reportedly given to the couple. Chapman was happy to supply the list he just happened to have written down in his log. It was not to be a long trial as George Chapman, so-called honest businessman, was up against Alfred Clark, a known criminal. Interestingly Maud Marsh would also testify that Chapman had paid for the stocks, which was of course also a lie. Her testimony had been reported in the local press at the time: "Mrs. Chapman said she was present when the prisoner asked for the money on both occasions and saw it handed to [Matilda Oxenford]." She had gotten out of her sick bed to go to court to help Chapman, even as he was slowly murdering her! It did not take long for the jury of 12 good men to convict Clark of "conspiracy to falsely obtain monies." He was sentenced to three years for his "crime" but he would not be in prison for long. As for Miss Oxenford, she was set free. The men of the jury felt that she had been set astray by the criminal Clark and was therefore not responsible for the fraud. The jury seemed to have forgotten that Miss Oxenford had been the one who actually stole the stock certificates in the first place.

After Inspector Godley's search of the Crown and his discovery of the notes in Chapman's locked drawer, the notes were kept in police custody. Godley had remembered the fraud case earlier in the year and, on a hunch, he checked the numbers on the banknotes. The numbers were the same ones Chapman had sworn he had given to Alfred Clark. It would not be long before Clark was once again a free man.

At about the same time Chapman was attempting to defraud the court, the fifth and final Thames Torso murder victim was discovered only 1,200 yards from his pub in a short alley known as Salamanca Place. It would be the final murder in a series which had begun 15 years earlier in the town of Rainham. Although it would be one of the bloodiest in the series, this single murder would not cause very much of an outcry. Possibly too much time had passed since the fourth victim had been discovered on Pinchin Street in 1889 to cause great concern. There were, after all, many more matters to be concerned about in the ghettos of London. More likely however, because this victim, like three out of four other victims, would never be identified it would be hard for some to feel much empathy. Nevertheless, it was indeed a very bloody affair.

"Oh, What's That?"—June 8, 1902

It was always quieter on the night shift at Messrs. Doulton's Pottery Works than the fast-moving and busy day shift. It was a good job and a good shift for Charles Whiting and his friend Robert William Muntzer. That cool Sunday morning of June 8 promised to be just one more relatively uneventful early day on the job. That was about to dramatically change. At around 4 in the morning both men could be seen walking along Broad Street, which ran parallel to the Albert Embankment. The small factory was within easy earshot of the always active Thames River and the two men could readily feel its presence in the light mist moving all around them. Speaking of the work to come and what skills would be needed for the upcoming project, the men turned into Salamanca Place, which backed up to the old red brick factory. They were not long in the alley before Whiting spotted the strange pile directly in their path. It had not been there earlier.

Charles Whiting stopped so fast in grabbing Muntzer by the arm that Muntzer thought his friend had been struck by something. It was not, however, a physical strike but a mental one as Whiting cried out, "Oh, what's that?" It took no time at all for Muntzer to focus his attention directly in front of him on a sight he would never forget and one he would have trouble discussing even days later. The men had found the dismembered and butchered remains of what had recently been a human being piled up near the front gate of Doulton's Works. It was reported, "What had stopped the men, literally in mid-stride, was the sight of a head placed on top of the pile, with the dead eyes looking directly at them with a glassy, terrifying stare."

This discovery, less than one and one-half miles from George Chapman's pub on Borough High Street, would be the only Torso Murder which indicated that the killer was by then living south of the Thames River. It had been a local kill and the killer had wanted to relieve himself of his burden with great haste.

After the men recovered a bit from their discovery they ran inside to inform John Cox, who was working as night watchman, of their find. Cox informed the men that he had taken his usual early morning walk from his post in the lobby around the building and the alley at around 3 A.M. The pile of body parts was not there at the time. He also told the men that he had seen and heard nothing from his post some 70 yards away from the remains. Once again no one had seen or heard anything. It would be John Cox who would run down Salamanca Place in search of a constable, leaving Muntzer and Whiting to guard the body pile.

It was at this point that two young men walked past the alley on their way to a local medical school. Much to Muntzer's surprise the "medical students" stopped to have a look at the pile. One of them stated "Oh, it's a woman's head." With that "report" the young men simply continued calmly on their way. During the investigation neither man would come forward to explain their seemingly bizarre behavior.

Mr. Cox was soon able to locate Police Constable Birton. Constable Birton was on his usual patrol route near the Thames Embankment as Cox excitedly ran up to him. Cox, however, was far too overwrought to give the officer a clear account of what had been found. He did stammer out the words "Come here, I want you!"

The excited and wild look about Cox alerted the officer that a major problem needed his immediate attention. He followed John Cox back to Salamanca Place. On the way the officer tried to get a more detailed report on exactly what was wrong, but Cox simply could not provide one. An explanation, however, was short in coming. "In the early morning light of a new day P.C. Birton viewed a sight he would never forget. The arms and legs had been crudely ripped off with great force. The backbone had been sawn in half, roughly, with evidently no great skill. The head and other portions of the body had been boiled in water, or roasted in some type of oven."

It did not take long for Constable Birton to realize that he needed as much help as he could get for this job. As more officers arrived along with the local police surgeon, the lamp lighter for the area was found. The man reported that he had gone down the alley at 3:10 that morning and had seen nothing out of the ordinary. The constable had also patrolled Salamanca Place around 3:30 and the area had been quite deserted. The killer had not spent much time in the dimly lit side street as he dumped his brutal cargo. He had left no trace of who he was, escaping into a dense London fog, which had rolled in off of the nearby river.

At the coroner's inquest, the public would learn of the great lengths the killer had gone to erase the identity of the victim. The report stated: "The head and face were in particularly bad shape, and badly disfigured. The 'cooking' had shrunk much of the skin, so much so, that one ear appeared much smaller than the other. Several front teeth were missing and most of the scalp on top of the head was gone." Nevertheless, the doctors determined the cause of death to be suffocation. They also reported that the victim had been from 25 to 30 years old, around five feet tall and slim. Coroner Dr. Michael Taylor would make one final observation, which would be critical to understanding the killer of this unknown woman. This was a serial murder conducted by the same man who had killed one in 1887, one in 1888 and two in 1889 before his long break. Dr. Taylor reported that the murder was "on all fours" with the other cases. (The same man had murdered all of the Thames Torso victims.)

Once again, we have the words of Inspector Abberline of Scotland Yard: "Indeed, if the theory be accepted that a man who takes life on a wholesale scale never ceases its accursed habit until he is either arrested or dies, there is much to be said for Chapman's consistency. You see, incentive changes; but the fiendishness is not eradicated. The victim, too, you will notice, continued to be women; but they are of different classes, and obviously call for different methods of dispatch."

POLICE COURT—MONDAY, OCTOBER 27, 1902

The face that Severin Klosowski presented to Paul Taylor at the Southwark Police Court on October 27, 1902, would be one of disinterest and cynicism. Klosowski would show to all the world that he cared little for the "silly little court." As time went on however, his opinion would change considerably.

He had been accused of the "Feloniously killing and slaying of Maud Marsh, aged 19, by administering to her a quantity of arsenic at 213 Borough High Street." The newspapers also reported on the immediate interest in the case by the public. "Naturally enough a widespread interest has been awakened in the case for, as, a morning contemporary remarked, 'The narrow margin which separates the grave from the gay has rarely been illustrated in a more striking manner' than in the events connected with his arrest."

Klosowski, of course, would state "I know nothing about it." But it would not take long for the authorities to discover much in the way of damaging evidence against the only real suspect in Maud's murder. As for Klosowski's solicitor, Mr. Sydney, he would have much work ahead. But for the time being the defense had no questions for Inspector Godley. However, Mr. Taylor had a few.

MR. TAYLOR—When did the woman die?
INSPECTOR GODLEY—On the 22nd.
MR. TAYLOR—At the Hospital?
INSPECTOR GODLEY—No, at his residence. I may add, from inquires, I have made that he was the only person who fed her. He would feed her himself, and he would allow no one in the kitchen while he prepared her food. I also found that this was the third woman that he has had die within five years. Two were his wives, and this one was represented as his wife.
MR. TAYLOR—The inquest is to-morrow? (Coroner's Inquest)
INSPECTOR GODLEY—Yes. I found five books and some white powders, which have not yet been analyzed.
MR. TAYLOR—Have you had any medical opinion as yet?
INSPECTOR GODLEY—I have seen a report that arsenic has been found in the body. The same doctor attended the wife, who died at the Monument under similar circumstances, and he is now of opinion that she also was poisoned.
MR. TAYLOR—The case may require three or four hearings?
INSPECTOR GODLEY—I should say it may require a dozen if we have to exhume the bodies of the two wives.

Klosowski was then ordered held on remand for eight days to allow investigators the opportunity to find out just what the white powder in those mysterious bottles was. It did not, however, stop Klosowski's attorney from trying to secure bail for his client.

MR. H.J. SYDNEY—I don't know whether, under the circumstances, you would accept bail. This is a man who holds a license, and there is really no evidence against him, except what the officer has told you. You see, there is an absolute denial on his part.

INSPECTOR GODLEY—I shall object to bail. There is nothing to stop this man from leaving the country. He came to America in 1893 (Godley had found the note at the Crown stating that Klosowski had arrived in 1893.), and there is nothing to keep him here. He has no banking account. I seized between £200 and £300 at his residence.

MR. TAYLOR—I shall not grant bail.

MR. SYDNEY—With regard to the money found in the house, of course, the police have no right to that.

MR. TAYLOR—I consider that all the money ought to be handed over. In a charge of this kind it is essential that the man should have the money for the purposes of his own defense. It is not a question of robbery in this case.

November 1, 1902
South London Observer
SOUTHWARK POISONING MYSTERY.

Publican Charged with Murder.

Great interest has been manifested in the strange story which was opened at Southwark Police-court on Monday before Mr. Paul Taylor, when George Chapman, 36, licensed victualler, of the Crown public-house, 213 Borough High Street, was brought up in custody... The deceased advertised about fourteen months ago for a situation as bar maid, and the prisoner replied. After a short time he asked her how she would like to be Mrs. Chapman. Her father understood that she was married.

Chapter 10

Coroner Waldo's Inquest: The Maud Marsh Matter

> *Fifty doctors won't find out.*
> — Alias George Chapman

Coroner's Inquest — Tuesday, October 28, 1902, Session 1

The second investigation into the murder of Maud Marsh began with the seating of 18 jurymen in the Mission Hall in Colliers Rents, Long Lane, Southwark. Doctor F. J. Waldo, coroner for the City of London and Southwark, began the work of detection at 11:45 in the morning to an overflow crowd of more than slightly interested individuals. The men of the press took note as the crowds grew each day:

> The public interest in this case has been evinced day by day in the gathering of large numbers of people in the vicinity of the Crown, who discussed from their particular standpoint the details of the case as made known through the Press, to which have been added many stories of greater or lesser trustworthiness, detailed by those who may have known the interested parties. On Tuesday a considerable number of persons gathered in the vicinity of Collier's Rents, Long Lane, wherein is situate the Mission Hall that serves for the Coroner's Court. It was anticipated that the accused would be brought into court for the purposes of the coroner's inquiry, but such was not to be on that day at least [*South London Observer*, Nov. 1, 1902].

Klosowski was represented by Thomas Sydney, who knew from the start that he would have his hands full defending a man who appeared to already have engendered a great dislike among a great many people. Representing the Marsh family was E. H. A. Newman. Newman had been hired by Mr. Marsh, who seemed to have come late to the conclusion that the man he knew as George Chapman had indeed murdered his second youngest daughter.

Also on hand to view the proceedings for official London were Detective-Inspector Godley and Detective-Sergeant Kemp. Backing up the two case detectives was bacteriological expert Doctor Emile Ludwig Freyberger, who was regularly consulted by the London County Council. It would be a brief first day of testimony as the men of the press took in all that was said.

Coroner Waldo informed the crowded room that "This inquiry will take some time. It relates to the death of a woman named Maude Elizabeth Marsh, who was a barmaid at the Crown public house in High Street. George Chapman, who keeps that house, has, I understand from the police, been charged with having caused her death under suspicious circumstances. I propose today to take merely evidence of identification."

Robert Marsh was then called to the bench to report that he had indeed identified the dead girl as his daughter, Maud, and that she had been only 19 years of age at her death.

CORONER DR. F. J. WALDO—Was she employed as a barmaid at the Crown public house?
ROBERT MARSH—I always understood that she was Mrs. Chapman, sir.
WALDO—Thank you. It will be necessary in this case for the contents of the viscera and other organs to be carefully examined, and a further post-mortem examination will have to be made. I propose, therefore, to adjourn the further hearing until Friday week, November 7th, at eleven o'clock. I do not suppose we shall finish that day, but by commencing early we shall be able to make some progress.

The inquest was then adjourned for the day.

FIRST AUTOPSY REPORT ON MAUD MARSH— OCTOBER 30, 1902

On October 30, Doctor Emile Freyberger, Dr. Stevenson and Dr. Stoker aided by "another medical man," conducted the postmortem on Maude Elizabeth Marsh. Even though the results would not be disclosed to the press or public until the coroner's inquest was resumed, there was still a great deal of interest and speculation as to what the results would show. The theories were beginning to fly:

> The fact that the body was in a remarkably good state of preservation bears out the theory that the girl died as the result of arsenic poisoning, for arsenic is a well-known preservative. Being a mineral, it is very easy of discovery by chemical analysis, no matter what the state of the body is or how long life has been extinct. Consequently, it is confidently anticipated that if the second Mrs. Chapman died from arsenic poisoning, some trace of the poison will still be found in her body [*South London Observer*, Nov. 1, 1902].

On hand for the police was the ever-vigilant Inspector Godley. Godley knew that he had the right man and wanted to make sure that there were no problems with any aspect of the investigation. He also wanted to be present in case there were any questions the doctors needed to have answered during the examination.

MAUD'S FAREWELL—NOVEMBER 5, 1902

As the investigation into the three poison murders was picking up speed the final victim of serial killer Severin Klosowski was laid to rest. By that time all of London could read of the case and "...the interest in the strange circumstances attending the death of Miss Maud Marsh at the Crown public house, High Street, Borough, is still maintained." Maud would be buried near her home in West Croydon and the service would be paid for by Klosowski who was still announcing his complete innocence in the matter. While he stood in the dock before a police court hearing he penned a short note, which would be placed with flowers on the coffin. "In Memoriam — From a devoted friend, G.C." It was, to say the least, a complete lie.

November 8, 1902
Southwark and Bermondsey Recorder and
South London Gazette,
THE BOROUGH MYSTERY.
BURIAL OF MISS MARSH.

The funeral of the deceased took place on Wednesday. It was just after twelve o'clock when the funeral procession left the premises of the Southwark Bridge Road undertaker, and by that time a big crowd, chiefly composed of women, had gathered. The only wreath placed on the coffin was that sent by Chapman himself, "From a devoted friend;" and the others were conveyed in the first of the two mourning coaches which followed behind. The coffin was taken to the home of the girl's parents in [West] Croydon, and from there to the cemetery.

The card sent by Klosowski was attached to a wreath of flowers made of pink chrysanthemums, camellias, lilies and tuber roses wrapped together with a wide violet ribbon. The card and flowers sent to the gravesite found disfavor with at least one individual, possibly Robert Marsh. An unidentified writer had contacted a local newspaper protesting any flowers or memoriam from Klosowski being allowed to be placed on the grave. The writer made it clear that any such display would not reach the gravesite. However, no untoward incident occurred as the coffin was lowered into the grave along with the flowered wreath and card sent by Klosowski. It would be allowed to rot while the rest of the flowers were handed out to Maud's family and friends. It was dutifully reported that her suspected killer was not among those who received any of the flowers.

For most of the afternoon a hard rain fell in the area but it was reported that it had "no deterrent effect upon the women of Croydon — there were few men present — who assembled in their thousands. They lined the streets leading from the residence to the parents of the deceased in Longfellow Road to the cemetery." Also, there were large crowds on hand at the entrance to the cemetery as well as all the way to the small chapel. Most impressive was the "mounted police Inspector" who had ridden in front of the funeral procession all the way to the cemetery.

Due to the anticipated overflow of people the service was conducted by two priests; Reverend E. Phillips who was the curate of St. Saviors Roman Catholic Church of Croydon and Reverend J. H. Crickmen the curate-in-charge of St. Phillips in Noerbury. So many attempted to view the service that when the coffin was placed "within the latter edifice [many of those nearby] made an unseemly rush for the doors, overcrowding being only prevented by the determined efforts of the officials, who had to close and lock the doors. Later, after the committed services were completed and the family departed along with their guests there was a second rush of spectators to view the new grave before it could be covered up." On seeing Klosowski's wreath, some felt that someone should go down to remove it, but in the end it was covered over with dirt.

With Maud now laid to rest it was time to shift official attention to the police court and coroner's inquest, both of which were still underway.

Coroner's Inquest — Tuesday, November 11, 1902, Session 2

At 10:45 A.M. a handcuffed and somewhat ruffled Klosowski, still professing to be one George Chapman, was brought into the Southwark Coroner's Court. There had been some type of incident, not announced to the court, because the prisoner was escorted into the courtroom by two "warders from Brixton Prison." The extra guards and handcuffs that he wore all the way into the courtroom is suggestive of a possible escape attempt by or a serious disturbance expected from Klosowski, but this would be only speculation as no official notice was given for the extra security. An attempt to escape would indicate that Klosowski was starting to believe that he might not make it out of his coming trial alive! The guards did not leave his side as they had before. It was reported: "The handcuffs were removed, and he took a seat between his custodians, facing the coroner."

Once again official London gathered to hear evidence against Klosowski, still known in court as George Chapman. Inspector Godley and Sgt. Kemp were on hand as were Police Superintendent Walters and Chief Inspector Bonner. They were present to give any required testimony but also to gather any medical information that may be released during the hearing in order to testify at the ongoing Police Court hearings. Also present were Dr. Freyberger for the government and Mr. Sydney, who would represent Klosowski and would cross-examine the witnesses.

Mr. Robert Marsh was first to be called by the coroner who asked Maud's father how it came to be that Maud worked at the Monument pub and then the Crown.

ROBERT MARSH — My daughter advertised in August, 1901, for a situation as barmaid. She had ten replies, one from a Mr. Chapman, at the Monument public house, Union Street, Southwark, offering her employment. He offered to pay her expenses, whether engaged or not. She came up some days after, and was engaged. I got no communication from her, but my wife did a few days after. I went up and saw her at the Monument. I asked her if she thought she suited, and she said "Yes," and that Mr. Chapman liked her very well. I visited her again about a fortnight [two weeks] after, and in conversation she said, "Mr. Chapman has asked me how I would like to be called Mrs. Chapman." I told her she had better wait and see how she got on. She asked me my opinion, and I told her it was too soon because she didn't know enough about the man. She said she would wait. I did not see her for some time afterwards, when she came home with Mr. Chapman. She said she was going to get married, and I told her not to do anything underhanded, but to let me know. I was in the Croydon Hospital afterwards, and my daughter and Mr. Chapman came to see me. No conversation of importance took place then, but at a subsequent visit she referred to the marriage, and told me that she was married. She had a wedding ring on, and said she had been married on a Sunday somewhere in Bishopsgate, at a Roman Catholic room. I asked why she did not let me know, and she Mr. Chapman did not want to make a fuss about it.

CORONER WALDO — Did you ask for the certificate?

MR. MARSH — Yes, and she said, "George has got it locked up." Some weeks ago she wrote to her mother saying she was very ill, and was in Guy's Hospital.

CORONER WALDO — What did she say to you?

MR. MARSH — I asked her what was the matter, and she said it was inflammation in the inside. She complained of pains in the stomach and retching. I next saw her in bed at the Crown public house on the 18th of October. She again complained of the pains. I asked her what caused it, and she said she could not tell me. She said she had had diarrhea.

CORONER WALDO — Did you see your daughter alone on that occasion?

MR. MARSH — Yes, but Mr. Chapman came in several times. Each time he came in he walked up to her and felt her pulse. I said she seemed bad, and Chapman said, "Yes, she was." She asked for water, and Chapman left the room and brought it to her. She used to drink a little, and vomit it immediately.

CORONER WALDO — What color was it?

MR. MARSH — It was a dark color, not any particular, but certainly not clear.

CORONER WALDO — When did you see her again?

MR. MARSH — I last saw her on October 21st, at the Crown, and still in bed. When I saw her on that occasion I thought she was getting better. I asked my daughter if she wanted anything, and she said no. She continued to vomit, and to complain of pains in her stomach. Later on I went back to the bedroom, accompanied by Chapman. I said to him, "I believe my daughter will get better now." Chapman said, "She will never get up any more." I turned to Mr. Chapman and asked if he had seen anyone else like it. He said, "Yes." I said, "Was your other wife like it? And he said, "Yes, just about the same."

CORONER WALDO — You still thought your daughter was his wife?

MR. MARSH — Yes.

CORONER WALDO — Was anybody else in the room at this time?

MR. MARSH — Yes, the nurse Jessie [Toon]. I had suspicions that my daughter was having foul play. Chapman said she was being attended by a doctor, but I was not satisfied, because his methods of coming in the room, feeling her pulse, and going to get the water, roused my suspicions. I consulted Doctor Grapple, of Croydon, telling him that I had a daughter ill in London, and I should be pleased if he would visit her. He went on the afternoon of October 21st, paying a surprise visit, and I saw him the next morning. He said my daughter was very ill, but he did not see why she should not get well if the sickness would stop, He said his opinion was that my daughter had been poisoned by arsenic, but how she got it he could not tell.

After Dr. Waldo thanked Robert Marsh for what must have been a difficult ordeal in discussing the slow death of his youngest daughter, Mrs. Marsh took the stand.

> MRS. MARSH— She was 19-years-old in February last. When my daughter inserted the advertisement she had been out of employment for about two months. She had been behind the bar before. I advised her to advertise, and she did so, getting nine answers, including one from the Monument. I went with her to see Mr. Chapman on the same evening. I saw Mr. Chapman, and said, "I have brought my daughter in answer to your post-card about the situation." Mr. Chapman asked my daughter if she had been in that line before, and she said she had a slight knowledge of bar work. It was arranged that she was to receive 7s a week to commence with, and it was also arranged, if my daughter's character was satisfactory, that should go in on the following Thursday. Chapman said he was a widower. I asked him if he was the only one in the house. He said all the upper part of the house was let to a family. Chapman said he thought she would suit. I went home with my daughter, and later on we had a communication that the character was satisfactory, and saying would she come in on the Monday. When she had been there a week she said Mr. Chapman had given her a gold watch and chain. I said to my husband, "It seems funny that he has given her that so soon. You had better go up and see her," and he did so on the Sunday following. When he came back he said it was quite true that he had given her this watch and chain, and that he had invited Mr. Chapman down on the following Sunday. They both came down on bicycles on the Sunday.
>
> CORONER WALDO— Was anything said about these presents?
>
> MRS. MARSH— Yes. I asked my daughter about it. She said it was all right, and that Mr. Chapman had given her the watch and chain and some rings which she was wearing.

The question now asked is whether or not these were the well-known rings torn from the fingers of a Ripper victim some 14 years earlier? More to the point, however, for modern-day investigators is whether or not they are in some old dusty box in Scotland Yard's Black Museum and can they be identified as coming from a Ripper victim so long after those crimes were committed? If they can be identified then ... perhaps a vital clue to another old case?

The coroner then had Mrs. Marsh identify and read several letters she had received from Maud. These were the letters that revealed Maud was being pressured by Chapman for sexual favors as he attempted to have Maud enter into a fraudulent marriage. It would not take long for Chapman's pressure to change Maud's tone as she attempted to calm her mother's fears with later letters. Mrs. Marsh testified:

> They came down on the following Sunday, and Chapman expressed a desire to marry my daughter, and went to the hospital to see my husband about it. On returning from the hospital Chapman took a will from his pocket, made in Maud's favor, which he signed, and I and my son signed it as witnesses. On October 13 I visited them at the Monument. There was a quantity of confetti outside, and my daughter told me that she had been married that morning. She said she had been married in Bishopsgate Street at a Roman Catholic church or chapel. I asked Maud where the certificate was, and she said, "George has got it."

From that point on Mrs. Marsh suspected that Chapman was up to no good, but it is doubtful she thought he might be in the process of slowly murdering Maud. Mrs. Marsh continued to explain to the coroner that she had received news of Maud's illness and the family did what they felt they could do to help.

> MRS. MARSH— My daughter wrote to say she was ill and was an inpatient at Guy's Hospital. I went and saw her and inquired what was the matter, and was told she was suffering from constipation and inflammation of the inside. Then Maud wrote from the Crown to my married daughter, and said she was very ill. That was last September. She said she must have someone with her and would she come. She said, "Don't let mother know, because she will worry so." My daughter Louisa went on the Saturday and stayed with her till the Monday. When Louisa came back she said Maud was very ill indeed. I could not leave my house, but my husband went up to see her. When he came

home he said that she was very bad, and would not live a couple of days. I went up and saw Mr. Chapman in the bar. I shook hands and said, "How is Maud?" He said, "No better." He invited me to go up, and I and my daughter Louisa went up to the back room on the second floor. The nurse said Mr. Chapman had given her an injection twice. I stopped there all night. Mr. Chapman was in the room all night lying on the spare bed with his clothes on.

CORONER WALDO— Did you ask her what had made her so ill?

MRS. MARSH— Yes, and she said she thought it was rabbit. I asked her if Mr. Chapman had some of the rabbit, and she said they all had some, but that none of the others were ill. When she died the doctor said my daughter had died of poison. When Dr. Grapple had seen my daughter he called me into a room and said, "Your daughter has been poisoned," or "Your daughter is being poisoned." I asked him if it was the rabbit. He said, "No, arsenic." After my daughter's death, Mr. Chapman asked Dr. Stoker for a certificate. Dr. Stoker said he did not feel justified in giving one then. Chapman asked why. Dr. Stoker said there was nothing to show what she had died from. Mr. Chapman said she had died from exhaustion. Dr. Stoker said, "But what caused the exhaustion?" Chapman said the continued vomiting and diarrhea. I suggested that there should be a post-mortem examination. Dr. Stoker said if we would agree to a post-mortem examination he would pay all the expenses himself. I asked Mr. Chapman if he would agree to a post-mortem examination, and he said, "Yes." Mr. Chapman asked me to stop [at the Crown] till the funeral. Inspector Godley told me my daughter was not married. I said to Mr. Chapman, "George, haven't you really married Maud?" and he said, "No!"

The coroner then went over two letters written by Maud in pencil while she was in the hospital. Maud had written to Klosowski, as "My dear husband," informing him that she would come home as soon as she could. One of the letters was signed, "I remain your ever true and loving wife, Maud." With the reading of the two letters Dr. Waldo adjourned the Coroner's Court until the next Tuesday at 11 o'clock in the morning.

CORONER'S INQUEST— TUESDAY, NOVEMBER 18, 1902, SESSION 3

Once again Dr. F. J. Waldo resumed his inquest into the Maud Marsh matter. As winter began to take hold of London crowds filled the hall as well as many of the approaches to the Southwark Coroner's Court. Interest in the case continued to increase as more and more details made their way into the London papers. Chapman/Klosowski was becoming a household name: "As is well-known, George Chapman, who held the license of the house and with whom the deceased had lived after being attracted to his service as a barmaid, is in custody on the charge of murdering her by administering the poison. The motley crowd outside were rewarded for their wait in the biting wind by a glimpse of Chapman as he was driven past in a four-wheeled cab and handcuffed to two stalwart warders. On getting into the court the handcuffs were removed, and the accused took his seat quietly between his two custodians, with whom during the long and weary inquiry he occasionally exchanged words."

The authorities would be taking no chances with the Borough Poisoner. And, if there were any problems at the inquest, Inspector Godley and Sergeant Kemp were also on hand to see that Klosowski behaved himself. It was clear that the hearings were starting to take a heavy toll on Klosowski. Klosowski knew the situation was grim and escape from custody was becoming less of a possibility.

A little after 11 o'clock in the morning Dr. Waldo called Maud's sister, Louisa Sarah Morris, to the stand to relate to the jury what she discovered during conversations with Klosowski, a man she knew only as George Chapman. Louisa, who had married a warehouseman, was at the time living with her parents at 14 Longfellow Road in West Croydon while her husband searched for work.

Louisa reported that she had visited her younger sister in the Queen's Ward at Guy's Hospital in bed number 17 on a Wednesday afternoon. The nurse and doctor had informed her that Maud was, "very bad," and that they had been unable to discover what was medically wrong with her.

Louisa had also been suspicious of the so-called marriage. Maud had earlier informed her older sister that she and "George" had been married "in a Roman Catholic room in Bishopsgate, but George had the certificate." When she again confronted Maud in the hospital, Maud would only say, "Yes, I am; so there." It was at that point that Louisa told Maud that she did not think Klosowski was treating her correctly.

Some time earlier, Louisa and Maud had gone on a day trip to Streatham, but the sisters had had such a fine time that they had not kept track of the time and were returning late. Louisa related to the court that Maud suddenly became distraught on realizing that she was late. "Witness asked her, 'What are you crying for?' and she said, 'Look how late it is. You don't know what my husband is.' Witness next said, 'Why, does he hit you?" She replied, 'Yes, he bangs me; he took hold of my hair and banged my head.' The witness said, 'Can't you pay him back?' and she said, 'Yes; I kicked him."

Louisa had also confronted Klosowski in the Crown about Maud's rapidly failing health. At the time a very confident serial killer nearly admitted what he was doing. It was about as close to a confession as Klosowski would ever make. It was a boast he would soon regret.

LOUISA — Isn't it funny the doctors can't find out what's the matter?
KLOSOWSKI — Fifty doctors won't find out.
LOUISA — What do you mean?
KLOSOWSKI — Never you mind.

Louisa then told the court of a visit she and her husband had made to the Crown ten days before Maud's death. Maud had written a note to her sister asking that she come, telling her that she was very ill and needed help. Interestingly, Louisa burned the letter from Maud, but she did come to the Crown and stayed for about two and a half days. It was during this visit that Maud told her sister that she felt that the medicine "George" was giving her "was the cause of her retching." Yet, Maud continued to take the medicine!

Louisa informed the court that during her stay Klosowski would make many trips upstairs to Maud's room bringing her things to drink, but Maud could not keep anything down. However, when Louisa gave her sister some bovil tea she felt much better and Maud was able to get up and wash herself. It did not seem to have occurred to Louisa that only when Klosowski fed or gave Maud something to drink did she bring up any food or drink.

Finally, Louisa testified about an incredible incident which occurred after Maud had been released by the hospital. Louisa, Maud, their mother and Klosowski were having tea. Klosowski could barely contain himself as he had failed to kill Maud during the first period of slow poisoning. Maud having been saved by the absence of Klosowski at the hospital, he was anxious to get back to the work of poisoning and almost said too much.

MAUD — What do you think? George says I shall not live to see 28.
LOUISA — Pooh, how does he know?
KLOSOWSKI — No more you won't.
MAUD — Remember I have been ill once, and this (pointing to her side) is a long liver.
KLOSOWSKI — We shall see. (At this point Klosowski shrugged his shoulders.)

The conversation had an electrifying effect on the court. Klosowski's legal council, Mr. Sydney, attempted to deflect as much of the effect as possible. It would be a losing cause but he did make a few points as he asked Louisa if her sister and Klosowski were happy. "Chapman and my sister appeared to he happy: they were always playing and larking. Chapman never prevented me from going when I liked to see my sister. There was no concealment about what Chapman did so far as I could see. The talk about my sister dying before she became 28 was like chaff; I did not think much about it at the time."

With that, another of Maud's sisters was called to the stand. Alice May Marsh lived near her parents in West Croydon and worked as a domestic servant. She had first met the man she knew as George Chapman 14 or 15 months earlier when Maud and Klosowski visited her father in the Croydon Hospital. "She went again in July [1902] to see her sister when she had a holiday. This was at the end of July. She first went on a Monday, and stayed with her sister. At the end of the week she returned to Croydon. On July 26 she went again in consequence of getting a post-card. She saw Chapman in the bar, and asked him how her sister was, and he replied, 'She's in bed, dying hard.' She went upstairs to her sister, who was holding a cup of sienna tea in one hand, and a lump of sugar in the other. She suggested that her sister should have a doctor or go into hospital, and deceased told the witness, 'George has made this, but I can't take it because it makes me sick.'"

During Alice's visit with her sister, Maud complained that "George would not let me go into a hospital." When confronted Klosowski said, "If she wants to go anywhere she can have a doctor; there's one round the corner." At that point Alice helped her sister to get dressed, which took the better part of an hour. When the pair were finally able to go downstairs Klosowski gave his "wife" half a crown (about $2.00) and, with help from Alice, she slowly and very painfully made her way to the nearby doctor's house, but he was not in. Alice continued to explain to the court that it was at this point that she suggested, rather strongly, that her ill sister go at once to Guy's Hospital, which they did but Maud expressed her fear that Klosowski would find out. "We must not let George see us going."

Of course Klosowski did find out that the women had gone to the hospital. In fact, no fewer than six doctors had seen Maud. She was in such great pain that any touch made her cry out. She had also fainted while being examined, yet all they would, or possibly could do was to give her a draught of beer and a prescription for some medicine. Despite her obvious pain and failing condition she did not stay at the hospital—such was the power and control over her of her tormentor. Maud still feared Klosowski finding out that she had visited the doctors at the hospital. In fact, Klosowski was indeed furious that for a short period of time he had lost control and that Maud had been away from the Crown for so long.

The last time Alice would see her sister alive was on October 20 as she lay on her deathbed in a small and dark back room at the Crown. She had written to her sister at Guy's Hospital but had received no answer so she decided to visit whenever she had the chance. "When I saw her she was looking very thin, and bad. At first she went to the front bar to speak with Klosowski who told her that Maud was 'very ill.'" When she went upstairs Klosowski made certain that the two were not left alone for any great length of time, constantly coming and going as he checked Maud's pulse. What he was checking, of course, was the progress of his "work."

The London papers were reporting developments in the inquest closely, especially any last visits by family members. "When she was leaving [Alice] said, 'Good-by, Maud,' and her sister replied, 'Good-by, you won't see me again.' She died on October 22, and the day after [Alice] went to the Crown, and went with Chapman to the mortuary, where she saw her sister."

Daisy Marsh was then called to testify that she had visited the Monument for two full months, early in the relationship. She had been surprised to learn from her sister that Klosowski had asked Maud to marry him. She would also witness the celebration of the fake wedding at the pub later that day.

The final witness of the session proved to be of great interest to the coroner as she had nursed Maud from October 16 until her death. Jessie Toon informed the inquest that while she was attending Maud, Klosowski had given her injections and would never allow the nurse to handle them. Later, as the doctor demanded a postmortem, which Klosowski had informed Mrs. Toom that he did not want, Klosowski told Toom to tell the doctor that "If he asked, that the injections consisted of beef tea, milk and egg."

The day before Maud died Jessie Toom had overheard a conversation between Mrs. Marsh and the doctor. The doctor told Mrs. Marsh that, if anything happened, he would pay for the postmortem. Jessie soon told what she had heard to Klosowski, who was, to say the least, very upset. "It's that wicked old cat (Mrs. Marsh). She has been raking all this up against me. If she dies she wants to have her cut about and show me up. Now, be careful, Jessie, what you say to her, and take particular notice of what she says to you, and ask her in the course of conversation — not to let her think you are inquisitive, or that I want to know — whether she thinks there is anything wrong or any foul play." The true voice of serial killer Severin Klosowski, alias George Chapman, was finally being heard — loud and very clear! As for Jessie, she would follow his orders to the letter. With good reason she feared Chapman.

With that dramatic testimony Dr. Waldo adjourned the inquest for the day until the next Tuesday. He informed the court that the all-important medical evidence would be given at that time. Despite the all-day session the crowds continued to block streets outside the hall so much so that it was not until 6 P.M. that Klosowski could be moved, under heavy guard, back to his holding cell. Those who stayed got a quick look at the man now being call the Borough Poisoner of Southwark.

CORONER'S INQUEST— TUESDAY, NOVEMBER 25, 1902, SESSION 4

As London papers reported the news of the exhumation of Bessie Taylor at Lymm Cemetery in Cheshire, coroner Waldo resumed his inquest into the death of barmaid Maud Marsh. The first to be called was Louisa B. Cole, who had been employed as a domestic servant at the Crown. Because Klosowski had told police investigators that Maud may have been poisoned by a piece of bad rabbit meat, Waldo felt it was necessary to put to rest that possibility. It would not take long for Louisa to end that speculation. She testified that others in the household had also eaten the meal, including Klosowski himself, and no one had become ill that night.

> [Louisa] ate some of the rabbit. Mrs. Chapman's (Maud) portion was not eaten at once, but was kept for her in the oven for a time. She was not aware that the rabbit caused Mrs. Chapman to be ill. Nobody was ill so far as she knew at the time. She always cooked and prepared the food. There was pork and cabbage with potatoes cooked and served with the rabbit. There was no strange taste about the rabbit. Two days afterwards Mrs. Chapman helped herself to cold meat and potatoes, but she did not eat the meat. She went upstairs and lay down, and in half an hour afterwards was sick.

Louisa then told the court that, before Maud went upstairs, Klosowski had prepared some medicine for her to take. It had a milky color, which seemed to make Maud vomit. Clearly whatever made Maud ill that day, it had not been the rabbit. At trial the rabbit story would be thoroughly gone over by the prosecution and completely dismissed as nothing more than an attempt by Klosowski to remove suspicions from himself.

Interest then focused on Frank L. Gilbert, the mortuary attendant from Long Lane who had been contacted by Klosowski to remove Maud's corpse as soon as possible. Klosowski was eager to put Maud in the grave and out of his pub as quickly as possible before the doctors could examine his "wife."

> On telling Chapman that I came from Dr. Stoker, Chapman said he knew all about what I had come for. Chapman said his undertaker was Smith, in the Southwark Bridge Road, but he wanted the body

removed that night. I told Chapman that I thought Smith might not be up at the time, and Chapman told me to go and see, and he would make it all right. I went to Smith's place and he said he could not remove the body that night. I went to Smith's foreman and arranged for the body to be removed at 5 A.M. I then went back to the Crown and told Chapman, who said it was very awkward, because he wanted the body removed that night. Next day, October 23rd, I went to the Crown at 6 A.M., and assisted in removing the body. While in the mortuary we suddenly saw Mr. Chapman come in. I then said to Chapman "Who is the lady?" and he replied, "She is my wife, and 20 years of age." Chapman said he would like the body buried as quickly as possible.

After the body of Maud was removed from the Crown and delivered to the small mortuary, Mr. Gilbert went to Dr. Stoker's office to inform him of the removal. Stoker was not at his office at the time as he was preparing to conduct a private postmortem, which he knew was not fully authorized by the authorities. Nevertheless, with Frank Gilbert in attendance, the examination began at 11 P.M. that evening. Dr. Stoker did most of the work but he was assisted by Doctors French and Cotter. Dr. Stoker wanted to have two professional witnesses to the work in case there was a need at some future time for any testimony in the courts. When completed Gilbert testified that the medical men carried away several samples in "sealed glass jars" for further examination.

Mr. Gilbert informed the court how concerned Klosowski was even after Maud's body had been removed. The next day Klosowski visited Smiths and spoke to Gilbert. "On the Saturday, Chapman came and asked whether the body could be buried from the mortuary, as he did not want a fuss made about his place. The burial was to have taken place on October 27th, but on receiving an order from the coroner the body was not removed. I was present at the second postmortem, which was carried out by Dr. Freyberger, Dr. Stevenson, and another doctor whose name I do not know. They made an examination of the same body as the other doctors."

Dr. J. H. Targett was then called to relate to the court his recollections of Maud's pain-filled visit to Guy's Hospital. At the time Maud could not be properly examined due to her sensitivity to touch but as her time away from Klosowski increased, her pain and suffering decreased.

> I had the deceased under my observation on Monday, July 28th. She remained there until August 20th. She said she had been married ten weeks (actually the claim was 10 months). She also told me that she had been seized with severe pains in the lower part of the body; they would come and go, but on the whole they were increasing in their severity. I did not know that she had been an out-patient previously. She stayed in bed at the hospital. She had a good deal of fever, and was exceedingly tender over the stomach — so tender that a proper examination could not be made. There was constipation present, but that was not an important symptom. There was a high state of fever, and the temperature was up to 106. About August 11th the temperature came down almost normal. The pain was severe, and they had to administer opiates. After the fall of temperature the pain subsided. On August 15th or 16th the temperature previously noticed passed away. Her condition improved steadily until August 20th, when she took her discharge. I never came to any conclusion as to the cause of the illness. But at one time I thought she was suffering from inflammation of the covering of the bowels. It never entered my head that she was suffering from an irritant poison.

The medical history of Maud's slow and painful decline was then continued by Dr. J. M. Stoker of New Kent Road. The doctor had been called into the case by none other than Klosowski on October 10. Klosowski, the practiced serial killer with his own medical training, felt he could use the old doctor to certify death when he had finished his work on Maud. At his arrival, Dr. Stoker was informed that Maud had been suffering from vomiting and diarrhea. The cause of the problem was, of course, not discussed. It is interesting to note that Maud was so badly served by the doctor that when he first visited Maud at the Crown he never even examined her, taking his cues from Klosowski alone. His first formal examination of Maud would come the next day.

Dr. Stoker soon came to the conclusion that Maud was suffering from inflammation of the stomach, yet he could not find any reason why. For six days he came and went as Klosowski continued to poison Maud, and if testimony can be taken at face value, while the doctor was present. On that day Stoker informed Maud that she needed to go to the hospital as she was by then unable to hold down any food. By that time, however, Klosowski's hold on Maud's mind was complete and she protested bitterly and cried. Maud would simply not allow anyone to remove her from the Crown and away from her "husband." Her fate was sealed.

Resigned to the fact that Maud could not be persuaded to hospitalize herself, Stoker convinced the now gravely ill woman that she should at least be tended to by a full-time nurse. Five days before Maud died Dr. Stoker again visited the Crown and consulted with Jessie Toon, who had been engaged to nurse Maud during what would become her last days. Stoker instructed Mrs. Toon to administer Bismuth powders, but Maud was unable to keep anything down. And despite her weakened condition, when Maud died on October 22, Dr. Stoker expressed his surprise to the coroner's court that Maud had passed so quickly. He did not yet know of the massive final dose of antimony, which had been administrated by Klosowski.

At the coroner's court reporters would record the moment, only a few weeks earlier, when Dr. Stoker confronted Klosowski and informed him that he would not sign the death certificate until a closer look at Maud had been completed.

> The mother, Chapman, and the nurse were present. Chapman told [Dr. Stoker] that she died about noon. He went on the landing with Mr. Chapman, and told him, as he could not account for the cause of death, he would like a post-mortem. That was all that passed. Then he went back into the bedroom with Chapman, and told the mother he could not account for the death, and would like a post-mortem. Chapman said she died from exhaustion, and [Dr. Stoker] asked him what caused it; to which [Chapman] replied diarrhea and vomiting. Then [Dr. Stoker] asked what caused them, and Chapman made no answer. He told Chapman that other doctors had seen the deceased, and they might also want to know the cause of the illness and death. The body, he told Chapman, would have to be removed to the mortuary, and after the post-mortem would be returned to the house for burial.

The next day Maud's body was removed as Dr. Stoker contacted Doctor Cotter and Doctor French. Both men arrived to witness the postmortem but none of the men could find anything medically wrong with Maud which would point to why the formally healthy young woman had become ill or why she had died so suddenly. Samples were placed into glass bottles. These bottles were then taken to the Chemical Research Association the following day where the samples were subjected to tests for poison. The report from the association was conclusive: "We have examined the contents of the stomach, and are of opinion that it contains an appreciable amount of arsenic."

That was all Dr. Stoker needed to confirm his recently held suspicion that Maud had met with foul play, and that Klosowski, under his alias of George Chapman, was the one and only suspect. His next move was to inform both the police and the coroner. He also recalled how similar the Maud Marsh case was to Klosowski's earlier "wife" Bessie Taylor. "After the postmortem on Maud Marsh the two cases struck me as being very similar, and the result of the examination confirmed my suspicions. I did not tell Chapman of the similarity of the symptoms of the two women. There was no arsenic in any of the drugs I prescribed for the deceased."

Finally, Dr. Grapel related his conversation with Dr. Stoker about Maud's condition and how he came to the conclusion that Maud was suffering from ptomaine poisoning. Dr. Grapel informed the court about his wire to Dr. Stoker stating: "Look out for traces of arsenical poisoning," but it would be too late to save Maud.

With that, Coroner Waldo adjourned for the day, informing the jury that Dr. Stevenson would not be ready to testify for three weeks as he was working on other matters. Dr. Waldo then called for the fifth and final session to begin on December 18.

Coroner's Inquest— Thursday, December 18, 1902, Final Session

The final session of the coroner's inquest into the death of Maud Marsh began with the calling of Detective-Inspector George Godley, who went over what he had found at the Crown and gave a brief description of how he arrested Klosowski, whom he knew at the time to be George Chapman, supposed American expatriate and pub lease holder. He would soon learn a great deal more as the overconfident serial killer had failed to secure or cover up even the most damaging evidence of his three poison murders. Godley did not find, in any case, there are no documents or reports which would confirm it, any solid evidence of his direct involvement in the Torso or Ripper murders. Only later, when a detailed picture of his antecedents came to light, would he become a very real, albeit unofficial, suspect in London's most infamous crime series.

Godley informed the court that he had located "a large number of medical and scientific works, including the *Pharmacopeia*, a *Latin Pharmacopieca*, several volumes of *The Family Physician*, *A Practice of Physics*," which he presented to the jury. He also located a rare copy of James Berry's book on his life as an executioner. Berry was a well-known London executioner who had written an account of his official duties.

In one of the medical books Godley located what would become *the* key piece of evidence against Klosowski. It would lead the police directly to the origin of the poison and end any hope that Klosowski was anything other than a multiple murderer. "In one of the medical books was a label bearing the name of W. H. Davidson, a dispensing chemist of Hastings, and the words, "Tartar-emetic poisoning."

Not unlike many serial killers, Klosowski was a man who collected trophies of his kills, but he had been, to say the very least, careless in his storage of evidence which, if discovered, would surely mean his life. The question is asked whether he was careless or simply grew tired of the constant running and hiding. After all, he had been at "the game" and on the run for well over 15 years. Whatever the reason, the police had found a gold mine of evidence, which would clearly point to the man in the box as the only true suspect in the case of the Borough Poisoner.

Inspector Godley also described the easy manner in which he and Sgt. Kemp arrested Klosowski at the Crown. Klosowski announced that he had no idea what had caused his young "wife" to die, even though poison had been suggested. "I don't know anything about it; I don't know how she got the poison. She has been in Guy's Hospital for the same sort of sickness."

At 10:15 P.M., after dropping Klosowski off at the police station and returning to the Crown for a second look, Godley made his way back to the station to inform Klosowski that he was under arrest for the poison murder of Maud Marsh. Klosowski was stunned as he blurted out, "She did not die suddenly; if she had been poisoned she would have done. I am innocent!"

Mrs. Marsh and Mrs. Jessie Toon were then recalled to restate the fact that food and drink had been served to Maud by Klosowski alone as well as to note Klosowski's callousness in the face of Maud's death.

Doctor Freyberger, a pathologist at the London County Council, then described the postmortem he had assisted at on October 30. He noted that Maud's skin was "a yellowish green hue and bloodless, but there was no eruption about the body." (This was a clear sign of some type of metallic poison.) "There was no combination of causes to account for the death."

Dr. Thomas Stevenson was then called to give his report on the chemical analysis he had done on Maud's body. The doctor was the Home Office analyst at the time and he detailed, as best he could, the particulars about the poison which had killed the woman. He had earlier given the same testimony at the police court, which would continue well into the first few weeks of 1903. He stated: "It [is] difficult to say what a fatal dose of tartar-emetic was; but [I have] come to the conclusion that 15 grains was an average fatal dose, while the amount found in the various organs was 20.12 grains. An ordinary person would not tolerate more than 3 grains; one or two grains were a very sure emetic; a person with inflammation of the lungs could take more. A grain or two given continuously would have a very bad effect. [I] was of opinion that Marsh took a large dose not many hours before death, seeing the quantity that was found in the bowel."

It would be Dr. Stevenson's testimony which would conclusively show that not only had Maud Marsh been slowly and deliberately poisoned but also that her killer had given her a massive dose of antimony just as the doctors were coming to realize that fact, which may very well have saved her life. In view of all the chemical evidence along with Maud's general condition of purging and "excessive vomiting" the doctor concluded that "he had no doubt that death was due to antimonial poisoning," and that it could not have been accidental due to the length of time it took to take the life of Maud Marsh.

In what appeared to be an ironic postscript, the coroner recalled Doctors Targett, Stoker and Grapel to discuss the by now well-known symptoms of Maud before her death. Each doctor in turn stated that, indeed, the symptoms they had all noticed in their dying patient had been consistent with those of antimonial poisoning. Yet none of the doctors had come forward in time to save Maud's life.

It would be left to Dr. Richard Bodmer, the public analyst for the borough of Bermondsey, to verify that his work at the Clinical Research Association did indeed find arsenic and antimony in the samples with which he had been supplied. He had tested Maud's stomach and liver from samples in sealed bottles, which had been given to him by Dr. Stoker. The case of poisoning was now airtight, and the coroner summed up the evidence for the jury.

Doctor Waldo first noted that Dr. Stoker had not been on firm ground performing a private postmortem as critical evidence could have been lost. As it turned out, however, the case was not compromised. The doctor continued:

> Having reviewed the evidence, he remarked that the inquiry resolved itself into their answering two questions—1: What in their opinion was the cause of death, and if they were of opinion, as they must be, that it was due to antimonial poisoning? Then 2: How and by whom, in their opinion, was the poison administered? They had to consider whether Maud took the poison herself for any illegal purpose, or to commit suicide, or whether any person or perhaps administered it. If they found on the evidence, which was circumstantial, that the accused administered it with intention to kill, then it would be their duty to return a verdict of willful murder against him. But if they thought evidence against him was not sufficient, then they could say that death was due to antimonial poisoning, but there was not sufficient evidence for them to come to the conclusion that he had administered it.

It would not take long for the South London jury to reach its decision. After only 20 minutes the men returned to a hushed inquest room "and announced that they had come to the conclusion that the death of Maud Eliza Marsh was caused by antimonial poisoning...."

December 20, 1902
*Southwark and Bermondsey Recorder and
South London Gazette,*
BOROUGH POISON MYSTERY
CORONER'S INQUEST.
VERDICT.

The inquiry as to the death of Maud Marsh was concluded by the Coroner, Dr. Waldo, on Thursday afternoon, when a verdict of WILFUL MURDER. was recorded by the jury against George Chapman.

With the work of the coroner's inquest now complete, London authorities could devote their full attention to the ongoing police court hearings and the investigation into the mysterious deaths of Mrs. Spink and Bessie Taylor as well as to a detailed examination of how and why Maud Marsh and the others had been murdered by a lone and very determined serial killer.

Unofficial London and the press, however, would begin to ask whether or not the man in the dock, soon to be fighting for his life, was none other than Jack the Ripper. And more importantly, would the investigators be able to finally prove just who had held title to London's most infamous and as yet unknown serial killer? To say the very least there was much interest in the proceedings and even more speculation as to what the outcome would be.

> "On Thursday afternoon Mr. Sydney himself had a long interview with his client, and found the accused confident that he will be acquitted."
>
> — News Reports

POSTMORTEMS OF THE BOROUGH POISONER VICTIMS

The official postmortems on the victims of the Borough Poisoner were conducted by Dr. Thomas Stevenson in the reverse order of their deaths. Dr. Stevenson was a medical doctor who would become the official medical analyst for the Home Office on these cases. At the time of the trial the doctor was a lecturer on forensic medicine at Guy's Hospital and he was well known for his abilities to analyze poison cases. He had represented the Home Office for 31 years when he was called to work on these murders. His investigation would become key to understanding the work of a cold-blooded serial killer.

Maude Elizabeth Marsh — Postmortem conducted on October 30–31, 1902
Elizabeth "Bessie" Taylor — Postmortem conducted on November 22, 1902
Mary Isabella Spink — Postmortem conducted on December 9, 1902

The following postmortem reports are taken from the testimony of Doctor Thomas Stevenson given during the poison murder trial of Severin Klosowski, alias George Chapman, as reported in *Trial of George Chapman*, edited by Hargrave Lee Adam.

Adam, who was acquainted with Sir Charles Warren, metropolitan police commissioner at the time of the Ripper murders; his assistant Sir Robert Anderson; Chief Constable Melville Macnaughten as well as Inspector Godley, would put together the most complete work ever written on Klosowski's trial. It is a vital first source to review before moving on to the story of the dark trial of serial killer Severin Klosowski.

Postmortem Testimony on Maude Elizabeth Marsh*
Murdered on October 22, 1902
Conducted by Doctor Thomas Stevenson — October 30–31, 1902

Assisted by Doctor P. G. Cotter, Doctor James Maurice Stoker and Doctor Emile Freyberger. (Dr. Freyberger had recently been appointed pathologist to the London County Council.)

The body had been dead fully eight days, but there was not much decomposition, much less than I should expect in a body so long dead, considering the time and season. The scalp covering the skull was dry. That indicated that there was little fluid in the tissues. The skull and brain were normal; there was no hemorrhage or disease in the brain. The spinal cord was normal, and there was no sign of disease there. The tongue was yellow, coated, and swollen. The air passages of the lungs were quite clear, and the lungs free from disease. There was a good deal of fat about the heart, but that would not have affected her health much unless it had gone much further. It invaded the muscles to the extent of about one-third. The mesenteric glands were much swollen. The stomach had been taken away, but it was given to me by the coroner's officer before the end of the post-mortem. The blood vessels of the bowels were unusually red injected with blood, but not to a very marked extent. The

---

*This evidence was given during the trial of Severin Klosowski alias George Chapman on March 18, 1903.

mucous membrane of the bowels was swollen and slimy, and was in the condition which we usually know as sub-acute enteritis, which is inflammation of the membrane lining the bowels. There was a good deal of liquid in the bowels, but only a little semi-solid fecal matter, which was about the sigmoid flexure of the colon. One of the glands showed that she had probably been a person subjected to habitual constipation. The whole of the rectum had been removed. I found no ulceration of the bowels. I examined the pancreas, the spleen, and the kidneys. They were all sound and healthy. The liver had been detached, but it was in the abdomen. A small portion had been removed. It was rather dry and greasy, but there was no condition which would affect her health materially.

I examined the womb and ovaries. They were perfectly normal. She had never apparently borne a child, nor were there any signs that she had been far advanced in pregnancy. Menstruation was just upon ceasing. I found no evidence of any natural disease which would account for her death.

I suspected that she had died from some form of irritant poison, which had set up enteritis. I had heard of the question of arsenical poisoning, but I came to the conclusion on making the examination that it was not arsenic, but some other metallic poison. I then removed the brain, some blood from the cavity of the chest, the spleen, the gall bladder, which was full of bile, the liver, the kidneys, the contents of the bowels, the bowels themselves, and also some blood from the abdominal cavity. They were all rather light in weight. The drain on the fluid caused by vomiting would account for that in a great measure.

On the 31st I examined the stomach from the jar. There were signs of putrefaction externally, and internally it was pink and injected with blood. The blood vessels were prominent and redder than usual. Internally it was coated with a good deal of yellow, slimy mucus, which became an orange color at the bowel end. I did not find any ulcers or loss of substance. I examined the contents in the stomach and portion of the liver and rectum in the jars.

I made an analysis of various parts of the body. Every portion of the body which I examined had antimony in it. I found antimony in the stomach and its contents, in the bowels and their contents, in the liver, bile, spleen, kidneys, the fluid which I took from the abdominal cavity, the blood from the cavity of the chest, and in the brain. I made tests for arsenical poisoning. I found traces of arsenic in a small quantity, and I formed the opinion that death had not resulted from it. Arsenic is sometimes found in antimony when it is impure. *I came to the conclusion that death was caused by poisoning with antimony in a soluble form — tartar-emetic or metallic antimony* (emphasis added). That is one of the scheduled poisons.

I did not find any bismuth, but the tests for bismuth are not so complete. If there was any it must have been infinitesimal. I have never heard in late years of a case where bismuth has caused such symptoms as these, or caused death. Bismuth is now purified from arsenic and other impurities. Five grains is an ordinary dose. In the cases I have heard of where death was caused by bismuth I think that 120 grains must have been taken. I found no trace of impure bismuth in this case. I found 0.32 of a grain of metallic antimony in the contents of the stomach and 5.99 grains in the contents of the bowels. That indicated to me that *there must have been a large dose of antimony given within a few hours of death*, as it is soluble in water. It had not been got rid of by purging or vomiting. In the liver I found 0.71 of a grain of metallic antimony, in the kidneys 0.14 of a grain, in the brain 0.17 of a grain — in all I found 7.24 grains, the bulk of which was in the bowel. I deduce from that there was a good deal more antimony in the body. Antimony can be made soluble in the form of tartar-emetic or emetic-tartar, which is a white powder, soluble in water. It does not change the appearance of the water. Emetic-tartar is not altogether antimony. 7.24 grain of metallic antimony would represent 20.12 grains of tartar-emetic, the proportion being, roughly, three to one.

I did not calculate the amount of tartar-emetic in the whole body, but from my experience I should put it at between 25 and 30 grains. When tartar-emetic or antimony is administered, as a rule the greater part of it is very quickly ejected; purging relieves it. The effect of the poison itself generally takes a very considerable time before it causes death. Death has occurred in many cases where it was given in repeated moderate doses. Vomiting and purging make people waste away. It produces gastro-enteritis, and they also appear to die from failure of the heart. Antimony depresses the circulation and quickens the pulse, but gives it a very feeble power. Two grains of tartar-emetic have killed, but that is not ordinary. I should put the ordinary fatal dose at probably 15 grains; others put it at 10, and even that might not be fatal if the greater portion of it is vomited.

People have taken tartar-emetic in much larger quantities and have recovered where it has been quickly vomited. I am of opinion that if 2 or 3 grains were given repeatedly to a healthy person it would eventually cause death. When doses of antimony are given from time to time the symptoms are great depression, profuse perspiration, followed by nausea and vomiting. Purging is set up with pain in the abdomen, and usually after a time there is a burning or metallic sensation in the throat and stomach; there is a great thirst. Spasms are quite common, and patients fall sometimes into a comatose or semi-comatose state. They are generally very pallid, and sometimes they get quite jaundiced and dark under the eyes, and thin and worn. It is sometimes the appearance, apart from other symptoms, which indicates that the patient is approaching death. In the case of Mr. Braywood, it was his appearance which excited the suspicion that he would die. Sir William Gull and others who saw him, although he was apparently going on well, thought afterwards he could not get on so well. That was a case of poisoning by tartar-emetic.

If tartar-emetic is taken in a strong solution it has a somewhat metallic, but sweetish taste, but when taken diluted it does not have much taste. It can be covered up by food or medicine. People take antimony wine, which is sherry with antimony in it, and yet not know that anything is wrong. If doses had been going on for some time so as to set up irritation of the mucous membrane that would set up the burning feeling in the throat. Antimony can be dissolved and given by injections, or put into injections. That would be very dangerous; it would be quickly absorbed into the rectum and then into the body. The vomit in a case of poisoning by antimony would be at first the contents of the stomach, and then it would become green or yellow.

I got a great number of bottles from Sergeant Kemp. I examined them. There was antimony or arsenic in one of them. Some of them had contained photographic chemicals. I examined the bismuth powders found in the room, proved to have come from Dr. Stoker. They were free from antimony and arsenic. I also examined the bismuth from Dr. Stoker's surgery. It was pure and a very good specimen. The two bottles which contained medicine had no trace of antimony or arsenic. The other one had two or three drops at the bottom of it. I do not know if it had been washed out. I found bismuth and antimony in it. I should say there was quite as much antimony as bismuth in it. There was enough antimony to give several full doses. Tartar-emetic can be dissolved in water, so as not to be apparent, and this could be mixed with a bismuth preparation. It is also soluble in brandy; brandy of ordinary strength will take up about 2 grains to the ounce. A tablespoonful of such medicine would be a full emetic dose. It is much more soluble in brandy and water than in plain brandy. These two bottles contain brandy and water, two parts water and one part brandy. There is tartar-emetic in one of them. This one, which contains an ounce, is probably a fatal dose. I could find nothing to account for death except poisoning by antimony. Antimony might be given to produce perspiration and for bad colds, but only from one-twenty-fourth to one-twenty-sixth of a grain to a dose. Half a grain to a grain would be an emetic. Death would not ensue from one dose of that strength or cause great pain. If vomited, it would not produce diarrhea. All the signs I found at the post-mortem would not be caused by such doses as that.

Postmortem Testimony on Elizabeth "Bessie" Taylor*
Murdered on February 13, 1901
Conducted by Doctor Thomas Stevenson — November 22, 1902

The body was covered with a mouldy growth, but otherwise was fresh. There was no putrefaction and no odor. The tissues were dry. The muscles had a red and freshest appearance. There was a fecal odor in the abdomen, but no putrefactive odor. Although the features had mould on them, one could follow the shape and general contour. The breast was shrunken and the whole body dry. Generally when bodies decompose they become wet and slimy. This [body was] extremely well preserved except for the superficial skin.

I made an examination of the various organs. On the base of the right lung I found old adhesions from old pleurisy. The lungs were shrunken and dry, but otherwise healthy and free from deposits or cavities. Adhesions are quite common in people of good health in middle life and after. The heart and its valves were healthy. The stomach was empty, but its vessels were filled with dark blood to an unusual extent. On the inner surface of the gullet end of the stomach there was a patch about four inches in diameter of a cinnabar red color which denoted gastritis. There was no ulceration or perforation or any loss of substance in the mucous membrane of the stomach. The cinnabar red color extended more or less through the bowels, indicating enteritis. The inner surface of the bowel was coated with a yellow paint-like stuff, which was sulphide of antimony. The pancreas, spleen, kidneys, and liver were all shrunken by time, but otherwise normal. The womb, ovaries, appendages, and bladder were quite normal. I found no trace of cancer nor uterine trouble. I could find no sign of any cause of death. I examined the brain. It was a good deal decomposed. There was no sign of hemor-

---

*This evidence was given during the final day of the trial of Severin Klosowski alias George Chapman on March 19, 1903.

rhage, or any other recognizable disease. I found no intestinal obstruction. *I formed the opinion that she died from gastro-enteritis, which was due to some irritant poison.*

I removed the stomach, bowels, liver, spleen, kidneys, heart, brain, and lungs, and subjected them all to analysis and examination. The analysis showed that antimony was present in all those parts. There was no other poison. In the stomach there was 0.12 of a grain of metallic antimony, in the bowel 8.43 grains, in the liver 1.64 grains, in the kidneys 0.30 of a grain, making a total of 10.49 grains. That represents of tartar-emetic in the stomach 0.32 of a grain, in the bowel 23.43 grains, in the liver 4.55 grains, in the kidneys 0.82 of a grain, making in all 29.12 grains. I cannot find any recorded case of such a quantity having been found in the bowel after death. *It suggests that she had some large dose not long before her death.* I examined the earth about the coffin, but found no poison.

Postmortem Testimony on Mary Isabella Spink*
Murdered on December 25, 1897
Conducted by Doctor Thomas Stevenson — December 9, 1902

I attended at St. Patrick's Cemetery, Leytonstone, on 9th December, 1902, and examined the body in the coffin bearing the name plate of Mary Isabella Chapman, who died on 25th December, 1897. I saw the lid removed. The body was altogether remarkable; the face and head were those of a woman who might have been coffined that day from the appearance. Even the eyes were un-ruptured, a very unusual circumstance. There was not the least difficulty in recognizing her. The muscles had a fresh appearance. All the parts of the body cut rather leathery, like shoe leather, and, of course, were drier than in a fresh body. All the parts of the body except the brain were preserved. The stomach was unusually pink externally. That was from the blood in the vessels being more than usually good. Its inner coat was of a peculiar cinnabar red color, and towards the bowel end there was a patch [of] blood which had been effused. There was no sign of perforation of ulceration, there was no loss of substance in the mucous membrane. Towards the bowel end there were some old scars of years' standing. The bowels were not ruptured. The tube was intact. Internally the bowel had the same red color as the stomach. There was no ulceration. The liver was pale, but firm in texture and fairly normal. The spleen, the kidneys, the bladder, the heart, and the lungs were all normal.

There was no sign of phthisis; that generally indicates disease of the lungs. The cause of death was gastroenteritis. There was no other cause. There was nothing to indicate that the woman had been a confirmed drunkard. If she had drunk it had not produced any serious injury to the kidneys or liver. The inflammation which I found in the stomach was not attributable to alcohol.

I removed the stomach, bowels, liver, kidneys, spleen, lungs, heart, brain, and some of the muscles, and submitted them all to analysis, except the lungs. They all contained antimony. It had permeated to the muscle of the thigh. In the bowels I found 0.41 of a grain of metallic antimony, in the liver 0.87 of a grain, in the kidneys 0.06, and in the stomach 0.03, which makes altogether 1.37 grains. That would represent as emetic-tartar 3.83 grains. There was more in her liver than I found in Maud Marshs. *That quantity points to a large amount of antimony having been absorbed into the body, and would indicate a considerable dose having been taken some hours before death,* or the continuous administration of small doses. The purging and vomiting would get rid of a good deal of the antimony.

I came to the conclusion that the cause of death was poisoning by antimony, and I attribute the preservation of the body to the antimony. It has not been thoroughly recognized that preservation is one of the effects of antimony, but it has been found in previous cases to be a preservative. The fact of antimony being found in the muscles would not indicate that doses of antimony had been going on for some time, because I think it would quickly pass to every vascular part of the body. I tested the earth round the coffin to see if it yielded any poison. Evidently the body had not been touched by water. The coffin and its contents were well preserved.

Testimony on Maud Elizabeth Marsh†
Murdered on October 22, 1902
Private post-mortem conducted by Doctor James Maurice Stoker at the
Southwark Mortuary — October 23, 1902
Assisted by Doctor P. G. Cotter and witnessed by Dr. French

---

*This evidence was given during the trial of Severin Klosowski alias George Chapman on March 18, 1903. Overseeing the exhumation of the body was Mr. E. Kearley, superintendent of Leytonstone Cemetery.

†This evidence was given during the poison murder trial of Severin Klosowski alias George Chapman on March 18, 1903, as reported in *Trial of George Chapman* edited by Hargrave L. Adam.

On 23rd October I made a post-mortem examination with Dr. Cotter. I examined the liver, the kidneys, the lungs, and the ovaries. They were healthy. I examined the intestines and the stomach externally. *I could not arrive at any opinion as to the cause of death.* I did not see anything to account for the symptoms causing the death. I had taken two glass bottles with me when I went to make the examination, and I had taken pains to see that they were chemically clean. I removed the stomach and its contents from the body without opening it. I tied it up and put it straight into one of the bottles. I also removed portions of the rectum and the liver and put them into the other bottle. The deceased was not pregnant. There were no traces of pregnancy or any affection of the womb. I took the bottles away myself and sealed them up, and the next day I took them to Dr. Bodmer, of the Clinical Research Association. I was present at the post-mortem examination made by Dr. Stevenson.

Chapter 11

The Police Court Does Its Work: The Case of the Borough Poisoner

Saturated with Antimony
— Doctor Thomas Stevenson

THE INQUEST DEBATES—NOVEMBER–DECEMBER 1902

The work of the police court would press forward along with the coroner's inquest despite the debate in government about evidence being given in coroner's court while a criminal investigation was ongoing. Mr. Archibald H. Bodkin, the director of public prosecutions, who was representing the government in this case would give his opinion to the Police Court magistrate, Cecil M. Chapman. Mr. Chapman had taken over from Paul Taylor, who had gone on vacation. Hargrave L. Adam would later describe Archibald Bodkin as, "Tall, broad shouldered, rugged of countenance, and commanding of respect. He has large gray eyes, which are capable of expressing a wonderful depth of retrospection. Bodkin, is a strong opponent of the premature holding of coroner's inquests in murder cases; he is of the opinion that they seriously impede the police in carrying out their difficult duties, and are detrimental to the true interests of law and justice and public security."

Mr. Bodkin would begin his work at the police court by stating, "So far as this day's proceedings are concerned, I do not propose to

Police Court Magistrate Cecil M. Chapman (original from *Trial of George Chapman*, 1930).

open the case or give any evidence which might be called controversial, for the reason that there is another inquiry proceeding, and I cannot help thinking somewhat unfortunately proceeding, contemporaneously with the magisterial inquiry, and that inquiry is not bound by the ordinary rules of evidence. I think it would be in favor of the defendant himself if the gentleman conducting that inquiry either completed it according to his discretion, or adjourned it until this inquiry is finished."

As would be expected the police were in agreement with Mr. Bodkin as he fought to keep as much out of the record as possible in order to present the main evidence during the expected upcoming trial. Coroner Doctor Waldo also made his feelings known after he had completed his inquest into Maud Marsh's death. He stated: "I went into [the case] as fully as I could with what evidence was available [during] the Chapman case. Dr. Stevenson was prevented from giving evidence before me until he had been before the magistrate [police court] and Mr. Bodkin, for the Crown, although the police from Scotland Yard had agreed to produce him before me when wanted by me. Mr. Bodkin apparently did not like my having so full an inquiry which was in Chapman's interest, and criticized me in the magistrate's court, which was reported in the *Times*. His feelings then, as now, [is] against the coroner and jury having a full inquiry into cases charged before a magistrate or bench of J.P.'s."

Coroner Waldo was also unhappy at new laws recently passed, which he felt placed an unjust burden on the accused. He affirmed: "I think the new Coroner's Act, clipping the wings of the coroner in cases in which there is a charge of a crime by the police, will be against the interests of the prisoner, especially before a legal coroner, as in London and in other big cities."

Despite the legal and legislative debates moving through the British government at the time, both the coroner's inquest and police courts continued their respective lines of investigation into the death of Maud Marsh. In the police court, however, investigations would include the murders of Mrs. Spink and Bessie Taylor, which gave a greater depth of understanding into the murderous career of one "George Chapman." Even though a few investigative toes would inevitably be stepped on, both investigations would be successfully completed with many surprising revelations into the life and times of the Victorian serial killer.

Counsel for the British government, A.H. Bodkin (original from *Trial of George Chapman*, 1930).

POLICE COURT— WEDNESDAY, NOVEMBER 12, 1902

Robert Marsh was first to be called to the dock to give essentially the same testimony he had given at the coroner's inquest the day before. When he had finished, Bodkin pressed the grieving father about the unwelcome (by Klosowski) doctor's visit to see Maud.

Mr. Bodkin—Did the accused say anything about Dr. Grapel's visit?
Mr. Robert Marsh—He said, "If one doctor cannot cure her, fifty cannot." He said he did not like the idea of Dr. Grapel's calling.
Mr. Cecil Chapman—What reply did you make?
Mr. Marsh—I said, "It is no good making a bother; I wished the doctor to come."

Mr. Sydney, who represented Klosowski stepped in to ask a few questions of Robert Marsh.

Mr. Sydney—From first to last did your daughter and the accused live on the best of terms together?
Mr. Marsh—I have had no complaints.
Mr. Sydney—There was never any friction, so far as you saw?
Mr. Marsh—No.
Mr. Sydney—During the time of her illness, did the accused give you and other members of your family every information?
Mr. Cecil Chapman—That is rather a difficult question. If you ask him whether the accused answered the question put to him.
Mr. Sydney—I put it further than that—that he volunteered information.
Mr. Cecil Chapman—He gave them such information as they received, but there might be other information which was not given.
Mr. Sydney—I will put it in another form. I think you made inquires about your daughter's health. Did he answer frankly?
Mr. Marsh—Yes.

Robert Marsh was excused and Magistrate Cecil Chapman called for the hearing to continue in a little more than two weeks, which would allow the police enough time to develop more leads into the unfolding case of the Borough Poisoner. As for the accused, he was once again ordered held without bail.

The delay would also allow the ongoing coroner's inquest to continue, and perhaps finish, so as to avoid any confusion or delays in prosecutor Bodkin's examination of the evidence before the police court.

Police Court—Friday, November 28, 1902

As rain fell on a chilly London, Coller's Rents once again played host to the Southwark poisoning case of Maud Marsh at police court. Maud's mother, Eliza Marsh, was sworn in and, as did her husband before her, reported that she resided at 14 Longfellow Road in West Croydon.

By this time Mrs. Marsh had already given evidence at the coroner's inquest, which she now repeated at the police court. Marsh informed the court that "in response to an advertisement inserted by the accused for a barmaid" she and her young daughter had visited the man she would know as George Chapman at his business at the Crown public house. Beyond the lie of his false name Klosowski informed Mrs. Marsh that the ring on his finger was indeed a wedding ring, but that he was "sadly a widower." He also informed Mrs. Marsh that he liked her daughter and she "would suit him nicely." He would say much more later.

Mr. Bodkin—Did he use any other word instead of "Like"?
Mrs. Marsh—I cannot exactly say. He said he had taken her about, and asked to be engaged to her.
Mr. Bodkin—Did you agree to it there and then?
Mrs. Marsh—I said I would ask her father about it.

After a brief discussion of the will being signed, which Klosowski had written in Maud's supposed favor under his alias of George Chapman, Bodkin focused on Maud's illness and last moments.

Mr. Bodkin — Did your daughter make some statement as to what she attributed her illness to? Did she mention anything which she had taken?
Mrs. Marsh — Yes; and I asked the accused if he thought the rabbit of which she had eaten part was the cause of the illness.
Mr. Bodkin — What did he say?
Mrs. Marsh — He said he could not tell, or he did not know. He also said they all had some of the rabbit. I stayed with my daughter all that night.
Mr. Bodkin — The next day did you say anything to Dr. Stoker?
Mrs. Marsh — I suggested calling in my own medical man, Dr. Grapel, of Croydon.
Mr. Bodkin — And he agreed?
Mrs. Marsh — Yes. I stayed all that day and night. The next morning I was suffering from sickness and diarrhea myself. I noticed a change in my daughter's condition, and saw that she was dying.
Mr. Bodkin — Did she say anything shortly before she died?
Mrs. Marsh — She said "I am going."
Mr. Bodkin — Was the accused in the room then?
Mrs. Marsh — Yes.
Mr. Bodkin — Did he say anything?
Mrs. Marsh — Yes, "Where are you going?"
Mr. Bodkin — Did your daughter say anything to the accused before she died?
Mrs. Marsh — "Good-bye George." Then she died.
Mr. Bodkin — Did he remain in the room?
Mrs. Marsh — He closed her eyes and then he went on the landing.
Mr. Bodkin — Did you see what he did?
Mrs. Marsh — He cried.
Mr. Bodkin — Did you tell the accused anything about a conversation you had with Dr, Grapel?
Mrs. Marsh — I told him Dr. Grapel said she was poisoned.
Mr. Bodkin — Did the accused say anything to that?
Mrs. Marsh — He said he did not know how, unless it was the rabbit.
Mr. Bodkin — Did you make any reply?
Mrs. Marsh — I said "Dr. Grapel says you do not find arsenic in rabbit."

To conclude the matter of the rabbit, William Bird of 88 Broadwall was called to the stand. Bird was a general dealer in rabbits and also rented out horses and carts. He stated that he had "bought my rabbits from Farringdon Market and never had any complaints about them." Chapman's servant, Louisa Cole, had purchased the rabbit in the New Cut Market from Mr. Bird and would testify that she had "cooked it in an enamel pan and served it in the first floor front room. Nobody became ill after eating the rabbit."

With the rabbit question answered and Mrs. Marsh's testimony complete, attention was drawn to Mrs. Louisa Sarah Morris, a married sister of Maud's, who related to the court a strange conversation she had had with Klosowski. Klosowski was, of course, at the time feeding Maud a continuous diet of poison when Louisa questioned him about Maud's condition. Klosowski informed her that her sister had constipation, prompting the following conversation:

Louisa — That is funny, because I saw her a short time before and she had diarrhea.
Klosowski — She should have done as I have told her, taken the medicine I gave her. If she comes out of this lot she will do as I tell her.
Louisa — It seems very funny that the doctors cannot find out what is the matter with her.
Klosowski — I could giver her a bit like that (snapping his fingers), and fifty doctors could not find out.

When Louisa challenged him on the meaning of what he had just said Klosowski was silent. Perhaps he knew at that point that he had said far too much. Indeed, it would be this statement, when reported to Maud's mother and father, which would solidify their distrust of Klosowski, alias George Chapman. Louisa would also inform the court that Klosowski would not allow anyone to be alone with Maud for long periods of time and would "frequently enter the room each time taking Maud's hand and feeling her pulse."

Alice May Marsh, another sister of Maud's, was then called to testify about the callousness of her sister's so-called husband. She related an incident at a tea house near the Crown the day after her sister had died. With his confidence fully restored, Klosowski asked Alice to work at his pub. "There's a chance for you as barmaid now, Alice; will you come?" A shocked and grieving Alice could only reply, "No, thanks, London does not suit me."

To end the day's testimony Mrs. Jessie Toon, who had been engaged by Klosowski to nurse his dying "wife," was called. She would confirm how Maud had been attended to by Klosowski. "The unfortunate woman vomited frequently, and the accused injected what he said was beef tea and milk, but I never saw him mix the food. (These green injectors now rest in Scotland Yard's infamous Black Museum, the name of which has now been changed in the interests of political correctness to the Museum of Crime.) One or two injectors were made a day. Maud Marsh would not take the medicine. Sometimes she appeared to have fits, and her limbs became rigid—she was in such pain. She was always thirsty and used to ask for water, but the accused gave her brandy. On the morning of the girl's death the accused brought up some brandy and water. I tasted it, and it burnt my mouth and throat."

Mrs. Toon had been a close up eyewitness to a slow murder and had not realized what she was seeing despite tasting the brandy, which had burnt her mouth and throat. She suspected nothing and had done even less. The day's testimony was complete.

Police Court—Wednesday, December 17, 1902

For most of December the police court continued with testimony, which mirrored, for the most part, that which had been given during the coroner's inquest with the exception of evidence given by chemist William Henry Davidson. Davidson's recollections and his little book of poisons would prove conclusively that the man he had known as George Chapman, local barber and trained man of medicine, was the man in the docket now identified as Severin Klosowski, the customer of his in 1897 who purchased a very deadly poison. Examined by Bodkin in the morning, Davidson's memory proved to be excellent as he recalled the morning of April 3, 1897, when "Chapman" came into his shop for some white powder.

The retired chemist from Hastings testified that he had kept an accurate "Poisons Book" in accordance with the Pharmacy Act. The act required any individual who purchased certain poisons to sign the book and to state what the poison was to be used for. Chapman had asked about some tartar-emetic the day before and had returned on the third to pick up his ounce of death. He signed "G. Chapman" and wrote "take" in the column used to indicate the reason for the purchase. The good Mr. Davidson then wrote out the instructions on the small red label with the warning that the contents should be "used with caution."

It would be that small label, which Klosowski had kept for years, which would lead authorities directly to Davidson, placing Klosowski firmly on the road to the gallows.

November 29, 1902
Southwark and Bermondsey Record and
South London Gazette
SOUTHWARK POISONING
CASE.

EXHUMATION AT LYMM.

FURTHER EVIDENCE

The mystery surrounding the death of Miss Maud Marsh at the "Crown Tavern," High Street, Borough, has received fresh development this week, first by the

EXHUMATION

of the remains of Mrs. Bessie Chapman, the second wife of George Chapman, the prisoner who stands charged with the murder of Miss Marsh, formerly a barmaid in his employ. The exhumation took place on Saturday morning at Lymm Cemetery, Cheshire. A force of a dozen constables was posted in the picturesque country cemetery from an early hour. The grave in which the second Mrs. Chapman lay beneath her mother and father was surrounded by a screen of white sheets, and at five o'clock in the morning three gravediggers commenced the task of exhumation with the aid of lanterns. The morning was bitterly cold, and the ground was frozen to a depth of several inches. The work of bringing the three coffins to the surface was accomplished at eight o'clock, and they were ranged in a row by the side of the grave. As the morning wore on curious villagers gathered round the churchyard, but they were told by the police that the exhumation had taken place on Thursday, and they passed on. At ten o'clock Dr. Stevenson, expert to the Home Office, drove up to the cemetery in a carriage, accompanied by two assistants. The trio immediately proceeded to a temporary mortuary, a hut at the far end of the cemetery, where the coffin containing the body of Mrs. Bessie Chapman was brought for examination.

At this time those present in the cemetery were Dr. Stevenson, his two assistants, the clergyman who holds the benefice of Lymn parish, Detective-inspector Godley, of the M (Southwark) Division of Police, who has charge of the investigation, Mr. W. Tulle, an assistant undertaker to Mr. A. Smith, of Southwark Bridge Road, two brothers of Bessie Chapman, and a husband of Bessie Chapman's sister. Mr. Tulle, at the request of the detective officers, scraped the dirt off the plate on the coffin, and displayed the simple inscription recording the death of Bessie Chapman in February, 1901, and at once proceeded to unscrew the lid of the coffin. The body was found to be in a fair condition, and the two brothers easily identified it. Under the personal direction of Dr. Stevenson, the two assistants removed the chief organs of the body, and placed them in square glass jars, which were duly sealed and labeled. The various jars were placed into a large box, which was in its turn sealed, and removed to Dr. Stevenson's carriage, and shortly afterwards distributed to London. In the meantime the remains of Bessie Chapman were replaced in the coffin, and the three coffins were again interred, the clergyman reading the funeral service over the fresh interment. The three gravediggers filled in the grave, and the stone was carefully replaced.

Chapter 12

The Police Court Continues: Focus on Mrs. Spink and Bessie Taylor

That he did feloniously kill and slay...
— Charge Sheet — Southwark Police Court

With testimony now complete into the Maud Marsh matter, the prosecution team pressed forward with evidence linking Chapman/Klosowski to the deaths of Mrs. Spink and Bessie Taylor (Mrs. Chapman I and II). Before the start of that inquiry, however, Detective-inspector Godley was called to give evidence of his investigation and his arrest of Klosowski at the Crown. He would also add that he had located "a revolver fully loaded, and a rough kind of diary." The location of those two pieces of evidence makes for interesting speculation to be sure. Can they still be found at the Black Museum and can that pistol be used to link Klosowski to the last American murder of Jack the Ripper? That investigation has never been conducted.

POLICE COURT — WEDNESDAY, DECEMBER 31, 1902

By this time the coroner's inquest had been completed and the verdict of "Willful Murder" recorded against George Chapman. The police court now had a set of powerful evidentiary statements as well as autopsy reports linking Klosowski to a series of brutal murders over a period of some years. What official London had yet to suspect was that they were dealing with a man who had been a serial killer for a great deal longer than that!

Once again Bodkin would step forward to introduce as evidence a brief history of the accused as it pertained to the murders of two women who had called Chapman husband. As before, the police court was filled to capacity.

> The accused has been charged with the murder of Mrs. Spink on 25th December, 1897 and of Bessie Taylor, or Chapman, on 13th February, 1901, these two women having each lived with him for some time as his wife. The evidence with regard to the death of Maud Marsh disclosed that the death was caused by the administration of antimony in its soluble form of tarter-emetic; and in the long list of cases which had been decided it had been held that evidence of previous similar cases was relevant to a specific case when the symptoms and the post-mortem appearances were the same.
> It would be shown that in the case of Mrs. Spink and Bessie Taylor the symptoms of illness which preceded their deaths were just the same as with Maud Marsh, and the post-mortem appearances

gave rise to the inference of antimonial poisoning, and, indeed, the evidence would show that the accused murdered both of them.

In regard to cases of poisoning, it [is] not altogether remarkable that in a great many of them the persons accused had belonging to, or had been connected with, the profession of medicine; and therefore, it [is] not surprising now to know that the accused himself had passed through various stages of examination in medicine and surgery in Poland, the country from which he came. From certain papers found in his possession it appeared that George Chapman was a name which he had adopted since living, in this country, and that his real name was Severin Klosowski.

In 1888 the accused came to London, and he became a jobbing hairdresser in Whitechapel. He soon afterwards had a small hairdresser's shop in the Whitechapel Road. (This statement confirmed that Klosowski was in the central Ripper area during the murders.) *In 1889 a woman and two children came over from Warsaw, and there was no reason to doubt that they were his wife and children.* He did not consort with them, and they were supported for a time in the neighborhood. Eventually the accused himself left Whitechapel, and was next heard of in a barber's shop at Pechham." (At this point investigators did not seem to know that Klosowski had been to America for about 14 months.) He later had a small shop in that district himself, but not for long, as it did not pay, and he took up a situation as a hairdresser's assistant in Leytonstone.

In 1895 the members of a family named Renton were living at Leytonstone, and one of them, Mary Isabella, married a porter named Shadrack Spink. They were both of intemperate habits, and lived a rather unhappy life. Ultimately Spink left with his son Shadrack, deserting his wife. Two months later the wife gave birth to another child. Then the accused and Mrs. Spink were seen 'keeping company' together, and when spoken to by his employer about the matter the accused said 'We are going to be married.'

In July or August, 1897, the accused and Mrs. Spink came to London, and became the tenants of the Prince of Wales beerhouse, St. Bartholomew Square. Mrs. Spink's illness increased, and the accused gave out that she was suffering from delirium tremens. The accused kept her in one room, and apparently tried to prevent all other persons in the house from doing anything for her. She gradually got worse, and death occurred on 25th December, 1897.

The accused next advertised for an assistant, and selected Bessie Taylor, a healthy looking woman, aged thirty-two, who had been a housekeeper at a Peckham restaurant. They lived at the Prince of Wales until August, 1898, when they moved to the Grapes, Bishops Stortford, staying there until May, 1899, then going to the Monument. Bessie Taylor was taken ill like her predecessor, the symptoms being exactly the same. Her mother nursed her for a time, and she got better; but she soon had another relapse and died on 13th February, 1901.

Then followed the engaging of Maud Marsh and her death. In each of the three cases the illness and death were the same. Tartar-emetic was a deadly poison which the accused had purchased in such a large quality at Hastings. It was a little curious that he should have called in Dr. Stoker again; but sometimes persons [underestimate] the qualifications of others, and perhaps he did not like to run the risk of calling in another doctor. But for the prudent and proper concerned to consent to a private post-mortem examination, this case would never have been before the Court. It had been suggested that when a doctor was not perfectly clear as to the cause of a death he should at once acquaint the coroner's officer, but such a course would be unreasonable and lamentable.

Having completed his brief background for the court on the deaths of Bessie Taylor and Mrs. Spink, Mr. Bodkin closed his remarks for the day. It was left for Detective-Inspector Godley to end the day's testimony with a report that the accused had just been charged with the murders of both Taylor and Spink.

Police Court—Wednesday, January 7, 1903

Charge Sheet — Southwark Police Court
Date: 7th January, 1903

George Chapman, thirty-six, licensed victualler; for that he did feloniously kill and slay Maud Marsh by administering arsenic to her on 22nd October, 1902 at 213 Borough High Street;

Severin Klosowski, thirty-seven, otherwise called George Chapman, His Majesty's Prison, Brixton, publican, feloniously, willfully, and of malice aforethought killing and murdering Mary Isabella Spink, otherwise called Isabella Chapman, on the 25th day of December, 1897, at the Prince of Wales beerhouse, Bartholomew Square;

further feloniously, willfully, and of malice aforethought, killing and murdering Elizabeth (Bessie) Taylor, otherwise called Bessie Chapman, on 13th February, 1901, at the Monument public-house, parish of St. Saviour.

Before testimony could begin this day the court was informed by Martin O'Connor, representing Alfred Clark, that Klosowski had been served "with a writ at the instance of Alfred Clark for malicious prosecution, false imprisonment, libel, and slander." The year before, Klosowski had accused Clark of falsely obtaining £700 from him in a stock certificate fraud deal. When the money Klosowski had claimed he had given to Clark was recovered at the Crown by Detective-Inspector Godley, Clark was released from his prison term with all charges dropped. The case would never see the light of day, however, due to the upcoming murder trial, but at least long-time criminal and local conman Alfred Clark was out of prison — that was more than could be said for Severin Klosowski.

Testimony would be heard today from one of the most interesting figures ever to come to light in the Borough Poison case. Wolff Levisohn can be called the dark horse in these matters as he seems to be the only individual with detailed, though scattered, views of Klosowski for most of the time this serial killer was active in the East End of London as well as before and after those murders known to history as the Jack the Ripper murders. Indeed, it is not beyond the realm of possibility that Levisohn may very well have been responsible for a murder or two himself during that crime spree. He certainly knew a great deal more about Klosowski than he was willing to share with the police, yet there is no known reason why he would not come forward with more information than he did when he was called to testify before the London courts. The question remains: Did these two men, at some time in the past, "work" together in some criminal venture or were they simply two men with similar backgrounds living in the same general area who continued to run into each other?

To be sure it has been suggested that Chief Inspector Abberline, Scotland Yard's chief investigator at the street level for the Ripper murders, had investigated, or at the very least interviewed, Levisohn during the 1888 series of murders.

Levisohn began his testimony by telling the court that he first met Klosowski in 1888 when the accused killer worked at the dilapidated barber shop under the White Hart public house, in the very heart of Whitechapel. Yet there is a possibility that the men met earlier in Poland when Klosowski was a student in Warsaw. Also, the 1888 reference to the White Hart location stands in stark contrast to some writers of Ripper books, who seem determined to place Klosowski at that location no earlier than 1890. The reason for these writers' reluctance to place Klosowski at that location is quite clear. If he were there in 1890 most of the Ripper murders were completed by that time; however, if he were there in 1888 his workplace would have been literally a half block from the first murder and right in the middle of the Ripper's killing ground. Writers who would like their own suspect to be the Ripper state that Klosowski was not in the area in 1888, but eyewitness testimony at the police court hearing in 1902, Klosowski's murder trial in 1903, and later reports by police officers who had worked the case say that he was. It is up to the reader to decide which sources contain the most truth.

Levisohn continued, telling the court that his conversation with Klosowski, conducted in Polish with a bit of Yiddish mixed in for good measure, focused on the medical field and that Klosowski informed Levisohn that his name was Ludwig Zagowski. This was the earliest date anyone had testified to, indicating that Klosowski had used an alias. Yet, in theory at least, Klosowski had not committed any known crimes by that period. He did, however, leave Poland in a great hurry, so it can be assumed that he was running from something or someone even at that early date. Did he in fact kill the "real" Severin Klosowski?

The court was then informed that Klosowski "was an assistant to a hairdresser at this shop. Then he became proprietor." "He appeared to be very clever with medicines. He asked me to get him some medicine once, and I said, 'No,' as I did not wish to get twelve years." (This is a reference to Klosowski's attempt to acquire poison around the time of the Ripper murders. He was unsuccessful in his quest at the time so other methods of dispatch would need to be found. The question is: why did he trust Levisohn enough to ask for the poison?)

Levisohn further informed the court that the man he knew at the time as Zagowski was still working at the pub in 1889 when Klosowski became the proprietor. That would seem to indicate that Klosowski could have been working at that location for perhaps a full year before moving to his own barber shop not far away on Cable Street. It should also be remembered that Levisohn not only lived in the East End of London but also for a time he lived in Whitechapel. He knew the area and the people in the barber/hairdressing business very well as he was also working as a traveling salesman of hairdressing supplies.

Finishing up, Levisohn informed the court about several moves he learned Klosowski had made while Levisohn ran into him on his sales route. He reported that "Zagowski" had moved to several places, including South Tottenham and Bruce Grove Station. He was also able to confirm that Klosowski "was living by himself, but after a time he was joined by a wife and two children. He did not support them, and now and again [myself] and another man gave the woman coppers." That would have been when Klosowski and his new wife were living at 123 Cable Street in late 1889. It was also then that the torso of a dead woman was dumped across the tracks from Klosowski's home and business on Pinchin Street. From that point on no one, including Levisohn, ever reported seeing the "wife and two children" again. In 1894, when Levisohn again ran into Klosowski at 5 West Green Road, South Tottenham (after his return from America), the "wife and two children were not with him then, but another woman." That other woman was Annie Georgina Chapman, possibly the daughter of Ripper murder victim Annie Chapman, and Levisohn seemed to know who she was. One thing Levisohn did not do was to go to the police.

When pressed by Thomas Sydney under cross-examination about how he "first read about this case in the newspapers" and about how he connected "Chapman" with the man he testified to know as Zagowski, Levisohn stated, "When I saw it for the first time I knew how he got the name of Chapman, but I did not like to push myself forward."

The testimony of Wolff Levisohn completed, the government attorneys continued trying to establish the true identity of the man in the dock by calling the brother and sister of Lucy Klosowski. Stanislaus Baderski informed the court that he had first met the accused "thirteen years previously as Severin Klosowski. [We] first met at a polish club in St. John's Square, Clerlenwell. The accused was not a member." [My sister Lucy] "became acquainted with the accused, who kept a barber's shop at Cable Street. Later [I] heard of a wedding having been celebrated between Lucy and the accused and [I] went to the wedding feast, but was a little late. Lucy told me the marriage took place in Union Street, Whitechapel, on 23rd October, 1889. My sister and the accused lived at Cable Street for about six months, and then took lodgings in Commercial Street." With the move in 1890 to Commercial Street Klosowski was once again in central Whitechapel, the Ripper's preferred killing ground.

Adding to her brother's testimony, Mrs. Stanislaus Rauch confirmed Klosowski to be the man who had married her sister Lucy in 1889. Mrs. Rauch had been able to easily pick out Klosowski earlier in the day during a police lineup. There was no doubt in her mind as to his identity.

To end the long days' testimony the court called Joseph Smith Renton, a cousin of Mary Isabella Spink and John Ward, who had rented separate rooms to Spink and Klosowski. Renton confirmed that his cousin and Klosowski had lived together as man and wife but in 1896 he had known the prisoner in the dock as Chapman while his cousin passed as Mrs. Chapman. Ward added that the man he knew as George Chapman had met Mary Spink at his boarding house and that after a while, around October 1895, Chapman and Spink returned. Chapman informed Ward and his wife that the couple had been married: "Allow me to present you to my wife." Later "Chapman" would complain to Ward that "he was unable to get hold of his wife's money, with which they wanted to buy a business." Later, that would not be a problem!

POLICE COURT—WEDNESDAY, JANUARY 14, 1903

The first part of the day's testimony consisted of several witnesses coming forward to confirm the identity of the accused as Severin Klosowski as well as Klosowski's residences and businesses in the heart of Whitechapel. One witness, a Mrs. Helsdown, was also able to throw some light on the temperament of Klosowski when he moved into a boarding house in Hastings with Mrs. Spink and her little son Willie around January 1897. Mrs. Helsdown knew the couple as Mr. and Mrs. Chapman and noted that she "had heard them quarrelling occasionally. Once or twice [I] saw Mrs. Chapman's face was very red, and she said her husband had smacked her. [I] was also shown marks on her throat."

Mrs. Harriet Greenaway, also of Hastings, related that she had met "Mr. & Mrs. Chapman and son" in February 1897, at yet another boarding house. And although the Chapmans had not been there for more than a month the "wife" confided a secret to Mrs. Greenaway: "On one occasion Mrs. Chapman showed me a little black bag which was kept by the accused. She brought it up secretly." Mrs. Greenaway was also clear on the fact that Klosowski "had a revolver in the house."

For whatever reason neither the police nor the prosecutors pressed for any details about the secret black bag nor the very unusual fully loaded American revolver, which was recovered during the search of the Crown in October 1902. It is perhaps noteworthy to mention at this point that the "little black bag" does not seem to have been recorded by the police. And unless that little bag is in some long forgotten box stored in Scotland Yard's Black Museum, any secrets it may have once held are gone forever. Yet the question remains: Why was it so important to a serial killer named Klosowski and what made Mrs. Spink believe that it held some dark secret?

Alice Penfold was then called to explain her acquaintance with Klosowski and the fact that she may very well have been targeted by her "friend" for a bit of poison herself had she not been suspicious of his actions. Alice had been working in Hastings as a domestic servant and was on one of her walks about town when she was approached by Klosowski. He had introduced himself as the manager of a pianoforte shop. Before long they were walking together and even though Klosowski, still using the alias of George Chapman, was supposed to be married he wasted little time in asking Alice to go out with him. Indeed, the couple went out three times. At that point Alice complained of being ill. "He said he would give me something to do my cold, and he added that he had been in a hospital. He sent a note and some powders. I threw them in the fire." Alice was then asked: "You were going out with him. Why did you destroy them?" She replied, "I did not want him, but he used to follow me about." This incident, occurring just after Klosowski purchased his poison, could very well have been a small test of his newfound ounce of death.

Klosowski's cruelty and secretive life well established now by the court, the proceedings moved on to a review of the background of Mrs. Spink's death as witnessed by a onetime customer of the Prince of Wales public house, Mrs. Martha Doubleday. Mrs. Doubleday lived nearby and became very friendly with Isabella Spink, whom she knew as Mrs. Chapman.

"After a time Mrs. Chapman began to look very ill and thin, and at last the accused asked [me] to stay up with her all night. The accused wanted to know who was the nearest doctor, and [I] gave the name of Dr. Rogers. Mrs. Chapman was very sick and complained of pain in the head. The vomiting was very frequent during the night. The accused used to give her brandy, but not any nourishment. After Mrs. Chapman took the brandy she was very sick."

Mrs. Doubleday recalled that Isabella "was a mere skeleton." When confronted Klosowski, would only say that his "wife" was simply "wasting away," yet he could give no reason why. On the morning of her death the witness called Klosowski upstairs as his "wife" looked very bad but he only "looked at her, shook his head, and then went downstairs without making any remark."

A short time later Mrs. Doubleday recalled, "Chapman, came up quickly. Your wife is dying. He came up soon afterwards, but he was too late as she had just died." After making a show of going into the next room and crying, Klosowski "then went downstairs and opened the public house." It would be business as usual that day despite the still warm corpse lying in the upstairs bedroom. Nevertheless, Klosowski did make time during that busy business day to visit the undertaker to make arrangements for the removal of the body as soon as possible. After all, he was now quiet finished with one Mary Isabella Spink!

Londoners were by now closely reading about this case as it unfolded in their daily newspapers. Klosowski was interviewed still holding on to his alias of George Chapman, an American citizen. Local Southwark residents could read the reports in the *Southwark and Bermondsey Record and South London Gazette* on Saturday, January 17, 1903, and an article on this date gives a clue to discovering when Klosowski arrived in America. In it, he gives the name of a ship he knew, relying on the fact that others would verify that it existed and thus perhaps corroborating his tall-tale. It would lead to the identification of the ship he actually arrived on some 12 hours before the first murder in the American Ripper series.

"The Sun" states that George Chapman has informed the American Counsel in London that he is an American citizen, and he denies that his name is Severin Klosowski or that he has lived in Warsaw. He states that he was born in the State of Michigan, his father being one Alfred Chapman, a carpenter, who went to New York when George was still a baby. His father died when he was seven years of age, and the lad began life as an errand boy in a grocery store in New York City. When twelve or thirteen years of age he took employment with an American who dealt in horses and lived in Jersey City Heights. He started his hairdressing experience in a shop in Ninth Avenue, New York. This shop was owned by a German, whose Christian name — Fredrick — is all he can recall. In addition to his work as a barber Chapman sold such articles as appertain to the hairdresser's business, and thus made some extra money. He was economical, and saved all he could, and his expenses were of the lowest.

In 1893, having gathered together some £300, Chapman decided to come to England. He crossed the Atlantic in a cattle boat — **the Westerland he thinks her name was** — paying £2 and doing some odd work for his passage (emphasis added). Shortly after his arrival in London he attempted to return on the same boat, but was unable to do so, and before he found a way of getting back to America that suited him he was induced to invest his little capital and remain in this country.

Chapman admits that he can remember no names of his American days, but asserts his confidence that if the story is given sufficiently wide publicity some of the people who knew him in America will come forward and prove its truth.

The American authorities have given Chapman to understand clearly that should he be found guilty of the commission of any crime in England the fact that he was born in the United States and was therefore an American citizen, even if clearly proven would have no effect whatever upon the course of justice.

POLICE COURT—WEDNESDAY, JANUARY 21, 1903

On this day Sydney would be unable to attend to the defense as he was suffering from rheumatism and was confined home. Klosowski's attorney, Mr. Hutton, would be retained and would stay on to aid in the defense of the Borough Poisoner. As before, the courtroom was packed and Klosowski was led in by two sturdy officers and placed in the dock. They would stay by his side.

The day's testimony began with witnesses detailing how Klosowski had acquired his funds from Mrs. Spink's trust fund as well as matching deposits and withdrawals from Midland Bank and Lloyd's Bank of London. Even though money was not the prime reason Klosowski killed, the fact that a woman had money would never dissuade him from "giving her a bit of that." It was for him an added attraction to his murder plans.

Following the cash flow testimony, Joseph Betrikowski, a 30-year-old Russian/Pole living in London, testified. Commissioned by the police to translate 16 documents which had been found in the Crown by Inspector Godley, Betrikowski testified that all of the documents "related to a person named Severin Klosowski." What Joseph Betrikowski did not translate was the diary which had also reportedly been found during the search of Klosowski's pub.

Counsel for "George Chapman," Arthur Hutton (original from *Trial of George Chapman*, 1930)

These documents, in Polish and Russian, translated for Klosowski's 1903 trial, were published by Hargrave Lee Adam in the historical work, *Trial of George Chapman*, part of the *Notable British Trials* series in April 1930.

1) Extract from birth certificate

On the 15th day of December, 1865, at ten o'clock in the morning, there appeared Antonio Klosowski, 30 years of age, a carpenter by trade, native of the village of Nagornak, together with two witnesses, Ludwika Zywanski, aged 32, and Jacob Rozinski, aged 56, both of Nagornak, and employed there. They stated that Emilie, the wife of Antonio Klosowski, nee Ulatowski, age 29, had given birth to a child the previous morning. The child was named Severin and that his parents are Polish subjects. The godfather of the child was Ludwig Zyanski and the godmother's name was Marianna Colimowski. That they were present at the birth and that they affixed their signatures hereto in testimony thereof.

(Then follow the signatures of the Clerical Registrar of Kolo, the Chief of the Parochial Registry of Kolo, and a magistrate of Kolo.)

2) Primary school

This is given by the teacher of the Krasseminsk rural public primary school, consisting of one Standard, to the effect that Severin Klosowski, son of Antonio, attended the Krasseminsk School from October 17–29, 1873, till June 6–13, 1880, and completed the full term of studies of the first department, and that his conduct throughout his attendance at the school was very good.—In witness thereof I affix my own signature, Merkish, teacher, village of Krassenin, December 7–19, 1880.

(The authenticity of the signature of Merkish is attested by two witnesses.)

3) Society of Surgeons

Receipt for one ruble, paid by Rappaport to the Treasury of the Society of Surgeons of the town of Radom on behalf of the surgical apprentice, Severin Klosowski.

Radom, October 23–November 5, 1882.—N. Brodnitski, Senior Surgeon.

4) Well behaved

The magistrate of the County of Zvolen hereby certifies that Severin Klosowski, resident of the village Zvolen, is a well-behaved man, and was never found guilty of any crime whatever. To which effect he bears testimony by his own signature and official seal.—Dushevitch, Magistrate of the County, Village Zvolen, November 16, 1882.

5) Registry of Surgical Pupils

October 23–November 4, 1885.—The Radom Surgical Society, of the town of Radom, hereby certifies that the surgical pupil, Severin Klosowski, was entered at the registry of surgical pupils by the Senior Surgeon, Moshko Rappaport, in the town of Radom, November 22—December 3, 1882. Subject No. 8, and in accordance with Article 17, letter b, of the Surgical Society. One ruble in silver was paid by him into the Treasury of the said Society.—In witness whereof, Brodinski, the Chief of the Society, testifies by affixing his signature and the seal of the Surgical Society.

6) Apprentice Certificate

Certificate issued to the surgical apprentice, Severin Antonio Klosowski, to the effect that he, Severin Klosowski, was in my surgery for the purpose of studying surgery from December 1, 1880, till June 1, 1885, and during the whole of the time he, Severin Klosowski, discharged accurately all his duties. He was diligent, of exemplary conduct, and studied with zeal the science of surgery.—In testimony thereof I affix my signature, Moshko Rappaport, Senior Surgeon and proprietor of the surgery in the village Zvolen, June 1, 1885.

7) Certificate of Employment

Certificate issued to Severin Klosowski, resident in the village of Tyminitsa, county of Nodga, district of Iltetsk, Government of Radom, to the effect that he was employed for a period of four-and-a-half years by the local surgeon, Moshko Rappaport, in the capacity of a practicing surgery pupil, and under the doctor's instructions rendered very skilful assistance to patients—i.e., in cupping by means of glasses, leeches, and other assistance comprised in the science of surgery. To all the above I am able to testify as an eyewitness.—(Signed) O. P. Olstetski, medical practitioner in village of Zvolen, October 10—22, 1885.

8) Instruction Certificate

This is given to Severin Klosowski, surgery pupil, to the effect that from October 1, 1885, till January 1, 1886, he received instructions in practical surgery at the Hospital of Praga, Warsaw, and his general conduct was good.—(Signed) Krynick, Senior Surgeon.

In accordance with the application of Severin Klosowski, and in consequence of inquiries ordered to be made, the present certificate is issued from the office of the Chief of Police of Warsaw to the effect that the applicant while residing in Warsaw was not observed by the police to be concerned in any improper conduct whatsoever. The present certificate is given to Mr. Klosowski under the proper signature and government seal for the purpose of submitting the same to the Imperial University of Warsaw. Stamp duties have been collected.—Warsaw, April 29, 1886. Kasievitz, Deputy Chief of the Department. (Seal) A. Darenskov, Manager.

9) Employment Certificate

Warsaw, November 15, 1886.—This is to certify that Severin Klosowski has been employed by me as surgeon assistant from January 20, 1886, up to the present time, and during the whole of that period he performed his surgical functions with a full knowledge of the subject, and his conduct was good. To this fact I testify with my own signature, and affix my stamp.—(Signed) D. Moshkovski.

10) Biography

I was born in 1865, in the village of Nagornak, district of Kolo, Government of Kalish. I lived with my parents until the age of 15, attending at the same time the primary school. In 1880 my parents apprenticed me for the purpose of studying surgery to Moshko Rappaport, senior surgeon of the town of Zvolen. Having served my term of apprenticeship till 1885, I came to Warsaw, and whilst employed by Mr. V. Olshanski I also attended a practical course of surgery at the Praga Hospital. Upon the termination of my hospital practice I entered the service of Mr. D. Moshkovski, by whom I am still employed. I present herewith all my documents.—Yours faithfully, Severin Klosowski, Warsaw, November 15, 1886.

11) Passport

Passport, given on November 24, 1886, to Severin Antoniovich Klosowski, residing in the Radom Government, district of Ilshetsk, county of Khotche, village of Tyshenitsa, Nova Nil to travel to the city of Warsaw from the above date till November 1–13, 1887, upon the expiration of which the said document shall be returned to me. The civil and military authorities shall allow the bearer a free passage, and if necessary render him legal assistance. Given in Khotche, November 24, 1886. Physical description. Age, 21; born in 1865; height, medium; hair, of a dark shade; eyes, blue; nose and mouth, medium; chin and face, longish; birthmarks, none. Passport within the limits and the Kingdom of Poland. Free.—(Signed) Mazur, Magistrate of the County of Khotche. (Seal) Godlevski, County Clerk.

12) Employment Certificate

Town of Praga, November 24 to December 6, 1886.—I hereby certify that Severin Klosowski was employed by me in the capacity of an assistant surgeon from August 20, 1885, till February 1, 1886, and during the whole of the time he fulfilled the whole of his duties with zeal, and was if good behavior. In witness whereof I have affixed my own signature.—(Signed) C. F. Olshanski.

13) Petition for Junior Surgeon Degree

Warsaw, December, 1886.—His Excellency, the Dean of the Medical Faculty of the Imperial University of Warsaw. Petition from Severin Klosowski, surgical pupil, residing at No. 16 Muranovskaja Street.

I have the honor to request your Excellency to grant me permission to undergo the examination for the purpose of receiving the degree of Junior Surgeon. I enclose herewith the required documents.—Yours faithfully, Severin Klosowski.

14) Acceptance for Junior Surgeon Degree

Ministry of Interior, Medical Administration of Warsaw, December 5, 1886.—In consequence of the application presented by Severin Klosowski, surgical pupil, the Medical Administration hereby testify to the effect that they do not see any reason to oppose his receiving the degree of a Junior Surgeon. The required stamp duties have been paid.—(Signed) Dr. M. Oreszaief, Collegiate Councillor and Inspector. A. Pominski, Secretary.

15) Hospital Fees

Severin Klosowski has paid to the Treasury of the Warsaw Society of Assistant Surgeons, Hospital fees four rubles per month.— Warsaw. February 28, 1887. Cobalski, Senior Surgeon. Paid up till March 3[1], 1887.

After these documents were published in London papers, along with testimony on January 7 by Mrs. Stanislaus Rauch that Klosowski had been trained at Infant Jesus Hospital at Praga, near Warsaw, a letter arrived at the *Southwark and Bermondsey Recorder and South London Gazette*, which was published on January 31, 1903. Was the man in the dock really Klosowski or was this just one more alias being used by a serial killer from Poland? If not Klosowski, then who was he? What happened to Klosowski and did this man really have the medical training shown in the documents?

The following letter has been published: —

Sir, — I must apologize for asking you to again be good enough to insert the following: —

Since the appearance of a statement that Klosowski was at Jesus Hospital, Warsaw, in 1888, and as my brother was for several years house physician at the same hospital, I asked him to make exhaustive inquiries about Klosowski's antecedents and relationship with the above institution. No such names— under which Klosowski appeared in England — are to be found in the register for the Feldschers for the last forty years. The searching was done both by my brother and the present official (the Registrar of Feldschers), who had been in that capacity for over thirty years.—I remain, Sir, etc., IGNATIUS KNASTER.

Cambridge, Jan. 22.

Clearly this individual known to history as Severin Klosowski held many more secrets than we will ever uncover. One thing, however, is very clear. This was a man who was constantly on the run and was always looking over his shoulders.

At this point the court heard from two witnesses who had attempted to nurse Mrs. Spink while she was being slowly poisoned. Mrs. Jane Mumford had lived next to the Prince of Wales beer house in 1897 when the "Chapmans" moved in. Before long, she said, Mrs. Spink "complained of feeling unwell and gradually got worse." Mrs. Mumford was with Isabella for the final 6 days before she died helping Mrs. Doubleday. She testified that she felt it was strange that Klosowski "used to lock the room door at night and sleep on the couch. There was never a fire in the room, although it was December."

> Mr. Bodkin — Was anything given her at night?
> Mrs. Mumford — The accused would not allow me to give her anything. He used to give her the medicine in a wine glass — I presumed it was medicine.
> Mr. Bodkin — Did you ever ask the accused what was the matter with her?
> Mrs. Mumford — Once I said, "She seems queer," and he said, "She drinks a good deal of brandy."

The second witness to Mrs. Spink's death was Elizabeth Waymark, who had been contacted by Doctor Rogers to nurse the by then dying woman, who had less than two weeks to live. Mrs. Waymark saw "Mrs. Chapman was in a terrible condition." Yet, she was never allowed to feed or give Mrs. Spink anything to drink. "They were all administered by the accused himself."

> Mr. Bodkin — When the accused gave her anything did he do anything?
> Mrs. Waymark — He used to go up to the bedside and feel her pulse. I sometimes said, "She is very bad," and he would reply, "Yes, I know what to do." She used to say, "Do, do, kiss me," and he would take her hand. She used to be very thirsty at night, and the accused used to give her a white liquid like milk.
> Mr. Bodkin — Did she get better or worse?
> Mrs. Waymark — After the sickness she used to go off into a stupor.

As Mrs. Spink lay dying Mrs. Waymark checked her pulse "and found that it was very low — scarcely beating. She got worse and worse, and [I] sent for the accused." Klosowski, however, did not arrive in time.

For most of the remaining day in court, testimony focused on Klosowski's attempts to rid himself of Mrs. Spink's son Willie. After several attempts Klosowski would finally place the child in a work home as he moved on to his next victim — Bessie Taylor.

Police Court — Wednesday, February 4, 1903

> "Detective-sergeant Neil, M division, said he had researched the records at Somerset House and found no entry of a marriage between the prisoner and either Spink or Taylor."

The last full day of testimony at the police court would focus on the events which led up to the death of Bessie Taylor on February 13, 1901. Once again Detective-Inspector Godley was called to the bar to give evidence at the court. He related that he had been at the churchyard at Lymm in Cheshire when the victim had been exhumed and presented evidence of Klosowski's relationship with the dead woman, referencing papers found by the police at the Crown, as well as other documents showing the couple's movements before Taylor's death.

By far the most interesting testimony on this cold and wet day came from salesman William Taylor, who was the older brother of Bessie. He would relate to the court the money which had been given to Bessie, which found its way into Klosowski's accounts, and a strange meeting more than a year after his sister's death with "the accused."

> Mr. Sims — One word on money matters. Was your sister a careful woman in money matters?
> Mr. William Taylor — Yes, very careful and saving.

After a brief description of his sister's work and the fact that she had left for London, Sims continued to solicit testimony about Bessie's finances and her failing condition. Taylor had visited his sister around December 1900 at the Monument and found her to be in very poor health.

MR. SIMS—How was she in appearance?
MR. TAYLOR—Thin; like a little old woman.
MR. SIMS—When did you last see her alive?
MR. TAYLOR—A week before her death.
MR. SIMS—After the funeral, when did you next see him?
MR. TAYLOR—In July, 1902, he called at my place. He said he had just been to the brewers. It was just after my father's death, and I remember asking if he had heard about it. He said he was very sorry to hear of the loss, and mentioned that he had a law case on about a lot of money.
MR. SIMS—This cheque for £50 which was paid into the accused's banking account was made out by your father in favor of your sister?
MR. TAYLOR—Yes.
MR. SIMS—Was your father tolerably well to do?
MR. TAYLOR—Yes, and my mother had a separate estate.
MR. SIMS—Your sister was a favorite daughter?
MR. TAYLOR—Yes, especially on my father's side.

The final two witnesses, Doctors James Maurice Stoker and Thomas Stevenson, focused on the final treatment and postmortem of Bessie Taylor. Dr. Stoker had been called into the case on January 1, 1901: "He prescribed a milk diet, and also medicines for the sickness, but he could not say now what they were composed of. He made inquires, but could not find any explanation for the illness, and in consequence he had a consultation with other medical men. He afterwards gave a certificate that death was due to intestinal obstruction, vomiting, and exhaustion."

Klosowski's counsel, Arthur Hutton, then questioned the elderly doctor about Bessie Taylor's final days.

MR. HUTTON—Did the accused appear to take an interest in her welfare?
DR. STOKER—Oh, yes; he was in the room every time I visited her.
MR. HUTTON—Do you remember, after the three consultations [with three other doctors], the accused saying he would like to have the best specialist in London called in?
DR. STOKER—No. I should probably have remembered it if he had, and agreed to it.
MR. HUTTON—To the best of your recollection, the medicines you gave were taken?
DR. STOKER—Yes.
MR. HUTTON—Did you order her brandy?
DR. STOKER—Probably.
MR. BODKIN—From first to last was there any thought of poison present in your mind?
DR. STOKER—None whatever.

Dr. Stevenson was then asked by Bodkin to explain to the court the results of his postmortem on the body of Bessie Taylor, which confirmed that she had been poisoned by long-term, relentless introduction of antimony into her system. "In every part of the intestines and organs which [I] removed for analysis [I] discovered antimony." News reports stated: "From the distribution of antimony through the various organs, he judged that it had been taken in a soluble form, and the highest probability was that it was tartar-emetic. A large dose must have been taken within three hours of death."

MR. HUTTON—Did you form any idea as to how many doses had been taken?
DR. STEVENSON—No.
MR. HUTTON—The smaller the dose the longer the time it would take to become fatal?
DR. STEVENSON—As a rule.

With the testimony of Dr. Stevenson, the police court ended its inquiry into the deaths of Spink, Taylor and Marsh. All of the evidence having been collected, the court now adjourned to consider whether or not to charge Klosowski, alias George Chapman, with capital murder or to rule that insufficient evidence had been found in the matter.

Police Court—Wednesday, February 11, 1903

On this day reporters would note: "The prisoner was seated in the dock between a warder and a constable. He seemed in better health than on previous occasions, and quite unmoved by his position."

It would be a short final hearing as Sims stood to address the court: "Since the last hearing I have had the opportunity of considering the evidence of the three doctors called in consultation by Dr. Stoker. It is not necessary to call them here, and if it is necessary to call them hereafter I will give Mr. Sydney notice. I now ask for the committal of the accused on the three charges."

Cecil Chapman then addressed Klosowski and asked if he had anything to say. Answering for his client, Sydney informed the court that Klosowski was pleading "not guilty" to all three charges. "He pleads not guilty, reserves his defense, and calls no witnesses."

"Mr. Chapman committed the accused for trial at the next Old Bailey Sessions," in London's Central Criminal Court. The trial would begin on Monday, March 16, 1903, and only a few suspected that this would be the trial which would give rise to the very real possibility that the accused serial killer was none other than Jack the Ripper!

On the charge sheet Cecil Chapman would write: "I think Inspector Godley and Sergeants Kemp and Neil, and the other officer engaged in this case, deserve special credit for the pains taken and skill shown in obtaining evidence in this case."

"It transpired that Detective-sergeant Kemp, the second officer in the case, has been promoted to be inspector, and appointed to Scotland Yard for special duty."

News Reports

Section IV — The King's Justice

Chapter 13

The First Day of Trial: The Case of the Borough Poisoner

I submit that no murder can be more determined and more malicious than that by poison.

— Solicitor-General Edward Carson

CITY OF LONDON, MARCH 1903

It was not considered the trial of the era, but then again very few people in London at the time understood that the man on trial for his life in the dock at the Old Bailey was none other than Jack the Ripper. Had the population of England suspected that fact, it would certainly have been one of the most sensational criminal trials in British history. In 1903, however, only the people of London were closely following the trial of a suspected and hated serial killer. Only later would Severin Klosowski, alias George Chapman, become one of the few serial killers suspected of committing the brutal murders ascribed to the Ripper in the East End of London. Even today there is a continuing debate as to who the author of that series was. The jury, as it is said, is still out on the final verdict, but perhaps in the very near future some very solid evidence will be discovered, or rather, rediscovered, which will place the figurative hangman's noose around the historical neck of Severin Klosowski and put that case to rest once and for all. For the time being however, we submit to the reader the poison murder trial of Severin Klosowski as we look towards what could very well have been the only trial for murder of Jack the Ripper.

OLD COURT NUMBER ONE

Newgate jail had a well-earned and frightful reputation from past years when those held within its stone walls were subjected to torture and death. It had been designed by George Dance and was constructed on old Roman stone foundations from 1770 to 1778. By 1903 the unspeakable crimes which had been committed in the past were no longer a daily horror and in fact the whole system would soon be condemned and demolished in a little over a year. Its condemned cell, however, would be preserved and incorporated into the basement of nearby Lancaster House.

In 1903 Newgate still held the Central Criminal Court for London, called the Old Bailey. For the trial of Severin Klosowski, Old Court Number One would see duty for one of the last times. The court was described as "looking more like an old large cellar than a courtroom; badly lit, with a large reflector placed outside of the single outside facing window and small internal lighting. A large wooden and stone dungeon would be called to mind, but the image would be far too cheery. In the center of the building, the court could be reached by walking up an old wooden staircase, which twisted into the court itself. The main entrance used by witnesses was reached by a dark side passage, which was never fully lit even on the brightest days."

Around the court and above the main floor visitors could view the proceedings by climbing a short flight of old and well-worn stairs to the public gallery. For this trial the gallery would be completely filled with many individuals waiting outside to claim any seats left vacant during the day's testimony. On the main floor the gallery had a full view of the witness box centered between the judge's bench on the left and the jury box on the right. They could also see the small one-man box where the court reporter would do his work.

Lead counsel for "George Chapman," George Elliott (original from *Trial of George Chapman*, 1930).

THE PROSECUTORS

For the trial of Severin Klosowski, by then referred to in the press as the Borough Poisoner, the Crown brought forth a truly formidable team of veteran prosecutors lead by the solicitor-general himself, Edward Carson. Carson would be knighted as Sir Edward and later become Lord Carson. Carson, described as "slim and eager, with flushed face, tense and determined," had prosecuted Oscar Wilde and many others. It is noteworthy to state that the solicitor-general rarely made personal appearances in court but he felt that this case required his full attention. It was one he was determined to win.

Working with Carson was Charles Mathews, who would himself be knighted as Sir Charles a few years after this case. Mathews would later become the director of public prosecutions. He was described as "a small, spare man, with a keen, alert face and an incisive manor. Being a prodigiously hard worker, his face was pallid and at times careworn. He was always in the most deadly earnest, having a masterly grasp of his case, which he had beforehand assiduously digested

Above: Sir Edward Carson, K.C., M.P. The solicitor-general and lead counsel for the British government. *Right:* Charles Mathews, counsel for the British government (both original from *Trial of George Chapman*, 1930).

in chambers. He had a peculiar voice, thin and high pitched when he raised it, but very impressive when he lowered it."

Rounding out this impressive team of prosecutors was Archibald Bodkin, who would also be later knighted. It would be Bodkin who would open the case against Klosowski as he had the most experience of the three, trying cases at the Old Bailey. Bodkin was described as "tall, broad-shouldered, rugged of countenance, and commanding of aspect. He has large gray eyes, which are capable of expressing a wonderful depth of retrospection, as though he were looking back over many years and recalling within himself some of the many strange cases with which he has from time to time been associated. He speaks in a clear, full voice, and every word he utters, one instinctively realizes, has been carefully thought out beforehand, for he never seems to arrive at a hasty conclusion."

Along with these three men the government added Mr. H. Sutton from the projectors office and Mr. Sims from the treasury.

THE DEFENDERS

Even before the case came to trial it was clear to most observers that Klosowski would be a very difficult individual to defend. Much had been published in the London papers and there had been large crowds outside of both the coroner's inquest and police court inquires. Nevertheless, a team of men came forward to defend Severin Klosowski in the capital murder trial for the poison death of Maud Marsh.

Leading the defense was George Elliott, a well-known and respected defense attorney who was very familiar with the workings of the Old Bailey. He was described as being a "short, stubby little man, with rosy cheeks. Possessed of a clear, precise delivery, he had a homely irrepressible sense of humor, which sometimes encroached upon his emotional moments, the transition from one to the other being so sudden. Occasionally he would endeavor, though not always successfully, to encourage appreciation by smiling contemplatively at his own witticisms."

Elliott was joined by Arthur Hutton, who had worked with Elliott on past cases and was also fully familiar with the workings of the court. He was described as "a tall man, who always wore a monocle. He seemed incapable of losing his temper or of getting excited. In his slow, persuasive speech, he relied more upon logical argument than forceful rhetoric. Mr. Hutton excelled in addressing a jury, with whom he made himself very ingratiating, taking them into his confidence in a sympathetic and genial manor."

Vyvyan Lyons also joined the team along with Klosowski's original attorney Thomas Sydney. However, most of the actual defense work in the courtroom would be handled by Elliott and Hutton for whom this was most decidedly their home ground.

THE JUDGE

Justice Grantham, trial judge for the case of the Borough Poisoner (original from *Trial of George Chapman*, 1930).

In 1903 Judge Justice Grantham could rightly claim to be one of the most popular judges in Great Britain. He formed his opinions with great speed and was not above expressing them throughout the trials he attended. Hargrave Adam would write, "For instance, he often arrived at a preconceived notion of a prisoner's guilt, and made no attempt to conceal it from the jury." In fact, the judge was well known for not only interrupting the questions of council but, in many cases, he would examine the witnesses himself, much to the distress of whomever was questioning at the time. At one point during an earlier case a defense attorney named Stephenson protested, "With great respect, my lord, may I be allowed to examine the witness in my own way?" Not missing a beat, Judge Grantham forcefully replied, "With all respect, Mr. Stephenson, I am judge here, and I am to see that justice is done, and when the witness says something startling I think it is my duty as judge to give the witness an opportunity of explaining it."

Klosowski's defense team would certainly have their work cut out for them as they prepared to defend him in Justice Grantham's court in Central Criminal Court of the Old Bailey.

Old Court Number One — Monday, March 16, 1903

By the time Severin Klosowski stood before the bar at the Old Bailey the case of the Borough Poisoner had become the trial of the season. Much had been published about the three murders. Whispers began to be heard that, just possibly, the hated Pole was much more than a poisoner. As for Klosowski, he was a broken man, fully aware that his life was in the balance. When he was escorted into the court the *South London Press* would report that he "looked pale and careworn, stepped quietly into the dock."

There were crowds outside, much greater than usual for a murder trial, and many had hoped to be able to acquire one of the few seats to view the proceedings up close. Handling the visitors and working press for the trial was Undersheriff Langton, adorned in full dress uniform, including his fully polished sword worn on his hip. Concerned that they not be replaced in their seats, the lucky few who had them brought food and drinks. Many had opera glasses to get an even closer view of Klosowski as he fought for his life. In the courtroom for the entire trial would be his wife, Lucy Klosowski.

> The court was crowded. Alderman Sir Joseph Savory occupied a seat on the bench, while in the body of the court sat the Earl of Dysart, the Public Prosecutor.

Just before Klosowski entered, Judge Grantham entered "his court" through a heavy crimson curtain situated dramatically behind his bench. The covering hid his private entrance to the courtroom from his office, adding an air of grandeur to the proceedings, which began at a little before 11 A.M. As Klosowski came into view it was clear to all in attendance that he held no special joy at being the center of attention. British justice was about to shine some light on the murderous career of a serial killer. The court was called to order.

Elliott speaking on behalf of Klosowski submitted that the "prosecution were not entitled to prove the deaths of any other women at previous dates, which were alleged to have been brought about by the accused as he was separately indicted for them." Precedents was sited but Solicitor-General Edward Carson would not be put off by this attempt to limit his case against Klosowski. Carson stated that he was "entitled to open the facts and give evidence of the death of other women whom the accused had lived" and reported that the cases submitted by the defense had already been overruled.

It did not take long for Mr. Justice Grantham to rule that "the evidence was clearly admissible." Grantham then faced Klosowski in a hushed and darkened courtroom and called upon him to plead to the three murder indictments he faced. In a soft voice barely audible in the small courtroom, Klosowski stated three times that he was "Not guilty, Sir." The jury was then charged to hear the case for the murder of Maud Marsh. If need be, the other two cases could be tried but very few in court that cold day expected any other cases to be called. But would the gathered hear anything which could place Klosowski in and around the area stalked by Jack the Ripper?

The Speech for the Prosecution

> With the full attention of the "12 good men" of the jury, Solicitor-General Carson rose to introduce the prosecution's case to the court. It was not to be an overly long speech by courtroom standards but it skillfully laid out the case against Klosowski of murder by poison.
>
> The accused and Maud Marsh had been living together as husband and wife at the Crown, High Street, Borough. Maud Marsh died on 22nd October under circumstances and with symptoms which induced the doctor who attended her to refuse to give a certificate of death, and the result of the post-mortem examination went to show that the body of the deceased woman was literally saturated

with antimony. I think it will hardly be disputed that Maud Marsh died from poisoning. No doubt a large dose was administered shortly before death, and there was every indication that she had been repeatedly dosed with it for some time before death. The real question you have to try is whether it was administered to her by the accused.

One extraordinary effect of the poison is that, if it is administered during the lifetime of the person, it preserves the body in a remarkable degree, so that even several years after death the body of the deceased person is easily recognizable. The poison causes constant vomiting and very often great purging spasms, occasionally emaciation, and it causes the person to whom it is administered to have a most anxious look. There is also frequent intense irritation of the throat.

The accused is a Russian Pole, and his name is Severin Klosowski.

He appears to have had considerable experience as a barber-surgeon—a profession not now known in this country. He came to this country about 1888, and worked as a barber in various places. In October, 1889, he married a woman named Lucy Baderski, who is still alive. At one time they went to America, and she appeared to have come back without him. In 1895 the accused purchased a house in High Road, Tottenham, still using the name Klosowski. At that time he had left his wife, and he appeared to have met a young woman named Chapman, and it is probable that this induced him to take the name of George Chapman, by which name he has gone up to the present time. In 1897 he purchased a barber's shop at Hastings, and there made the acquaintance of a married woman named Spink, with whom he subsequently lived, they passed as Mr. and Mrs. Chapman.

While at Hastings we find the accused buying an ounce of tartar-emetic on 3rd April, 1897, which contained 146 grains at least of antimony, from Mr. Davidson, a chemist, whose book containing the entries of the sale of poison, with the accused's signature to it, will be produced.

At Easter, 1898, the accused took into his employ at [the Prince of Wales beer house] a girl named Bessie Taylor, the daughter of a Cheshire farmer. They appear to have gone through some form of marriage, and in March, 1899, they removed to the Monument public-house, Union Street, Borough, where on 13th February, 1901, Bessie Taylor died.

After the death of Bessie Taylor the accused made the acquaintance of Maud Marsh, a young woman eighteen or nineteen years of age, whose parents resided at Croydon.

During the course of her illness Maud Marsh was taken into a hospital, and speedily recovered, but her illness returned after she went back to the accused, who, once referring to her illness, said, "I could give her a bit like this and fifty doctors would not find out."

An important witness in this case is Jessie Toon, who was engaged to nurse Maud Marsh. After Maud's death she had an important conversation with accused, who told her to be careful and watch the deceased girl's mother, whom he described as an old cat who was desirous of showing him up.

As a result of the post-mortem examination, 20.12 grains of antimony were discovered in the body of the deceased, and, when I tell you that 2 grains have been known to kill a person, you will see that ... the body of Maud Marsh must have been literally saturated with antimony.

I submit that upon this evidence there can be no doubt that Maud Marsh died from antimony poisoning. Only three or four persons could have administered the poison, and as to two or three of them it is impossible that they could have done so. It was the accused who alone was in very close contact with the girl, and who took upon himself to introduce into the room the only food and drink she received, and it was the accused who in 1897 purchased, as I have said, a very large quantity of the very poison which this woman had taken. It is to this man that the evidence all points—a man whose early training made him acquainted with drugs and poisons. It is in this direction only that the evidence points, and I submit that the accused's was the master hand, and that it was the accused's previous experience which led him to believe that he could safely run the risk of deceiving the doctors. There is no reasonable hypothesis which can lead you to come to any other conclusion.

I desire to state the facts absolutely without feeling and with moderation, because we are engaged in the trial of a man against whom the verdict may mean the loss of his own life. These cases of poison (Spink and Taylor and others not connected to this case), although rarer, are perhaps more important than other cases of murder which more frequently come before the Courts, because of the difficulty there is in tracing them out. But if a distinction can be made in degrees of murder, I submit that no murder can be more determined and more malicious than that by poison, such as the one we are now inquiring into. Certainly no murder could be more demonstrative of the cruelty of the person perpetrating it than that of a man standing by the bedside, day after day, of the person he professed to love, and seeing her suffering torture and gradually sinking away from what he had by his own hand administered under the pretence of treating that person for maladies with which he professed to be acquainted.

Wolff Levisohn

After the introduction speech the prosecution team called to the witness stand one of the most intriguing and shadowy figures ever to come to light during the investigation of Severin Klosowski — Wolff Levisohn. Levisohn has been called the dark horse of this case as he appears to shadow Klosowski in many ways. He seems to have popped up in Klosowski's life at many critical points and then fade from view, only to reemerge as Klosowski changed his name, his job and his many addresses. Surely Wolff Levisohn knew much more than he was willing to state about Klosowski in a court of law. They must have shared some dark secret, which neither could ever reveal. Did he know for a fact that Klosowski was Jack the Ripper? And if he did know, how did he learn of his secret? The only words we have from Levisohn on the subject of Klosowski are his testimony on the first day of Klosowski's trial and his statement during the Police Court proceedings. "Jack" was never mentioned, but Levisohn was able to place Klosowski at the right place at exactly the right time, with all the right skills.

> I live at 135 Rosalyn Road, South Tottenham, and am a traveler in hairdressers' appliances. I have known the accused since 1888, when I met him in a hairdresser's shop in Whitechapel. I spoke to him in Yiddish. He said he came from Warsaw. I knew him as Ludwig Zagowski. We met from time to time up to 1890. He told me that in Warsaw he had been practicing in the medical line as a "feldscher" at the Praga Hospital. I have been a "feldscher" myself. I had seven years' training in the Russian Army. A "feldscher" is an assistant to a doctor. I talked to the accused about medicines, and he asked me if I could get him a certain medicine, but I said no, I did not want to get twelve years. I had a customer named Haddin at 5 West Green Road, South Tottenham. About 1894 or 1895 I called at Haddin's and saw the accused there. He was then an assistant, but he afterwards bought the shop which had once belonged to Mr. Haddin, in High Road, Tottenham. Later on he sold the shop and went away for several months, when he came back to a shop opposite Bruce Grove Railway Station. I called upon him there. I lost sight of him for a time, and I next saw him in custody. When a man becomes a "feldscher" in the Russian Army he gets a book given to him which contains his progress right through the service, and in civil hospitals he gets a certificate. The accused could not have been a soldier, because he was too young when he came over here. I did not see him from 1895 till 1903.

It had been shown during the Police Court proceedings that Klosowski had his hairdresser's shop at 89 High Street, Whitechapel, under the White Hart public house. The pub was only a few yards away from the first Ripper murder site, in the building Klosowski called home! As for the "certain medicine"— poison — which Levisohn refused to sell to Klosowski? The sale had been refused only a few short weeks before the Ripper turned to his blade to take his first victim — Martha Tabrum — on the first floor landing of the George Yard dwellings. Klosowski lived upstairs! No other suspect can be placed closer to a Ripper victim!

Mrs. Ethel Radin

The next witness firmly established that Klosowski was not George Chapman and confirmed that the prisoner had worked in the East End of London just before the first Ripper murder. The witness was also able to establish that Klosowski was very familiar with West India Dock Road in Poplar, East End. Although this area was fully two miles to the east of Whitechapel and the Ripper's primary killing ground, one victim who lived only yards from Klosowski in Whitechapel in 1888, as did all of the Ripper victims, had been murdered and dumped in Poplar, East End, on the night of December 20, 1888. Klosowski knew both areas intimately.

> I am the wife of Abraham Radin, of 82 Riveter Street, Shoreditch. About fifteen years ago, when we kept a hairdresser's shop in West India Dock Road, we had an assistant named Klosowski. I identify the accused as that man. He said he had been a feldscher in Warsaw. He had some papers with him, which he read to me, which were in the Russian and Polish languages. They had reference to his studies. He was with us for five months, during which time my baby was ill, and he helped me in the treatment of it.

Question — Before you identified the accused did a gentleman come to your place with a photograph?
Answer — Yes.
Q — And did you then go and pick out the accused?
A — Yes. I am quite sure about him.
Q — When you saw the photograph were you quite sure it was Klosowski?
A — Yes.

Stanislaus Baderski

It was then time to call humble tailor Stanislaus Baderski to the stand. Baderski had been a long time member of the local Polish club. It would be at this club in 1889 that he would meet and then introduce his sister Lucy to a local Polish barber named Klosowski.

> I come from Poland, and I have known the accused for thirteen years. I first met him in a Polish club in St. John's Square, Clerkenwell, in 1889. He was introduced to me as Severin Klosowski. He told me he had a barber's shop. I have two sisters, one of whom was named Lucy Baderski. She met the accused at the Polish club, and they kept company together four or five weeks, after which they got married. I was not at the wedding, but I went to the party in the evening after it. The accused and my sister were present at the party. It was on August Bank Holiday, 1889. They lived together in Cable Street and then in Greenfield Street, and they were known as Mr. and Mrs. Klosowski. There was one child of the marriage, a son. My sister left the accused about eighteen months after their marriage. She is alive now. I last saw her two or three months ago at Southwark.
>
> Question — Was the accused a member of the club?
> Answer — The accused was not a member of the Polish club, but he came there every Sunday night. I went to his house once or twice after he married my sister, but I did not have much to do with him. I did not see him again after he left my sister until I saw him in custody. I saw his name in the papers.
> Q — Did the police come to you?
> A — Yes.
> Q — Did you go to Southwark Police Court and identify the accused?
> A — Yes.

Mrs. Stanislaus Rauch

The final member of Lucy's family to be called that day was Mrs. Stanislaus Rauch. She was the married sister of Lucy and she would be able to estimate the time Klosowski and her sister lived together to include a trip of several months to the United States before her sister would return alone. She would provide evidence as to the gap in time during 1891–92 when Klosowski was no longer in London. The press would report: "Later in the day, while Mrs. Ranch, the sister of his Polish wife, was under examination, the occupant of the dock looked fixedly at her. On being asked to point out the man who she believed had married her sister, Mrs. Ranch stretched forth an accusing hand towards Klosowski, without, however, looking at him."

> I am the wife of William Rauch, of 292 Burdett Road, and I am the sister of the last witness. I have a sister named Lucy. I last saw her about four weeks ago. She left German Poland before I did. I only came over about [thirteen] years ago, and at that time my sister was married. Her married name was Lucy Klosowski. I met her husband in a public-house in Whitechapel Road. I think he is the accused. When I came to London my sister was living with him in Greenfield Street, and I used to go and see them there. When their first baby was born I saw the accused washing it just like a nurse. He said he had been a feldscher at the Hospital of the Infant Jesus at Praga, near Warsaw. I remember him and my sister going to America. She came back alone in February, 1891. Another child was born on 12th May. When the child was about a fortnight old the accused came back from America, and I then left my sister, as they were going to live together. I left them together in the same lodgings. That was the last I saw of him.
>
> Question — Were you shown a photograph before you went to court?

Answer — Yes, by Mr. Godley.
Q — Had you seen the accused very often before he went to America?
A — Yes. I came over here in August, and they went to America about the following Whitsuntide (seventh Sunday or 50th day after Easter).

Alfred Wicken

Hairdresser Alfred Wicken was next called to testify that he not only knew the accused by yet another alias, but that he also knew Klosowski had returned to England from America.

> I am a hairdresser at 2 Market Terrace, Lea Bridge Road, Leyton. Some years ago I was employed by Mr. Haddin, who had a hairdresser's shop in West Green Road, Tottenham, and accused was also employed there. We used to call him "Schloski." He worked there for about nine or twelve months with me, after which he took a shop in High Road, Tottenham, which had formerly belonged to Mr. Haddin. I left the neighborhood before the accused. I next saw him at Southwark Police Court a few months ago.
>
> Question — Have you ever heard the accused called Ludwig Schloski or Severin Klosowski?
> Answer — No. It was in 1892 or 1893 that I met him. I only know Levisohn. I did not know any of the others. I may have known Levisohn at the time I knew the accused. I did not know that Levisohn knew the accused as Ludwig Zagowski until after this case commenced. I never heard the accused called by any name except "Schloski."
> Q — Were you shown two photographs before you went into Court?
> A — Yes.
> Q — When you identified the accused was he in the dock?
> A — Yes.

William Lemain Bray

Clerk William Lemain Bray's testimony brought to light Klosowski's movements up to early 1895. Bray would also remember a young lady who visited with Klosowski.

> I am managing clerk to Mr. Braud, solicitor, of 6 Gray's Inn Square, and I live at 82 Park Lane, Tottenham. I know a Mr. Pincott; he is a personal friend of mine. In 1895 he was the owner of the shop at 518 High Road, Tottenham. About December, 1894, I was consulted by him with reference to the letting of that shop. The man who proposed to take it came alone to see me on several occasions, and he gave his name as Severin Klosowski. After giving me some references, an agreement was drawn up, which he signed in my presence. On 14th January I was at Southwark Police Court when I saw several men, and I picked out the accused from amongst them as the man who had signed the agreement. I have no doubt about him. I remember a young woman coming to me on several occasions. I have no doubt she gave her name, but I do not remember it now. It may have been Annie Chapman. The accused called on me eight or nine times, and I afterwards collected his rent as it became due. That was eight years ago.

After a break the court would hear from Inspector George Godley, who would describe for the court the many items he had found in searching Klosowski's bar and rooms, including a diary reportedly from 1893. Godley would read from some of the pages, including one interesting entry for a job. "Hairdresser wanted, indoors, 30s., to W. Holton, Clifton Baths Market." It was not reported whether or not Klosowski had applied for the job. Godley would also read from a sheet of paper which Klosowski had written as a cover story in an attempt to show that he had not arrived back in England in 1892. The note stated: "Came from America in 1893, independent. Deposits £100, when from America I had £1000." It was clearly a lie but the reason for the cover story was never pursued.

The good inspector would also report on the many documents he had found related to "one Severin Klosowski." For a translation of these documents the authorities would turn to Joseph Betrikowski, who lived at 30 New Street, Kennington Park Road, London. These documents would conclusively prove that publican Chapman was, in fact, a very skilled junior surgeon named Severin Antoniovich Klosowski from Poland. However, one document would show a very interesting date. Klosowski's birth certificate recording his birth on "15 December, 1865," was dated "29 October, 1882." Why it took 17 years for this document to be produced is not known. One intriguing suggestion is that this man was not Klosowski after all, and that he simply acquired the document as some type of cover in 1882. Did he do away with the real Klosowski? Is it possible that the "real" Severin Klosowski was long dead and that this man was more of an enigma than anyone could possibly have guessed? At this late date it is close to impossible to determine the truth, but it is, to say the least, not beyond the imagination.

The documents included:

- Birth Certificate
- Primary School attendance record
- Society of Surgeons' Receipt
- Well Behaved Certificate
- Registry of Surgical Pupils Document
- Surgical Apprentice Certificate
- Certificate of Surgical Employment
- Surgical Instruction Certificate
- Surgical Assistant Employment Certificate — Warsaw
- Biography written by Klosowski
- Passport
- Surgical Assistant Employment Certificate — Praga
- Petition for Junior Surgeon Degree
- Acceptance for Junior Surgeon Degree
- Hospital Fees Receipt

One must ask why Klosowski felt he needed to document the supposed fact that he had not been convicted of any crimes. Yet on November 16, 1882, he received just such documentation from the local magistrate.

> The magistrate of the County of Zvolen hereby certifies that Severin Klosowski, resident of the village Zvolen, is a well-behaved man, and **was never found guilty of any crime whatever** (emphasis added). To which effect he bears testimony by his own signature and official seal.—Dushevitch, Magistrate of the County, Village Zvolen, November 16, 1882 (author's emphasis).

George Schumann

Having established who the defendant was and detailing his many movements both during and after the Ripper period, the prosecution called George Schumann to the stand. Schumann was a barber who could also place Klosowski in Whitechapel during the Ripper murders who worked below the White Hart pub and who had seen the ever on the move Klosowski in Hastings after he returned from his adventures in America. This witness was a vital link between the two periods of the serial killer's life and it firmly placed Klosowski in Hastings, where the little bottle of poison was purchased for his new series of death.

> I am a barber at 33 Hill Street, Hoxton. I know the barber's shop underneath the public house in High Street, Whitechapel, which was occupied by the accused. I saw him twice. The first time was twelve years ago, and it was eight or nine years before I saw him again. The second occasion was at Hastings, outside a barber's shop. There was a short woman assisting him in the shop. I am not sure of his name; it was some foreign name like Klosowski.

William Henry Davidson

By far the most damaging witness against Klosowski was chemist William Davidson. Inspector Godley had found the small red label in one of the books seized from the Crown on October 25, 1902, but it would be up to Davidson to place the label and the poisons about which it warned clearly into the hands of one Severin Klosowski, alias G. Chapman.

> I am a chemist, and I now live at 49 Upper Lewes Road, Brighton. In 1897 I was living at 66 High Street, Hastings, and carrying on the business of a chemist there. I have now retired. I was at Hastings for about eighteen years, and while there I used frequently to go to a barber's shop to get shaved. The accused was employed there, and he shaved me on many occasions. One day he bought several things from me, and asked me to let him have a particular poison. He purchased 1 ounce of tartar-emetic. We have to keep a copy of the sale of poisons. I produce my poison register book. The entry relating to the tartar-emetic sold to the accused is as follows: "April 3rd, 1897, name of purchaser, Mr. G. Chapman, 1 ounce of tartar-emetic." That is my writing. Then there follows: "Purpose for which it is required," but I cannot make out what is written here; it is in the accused's handwriting. It looks like "take" or "teke." He wrote that in my presence after he signed "G. Chapman." I knew him as Chapman, but I do not recollect his Christian name. I gave him the ounce of tartar-emetic, which is a white powder, and I wrote out the label which was put on the bottle in my own handwriting.
>
> > W. H. Davidson, dispensing chemist.
> > Poison, Tartar-emetic.
> > Dose, $\frac{1}{16}$th grain to $\frac{1}{4}$.
> > To be taken with caution.
> > 66 High Street, Hastings.
>
> The word "POISON" is printed, and I used a red label to indicate poison. I also sold the accused two or three old editions of medical books. I cannot find any other sale of tartar-emetic in my book. I saw in the newspaper an account of a woman named Chapman having died of this poison, and I went to the police and gave such information as I had.
>
> Question — Can you recollect having sold so large a quantity of tartar-emetic as this in any one year?
> Answer — No. If I sold it, it would be entered in the book. It is very seldom asked for.
> Q — Have you during your professional life sold as large a quantity as this?
> A — Yes, several times.
> Q — Was it not a very unusual request to have made to you?
> A — No, because the accused had had several transactions with me.
> Q — Did he get some other poisons from you?
> A — I think he did have some other poisons, but they would not come under Schedule I.
> Q — Did you demur at his wanting so large a quantity?
> A — I do not know that I did. I cannot say what was passing through my mind at the time, but from my conversation with him I knew he had a good knowledge of medicines, and so I let him have it.
> Q — You knew he was not practicing as a medical man?
> A — Yes, but no doubt he gave me a cogent reason why he wanted it, although I cannot say what it was now.
> Q — Did you ask him what he required the poison for?
> A — No doubt I asked him what he required it for.
> Q — Is the dose you name an infinitesimal quantity compared to the quantity you sold to him?
> A — Yes.

After Inspector Godley testified that he found the poison label at the Crown the court adjourned for the day.

Chapter 14

The Second Day of Testimony

There is a chance for you as barmaid now
— Alias— George Chapman

OLD COURT NUMBER ONE—TUESDAY, MARCH 17, 1903

On the second day of the trial the Marsh family would be called to the bar to explain not only Klosowski's actions but also their own lack of action on behalf of Maud. Certainly no one in the courtroom was going to press Maud's grieving family, but it soon became clear that little had been done to remove Maud from Klosowski's deadly grip. Despite all of the clues to Maud's poisoning, they seemed to have been completely missed by all those around her.

Mrs. Eliza Marsh

Maud's mother would be the first to testify at court this day as she detailed what she knew of the events which had cumulated with the death of her young daughter.

Married: On 13th October I went to the Monument and saw some confetti lying about. My younger daughter Nellie was staying there on a visit at the time. On my arrival I saw Nellie, Maud, and the accused, and in the accused's hearing Nellie said, "Maud was married this morning." That was the first I heard of any marriage having taken place. The accused asked me to stop and have some dinner, which I did, and in his hearing again it was said that the marriage had taken place at the Roman Catholic Church. Maud was wearing a new wedding ring, and several other rings which the accused had given her. I asked about the certificate, and Maud said, "George has got it, and has put it with his other papers."

Injections: I have seen the accused administering the injections to my daughter. I did not see any liquid injection. The accused was frequently in the room during the daytime. When he came in, as a rule he went to her bedside and felt her pulse. I asked him what made Maud so bad, and he said he did not know, unless it was a rabbit she had eaten.

Poisoned: I attended to my daughter during the night. The vomiting continued. It was still green. Only drink was given to her during the night. Sometimes she wanted brandy and water, and sometimes only plain water, as long as it was cold or with pieces of ice in it. The accused gave it to me. Maud vomited every time she took it.

Early on Tuesday morning I made some gruel for my daughter and gave it to her, but she did not retain it. I got the gruel out of the kitchen; the servant, Louisa Cole, got the milk for me. I saw Dr. Stoker towards midday, and shortly afterwards my own doctor from Croydon, Dr. Grapel, called, at my husband's suggestion. He saw my daughter with Dr. Stoker, and, after they had examined her,

Dr. Grapel made a statement to me. I afterwards said to the accused, "Dr. Grapel thinks Maud has been poisoned." He said he could not think how, unless it was the rabbit. I said, "Dr. Grapel says you don't find arsenic in rabbits." The accused said, "I cannot think what it was then."

The Brandy: She had nothing to drink except water, or brandy and water. The accused generally brought the brandy. Sometimes I went down into the bar and asked him to give me a little.

During the early hours of the morning my daughter slept. She woke about 3 or 4 A.M. and asked for some drink. I gave her a little brandy and soda, which was kept in a small bottle on the landing outside. I only gave her about a tablespoonful of brandy. After she had taken it she vomited, and that was the last time she did so. Between 5 and 6 A.M. I took a little of the brandy myself in some iced water. After I had taken it I had severe diarrhea and sickness and pain in the lower part of my stomach, which continued till about 7 A.M. I had about six attacks of diarrhea and vomiting during that time.

Her Final Moments: When I got back to the room the accused was standing by the bedside. I do not know if he had anything in his hand then, but he got a little more brandy for Maud, because she said she was thirsty. I had told the accused what I was suffering from, and that he must send for the nurse. I told him I had both sickness and diarrhea. I do not know what he said; he did not suggest any cause for it. He said that it was perhaps from sitting up two nights and having had no rest. He did not stay in the room after Toon came, and when he had gone Maud asked for something to drink. Toon offered her some brandy in the glass which was standing on the safe. As Toon offered it to Maud she put up her hand and said, "No, no, no." Toon then gave her a little water. Toon then tasted the brandy, because she thought it was too strong. That was about 9 A.M., and about that time Maud had a kind of fit. There had been purging since the early morning, but not from the back passage. That which came away from her was green. Her lips and hands were dark and had changed colour. I went and told the accused, and he came upstairs. He did not bring anything with him. He went to the bedside, and Maud said, "I am going, George," and the accused said, "Where?" She said, "Good-bye, George," and that was all she uttered.

Severin Antoniovich Klosowski, alias George Chapman (artwork re-created by Robert DeLaCruz from an original March 1903 set of Severin Klosowski trial sketches presently held in Scotland Yard's Black Museum file on George Chapman).

Certificate: Maud had died at 12:30, and a little while afterwards Dr. Stoker came. I heard the accused ask him for a certificate of her death. Dr. Stoker said he could not give one. I asked why. He said he did not feel satisfied about the way she had died, and he was surprised to find her dead. The accused said, "Why not?" Dr. Stoker said because he could not think why she had died so suddenly. The accused said she had died from exhaustion caused by diarrhea and sickness. Dr. Stoker said he should like a post-mortem, and also said, "What caused the diarrhea and vomiting?" The accused did not make any answer.

Question — Was Maud ill while at the Monument?
Answer — Yes, for about three days, but I do not know the date. I did not visit her there.
Q — Did Maud not have severe pains in the stomach while at the Monument?
A — Yes, and a Mrs. Bolling attended her. It was a kind of flooding, Maud told me.
Q — Were the symptoms not something of the same kind as she had in her last illness?
A — Yes. She got quite well again. That was a long time before November, 1902.
Q — Who suggested that Dr. Grapel should be called in?
A — My husband. I did not speak to the accused about him; I did not know he was coming. I was surprised at Dr. Grapel coming, and so was the accused.
Q — Did you not know that the accused had arranged with Dr. Stoker to meet Dr. Grapel In consultation?
A — No. When Dr. Grapel came the accused sent the servant [Jessie Toon] to Dr. Stoker to say that Dr. Grapel was waiting.
Q — Where was the brandy that you gave to Maud obtained?

A — It was obtained from the bar. It was the best the accused had got. I do not know if it was Mortall's *Three Star* brandy. He got it out of a bottle, but he generally brought it up in a glass.
Q — Did you see the brandy poured from the bottle into the glass in the bar?
A — No.
Q — Did you fetch some?
A — Yes. He took it from a bottle in the bar.
Q — Was there anything in its appearance which excited your suspicion?
A — No.
Q — When you drank some yourself did you suspect it was wrong?
A — No.
Q — How long afterwards was it that you took ill?
A — About two hours afterwards, and it was not until I suffered discomfort that I knew it was the brandy and water which caused my illness.
Q — Did you ask Maud what she thought had made her bad?
A — Yes, and she said she did not know, unless it was the rabbit.
Q — Did you tell the accused that?
A — I think I did. When Toon drank some brandy and water on Wednesday morning she said, "Good God that has burnt my mouth." She had only sipped it.

Mr. Robert Marsh

Maud's father Robert was then called to the stand to tell the court what he could about the events leading up to the death of his daughter. He was not in the best of health and was unable to fully inquire about Maud's welfare. He had recently been in and out of the hospital and was still quite weak during the trial. He spoke in a soft voice.

At the Hospital: I left the hospital just before Christmas, and I went to the Crown. I went there again in July, 1902. Maud was then in Guy's Hospital. I saw the accused and asked him how Maud was. He said she was ill and in Guy's and asked me if I wanted to see her. I said, "Yes, that is what I have come for." I did not ask him what was the matter with her, and he did not tell me. I went to the hospital that same evening and saw Maud. She complained of vomiting and pains in her stomach.

At the Crown: I went upstairs to Maud's bedroom on the second floor. The accused went upstairs in front of me, and when we got into the room he took hold of Maud's hand. He did not say anything. She often showed signs of thirst. The accused gave her some water. He came up and down stairs every few minutes the whole time that I was there. When she asked for water the accused went out of the room to get it. He was not long absent. When he gave her the drink she vomited it nearly every time.

One Last Time: I thought Maud was better. I went up to the room twice. I went down again and saw the accused in the bar, and I said to him, "Maudie is very bad, is she not, George?" He said, "Yes." He did not say any more. I went upstairs again with him and I said to him, "I think my daughter will pull through now, George," and he said, "She will never get up no more." I said, "Have you seen any one else like it?" And he said, "Yes." I said, "Was your other wife like it?" and he said, "Just about in the same way." He told me that Dr. Grapel had been, and said that he had already got one doctor in attendance, and he did not know what we wanted another for; we did not want fifty. I told him it was no good to make a fuss about the doctor, as I had sent him up. Before I had gone downstairs I thought Maud some better; I was quite pleased at the way she spoke to me. That was the last time I saw her alive. The next day, about 4 P.M., I had a telegram announcing her death. I showed it to Dr. Grapel about five o'clock.

Question — Were you always on the best of terms with the accused?
Answer — Yes. I minded his house for him on two occasions.
Q — Did you always find him pleasant and agreeable?
A — Yes; he always answered my inquires about my daughter perfectly frankly. I thought he treated her well.
Q — When you said to him, "Have you seen anyone else like it?" did he say "Yes." quite readily?
A — Yes, and he had no hesitation in saying about his other wife, "Just the same way."
Q — Why did you get Dr. Grapel to come?
A — I suspected the accused on the 18th, and that is why I told Dr. Grapel to go. I did not like him getting the water and giving everything to her himself.

Q — Did you offer to do it?
A — No, the woman was there to do it, but he would not let her. I did not do it, because I did not know where the things were.
Q — Did you see any of the brandy which was for Maud poured out?
A — No. I did not know what class of brandy it was. I was not left alone with Maud for more than five or six minutes at a time.
Q — Did you call in Dr. Grapel because the accused had said that his former wife had suffered in the same way?
A — No; I was suspicious before that.

Mrs. Louisa Sarah Morris

The court then turned to an examination of Mrs. Louisa Morris, the married sister of Maud. She had been a frequent visitor to her sister at both the Monument and the Crown pubs and had been the family member closest to events as her sister was slowly killed by the Borough Poisoner.

A Finger Snaps: On one occasion he told me that Maud was suffering from constipation. Maud had told me it was diarrhea. I said it was funny, and I could not make it out. He said, "She should have done as I told her." I asked what that was, and he said, "She should have took the medicine I gave her." I said, "She never would take medicine," and that it was funny the doctor could not find out what was the matter with her. He said, "I could give her a bit like that" (snapping his fingers), "and fifty doctors would not find out." I said, "What do you mean?" He walked away and said, "Never mind."

Quite Helpless: For dinner she had pork, potatoes, greens, a piece of bread, and a glass of ginger beer. That meal stayed on her stomach. When I left she appeared to be pretty well; she was propped up in bed reading the paper. I did not go out of the house, but I was out of her room for about an hour and a half. I left the accused in the room with her, and when I came back she was very bad and quite helpless.

Her Last Time: I returned to the house on Monday, the 20th, and I found Maud very bad. She did not speak to me. Maud vomited during the day. She had diarrhea, and was in great pain. The vomit was green. I left that evening, leaving my mother with Maud. I never saw her alive again.

Question — Did you see a good deal of the accused and Maud when they were living together?
Answer — I did.
Q — Were you on very good terms with Maud?
A — We were on very good terms indeed, and she took me into her confidence.
Q — Up to the time of her last illness did she seem happy and contented?
A — Yes, at times. She used to complain that the accused would not let her go out; she had to stay in the bar or up in the house.
Q — Was Maud not very much distressed about not having a family?
A — Yes; she told me she was very unhappy to have no family. I used to take my baby to the house when I went to see her, and she would sometimes on such occasions get very distressed and cry a good deal.
Q — Was she very fond of children?
A — Yes, she said how grieved she was that she had not a baby of her own.
Q — Did Maud tell you that the accused had given her some medicine and she would not take it?
A — Yes.
Q — When the accused brought up the champagne did you have any of it?
A — I sipped it, but I did not like it. I have had some champagne which I liked.
Q — Did the accused have any?
A — No. He gave Maud two or three lots. I drank out of the same glass as she did. He poured a drop out, and I tasted it. I said, "I don't like that," and I pushed it away.
Q — Who had cooked the pork and vegetable for the dinner?
A — The servant and I, and Maud said she would like to have some. She seemed so much better I had a good mind to go home that night. She had her dinner, and seemed all the better for it.

Daisy Harriet Helen Marsh

Maud's younger sister, 15-year-old Daisy, was then called to give a short testimony about the fraudulent wedding ceremony she witnessed as she visited her sister at the Monument. She had been on an extended two-month visit but had not been taken into confidence by her sister that all was not right at the pub.

> Question — Did Maud say that she had been married at the Roman Catholic Church in Bishopsgate Street?
> Answer — Yes.
> Q — Had you seen a ring on her finger before that Sunday?
> A — No.
> Q — Was the accused kind to you?
> A — Yes.
> Q — Did he and Maud seem very happy together?
> A — Yes; he seemed to be kind to her.
> Q — Did you help your sister in the house?
> A — Yes.

Alice May Marsh

Next called was another sister, Alice, who witnessed Maud's decline and was the subject of Klosowski's next attempt to obtain a woman. Alice did not fall for his "charms."

> A Sickness: I went to the Crown last summer and saw my sister and the accused there. I took her to Guy's Hospital, and after she came out I got a postcard from her and went again to the Crown. I saw the accused in the bar. I did not expect to see him. I said, "I thought you were ill in bed," and he said, "It would not do for both of us to be in bed." He did not look ill.
>
> The Offer: On 23rd October I went to the Crown again. Maud's body had then been removed to the mortuary. I had tea with my mother and aunt and the accused. While we were having tea the accused said to me, "There is a chance for you as barmaid now. Will you come?" I said, "No. thanks, London does not suit me."
>
> Question — Did you take it as a joke when the accused said there was a chance for you as a barmaid?
> Answer — I do not know whether I took it as a joke or not. The accused had asked me to go and live with him and my sister.

Mrs. Jessie Toon

After a break the day's testimony continued to focus on individuals who could report on how Maud was cared for and who had access to her when it came to food and drink. One individual who was close to these events was Jessie Toon, who was hired to care for Maud even though she had no experience as a nurse.

> Crying: The accused asked me to go and see Maud, and I went upstairs. She was in bed and crying. I asked her what she was crying for, and she said she was ill, and that if she could not get anyone to look after her she would have to go to the hospital, which she did not want to do.
>
> Syringe: The accused told me she was fed with a small syringe, with a rubber thing, with beef tea and egg and milk in it. He prepared the injections in the kitchen and administered them himself. He brought them up into the bedroom in a half-pint tumbler. After he had given the injections he took the tumbler and the syringe and washed them himself. The injections did not stay with the deceased, they came back again quickly, and she was in terrible pain.
>
> She Talks: He said he would not give me any rum to drink. I said, "What for?" and he said, "Because you talk, Jessie, when you have rum." I said, "People ask me about Mrs. Chapman," and he said, "Well, I don't want you to have anything to say." I said, "Very well, if it is your wish I won't say anything; if they ask me no questions I won't tell them no lies." He said, "That is right, Jessie, I don't want you to say anything of what occurred upstairs."
>
> Question — Did you tell him that she refused to take the brandy because it burned her mouth?

Answer — No, because she was dead when he came again. I burned my mouth with it about a couple of hours before she died.
Q — Did you see the doctor after her death?
A — I did.
Q — Did you then tell him anything about it burning the deceased's mouth or your own?
A — No.
Q — Did you tell the accused about it?
A — No, I told Mrs. Marsh. I did not tell the accused because I did not think it important.
Q — When did you first mention it?
A — When I saw Godley. I did not tell him of it the first time I saw him. I made a statement to him, which he took down in writing.

Dr. James Henry Targett

The first medical man to be called to testify at the trial was Dr. Targett, who had seen Maud at Guy's Hospital in late July 1902. It would soon be clear to the court that Dr. Targett had no idea what was really wrong with a greatly suffering Maud Marsh.

I am assistant obstetric surgeon at Guy's Hospital. I remember a woman named Maud Chapman being admitted to a ward at Guy's on 28th July. I do not know the address she gave. She remained an in-patient till 20th August. I attended her.
Question — What did she complain of?
Answer — She complained of great pain in the lower part of the abdomen. It came on in attacks of great severity. At times she had considerable fever.
Q — What were the symptoms?
A — Her pulse was more rapid than it should have been. She had occasional sickness, and her abdomen was extremely tender to the touch, so much so that I could not make a complete examination. She began to improve about 10th August. During the first fortnight her temperature went up to about 102. On 10th August her temperature began to fall, her pulse also began to improve, and there was a general improvement until she left.
Q — What did you discover was the matter with her?
A — I thought she had peritonitis, but we never discovered any cause for it.
Q — Why did you not discover the cause?
A — Partly because she was so tender, and there may not have been any cause. We could never form any clear idea what she was suffering from. Her temperature was normal when she went out. When she came in she was very ill.
Q — Had you heard the history of her illness before she came to you?
A — I had heard the history of her illness before she came to us from the student in the ward. He would get from her an account of her illness.
Question by Judge Grantham — Have you had any experience of antimonial poisoning?
A — No. I should think that ten days would be a reasonable time for a person to recover from that poison if during that time no more was administered.

Florence Rayner

Even before he had dispatched Maud, Klosowski had his eye on his next victim along with a plan to go back to America. It was time again to "cut and run." In the press Miss Rayner would become known as "the Peckham barmaid."

Last June (1902) I became acquainted with Maud Marsh, whom I knew as Mrs. Chapman. I was afterwards retained to go as barmaid at the Crown. When I went there in June the deceased was apparently in good health. After I had been there about a fortnight (two weeks) the accused kissed me and asked me to be his sweetheart and go to America with him. I used to take my meals with him alone. When he asked me to go to America with him I said, "You have got your wife downstairs; you don't want me." He said, "If I gave her that" (snapping his fingers) "she would be no more Mrs. Chapman."
Question — Were you employed by the accused as barmaid and servant?
Answer — Yes.

Q — Did you take much notice when he asked you to go to America with him?
A — No; my dignity was hurt at the idea of a married man asking me to do such a thing.
Q — Did the accused kiss you often?
A — He kissed me constantly when we were at meals together. He did not kiss me in front of his wife.
Q — His kissing was a matter of daily occurrence?
A — Yes.
Q — Did you not object?
A — I did not object; I could not help myself.
Q — Did you want him to go on kissing you?
A — I do not know if I wanted him to go on kissing me.
Q — How long did you stay?
A — I stayed on three or four weeks, and then the deceased told me that the accused said he must have some one stronger. I had fainted on the Saturday night from the stuff the accused had given me.
Question by Justice Grantham — What happened when you went to the accused to get a reference?
A — When I went to get a reference he took me by the throat and threw me out.

Annie Chapman

On September 8, 1888, Jack the Ripper murdered Annie Chapman. Chapman left behind a daughter named Annie Georgina Chapman. It has not yet been proven that the woman who lived with Klosowski as man and wife and had a child by that union is *the* Annie Georgina Chapman. However, if it can be proven that she was the daughter of a Ripper victim and the woman whose name was taken for his own it would show a direct link between a Ripper victim and Severin Klosowski. No other suspect in the Ripper case would ever come closer to a family member of a Ripper victim and, as history has already shown, no other suspect ever came closer to living and working in "Jack's" killing fields!

I first became acquainted with the accused towards the end of 1893, when he was going under the name of Klosowski. He was employed as an assistant at Mr. Haddin's hairdresser's shop, West Green Road. I went there one day and saw the accused there and made his acquaintance. After that I went out with him for a little while. I think he said he was either single or a widower. He was living at Haddin's, and he proposed I should go as his housekeeper, and after a time I did so. I lived with him as his wife; we passed as Mr. and Mrs. Klosowski. I went to live with him in November, 1893, and left him in November or December, 1894. At the time I first met him my name was Annie Chapman.

Question — Did you see the accused in February or March 1895?
Answer — Yes; he came on a bicycle one day to Albert Road, Tottenham, where I was living.
Q — Have you had any letter or communication from him since February, 1895?
A — No.
Q — How did you come to know about this case?
A — My sister read this case to one in the newspaper, and I went to the police court, but I did not give evidence there.
Q — Where did you identify the accused?
A — I identified the accused in a passage at the Court from about ten other men.
Q — And did you go there expecting to see a man like him?
A — Yes.
Q — Was he very much the same as what he was when he left you eight years ago?
A — Yes.
Q — How long did you live with the accused?
A — I lived with him for a year.
Q — And you have no doubt the accused is the man?
A — I have no doubt.
Q — Do you recognize that woman (pointing to Lucy Klosowski)?
A — Yes, he brought her to the shop where I was living with him. He said she was his wife.
Q — Did you all three live in the house for some weeks after that?
A — Yes, and then I left. That was the reason why I left.
Q — Is the accused the father of your child?
A — Yes.

Dr. Francis Gasper Grapel

If there can be a hero in this case the title would go to Dr. Francis Grapel who came to the correct conclusion that Maud Marsh was being poisoned and most likely by her so-called husband. It would take but one day for this medical man to discover the deadly truth and even quicker to act. It is to his great credit that he acted, even though he knew there would be risks to his reputation if he accused anyone of criminal activity.

I am an F.R.C.S., and I practice at 103 London Road, West Croydon. I asked to see Mrs. Marsh. I stayed in the bar, and then saw Dr. Stoker, and together we examined the deceased. Her skin was sallow, jaundiced and muddy in appearance, tongue coated, her pulse fairly quick, and her breathing shallow. She was in a semi-comatose condition. I examined her stomach and found it was extremely tender to touch; when I touched it she groaned and retched. I had a consultation with Dr. Stoker downstairs, and then saw Mrs. Marsh. Dr. Stoker and I were of opinion that she was suffering from some acute irritant poison, probably ptomaine. Later on the suspicion crossed my mind that it was not ptomaine poisoning, but repeated doses of arsenic.

Question — When did it cross your mind that it was arsenical poisoning?
Answer — It crossed my mind on my way home.
Q — Did you not go back and tell Dr. Stoker or send any communication until after she was dead?
A — No. Bringing in a diagnosis of repeated doses of arsenic is tantamount to accusing some one of murder, and I had no proof whatsoever.
Q — Did you believe she was likely to die them?
A — No. I was going to communicate with Dr, Stoker next day.
Q — Who was the first person you saw at the Crown?
A — The accused. I had a desultory conversation with him.
Q — Did he send for Mrs. Marsh?
A — Yes, he sent for Mrs. Marsh before I saw Dr. Stoker.
Q — Did you question him about the symptoms?
A — No. He said she had been suffering from constipation.
Q — And did he tell you how she had been treated?
A — No. I did not say more to him than I could help. On the Wednesday morning I told Mr. Marsh that I was going up to London as early as I could on that day to see Dr. Stoker, with the idea of having the excrete saved and examined.
Q — Did you not feel justified in at once telling the father what your suspicions were?
A — No; even a doctor must have time to think about a case before he renders himself liable to anything legal.
Q — Why did you not go to London on the Wednesday?
A — Because I heard of the deceased's death.

The Court was adjourned for the day.

Chapter 15

Requiem for a Serial Killer

I found no evidence of any natural disease which would account for her death
— Dr. Thomas Stevenson

OLD COURT NUMBER ONE — WEDNESDAY, MARCH 18, 1903

On the third day of Klosowski's short trial the doctors would take center stage during the first part of the day. Their testimony and autopsy reports would show conclusively that all three of Klosowski's "wives" had died by antimony poisoning. Their words would also show how little they had really done to save the life of Maud Marsh. Later in the day the details of Mrs. Spink and Bessie Taylor's deaths would come in testimony by several witnesses who were able to relate their personal contacts with a serial killer they thought they knew as George Chapman, expatriate American.

Dr. Stoker, the medical man from Southwark who attended Maude Marsh and Bessie Taylor, gave his version of the illness and the story of the death of Maude — a retold catalogue of grievous suffering, useless remedies, and professional perplexity. The post-mortem that followed the girls' death made him none the wiser, and he sent the internal organs, to the Clinical Research Association... [*Pall Mall Gazette*, March 24, 1903].

Dr. James Maurice Stoker

I am an L.R.C.S., and I practice at 221 New Kent Road. On 10th October, about 5 P.M., the accused called at my surgery, which is about half a mile from where he lives, and said he wanted a bottle of medicine for diarrhea and vomiting. He led me to believe it was for his wife. He said she had been at Guy's Hospital suffering from the same thing.

The deceased told me that they (the doctors) said she had peritonitis. The symptoms she complained of would be consistent with peritonitis.

About the fifth day I noticed she had spasms; they came on with great pain in the stomach; she got rigidity of the muscles of the leg, and they passed off in about half a minute. They did not synchronize with the sickness; they came on independently. On one occasion she had two in about five minutes.

She was very much worse on the 15th, and on that day I stopped all food through the mouth except the bismuth powders. She could not even keep the medicine down.

I suggested to the accused that she should be taken to the hospital, but the deceased objected and began to cry. I suggested a nurse, and the next day, finding there was still no one there, I spoke to the accused about it.

When I saw her on the Tuesday I had no reason to anticipate she would die so soon. On the Monday she was about as bad as she could be, and I could not say if she would get well.

On Wednesday I went into the bedroom. The accused and Mrs. Marsh were there. The accused was wiping his eyes. I asked when the deceased had died, and I was told. I then went out on to the landing and had a conversation with the accused. I said I should like a post-mortem, as I could not account for the cause of her dying. He said, "What use is it?" I said that I did not know what was the cause of death, and I might be asked what had caused her death. The accused said she had died from exhaustion. I asked what caused the exhaustion, and he said, "Diarrhea and vomiting." I asked what caused the diarrhea and vomiting, and he made no answer.

I had a consultation with Dr. Cotter, and, as a result, in the early morning of Saturday, the 25th, I communicated with the police.

Question — Have you ever had practical experience of the tartarisation of antimony?
Answer — No, and I do not think I should recognize it if I came across it in a post-mortem. If antimony was present in the deceased's stomach when I took it out and placed it in the glass jar I should not recognize it.
Q — Should you not have analyzed the deceased's vomit yourself?
A — No.
Q — Should you not have tried to trace the presence of antimony?
A — No.
Q — Have you ever had a case of poisoning from bismuth?
A — No.
Q — Do you know that there are such cases?
A — I know there are such cases, but you would want an enormous quantity.
Q — And do you know that you can get diarrhea and vomiting from an overdose of bismuth?
A — Yes.
Q — And might you get spasms in the arms and legs?
A — Yes.
Q — When did you first meet the accused?
A — I think I first met him in January, 1901, in connection with Bessie Taylor, who at that time was living with him as Mrs. Chapman.
Q — Did you not think of submitting the vomit to chemical analysis because suspicion was entirely eliminated from your mind?
A — Yes; I had no idea of any irritant poison, and it would not have been possible for me to recognize when examining the body.
Question by Judge Grantham — You know that Bessie Taylor died at the Monument?
A — Yes.
Q — Were her symptoms something similar to those of Maud Marsh?
A — Yes.
Q — And even did not make you think that you ought to make further inquiry into this case?
A — No, not until after death.
JUDGE GRANTHAM — I think it was the duty of the doctor to have told Mrs. Marsh, after her daughter's death, that he knew the accused was not her husband.
SOLICITOR-GENERAL CARSON — Does your lordship not think the doctor was placed in a rather difficult position?
JUDGE GRANTHAM — Certainly not. The doctor ought always to let the parents know the true position of affairs.

Dr. Richard Bodmer

I am a fellow of the Institute of Chemists, and am public analyst for the borough of Bermondsey. I am also consulting chemist to the Clinical Research Association, 1 Southwark Street. I received two sealed jars from Dr. Stoker, one of them containing a human stomach and a small piece of human liver, the other containing a lower part of the bowel and some pieces of liver. I discovered arsenic was present. On Monday, 27th October, Inspector Godley saw me, and in consequence I subjected another portion of the contents of the stomach to Marsh's test, which is also a test for arsenic and antimony. I discovered both present by that test, and also found that there was far more antimony present than arsenic.

Mr. Frank Lovell Gilbert

Next up came Frank Gilbert, the mortuary keeper at Collier's Rents, Southwark. The prosecution team wanted the jury to understand just how fast Klosowski wanted Maud's corpse removed from his business. Now that he was done with her it was time to move on to more pressing matters. There were many more women out there for him to own!

On 22nd October, just before midnight, I saw Dr. Stoker, and in consequence of what he said I went to the Crown. I saw the accused, and asked him if he was Chapman. He said, "Yes." I told him I had been sent by Dr. Stoker to remove the body to the mortuary. He said he required it removed that night, but I said it was rather late. Having paid a visit to the undertaker, the removal was arranged for 5 A.M. the next day. The accused went to the mortuary with me then. We got there about 5.55. After we had taken the body from the shell I asked him who she was, and he said, "Maud Marsh, my wife." I asked him her age, and he said "twenty." On 25th October I again saw the accused at the Crown. He asked me if the funeral could start from the mortuary at 9 A.M. on the Monday; he said he had a business in the High Street, and he did not want any fuss outside the Crown.

Dr. Thomas Stevenson

The prosecution then got down to the core medical evidence in this case by calling to the box Doctor Stevenson. His testimony would clearly show that Maud had been slowly murdered by a long and continuous process of poison introduced into her body, ending with a final deadly dose.

I am an M.D., and I am one of the official analysts to the Home Office. I am also lecturer on forensic medicine at Guy's Hospital. I have had experience in analysis, particularly with reference to poisons, and have acted for the Home Office for thirty-one years. On 30th October I attended St. Georges's mortuary to make a post-mortem examination on the body of Maud Marsh. Dr. Freyberger, Dr. Stoker, and Dr. Cotter were there. There had been a previous post-mortem.

The doctor then gave a detailed summation of his postmortem on Maud Marsh, which indicated that she had been poisoned by antimony, and he was then questioned for more details of the case.

Question — Is there enough antimony left in this bottle for a fatal dose?
Answer — No, but if the bottle had been full of the same preparation of bismuth, antimony, and water, I think there would have been sufficient for a fatal dose, but I am not positive.
Q — How many doses did it contain?
A — Six doses. Each dose of itself would not be a fatal one, but I cannot say what would be the effect of six successive doses. I should expect a person to be very ill after taking them.
Q — Did you examine the syringes?
A — Yes.
Q — Is one of them covered with an insoluble preparation of antimony, which is used in its manufacture?
A — Yes. Apart from that, I did not find any trace of antimony on either of them.
Q — Did you hear they were used for the injecting of liquid beef tea?
A — Yes, and also that they were soaked and washed afterwards.
Q — What was the immediate cause of death?
A — Acute gastritis. I have had to be with a good many cases, but I never saw such extensive gastroenteritis from ptomaine poisoning.
Q — Do persons who have died from ptomaine poisoning suffer from sub-acute enteritis?
A — Yes; it is a question of degree.
Q — Can you say if the whole of the last dose of antimony was due to rectum administration?
A — I cannot say, but I think that she must have had during the last few hours of her life some given by the mouth. If brandy was pure it would not take up enough antimony to give it any extra test, but I should not like to take a mouthful of this brandy and water and antimony.

Cross examined, Dr. Stevenson admitted that antimony was sometimes used as a drug for the care of drunkenness. On this point the Solicitor-General immediately put Mrs. Marsh into the box again, and asked her if her daughter had been addicted to drinking habits. Mrs. Marsh declared that the unhappy girl never drank too much. Mr. George Elliott hastened to assure the court, in respect for the memory of the dead girl that he never intended to suggest for a moment that she was a drunkard [*Pall Mall Gazette*, March 24, 1903].

Richard Bodmer (recalled) — Question — Did you take part with Dr. Stevenson in the chemical analysis of the different parts of the deceased's body? Answer — I did. I have been in Court while he has been giving evidence, and I agree with him absolutely.

Dr. Ludwig Freyberger (examined) — I am an M.D. and M.R.C.P. I was present on 30th October at the post-mortem conducted by Dr. Stevenson. I have heard him describe the various organs of the deceased's body, and I agree with his evidence. I took no part in the chemical analysis.

Inspector George Godley (recalled) — I found the bottle which Dr. Stevenson has referred to. Nos. 2, 3, and 4 I found in the deceased's bedroom. I took them to my office and handed them over to Sergeant Kemp, with instructions what to do. I took everything that was there.

The court would then turn to testimony examining the life and death of Mary Isabella Spink, even though Klosowski had not been brought to trial for her murder. However, Judge Grantham had earlier ruled that testimony could be taken in both the Spink and Taylor murders in order to establish clearly in the minds of the jury that a pattern existed leading to death in all three poison cases. By focusing on Klosowski's prior actions the prosecution was marking new ground in British law. For that reason this case would become one of the "notable British trials" and required reading for all who pursued the legal profession in Britain. Indeed, *Trial of George Chapman* may still be found in many law libraries in Britain as well as the United States.

Detective Sergeant Arthur Neil

I searched the register of marriages at Somerset House from the beginning of 1895 to 1897, and I found no record of any marriage between anyone named George Chapman and Mary Isabella Spink, or between Severin Klosowski and Mary Isabella Spink, or between Klosowski and anybody else.

Mrs. Anna Helsdown

I am the wife of Frederick. For some years we lived at 10 Hill Street, and I remember a Mr. and Mrs. Chapman, and a little boy named Willie, coming to live in the house. The accused is Mr. Chapman. I did not know him before that. The boy was about five or six. After they had been there some time the accused opened a barber's shop in George Street. He and his wife had their meals there. I heard her cry out once or twice, and I went to her next morning and she showed me a mark on her throat. She made a communication to me. She was not so well during the latter part of the time as she was at first. She was sick, and said she had dreadful pains in her stomach. That was in 1896. I saw her vomit; it was greenish. No doctor was attending her. I left them there in 1897.

Mrs. Martha Doubleday

The accused came to me a fortnight before Christmas and asked me if I would go over and sit up with his wife at night, as she was very ill. I said I would, and I went up to see her. There was no doctor there. I asked if I would fetch a doctor. The accused said, "Who is the nearest?" I said, "Dr. Rogers." He gave me a paper, and Dr. Rogers came.

Question — Were you a customer at the beer-house?
Answer — I was not a customer at the beer-house until about six months after the accused took it.
Q — And at that time Mrs. Chapman was a very healthy woman?
A — Yes.
Q — Did you know that she was suffering in any way?
A — No.
Q — Did she not say that she had been ill at Hastings?
A — No, neither did the accused. The first symptoms that I noticed of her becoming ill were that she began to get thin.

Q — Did Dr. Rogers come regularly?
A — Yes.
Q — What had you to drink while you were in the house?
A — The only thing I had to drink while I was in the house was a drop of stout, which the accused brought up to me. I did not taste the brandy.
Q — Did you drink the stout?
A — I did not drink the stout, because I did not care for it.
Q — Did you have much to say to the accused?
A — No.
Q — Dr. Rogers saw Mrs. Chapman before she was dead?
A — Yes.

Mrs. Elizabeth Waymark

I go out nursing sometimes. I knew the late Dr. Rogers, of Old Street. Towards the end of 1897 he sent me to the Prince of Wales to nurse Mrs. Chapman for a fortnight before her death. I very often saw her vomit. It was slimy and green, and as she vomited she was purged; she had diarrhea. She did not take much food, only a little beef tea, brandy, milk and soda, and water. The accused generally gave them to her. When I saw she was dying I sent down two or three times for the accused. At first he did not come up, and when he did she said to him, "Do kiss me." She put her arms out for him to bend over to kiss her, but he did not do so. The last time I sent for him just before she died he did not come up in time. I prepared the body for burial. It was a mere skeleton. She died on Christmas Day, 1897.

Question by Judge Grantham — What was the appearance of the body when you saw it after it had been exhumed?
Answer — When she was exhumed she looked as if she had only been buried about nine months. The only difference was that her hair had grown a little longer on the forehead. The face was perfect.

After Mrs. Waymark completed her testimony the court called undertaker Henry Edward Pierce to the stand, who testified to Klosowski's demands that Spink be buried as soon as possible. On December 9, 1902, Pierce would be on hand to identify the body of Mary Isabella Spink as she was removed from her grave for a long overdue postmortem examination.

Inspector George Godley (recalled) — I found this undertaker's bill at the Crown. I also produce the certificate of registration of the death of Mary Isabella Chapman on 25th December, 1897. The cause of death is certified by Dr. Rogers to be phthisis.

Early in the afternoon the sad story of Maude Marsh was ended, and the Crown turned to the history of Isabella Spink, the first Mrs. Chapman. Dr. Stevenson, once more in the box, explained the extraordinary state of preservation of the body. "The body was so fresh that it might have been buried that day [*Pall Mall Gazette*, March 24, 1903].

Dr. Thomas Stevenson (recalled) — Once again the doctor's testimony would clearly show that Spink had also been slowly murdered by a long and continuous process of poison introduced into her body, which ended with a final deadly dose. He had rightly concluded that she had died by antimony poisoning and that it had been administered over a long period of time.

There was no sign of phthisis; that generally indicates disease of the lungs. The cause of death was gastroenteritis. There was no other cause. There was nothing to indicate that the woman had been a confirmed drunkard. If she had drunk it had not produced any serious injury to the kidneys or liver. The inflammation which I found in the stomach was not attributable to alcohol. I came to the conclusion that the cause of death was poisoning by antimony, and I attribute the preservation of the body to the antimony.

Question — Does the condition of preservation in a measure depend on the surroundings of the body, quite apart from anything internal?
Answer — Yes.
Q — And was the grave 18 feet deep?
A — Yes.
Q — Does the depth of the grave to some extent help to preserve the body?
A — Yes, but if this body had begun to decay at the time it was buried the depth of the grave would not have retarded it. The air generally reaches a body before it is buried.

Q — There were seven other coffins above; this one was at the bottom?
A — Yes.
Q — What was the appearance of the body?
A — The body was almost lifelike.
Q — Did you analyze the lungs?
A — No, because I was told the woman had died from phthisis, but when I found no traces I put them aside in case questions were asked.
Q — If you had not known the history of the woman, and were told that a certificate of death from phthisis had been given, would you have found that consistent with her condition?
A — I might possibly have found that consistent with her condition.
Question by a juryman — Would antimony given in gradual doses for a long time be more likely to preserve the body than a sudden dose?
A — I am of opinion that antimony given in gradual doses for a long time would be more likely to preserve the body than a sudden dose. It would get more into the system.

William Taylor

Testimony then focused on Bessie Taylor. Her brother was called to inform the court of what he had seen of the man he knew as George Chapman. "For this case three extra doctors were called in to consult with Dr. Stoker, Chapman's medical advisor. In fact, the prisoner seemed to court inquiry. The doctors could make nothing of the case."

I live at 62 Lausanne Road, Hornsey. Bessie Taylor was my sister. She was about thirty-six when she died. About four years ago she introduced me to the accused as her husband. I cannot fix the date. I recognize the photograph now shown me as a photograph of my sister. She looked strong and healthy. When I saw her at the Monument she appeared to be very ill and shrunken; she had gone like a little old woman. I was at the graveside in November, 1902, and saw her grave opened and the coffin in which she had been buried taken out.

Question — How often did you see the accused and your sister together?
Answer — About six times.
Q — Did he treat her kindly and properly?
A — Yes.
Q — Did she seem to be fond of him?
A — Yes, and they seemed to be happy.
Q — Did you ever hear your sister make any complaint about him?
A — No.
Q — Did you know that she was being attended by a doctor?
A — Yes.

Mrs. Elizabeth Ann Painter

Elizabeth Painter had been a longtime friend of Bessie and would see firsthand how cruel Klosowski could be to the many women who crossed his path. She did not however, suspect that Klosowski was putting anything in Bessie's food. One thing was clear — Klosowski could not keep his roving hands off of any woman he wanted to own.

I was acquainted with Bessie Taylor for many years. I remember her being in a situation at Peckham. About Easter time, 1898, she left there and went to live at the Prince of Wales. I understand that she had been married. I visited her there and saw the accused. They were living as Mr. and Mrs. Chapman. She was in good health.

Question — Were Bessie and you great friends?
Answer — Yes, we had been in service together.
Q — How long had she been at the Monument when you first noticed anything the matter with her?
A — I do not know. I think that when she came from Bishops Stortford her health began to fail.
Q — Did you sometimes assist in the business?
A — Yes; Bessie took a prominent part in the bar.
Q — When the accused said, "Your friend is dead," did you take him seriously?

A — I did not. I thought it was just his way of putting it.
Q — When you visited Bessie and she was ill, did you have something to drink?
A — Yes.
Q — Did you always find it all right?
A — I always thought it was all right.
Q — Did you ask for it?
A — Sometimes I would ask for it, and sometimes the accused would give it to me.
Q — Was it what had been got for Bessie?
A — No. The brandy and things for her were always in the room when I got there.

Questions by a juryman — Did the accused ever kiss you?
Answer — He kissed me once or twice.
Q — Did he ever make any overtures to you?
A — No, he never made any overtures to me nor said that I could be Mrs. Chapman.
Q — Did he kiss you while Bessie was about?
A — Yes.

Mrs. Martha Stevens

I live at 22 Fanshaw Avenue, Barking, and have been a nurse for a number of years. I used to live at Union Street, Borough. Two or three months before Christmas, 1900, I got to know the accused and Bessie Taylor at the Monument. When I first knew Bessie she seemed pretty well in health. Later on she complained to me of being fatigued, languid, and having pains in her stomach. I suggested that she should go to the doctor. She made a complaint to me, and I mentioned Dr. Stoker's name. I went with her to his surgery more than once. He gave her some medicine. She seemed to rally, but not for long.

I was with Bessie on the 13th of February, and about 1:30 A.M. I thought she was dying, so I called the accused. He came up just as she was dying. He looked at her, and I think he said, "Oh, she has gone," and he commenced to cry. I stopped a day or two in the house, and on the 15th the body was removed in a coffin to the railway station.

Question — Did you know Dr. Stoker before you went to the Monument?
Answer — I did.
Q — Did you introduce him to the Chapman?
A — Yes.
Q — Were three specialists also called in while you were there?
A — Yes.
Q — Altogether there were four doctors?
A — Yes. They examined Bessie, and had a consultation in the clubroom.
Q — Was the accused present?
A — The accused was not present; he came up afterwards.
Q — During that time did Bessie have everything that was prescribed for her?
A — Yes; she was looked after with every possible care.
Q — Did the accused seem to be willing to have everything done that could be done?
A — Yes; he got everything that was suggested.
Q — Who generally prepared the food?
A — Mrs. Taylor.
Q — Had the accused always access to the bedroom?
A — Yes.

Dr. James Maurice Stoker (recalled) — Once again doctor Stoker was called to the box to testify about what he had learned about the death of Bessie Taylor and Klosowski's actions leading up to her murder.

Question — What did you think was the matter with Mrs. Chapman (Bessie Taylor)?
Answer — At first I regarded the case as one of constipation, and I directed my treatment with the view of removing that. I attended her at her home for excessive diarrhea, so the stoppage must have given way.
Q — How often did she come to your surgery?
A — I think she came twice.
Q — Do you remember what you gave her?
A — I do not remember what I gave her, but it would be most likely a dose of salts.

Q — And I believe that Dr. Sunderland came to the conclusion that she was suffering from some uterine trouble?
A — Yes, I believe he did, but I have no record of it.
Q — Did the accused see Dr. Sunderland when he came, and ask him what was the matter with his wife?
A — Yes.
Q — Was he dissatisfied with your opinion?
A — I do not remember that he was dissatisfied with our opinion.
Q — Whom did you consult with?
A — Dr. Thorpe.
Q — What did Dr. Thorpe tell the accused?
A — I think he told him that the woman had hysteria.
Q — And did he accept that opinion?
A — Yes, he accepted that opinion as he had accepted Dr. Sunderland's.
Q — What did Dr. Cotter say?
A — Dr. Cotter said it was some cancerous disease of the stomach or intestines.
Questions by Judge Grantham — Did it occur to you that she was not suffering?
Answer — No.
Q — What was the primary cause?
A — Constipation.
Q — And what caused her death?
A — The vomiting and exhaustion had caused her death.
Q — Would it not have been wise to have had a post-mortem?
A — It would probably have been wise to have a post-mortem before giving a certificate, as all the doctors were evidently wrong.
Q — Have you ever known a case where four doctors gave four different opinions, and when the patient died still there was no post-mortem?
A — No.

Detective Sergeant Arthur Neil (recalled) — I have searched the records at Somerset House between January, 1898, and March, 1900, and I can find no record of a marriage between George Chapman and Bessie Taylor, or Severin Klosowski and Bessie Taylor.

To end the day's evidence William Tull and William Kelsall were called to inform the court that they were both present when the body of Bessie Taylor was exhumed from the grave at Lymn Churchyard. Both men would be able to identify the body as that of Bessie Taylor. The court would not want to sentence anyone to hang because of an error in having exhumed the wrong corpse from the ground.

By the end of the third day of testimony there could not have been any real doubt that British justice was about to close the books on the Borough Poisoner. There could be no doubt that Klosowski, alias George Chapman, was indeed a most effective and brutal serial killer. There was also a great deal of speculation that none other than Jack the Ripper was also having his day in court!

Chapter 16

"You've Got Jack the Ripper at Last!"

What is the use of seeking for motive when we have the actual fact of the murder?
— Edward Carson

OLD COURT NUMBER ONE — THURSDAY, MARCH 19, 1903

On the final day of Klosowski's trial the prosecution would spend very little time with their final witnesses. For the most part the prosecution team had proved their case. It would be up to the defense team to bring forth evidence on behalf of their client. The only problem — there was no evidence for them to show!

The *South London Press* would take Klosowski's measure as he entered the small and darkened courtroom for the final time. As before, all eyes were on the prisoner and the room grew silent. "On Thursday for the first time the prisoner appeared to realize his terrible position, and abandoning his attitude of passiveness, he displayed a keen, indeed a feverish, interest in the proceedings. When he entered the dock he was ghastly pale, and even the dim light of the court failed to hide the heightened pallor of the face. The restless movements of the hands, the twitchings of the mouth, all betrayed the emotion which he would fain conceal." Klosowski seemed to finally realize that he was caught.

Dr. Thomas Stevenson (recalled)

Dr. Stevenson was called to report on the autopsy of Bessie Taylor and the condition of the body. Needless to say, the good doctor found the remains saturated with metallic antimony. The poisons, having done their work, had also kept the body in a very good state of preservation.

Question — How long had the woman been buried?
Answer — About twenty-one months.
Q — How long had Isabella Spink been interred?
A — Practically five years.
Q — And neither body was putrid?
A — No.
Q — What was the mould you referred to?
A — Taylor was covered with ordinary vegetable fungi. There were conditions about the body that I identified with the case of Spink.

Q — How did you know it was the body of Bessie Taylor?
A — I compared Taylor's features with a photograph which I was told was hers, and I could recognize the general contour. The nose and cheeks had preserved their shape, but could not distinguish the eyes.
Q — There had been a change in her?
A — Yes, there had been a change in her which was more remarkable in the case of Spink, where there had been practically none. I think Taylor's body contained more antimony than Spink's.
Q — Given the same conditions as far as the coffin and grave were concerned, would you have expected to find that a woman who had only been buried twenty months, and had more antimony in her body, would be less subject to change than a woman who had been buried five years and had less antimony?
A — Yes.
Q — What kind of coffin was it?
A — Taylor's coffin was a dry elm one, and, as far as I could judge, the body had not been contaminated by contact with the soil, which was very dry and sandy loam.
Q — Where does putrefaction generally begin?
A — Putrefaction generally begins through the nose, mouth, and anus, and spreads outwards. There was none of that in either of them. The superficial decomposition of the body was due to the growth of mould.
Q — Does the presence of antimony not prevent the growth of moulds?
A — No; in fact, they will grow in a strong solution of tartar-emetic.

The prosecution wrapped up its case against Klosowski by calling Inspector George Godley and Detective-Sergeant Kemp to the stand to discuss how they had taken Klosowski into custody and what they had found during their inquires at the Crown public house. With what must have been a great satisfaction with their efforts the prosecution team then closed their interrogation and rested the Crown's case against Severin Klosowski.

In Defense of a Serial Killer

As Mr. George Elliott stepped forward to defend his client the small tomblike courtroom was silent. Klosowski's attorney knew that the evidence against his client was overwhelming and his team had been unable to locate any evidence or witnesses who could contradict any of the prosecution's witnesses. With that knowledge well in hand, Elliott informed a transfixed court that he "did not intend to call any evidence." He then went directly to his closing speech in the defense of a serial killer.

An eyewitness report would show the prisoner's despair as the trial drew to a close. "While his counsel was speaking he swayed backwards and forwards, pendulum-like, in his chair. If he diverted his gaze from Mr. Elliott it was to shoot a penetrating glance at the jury, trusting to detect some gleam of hope there, or some sign that the impassioned appeal of counsel was making an impression upon their minds. There was not a scrap of evidence directly favorable to the prisoner. At most Mr. Elliott could but ask the jury to weigh negative conclusions."

Elliott addressed the jury:

> I fully admit the magnitude of the task before me, especially as the Solicitor-General, by virtue of his position as an officer of the Crown, has the right of reply. The case, unfortunately, has been surrounded by a storm of prejudice which in any other country might have imperiled the calm administration of justice. There is also the fact that the accused is an alien, and we all know the feelings which at the present time are entertained generally against the immigration of aliens into this country. Thus, in addition to the prejudice I have referred to, I have the great difficulty of the accused's nationality to deal with.
> The accused undoubtedly stands before you under circumstances most lamentable. His is a crime, if guilty he be, which has ever been regarded with the utmost horror, and no doubt, gentlemen, during the four days you have been occupied upon this case, you have been wondering what could have

been the accused's motive. There are not the usual inducements present in cases of this kind. There was no necessity for the accused to resort to any act of this sort to free himself from the one woman so that he might live with another. None of the women appears to have thrown any difficulty in the way of living with the accused, so that of any adequate motive for the crime there was none. I would ask you, gentlemen, to remember that I am not here to prove the accused's innocence. I am here to refute the proofs of guilt put forward by the Crown, and unless you are satisfied beyond all human doubt that this hideous charge has been substantiated against the accused — if I can show that the Crown have not proved their case — I feel sure it will be your duty and your pleasure to free yourself from the responsibility of having to send to his doom a fellow-creature, however loathsome and revolting you might in other respects regard him.

The purchase of the tartar-emetic at Hastings is undoubtedly a most important incident, but I cannot help thinking that Mr. Davidson, the chemist, was singularly accessible in the easy sale of poisons, and that his memory must be somewhat defective. You have heard throughout that the accused had offered no objection to the free access of doctors to the deceased persons. Nor did he in any way attempt to disguise his movements. Indeed, when he was arrested he was in possession of a list of the houses he had kept and the dates he had occupied them. Again, none of the women appeared to have made any serious complaint of the accused's conduct towards them. Indeed, some of the witnesses had spoken strongly of his affection for the women and the solicitude he always showed for their recovery. He did not even select for himself the doctors called in to attend the women. In the case of Maud Marsh it had been suggested he had deliberately murdered her to marry Florence Rayner, but why should he have done this? He had but to tell Maud Marsh to go, and she must have left, as she had no claim upon him. Or he might have gone away himself, as he suggested to Florence Rayner he was willing to do, to America. The illness of Maud Marsh had in truth nothing to do with the appearance on the scene of Florence Rayner. In Dr. Stevenson's evidence I admit I have an overwhelming case to meet, but I think you will pause before you condemn a man merely upon the scientific evidence of a gentleman, however eminent he may be, without strong corroboration.

In conclusion, gentlemen, I would remind you that if you condemn the accused by your verdict it will be impossible to repair the mistake, if mistake has been made. Your verdict will be irrevocable, and I beg you to pause long before finding the accused guilty. The accused is a hated alien, and has all the prejudice against him which lies in that term, but I confidently appeal to you to exercise that wise and prudent consideration which always in this Court holds the balance between right and wrong.

A witness in the court would later tell news reporters about Klosowski's reaction to his attorney's defense speech, and Klosowski's distress as the prosecutor ended his rebuttal. "As his advocate was drawing to a close, Chapman burst into tears and covered his face with his handkerchief. The warders on guard in the dock, fearing a collapse, moved nearer the prisoner. More tears flowed when the Solicitor-General said the last word on behalf of the Crown."

A Final Prosecution Speech

Carson, the solicitor-general, then rose to speak his final words to the men of the jury as he finished up the Crown's case against serial killer Klosowski:

I have to congratulate my learned friend, Mr. Elliott, upon his able defense. In this Court we know no difference between the alien and the stranger and a citizen of this country. It is our proud boast that here, at all events, whatever it may be in other countries, it matters not to us who is the person on his trial, as all are entitled to the same law and the same justice.

Learned counsel has commented upon the absence of motive, but what is the use of seeking for motive when we have the actual fact of the murder? In this instance there was the most ample motive, for the prisoner's was a history of unbridled, heartless, and cruel lust. The case does not rest merely upon scientific evidence. There is the most ample corroboration. It is the prisoner who has been shown to have purchased a large quantity of antimony — we have the very label — and the poison is the poison which was common to all the persons whose deaths we are inquiring into. There is the same hand in each of the poisonings, and the little risk he ran in calling in the doctors is shown by the number of surgeons who were actually called in, and all of whom were deceived as to what these women suffered from. The prisoner's skill in medicine showed how far he could go. The doctors thought they were dealing with a respectable man, and hence they were deceived into giving certificates of death.

It is a most serious thing for a doctor to throw suspicion upon a household, and the prisoner in his statement showed conclusively how accurate he was in his power to deceive the doctors, and it from some cause or other Dr. Stoker had not desired further explanation and had given the prisoner a certificate of death in the case of Maud Marsh, it is shocking to contemplate what might still be going on at the Crown. The attentions paid by the prisoner to these women were the necessary mask for all that foul plot. We have now to do justice in the matter, and the exigencies of public justice and public law require you to do your duty like men.

Final Words from Judge Grantham

Certainly the longest dissertation on that final day was Justice Grantham's summation. Speaking from few notes Grantham evidenced an encyclopedic knowledge of the case as he detailed the events in chronological order to the silent courtroom. Having gone over the evidence brought forward he then charged the jury with their serious task.

Gentlemen, my task is over. I was going to say your task begins, but the painful part of your duty will be to say what your verdict will be. Think over the evidence which has been given and come to a proper conclusion in the case, namely, a clear conclusion if you can one way or the other, is the prisoner guilty or not? If there is any doubt in your minds, by all means give the prisoner the benefit of it. If you have no doubt about it, then, gentlemen, you have one duty, a painful one it must be, in the verdict you must find.

Gentlemen, will you consider your verdict?

When his lordship had summed up and Chapman saw that his last hope had gone, he sank back on his seat and his head dropped upon his breast. He had to be helped from the dock when the jury retired. When they returned he had to be similarly assisted.—News report.

The Verdict and Sentence

The men of the jury were then escorted to the side room to deliberate the fate of Severin Klosowski. The prisoner was taken to a small holding cell within a few feet of the men who held his fate in their hands. Klosowski would not have long to wait.

To a stunned courtroom the jury signaled that they had come to a unanimous decision in the case. They had been out of the courtroom for only ten minutes. It was 5:10 P.M. as the Clerk of Arraigns rose and faced the jury foreman.

CLERK—Have you agreed upon your verdict?
FOREMAN—We have. We find the prisoner guilty!

The verdict came as no surprise to anyone in the room, certainly not Klosowski's defense team. The only one who seemed to react with emotion at the verdict was the prisoner himself. According to the March 20 edition of the *South London Press*, "He heard the death sentence clinging to the dock railing, with warders supporting him on either side. His physical collapse was complete, and when the last dread scene was over, the murderer of Maud Marsh quitted the dock for the condemned cell, half-supported, half-carried by the warders."

British justice moved with lightning speed as the judge donned the black cap to face the now terrified prisoner standing in the dock. His sentence would be sharp and to the point.

Severin Klosowski, for I decline to call you by the English name you have assumed, the only satisfactory feature in the case we have just completed is that I am able to address you as a foreigner and not as an Englishman. The jury have come to the only conclusion which I am sure every one who has heard the case would have come to. It is not necessary for me to go through the harrowing details of this case, or refer again to the frightful cruelty you have been guilty of in murdering year by year women on whom you have gratified your vile lust. I have but one duty to perform — and it is not necessary for me to say more — it is the duty of sentencing you to death.

March 20, 1903
South London Press
THE SOUTHWARK POISONINGS

On Thursday, the fourth day of the trial at the Old Bailey, the cold-blooded murderer Severin Klosowski, the Russian Pole, who assumed the English name of George Chapman, was sentenced to death by Mr. Justice Grantham, who in passing judgment said, "The only satisfactory feature of the case just completed is that I have been able to address you as a foreigner and not as an Englishman.

NO POISON THAT CANNOT BE TRACED

The miscreant, Chapman, was only a clumsy poisoner after all. That snap of his thumb and finger and that statement of his to the sister of his last victim, Maud Marsh, that he could "give her a dose which sixty doctors could not discover," exhibits the depth of his ignorance of modern scientific analysis, and the wantonness of his criminal folly. It forged an important link in the chain of evidence which hands over a depraved murderer to the common hangman. The truth is that there is no poison today the administration of which to a human subject cannot be traced, and in this fact lies the public safety.

South London Press
Saturday, April 11, 1903.
THE FINAL SCENES

Billington was the executioner, assisted by Pierrepont, and in accordance with the custom slept in the prison on Monday night. The convict was aroused shortly after 6 o'clock, when he dressed and took mass, after which at 7 o'clock he was offered his breakfast of bread and butter and coffee, but scarcely ate anything. He was then very moody and depressed. As the dread hour approached, Chapman displayed a nervous fear of his approaching fate, and the slightest sound caused him to start.

Shortly before the time appointed the condemned cell was entered, and as Chapman was told to stand up he faltered, but soon pulled himself together. Billington quickly proceeded with the pinioning process, and the melancholy procession walked slowly to the execution shed, about 50 yards across the yard.

As Chapman went to the scaffold he was ashen pale, and almost stumbled more than once, and the dread of his rapidly approaching end seemed too great a strain to his nerves.

Just before leaving the cell he appeared faint, and drank a glass of water, and during the pinioning process he appeared to tremble. When actually on the scaffold Billington quickly strapped his legs and adjusted the cap, and instantly on the signal pulled the lever, death being instantaneous.

On the way to the scaffold, and also on the scaffold, Chapman made frequent ejaculations, and muttered inaudibly, rendering the last scene a peculiarly painful one.

After the execution Dr. Beamish examined the body, and pronounced life extinct, and it was left to hang for an hour. Chapman was of ordinary build, and was given a drop of 6 ft. 6 in.

In the crowd outside the gate were seen many of the foreign witnesses who figured in the case, and Chapman's reputed wife, Lucy Klosowski, was said to be in the immediate vicinity with her brother and sister.

Section V — The Future of Jack the Ripper

Chapter 17

A Century of Speculation and a Pub called the Crown

I cannot help feeling that this is the man we struggled so hard to capture fifteen years ago

— Inspector Frederick George Abberline

How Close Did They Really Come? First Light — 1903

It did not take long for speculation to begin, and with it would come the inevitable debate. Even before Klosowski could be dragged to the gallows for his richly deserved hanging, some of the men who had been engaged in the hunt for this serial killer years earlier began to publicly state that Jack the Ripper was about to meet his fate. The first to step forward was retired Chief Inspector Frederick George Abberline, Ripper chief investigative officer at the street level. And once again the London press were on top of the story.

Daily Chronicle
March 23, 1903

The police officers who have been engaged in tracing Klosowski's movements in connection with the three murders with which he was charged, are forming some rather startling theories as to the antecedent history of the criminal. These theories are connected with the Whitechapel murders which startled the world some fifteen years ago, and were attributed to "Jack the Ripper." The police have found that at the time of the first two murders Klosowski was undoubtedly occupying a lodging in George Yard, Whitechapel Road, where the first murder was committed.

To be sure, once the investigators into the poison murders had confirmed that Klosowski had lived in the very building that had held the first Ripper victim it was only a matter of time before they would take a much closer look at this now convicted serial killer. And the boys of the press would be right there with them. On March 23, 1903, a reporter for the *Pall Mall Gazette* would travel to the southern English town of Bournemouth (this writer's adopted hometown) and sit down to interview Inspector Abberline, who by then was enjoying his well-earned retirement in the coastal town.

The newspaper would tell its readers: "Should Klosowski, the wretched man now lying under a sentence of death for wife-poisoning, go to the scaffold without a 'last dying speech of confession,' a great mystery may forever remain unsolved, but the conviction that Chapman and Jack the Ripper were one and the same person will not in the least be weakened in the mind of the man who is, perhaps, better qualified than anyone else in this country to express an opinion in the matter. We allude to Mr. F. G. Abberline, formerly Chief Detective Inspector of Scotland Yard, the official who had full charge of the criminal investigations at the time of the terrible murders in Whitechapel."

Mr. Abberline was way ahead of them as he had already compiled a good many notes and was in the process of informing the British government of his thoughts on the matter. "What an extraordinary thing it is that you should have called upon me now. I had just commenced to write to the Assistant Commissioner of Police, Mr. Macnaughten, to say how strongly I was impressed with the opinion that Chapman was also the author of the Whitechapel murders." The good inspector, it would seem, had not only kept in close touch with Scotland Yard, but he had been following the poison trial with great interest and was busy compiling a file on Chapman and the recent murders.

Before long Mr. Abberline detailed some of the reasons why he felt that Klosowski was the man: "I have been so struck with the remarkable coincidences in the two series of murders that I have not been able to think of anything else for several days past — not, in fact, since the Attorney-General made his opening statements at the recent trial, and traced the antecedents of Chapman before he came to this country in 1888. Since then the idea has taken full possession of me, and everything fits in and dovetails so well that I cannot help feeling that this is the man we struggled so hard to capture fifteen years ago."

Abberline made several more points: "There are a score of things which make one believe Chapman is the man.... For instance, the date of the arrival in England coincides with the beginning of the series of murders in Whitechapel; there is a coincidence also in the fact that the murders ceased in London when Chapman went to America, while similar murders began to be perpetrated in America after he landed there. The fact that he studied medicine and surgery in Russia before he came over here is well established, and it is curious to note that the first series of murders was the work of an expert surgeon, while the recent poisoning cases were proved to be done by a man with more than an elementary knowledge of medicine."

It was at this point that the former chief inspector tied Klosowski to the actual murder site of the first Ripper victim, which was far more than any previous investigative work. "There are many other things extremely remarkable. The fact that Klosowski when he came to reside in this country occupied a lodging in George Yard, Whitechapel Road, where the first murder was committed, is very curious, and the height of the man and peaked cap he is said to have worn quite tallies with the description I got of him. All agree, too, that he was a foreign-looking man, but that, of course, helped us little in a district so full of foreigners as Whitechapel."

Even before the ink was dry on the newspaper interview, critics stepped forward to attack Abberline's thoughts on the case, but they really could not dispute his chronology of the events or the facts he discussed. Rather, discussion focused on assertions that a man who kills with a knife could not set it aside and pick up a bottle of poison. We now know from many case studies of serial killers, as well as reports from the FBI's own serial killer task force, that serial killers do indeed change their methods to suit events. The inspector put it this way on March 30, 1903, once again to a reporter from the *Pall Mall Gazette*: "As to the question of the dissimilarity of character in the crimes which one hears so much about," continued the expert (Abberline), "I cannot see why one man should not have done both, provided he had the professional knowledge, and this is admitted in Chapman's case. A man who could watch his wives being slowly tortured to death by poison, as he did, was capable of anything; and the fact that he should have attempted, in such a cold-blooded manner, to murder his first wife with a knife in New Jersey, makes one more inclined to believe in the theory that he was mixed up in the two series of crimes." "Indeed, if the theory be accepted that a man who takes life on a wholesale scale never ceases his accused habit until he is either arrested or dies, there is much to be said for Chapman's consistency."

We don't really know if any active members of Scotland Yard believed that Klosowski had been Jack the Ripper. Years later some of those officers would state that they believed that the Ripper had been Klosowski, but there are no known records of any official investigation into that possibility. Official London, it would seem, had lost interest in solving one of the greatest murder mysteries of all time. Indeed, one may wonder at what they would have discovered if they had only tried. Eyewitnesses were still alive! As for any possible interrogation of Klosowski — all that would stop at the end of a rope on April 7, 1903.

London Times
April 8, 1903

Execution.—Severin Klosowski, otherwise George Chapman, 37, a Russian Pole, described as a licensed victualler of the Borough, was executed yesterday morning within the walls of Wandsworth Prison for the wilful murder of Maud Eliza Marsh by poisoning her with antimony in October last. Billington was the executioner, and death was instantaneous. At the inquest which was afterwards held by Mr. Troutbeck, Major Knox, the prison governor, said that the convict made no confession. The jury found that Chapman had been duly executed according to law, and a notice to this effect was afterwards posted outside the gaol.

Inspector Abberline died on December 10, 1929, in Bournemouth, Hants, England, and he never wrote any detailed accounts of his Ripper investigations nor published any reports describing his private search for clues after he left Scotland Yard. Writing out his reminiscences it would seem, was simply not his style. The only written note of explanation he would pen can be found in a two-page note written to a friend, Mr. Walter Green, in a scrapbook he was compiling for his friend.

Why I did note write my Reminiscences when I retired from the Metropolitan Police. I think it is just as well to record here the reason why as from the various cuttings from the newspapers as well as the many other matters that I was called upon to investigate — that never became public property. It must be apparent that I could write many things that would be very interesting to read. At the time I retired from the service the authorities were very much opposed to retired officers writing anything for the press as previously some retired officers had from time to time been very indiscreet in what they had caused to be published and to my knowledge had been called upon to explain their conduct and in fact they had been threatened with actions for libel.

Apart from that there is no doubt the fact that in describing what you did in detecting certain crimes you are putting the criminal classes on their guard and in some cases you may be absolutely telling them how to commit crime.

As an example in the finger print detection you find now the expert thief wears gloves.

America was also paying close attention to the Ripper matter. On March 23, 1903, the *Fort Wayne News* ran the headline "He Is 'Jack the Ripper.'" Their readership could take their evening meals while reading that "Jack" had not only been busy tending business in London, he had also made the crossing to America. "The [London] police have unearthed circumstantial evidence a story printed here relates, tending to prove that George Chapman, convicted of murder last Thursday, is 'Jack the Ripper,' the mysterious perpetrator of the revolting Whitechapel murders of 1888. Chapman, it is shown, is really a Pole named Klosowski. The discovery has been made that Klosowski, soon after the Whitechapel atrocities ceased, went to Jersey City and opened a barber shop there and that while there several mysterious murders of women occurred. It is stated that Klosowski's real wife informed the police since her husband's trial that he, after a quarrel, tried to murder her in a bedroom back of the barber shop in Jersey City."

There was also news in 1903 that at least the Jersey City police took the news of possible Ripper murders in America seriously, but it seems that they did not bother to even discover where the illusive Pole had worked. The *Atlanta Constitution* would come right to the point with its headline into their coverage: "Original Jack the Ripper Under Sentence of Death in London

Why I did not write my Reminiscences when I retired from the Metropolitan Police.

I think it is just as well to record here the Reason why as from the various cuttings from the newspapers as well as the many other matters that I was called upon to investigate that never became public property — it must be apparent that I could write many things that would be very interesting to read.

At the time I retired from the Service the Authorities were very much opposed to retired Officers writing anything for the press as previously some retired Officers had from time to time been very indiscreet in what they had caused to be published and to my knowledge had been called upon

Above and opposite: Handwritten note by Inspector Fred Abberline on why he never wrote his "Reminiscences."

for Killing Women." With the dateline "New York, March 23," the paper reported, "A London dispatch was printed here today alleging that George Chapman, who was convicted of the murder of several women in London, was the original Jack the Ripper. It was further stated that Chapman had opened a barber shop in Jersey City some years ago and that soon after his arrival there a repetition of these Jack the Ripper murders occurred in Jersey City. Investigation by the

> 45 upon to explain (?) their conduct and in fact they had been threatened with actions for libel.
>
> Apart from that there is no doubt the fact that in describing what you did in detecting certain crimes you are putting the Criminal Classes on their guard and in some cases you may be absolutely telling them how to commit crime. As an example in the Finger-Print detection you find now the expert thief wears gloves.
>
> F.G. Abberline

Jersey City police today failed to show any trace of Klosowski or Chapman." The question of course must be: Did he use yet another alias when he opened up his Jersey City barber shop or did he simply work for someone else as a simple barber?

Continuing their coverage, the *Atlanta Constitution* on April 5, 1903, led with a headline: "Jack the Ripper To Die on the Gallows." From their special correspondent in London on March 25 the paper's readers were given a very good general review of Klosowski's background and some case details. "It is doubtful if a more extraordinary development ever took place in connection with the prosecution of a criminal than that by which Severin Klosowski, alias George Chapman, just condemned to die on April 6 for poisoning three women in succession, is indicated as the world famous assassin, Jack the Ripper, as well as the author of similar crimes in America." There was no question—Jack had killed in America.

Readers in Georgia were given not to doubt that Klosowski had been right in the thick of the Ripper murders and, indeed, had lived far closer to the victims than any other so-called suspect ever had. "It was first suggested that Klosowski might be Jack the Ripper when at his trial it came out that when the Pole reached London in 1888—the year of the Ripper crimes—he went to live in George yard, Whitechapel, where the first of the famous murderer's many victims was found dead, and that this [building] was his home during all the time when the assassinations were being committed."

And despite numerous attempts by later writers to downplay Klosowski's move to America, readers of the *Atlanta Constitution* would be well briefed on developments in 1903. "For one of the most sensational developments of the Ripper mystery was that, shortly after the murders ceased in Whitechapel, a series of crimes of the same sort began in America. At the time it was supposed that some American pervert merely had been inspired to imitate the London assassin example."

It was even hoped by probably more than just a few who had heard about the Ripper murders that Klosowski would confess to being the killer. "His lawyer who visited him in the condemned cell the other day, reported that the criminal was employed in writing out a lengthy statement of some kind, so there is a possibility that Klosowski has decided to reveal himself as one of the most famous of modern criminals and is the man of all men upon whom the London police have, since the commission of the ghastly series of butcheries in Whitechapel, been most anxious to lay their hands." What happened to that handwritten statement?

As of this writing there is no known confession by Klosowski that he was Jack the Ripper. Perhaps he saved that confession for the priest who visited him in his cell just before he was executed. Or was there really some sort of unknown and yet unsuspected conspiracy to remove any confession Klosowski may have written? Perhaps, yet all we know now is that he was writing a good deal before he died and no one seems to know where all of that writing ended up — one more twist perhaps in the case of Jack the Ripper.

The First Writer — 1930

After Klosowski's execution, official London seems to have lost much of its interest into the Ripper murders. This is not really surprising. After all, the Ripper had supposedly not killed for some fifteen years and no one was really pressing hard for a real investigation. Much of the population had moved on, busy with the daily struggle for life, especially in the East End, and there were certainly more pressing matters much closer at hand than an old, and for most, best forgotten murder case. Not even the ravenous press could resurrect any sustained interest in the case. For the next few years only the dust in a Scotland Yard room of records would cover the file folders of Jack the Ripper. In 1930, however, some of that dust would be brushed away by Hargrave L. Adam.

In April 1930, *Trial of George Chapman* was published as part of the *Notable British Trials* series by William Hodge & Company in London, England, and Canada Law Book Company out of Toronto, Canada. This volume, edited by Hargrave Lee Adam, was intended as more of an instructional work for attorneys than as a dissertation on the Ripper matter. It focused on the three poison murders in the case of the Borough Poisoner — George Chapman. However, Adam was so impressed that Chapman was the best suspect to fit the Ripper crimes that he devoted a full section dealing with the Ripper case. Adam's work would be the first to lay out the case, albeit neither fully nor completely accurately, against Severin Klosowski as the killer. It had only been a few months since Abberline's death and of course the papers had reported on the inspector's involvement in his most famous case 41 years earlier. For his work on the book, Adam would seek out the most reliable source on the murders, namely, retired Chief Inspector George Godley.

In the introduction to the poison murders, Adam writes: "After the investigation had been completed and the case against Chapman was fully established, the police authorities entertained a strong idea that some sinister connection existed between the Borough Poisoner and the mysterious murders of Whitechapel, popularly known as Jack the Ripper. Circumstantial evidence to support this belief was not lacking."

Adam then briefly described the general Ripper murders, starting with the murder of Mary Ann "Polly" Nichols on August 31, 1888. He seems to have discounted the murder of Martha Tabram three weeks earlier. Perhaps if he had begun with Tabram's murder he could have found an even closer connection to Klosowski, who, as we now know, lived in the building where she was stabbed to death. Continuing on he profiled, albeit not fully or accurately, the deaths of Annie Chapman, Elizabeth Stride, Catherine Eddowes, Mary Jane Kelly, Alice McKenzie (reported as an "unknown woman" in his book), and Frances Coles (reported as "one last murder in the series"), killed on February 13, 1891. He seems to have discounted the death of Rose Mylett, who was strangled to death by a cord on December 20, 1888, perhaps due to the controversy in placing her in "Jack's" column or because her body was found fully two miles east of the Ripper's preferred killing ground.

After the brief retelling of the murders, Adam lamented that the case was never "cleared up" even though some officials firmly connected to the police force had attempted to assure the public that they either knew who the killer was or had in fact knowledge which had been destroyed! Adam states:

> As everyone knows, who this mysterious criminal was has never been cleared up. Several prominent officials have from time to time asserted that they had established his identity. The late Sir Melville Macnaghten, the late Sir Robert Anderson, Sir Henry Smith, and many others of less importance have assured us regarding this. Sir Melville Macnaghten even went so far as to declare that he had once possessed documentary proof of the identity of the criminal, but that he had burnt the papers. An unprecedented thing, surely, for a police official to do! These declarations, as mere declarations without evidence to support them, are unsatisfactory. It is quite certain that nobody ever did know for certain who Jack the Ripper was.

Having said that, Adam then pushed forward the circumstantial case for Klosowski, alias George Chapman, as his prime suspect even though some, but not all, of his reasons would later prove to have been incorrect. "It is now proposed to present the case for supposing—one cannot put it in stronger terms—that George Chapman, or Severin Klosowski, was actually Jack the Ripper."

- Chapman arrived in London sometime in 1888; worked and lived in Whitechapel. (Actually he arrived in late 1887 or very early 1888—best guess.)
- Other murders during 1888. During this time Chapman was within easy reach of the scenes of these murders.
- It was thought that Jack the Ripper had medical knowledge. Chapman had been a medical student. (Actually, Klosowski had qualified as a junior-surgeon in Poland in 1887.)
- Description given of the man seen with the woman Kelly. This is a most faithful description of Chapman.
- The Americanisms in the letter and card written to the police. Chapman passed himself off as an American and used Americanisms in conversation. (In truth the so-called Ripper letters cannot be linked to the killer or anyone for that matter and at the time of the Ripper murders Klosowski had yet to visit America.)
- The grim and callous joking tone of the messages. Chapman was very callous, and was in the habit of indulging in pleasantries of this sort. (Caution taken here as only one message could possibly have come from the killer; the well-known "letter from hell" sent along with a small body part, and it was callous, but it cannot, as yet, be linked to any one suspect.)
- No Ripper murders in England, but similar murders in America, in the locality of Jersey City. Chapman and his wife left in May, 1890, for America, where Chapman opened a barber's shop at Jersey City. (Actually, it can be shown that Klosowski arrived in New York City on April 23, 1891, some 12 hours before the first Ripper murder in New York City. He did however, eventually move to New Jersey where two Ripper murders were committed in 1892.)
- At the beginning of 1892, Ripper murders cease in America. Chapman left America and

returned to London in May, 1892. (Actually, he could have arrived in London no earlier than mid June 1892.)

Adam then turned to Inspector Abberline and Inspector George Godley who he had interviewed for *Trial of George Chapman* and to whom he thanked in his preface in stating "...and, lastly, for much information, to ex–Chief-Inspector Godley, who probably knows more than any one else about the life and career of this criminal."

> Chief Inspector Abberline, who had charge of the investigations into the East End murders, though Chapman and Jack the Ripper were one and the same person. He closely questioned the Polish woman Lucy Baderski, about Chapman's nightly habits at the time of the murders. She said that he was often out until three or four o'clock in the morning, but she could throw little light upon these absences. Both Inspector Abberline and Inspector Godley spent years in investigating the 'Ripper' murders. Abberline never wavered in his firm conviction that Chapman and Jack the Ripper were one and the same person. When Godley arrested Chapman Abberline said to his confrere "You've got Jack the Ripper at last!"

Summing up, Adam would write: "That Chapman's career coincides exactly with the movements and operations of Jack the Ripper must appeal strongly to all who endeavor to throw light upon the shadows of the latter's obscurity. The whole of Chapman's life cannot be made quite clear. At his trial the prosecution proved that he murdered Mrs. Spink, Bessie Taylor and Maud Marsh; but as they made no effort to discover others no one can say, with confidence, how many murders he committed. A reasonable case for supposing that Chapman was Jack the Ripper has, at least, been furnished. At that the subject must be left without material proof of the connection. Upon that strange period of Chapman's career, when he worked and lodged in Whitechapel, no new light can be shed, and the identity of Jack the Ripper will forever remain a mystery."

Perhaps!

Arthur Neil—1932

In 1903, it would be Detective Sergeant Arthur Neil's job to track down Klosowski's real wife Lucy Baderski for the 1903 murder-trial investigation. He would soon find himself searching the streets and darkened places of Whitechapel, which had little changed since the Whitechapel killer walked its fog-choked lanes. For Neil, his search covered many of the familiar places the killer had surely walked, and he did not believe it was only a coincidence. He soon learned that the background, skills and movements of serial killer Klosowski matched that of the illusive Jack the Ripper. Having never forgotten his work on the case some 29 years later and 44 years after the Ripper murders began, ex–police superintendent Neil published his book *Forty Years of Man-Hunting* in 1932. He would come right to the point and name Klosowski as Jack the Ripper:

> The first "Ripper" crime occurred in August 1888. Chapman worked in Whitechapel at this time, and was there during the whole period of these wholesale killings. "The Ripper," by the account of four medical men, was testified as to having surgical knowledge. Severin Klosowski, alias George Chapman, had this qualification. Also it was thought, by the expert manner of the mutilations examined on the various bodies of his victims, that the "Ripper" was ambidextrous, that is left and right-handed. Chapman was seem to use his hands in this way during the time he lived in the Borough. The only living description ever given by an eyewitness of the "Ripper," tallied exactly with Chapman, even to the height, deep sunk black eyes, sallow complexion and thick, black moustache.
> Towards the end of 1888, Severin Klosowski left Britain for the United States. (Actually the year was 1891.) The "Ripper" murders had by this time ceased, so far as London was concerned. But a series of equally terrible crimes, causing a precisely similar reign of terror, began in America. (In truth the panic was short lived and only occurred in a small area of lower Manhattan slums.) These crimes ceased when, in 1892 Klosowski returned to this country (England).

We were never able to secure definite proof that Chapman was the "Ripper." But the theory remains just the same. No one, who had not been trained as a surgeon and medical man, could have committed the "Ripper" crimes. As we discovered, Chapman had been a surgeon in Poland, and would, therefore, be the only possible fiend (of known or suspected individuals) capable of putting such trained knowledge into the use against humanity, instead of for it. "Jack the Ripper" was a cold-blooded, inhuman monster, who killed for the sake of killing. The same could be said of Severin Klosowski, alias George Chapman, the Borough Poisoner. Why he took to poisoning his victims on his second visit to this country can only be ascribed to his diabolical cunning, or some insane idea or urge to satisfy his inordinate vanity. In any case, it is the most fitting and sensible solution to the possible identity of the murderer in one of the world's greatest crime mysteries ... as every detective very quickly learns there are things you cannot prove in a court of law but of which you feel quite curtain in your own mind.

[1951—Scotland Yard transfers Ripper files to the Public Record Office.]

THE THEATRE OF THE MIND—1952

Old-time radio shows have long been referred to as "Theatre of the Mind" for a very good reason. With no still or moving images to wash over the minds of the listeners the only images presented to radio listeners were the ones they created themselves as they followed the many tales featured on radio during an age gone by. As radio mysteries, along with other shows, were losing their battle to the new kid on the block—television—radio and movie personality Orson Welles, who was living in Europe at the time, put together and presented a new series, which was aired over the Mutual network from January 1 through December 30, 1952, originally produced for Radio Luxembourg. The series was called *The Black Museum* and, as one would suspect, it featured half-hour mystery stories based on the collection of criminal artifacts housed in Scotland Yard's basement, known as the Black Museum. The show's announcer addressed the audience at the beginning of each show:

> The Black Museum, a repository of death, here in the grim stone structure on the Thames which houses Scotland Yard is a warehouse of homicide, where everyday objects; a picture frame, a wicker chair, a telephone directory, all are touched by murder.

Indeed, each show chronicled a well-known murder case, which related to some article stored at Scotland Yard's private museum. To be sure, articles housed at this museum were fodder for Orson Welles and his radio crew, and, in fact, Welles was given a rare personal tour of the small, but very well-known collection of death. Keeping in mind the words of the radio announcer that "Only the names were changed to protect the innocent," we explore one episode titled "The Straight Razor."

In mid series Orson Welles once again began to tell a story based on an item on a museum shelf. His introduction began:

> Straight Razor; it's a familiar object, straight razor, perhaps your father used one like this, mine did. Straight keen edge, a bit of steel, beautifully sharpened and strapped to remove a man's whiskers or perhaps...

The story then flows to a bit of conversation between two men who will be speaking these same few words at the end of the show as well. This was a preview.

> A most efficient bit of Sheffield, isn't it Sergeant?
> Yes Inspector, for its original purpose as well as ... the other. Matter of fact, I use one exactly like it every morning.
> A grim thought Sergeant. A very grim thought.

Orson Welles then comes back to the microphone to insure the listener where the artifact may still be found.

Today, that razor can be seen in the Black Museum.

And as if to press home the point to the radio listener so that they could not possibly miss the point that the location of these case objects are in official custody, the announcer once again comes on, along with background music.

> From the annals of the Criminal Investigation Department of the London Police, we bring you the dramatic stories of the crimes recorded by objects in Scotland Yard's gallery of death—the Black Museum.

The radio play then begins in earnest as we find Welles walking the badly lit room, which houses the museum's collection on shelves, on the floor or propped up against walls—all marked very properly, by date, crime and victim. He soon comes to the show's object.

> Here we are, the razor. It's one of a set of seven. They used to come in wooden cases. Remember the seven straight keen blades marked one for each day of the week. And this one, well, it was used by a good looking fellow about forty who had a way with the ladies. And no matter where, at home, in the parlor and even in a Hansen Cab...

Welles then moves on as the story begins and the listener soon realizes that, although the date of the story is 1896, a few years off and the names (Wilson and not Klosowski) and ages of the characters have been changed, the story is decidedly not about razors. The story is about the Borough Poisoner and Severin Klosowski, and poison is the weapon, not a razor. The radio audience of 1952, it would seem, must have been wondering why the title was "The Straight Razor." Indeed, in the middle of the show Welles breaks in to tell the audience that the most important clue to this poison murder case will be a case of razors and not the poison bottle, which held the solution to the actual murder!

It is interesting to note that the show makes certain that we hear that the suspect came to England in 1888, had no memory of 1889 and had gone for a while to America before returning to England to begin a new crime spree. At this point the case moves once again away from poison and the sergeant, having searched the pub, comes back to the police station with the case of razors, which had been hidden.

> Where did you find those razors, Sergeant?
> Hidden Sir. Hidden in the bin on top of a spare bedroom closet, Sir.

Welles then comes back on to explain that it was the inspector who was a bit confused since "here was a case of poison," yet the suspect had hidden the razors where only a very good search would locate them. At any rate, the suspect is held for the customary 24 hours to await the toxicology report on his latest victim. It was not a surprising result.

> The girl was poisoned alright but not with arsenic. Her body was full of antimony.

The radio drama continues with the discovery of the location where the poison was purchased and, of course, a trial in which the suspect is convicted in only 10 minutes by a jury of twelve. At the end of the show we find the inspector once again in his office thinking about "Why did he hide them?" as he calls in his sergeant for a chat.

> Sergeant I may have hit on an angle. I sent over to criminal records for this file. Look at it.
> I see Sir. The description of this man fits Wilson perfectly. Of course this man was seen only once.
> True enough, but it's the identical coloring, height, weight, even the deep sound of the voice.
> It proves nothing Sir.
> I know, but there is more. The cases in this file began in '88, Wilson came to Whitechapel in '88. The cases stopped in '90, when Wilson went to America, but in that year—it's noted here—there were three identical cases in New Jersey. They stopped in '91 when Wilson came back here.

Finally, Welles and his 1952 radio team get down to who they are really talking about in this show as the inspector presses his sergeant to speculate on the identity of the author of the mysterious murder file he has been discussing.

> Would you Sergeant, in this room and having seen this record and knowing about those razors, hazard that Larry Wilson is—Jack the Ripper?
> I'd hazard it Sir, I couldn't prove it.
> Neither could I, but I'm convinced all the same. Perhaps if ... ah well, we've got him on other matters. We can hang him only once in any case.

The final narrative is delivered by Welles as he sums up the story about "The Straight Razor."

> We shall never know the full story, but most people would agree with the Inspector there was more than a reasonable chance that justice had finally caught up with Jack the Ripper. Certainly that case of razors deserves its place of honor in the Black Museum. They were sure but they never proved it. Larry Wilson was hanged for the death of poor little Mabel Dill legally and technically for the deaths of his other two wives as well, there was no question.
> The jury deliberated for exactly ten minutes. But the additional fact remains that never again from the date of Wilson's arrest was there a murder in the technique of Jack the Ripper; not in London, not in America. His terrible signature never appeared again on the body of any murdered woman. The case of razors remains in its customary place in Scotland Yard.

This is, of course, a radio drama, but it portrays the case of the Borough Poisoner, alias George Chapman, and it is highly recommended that anyone interested in the Ripper murders pick up a copy of the show and listen for themselves. Having said that one must ask a few questions: The names were changed for this half-hour program, but were the razors also changed? And if so, could the items referred to by Orson Welles be the black medical bag and knives proven to have been owned by Klosowski before he was arrested for murder? If so, and if these radio shows were based on items housed at Scotland Yard, then the next obvious question is: What happened to those items and are they now hidden away in some storage closet in the same building where detectives work, the very men tasked to hunt down Jack the Ripper? Could it really be so easy after these many years for any Scotland Yard detective to drop into the office of, Mr. Ross, the official formerly in charge of the Black Museum, and find those blades—razors or not— and test them for DNA? If there is blood under the handles or in the bag or case and it matches DNA taken from a living relative of a Ripper victim, could this most interesting of all cases finally be closed in one fell swoop? Indeed, a match of the DNA with a Ripper victim would constitute definitive proof that Severin Klosowski was beyond a shadow of a doubt Jack the Ripper, and Klosowski would have been convicted of those crimes in any court of law.

With his fame and worldwide reputation, Orson Welles would have certainly had the time during his private tour to handle any item he wished. Did he actually hold the weapon that Jack the Ripper used during that "Autumn of terror"? Perhaps we will know the answer to that and many other questions concerning that case in the very near future.

THE RIPPER PRESS CONTINUES

April 16, 1966—*Daily Telegraph*, "Letters By Jack the Ripper Published, Skill Theory Rejected. Letters and postcards purporting to have been written by Jack the Ripper, the killer who terrorized the East End of London nearly 80 years, were published yesterday. They appeared with contemporary medical sketches and scene-of-the-crime maps in an article by Prof. Francis Camps, the pathologist, in the *London Hospital Gazette*. The sketches and maps, hitherto undisclosed, were from the hospital's archives."

August 19, 1988 — *Times* of London, "Ripper Papers Unveiled, 100 Years on. Almost a hundred years after Jack the Ripper struck down his first victim on the east London streets, the case remains, according to one of the many investigators, 'as fresh as new-spilt blood.' For the first time, the police yesterday showed rediscovered papers and pictures missing from the voluminous Ripper files for an unknown number of years. The gaps were noticed last year when family of a former senior policeman gave the Yard a thick album of photographs he used in lectures. Yesterday, Mr. John Dellow, deputy commissioner, would not be drown on the latest Yard theories about the case as he sat under one of the police posters which reproduced the letter. Mr. Dellow said the discoveries did not take investigators any nearer the identity of the killer."

September 21, 1988 — *Maclean's*, "A Grisly Allure, Jack the Ripper's Mystery Defies Explanation. Since the crimes were committed, about 250 books and countless articles as well as 50 plays, films and television programs have appeared on the subject. Board games and computer games have recently appeared, and firms in London that provide tours through the Whitechapel area, where the murders took place, are doing a brisk business—especially among Canadian and American tourists. During the past year, the recovery of key documents and photographs relating to the Ripper murders have sparked renewed interest in the case. Last month, descendents of a Scotland Yard inspector who investigated the Ripper murders sent police other documents that they found among his papers, including photographs of the slain women and post-mortem records."

July 16, 1995 — *Sunday Magazine*, "Was This Jack the Ripper? In February 1993, Suffolk police officer Stewart Evans, who had studied the 1888 Whitechapel murders since he was 16, hit on sensational evidence that finally pointed to the identity of Jack the Ripper—an American doctor. Stewart Evans re-read the yellowing letter he held in his hand. Dated 1913, he was convinced it finally revealed the identity of Jack the Ripper. The letter had been sent by Chief Inspector John Littlechild to leading journalist George R. Sims. At the time of the Whitechapel murders, Littlechild was head of Scotland Yard's Special Branch, working closely with the team trying to catch the Ripper. It read, 'Amongst the suspects, and to my mind a very likely one, was a Dr. T. He was an American quack named Tumblety.'"

April 20, 2001 — *Daily Telegraph*, "Lost Jack the Ripper Letter Remains a Riddle. A letter allegedly penned by Jack the Ripper has re-entered the public domain decades after disappearing from the archives of the Metropolitan Police. The macabre note, scrawled in black ink signed 'Jack the Ripper,' was written in October at the height of the hysteria surrounding the Whitechapel murders, and when the last of the serial killer's known victims still had 10 days to live. The letter, posted in the East End on October 29, 1888, adopts a kind of written Cockney. It was sent to Dr. Thomas Openshaw, a pathologist at the London Hospital, who had been asked to examine a piece of human kidney contained in another supposed Ripper letter."

THE BLACK MUSEUM

London's Metropolitan Police Web site proudly proclaims that "The Black Museum," renamed "The Crime Museum," is the "oldest museum in the world put together purely for recording crime." However, even before that official claim to fame is made a bold framed warning is posted at the top of the Crime Museum's notice page.

> [The Crime Museum is a private museum—it is NOT open to the general public.
> It is open to police officers by prior appointment.]

So much for the friendly welcome.

In 1967, authorities moved the museum, along with the rest of Scotland Yard, to new offices on Victoria Street and the museum collections were deposited in some rooms on the second floor. In 1981, a newly designed facility was completed, consisting of two distinct parts. According to the description of the Black Museum on Scotland Yard's Web site, the first, known as the "old room," is "meant to capture the feel of the old room as it was in about 1880." The second room is where the cabinets are kept. We learn from the Web site that the "old room contains an extensive collection of weapons, all of which have been used in murders or serious assaults in London, and displays items from famous cases, generally, prior to 1900, such as *Jack the Ripper* and Charlie Peace." We also find that the second room "contains cabinets under the following categories: Famous Murders— Notorious Poisoners..."

One would think after those introductory words that we could expect to find something of interest in these old cases, shelves and cabinets about two very famous cases— Jack the Ripper and the Borough Poisoner. However, that is apparently not the case. At least as far as official policy is concerned, there is nothing held at the Black Museum relating to these two murder series. But is that really the case?

Researchers, including those who have had direct contact with the Metropolitan Police, have spoken to this and other writers about the changing responses given by the former curator of the Black Museum during visits, phone calls and letters. In July 1999 it was reported that the famous museum had very few papers or files on the Jack the Ripper case. This, of course, is a far cry from none. Later that year, it was reported that the museum held within its dusty bins the original equipment that was used by Klosowski to kill his common-law wives. That equipment was reported to be the old poison bottles as well as the green syringes he used for his poison work. Considering the fact that the Borough Poisoner case was well known at the time (1902–03) it is not too surprising to learn that these murder artifacts were held for display. It was also speculated that the Black Museum may very well hold Klosowski's diary discovered by Inspector Godley at the Crown Public House. However, the former curator, John Ross, would not allow any photos to be taken of the equipment nor would he allow any writers or researchers to even view those items. Ross was, however, good enough to explain that it is Scotland Yard's policy not to allow photography of any exhibits in his care. But why would he not allow any viewings? Perhaps plausible deniability is the answer.

In March 2000 Ross was again contacted for information on any evidence he may have in the Borough Poisoner case. It was reported at the time that the museum held no exhibits from the case, but it did possess a line drawing of Klosowski during his 1903 murder trial. This drawing, which turned out to be a composite of several courtroom sketches, has found its way into this series of books, so we do know that it had to come out of some kind of file on Klosowski at the museum. The official position, stated by the former guardian of the Black Museum in a letter to this writer, is that "the only files on the Ripper and Borough Poisoner cases are held in the Public Records Office at Kew."

In order to uncover some semblance of truth about the Borough Poisoner case, Ross was again contacted for information in late 2003. At this point in time the good Mr. Ross was willing to admit that the syringe and poison bottles did still exist and that they were held at the Black Museum. However, in later communications by mail the existence of these artifacts was again denied. In true governmental fashion the former Black Museum gatekeeper would deny all knowledge of these items. The new curator is Mr. Alan McCormick.

So what are we to make of Ross and the mysterious Black Museum? Simply this: it is unlikely that those who hold these artifacts of crime will willingly step forward and allow writers and researchers the opportunity to not only see and photograph these pieces of evidence but also to have them tested for what could be critical lines of research into those cases. Yet, what after all these years could these officials be hiding which could possibly affect the final outcome of these historical cases? Speculation has it that if Klosowski were ever proven to be

Jack the Ripper, then the descendents of his victims may press the British government for some kind of compensation if it could be shown that the police somehow missed a critical opportunity to solve this case. Yet, it would seem to this writer that the opportunity for Scotland Yard to be able to declare the case "closed" and so put the matter to rest would be much more important than any monetary compensation that possibly could be forthcoming.

THE NEW AGE OF "JACK"

After the release of the bulk of the Ripper documents by official London in the mid 1970s a new period of interest in the Jack the Ripper murders began. Writers and researchers were soon poring over the Home Office and police records in search of details for numerous new books and articles. Needless to say, many books were published, but very few are accurate in most details and the authors of even fewer have managed to whittle down the long list of supposed suspects to a few very good ones. However, several volumes are well worth a close look by all who wish to become informed about "Jack."

The first text, *The Jack the Ripper A to Z*, was published in 1991 by three research writers who have long sought the truth about these serial murders— Paul Beggs, Martin Fido and Keith Skinner. As the title infers, this work is written in an encyclopedic format covering most aspects of the case alphabetically from Abberline to Zverieff with summary reports on most aspects and longer reports concerning primary areas such as victims, suspects and murder sites. There is a nearly two-page entry on Klosowski, but it is so brief, as are most topics covered, it provides only a glimpse into the life and times of this career serial killer.

The second book, which has become one of the standard accounts of the general Ripper tale, is *The Complete History of Jack the Ripper* by Philip Sugden, published in 1994. It is indeed a well-written tome and does report on most, but not all, events surrounding the Ripper murders. Most interesting about this work is the reporting done on four of the most discussed suspects to hold history's claim to be Jack the Ripper — Montague John Druitt, Aaron Kosminski, Michael Ostrog and, last but certainly not least, Severin Klosowski, alias George Chapman. To his credit, Sugden does give both sides of the story when he reports on these individuals and their histories, not wanting to point the final accusing hand at any one man. However, he does seem to find Klosowski to be the best candidate of a bad lot. He writes, "George Chapman could have been Jack the Ripper. We have uncovered nothing to eliminate him from our inquiry. And he fits the evidence better than any other police suspect."

There is one area in which Sugden does indeed leave an opening and for that we travel to New York City and the murder of Carrie Brown. The Brown murder on the night of April 23–24, 1891, is well covered in Sugden's work, but he correctly refuses to tie one Ripper suspect to it for the moment as he writes: "Clearly it will take nothing short of proof that Chapman was in the city when Carrie died to invest the American connection with real credibility. The matter must rest there for the present." It would not take long for "the matter" to come up again. In this author's work *The American Murders of Jack the Ripper*, published in 2003, reported for the first time are the date and ship of arrival of Severin Klosowski into New York harbor. His name has been located on the passenger list of the S.S. *Waesland* arriving at 1:50 P.M. on April 23, 1891, less than 12 hours before Carrie Brown was murdered. "Real credibility" has now been fully established.

Sugden writes: "I have little hesitation in declaring Druitt, Kosminski and Ostrog 'Not Guilty.' In the case of Chapman I prefer recourse to a verdict long recognized only in Scottish law — 'Not Proven.'" Perhaps with the new information about Carrie Brown "Not Proven" will move to "Prime Suspect" in the mind of Sugden as well as other writers and researchers.

The final reference, and certainly required reading, appeared in 2000 with publication of *The Ultimate Jack the Ripper Companion*, by Stewart P. Evans and Keith Skinner. As stated by its authors the work is "a compilation of the major primary sources, indispensable for any writer or researcher tackling this enigmatic series of killings." Indeed, this work focuses on translating and placing in book form many of the documents and reports on Jack the Ripper. It may not bring to light any new information but it certainly has made access much easier for future researchers looking into these cases.

THE CROWN PUBLIC HOUSE

There is nothing like a murder mystery to raise the awareness of a building or other site. Such is the case at 213 Borough High Street in Southwark, London. The Crown had stood its ground here since around 1840 as a local pub and gathering place, not much different from the thousands of others throughout London and the rest of Great Britain. In 1902, this pub would become the focus of one of Britain's most notable trials as Severin Klosowski went on trial as the Borough Poisoner. But its fame would not last. The locals went about their busy lives after Klosowski was hung, and after all, there was much to be busy about in Georgian England and afterward, especially in the poorer areas of London's East End. And so the pub, under new management and several new owners, continued to sell a pint or two to the locals until September 1976, when it closed its doors as a working pub for the last time.

The final licensee, Richard Gunner, had run the place for the previous 10 years and had some interesting stories to tell about his business. In an interview conducted in 1976 at its closing, Gunner reported that, when he arrived in 1967, he "opened up four rooms which looked as though they had been boarded up for at least 40 years." He also reported that there was no indication as to why the rooms had been locked up for so long. He had also heard stories of mysterious things about the place: "I have heard all the stories of people hearing and seeing things, but I have never experienced anything myself." Nevertheless, he said, members of his family certainly experienced a few "bumps in the night."

Mrs. Bet Gunner, Richard's 63-year-old mother at the time, reported hearing "footsteps in some of the empty rooms, and the whistle of what sounded like a kettle boiling." In fact, she had told her son at the time that she would no longer stay overnight at the pub since, two years earlier, she had "caught a glimpse of a man in one of the upstairs rooms. He walked up the stairs laughing, then vanished!"

She is not the only one to experience strange sights and sounds at the old Crown. Richard's wife Barbara reported hearing the "sounds of crying upstairs." However, the cries ended when Richard tossed out an old baby carry-cot he had located in the attic. It was also two years earlier when a longtime friend, Mario Dempsey, reported an event which had occurred after closing. He said: "One Saturday night, when everyone left the pub quite early, I decided to fill up all the bottles and clean the place before I went to bed, so there would be nothing left to do in the morning. When I went to bed the place was spotless, but in the morning there was a glass on the counter, as if someone had pulled up a chair and had a drink."

Since 1976 no one, at least in physical form, has been able to pull up a chair at the pub and draw a pint. In its new form the building was used for a time as a canteen for a nearby company, which needed a place for its staff to eat during the lunch period. Later, the site would play host to an archaeological dig, which did indeed, according to reports, find part of an old Roman road beneath the basement floor of the old pub. Even later, we are told by local residents, the main structure behind the facade was replaced with a new three-story building, which incorporated the front of the pub albeit on a somewhat changed format at the street level. We are even told that the police, a few years ago, had taped off the building for some three days during an investigation into a fraud case — no reports yet if they checked out the basement.

But what about the future of 213 Borough High Street, and will we yet find anything at that site even remotely related to the Ripper murders? The answer may surprise us all. It seems that two areas *which still exist today* have yet to be fully searched — the small backyard and the walls of the old basement! There are no known reports dealing with a systematic search of the basement by officers during the 1902 search of the Crown nor are there any reports of police digging up the backyard for clues. It seems Klosowski had left so many easy-to-find clues into his three poison murders in the rooms of the Crown that there was no reason for investigators to go digging anywhere. Yet, we know he was a serial killer who collected artifacts of his murders. If he was Jack the Ripper, as so much of the circumstantial evidence seems to point, then he would have *needed* his hard-earned "collection" close at hand. For him, it would not have mattered that they were placed in an area not easily accessible, it only mattered that *he knew* they were close by. The backyard and basement walls would have been perfect storage places for his legacy of terror. Scotland Yard please take special note!

Remember, nothing was found in the Crown to point to his identity as the Ripper, but what happened to his secret black medical bag and the instruments held within? One thing is very clear — Klosowski would never have thrown it away. That black bag was a prized possession because it showed that he was a medical man and one to be respected, and it has not yet been found — at least officially. Perhaps a bit of digging or a little ground penetrating radar, put to good use, is in order? Is there a part of that basement wall which has an old but crude patch that does not quite match the rest of the wall? After all, what do we have to lose? Find the bag or perhaps a small jar with human remains sealed and preserved in red wine and the mystery of who Jack the Ripper really was is solved forever.

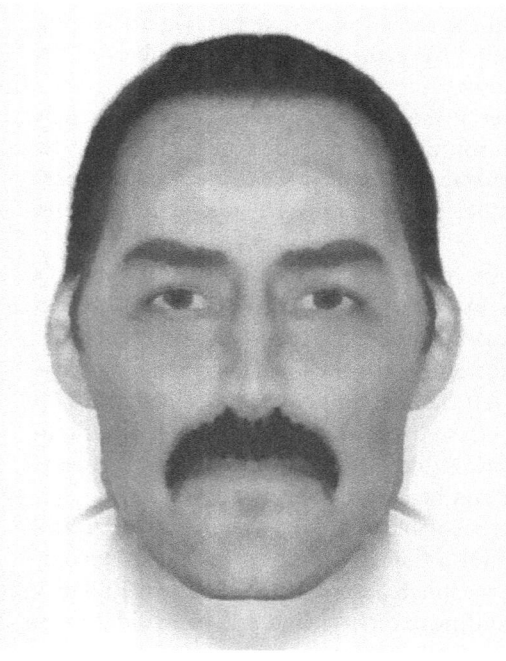

Computer composite of Jack the Ripper developed by Scotland Yard — 2006.

Scotland Yard Investigates — 2006

Rumors ran rife for a while that Scotland Yard had assigned a new investigator to the Ripper murders but no one could point to that individual nor could anyone outside of Scotland Yard discover why, after 118 years, the "Yard" would assign an officer to this case. In November 2006 the world would discover at least part of the answer. Scotland Yard investigators under the command of Laura Richards from the Violent Crimes Command had conducted a geographic, psychological and computer composite profile of the most infamous serial killer in history — Jack the Ripper.

Not surprisingly the computer generated profile bears a striking resemblance to Severin Klosowski and it closely resembles the composite developed by London investigators in 1888. The psychological and physical profile developed by the Violent Crime Command reads like a personal biography of Klosowski but neither one of these profiles proved as dramatic as the results achieved by the geography team, whose job it was to pinpoint the location of the killer during the 1888 "Autumn of Terror."

Scotland Yard team members were able to pinpoint a location which they felt was central to the murders— the infamous Flower & Dean Street located in the heart of Jack's killing grounds, the street the killer most likely lived on. Three Ripper victims lived on Flower & Dean Street and three lived around the corner, but the most important link to the murders is the fact that, across the street from where these victims lived, was a barbershop! Severin Klosowski worked as a floating barber in the area and he lived on George Yard, only two blocks away from Flower & Dean Street! Killer and victim could easily have stood face to face. And where was Alice "Clay pipe" McKenzie spotted before she was murdered? She was seen walking past the barbershop on Flower & Dean Street!

The questions now asked are: Does Scotland Yard have solid evidence proving the identity of Jack the Ripper? If not, why would they spend the time and money to investigate a 118-year-old murder? Why open this case? Did they find body parts or a murder weapon at 213 Borough High Street? Did they finally match DNA from the body parts or a weapon to a Ripper victim? Did they match the handwriting on the "letter from hell" to a prime suspect? Did they match DNA from the Pinchin Street torso to a relative of a prime Ripper suspect? Did investigators finally dig up the backyard at 126 Cable Street and find a skull related to the torso murders? Were investigators able to match Klosowski's American pistol to the final American murder in the American Ripper series? There are many more questions needing new answers.

Perhaps in the months and years ahead many of these questions will be answered by one of the finest law enforcement agencies in the world—Scotland Yard. Whom will they name as Jack the Ripper? My money is on Severin Antoniovich Klosowski, alias Jack the Ripper, who remains far and away beyond the usual Whitechapel suspects.

Appendix I

A Chronology of the Borough Poisoner

Severin Antoniovich Klosowski

May 15, 1892	Second child of Klosowski, a little girl named Cecilia, is born in Whitechapel, East End, London.
Mid June 1892	Klosowski arrives back in London for a short reunion with his wife. May have lived at 26 Scarborough Street, Whitechapel.
Summer 1892	Ripper case is inactive and is closed by Scotland Yard without any prime suspect for the murders in custody.
November 15, 1892	Thomas Neill Cream is executed in England—claimed to be Jack the Ripper.
Late 1892	Klosowski leaves no trace for last half of 1892 and most of 1893! Police unable to locate anyone who knew his location during this period. Wife may have been with him for a while.
Late 1893	Annie Chapman meets Klosowski. He was working at Haddin's hairdresser shop at 5 West Green Road, South Tottenham.
Nov 1893/Dec 1894	Annie Chapman lives with Klosowski, possibly at Haddin's shop.
Fall 1894	Klosowski brings in his wife Lucy to live with him and Annie Chapman.
December 1894	Annie Chapman leaves Klosowski because of wife Lucy's return. Annie is pregnant with his child.
Early 1895	Klosowski bought a house on High Road, Tottenham.
February 1895	Annie Chapman seeks support from Klosowski for his third child, he takes no notice. Lucy leaves Klosowski for the last time.
Early 1895	Klosowski now takes on the alias of George Chapman, lives with Renton family. Klosowski continues to move around a great deal.
Mid 1895/Early 96	Klosowski becomes assistant barber at 7 Church Lane, Leytonstone owned by Wenzel. Worked for 6 or 7 months.
c. October 1895	Klosowski lodges at a house on Forest Road owned by John Ward.
October 27, 1895	Klosowski and Mrs. Spink report that they have been married. She hands over £250 from trustees to Klosowski. He quits his job.
c. March 1896	Klosowski uses Spink's money to lease a barbershop in Hastings.
February 1897	Klosowski and Spink move to 1 Cobury Place, Hastings.
c. February 1897	Klosowski buys a boat, which capsizes and Spink almost drowns.
February 1897	A servant girl named Alice Penfold is courted by Klosowski. He informs her that he is single and that he is the manager of a pianoforte shop. He now plans to murder Mrs. Spink.

A Chronology of the Borough Poisoner

April 3, 1897	Klosowski purchases one ounce of tartar-emetic poison at William Davidson's chemist shop at 66 High Street, Hastings. This would be the smoking gun evidence at his trial as he keeps the poison label in his death file.
Fall 1897	Klosowski returns to London and leases the Prince of Wales public house in Bartholomew Square off of City Road.
Fall 1897	Balance of Spink's money is paid to "Mr. & Mrs. Chapman." Spink becomes ill from slow poison.
December 25, 1897	**Mary Spink is murdered by poison.** After she is dead Klosowski goes to open his pub on same day. Body is removed as soon as possible.
April 1898	Klosowski advertises for a new barmaid. Bessie Taylor answers the ad and is hired. Klosowski soon demands a sexual relationship.
c. June 1898	Klosowski and Bessie Taylor create a bogus marriage and are now "Mr. & Mrs. Chapman."
Late 1898	Klosowski and Taylor move for a short stay in Bishops, Stortford.
Late 1898	Klosowski gives up the Prince of Wales and leases the Grapes.
Before Christmas 98	A friend of Bessie's visits, Elizabeth Painter. Later reports that Klosowski threatened Bessie with a revolver. (First confirmation of gun in England.)
March 1899	Klosowski and Taylor move to Monument public house on Union Street, Southwark, London.
December 1900	Bessie's brother, William, visits at Monument. Klosowski begins to beat Bessie, but not in public.
February 13, 1901	**Bessie Taylor is murdered by slow poison.**
August 1901	18 year old Maud Marsh is hired by Klosowski as new barmaid at the Monument. Klosowski soon demands sex from Marsh.
September 13, 1901	Klosowski again creates a bogus marriage with Marsh. Now living as "Mr. & Mrs. Chapman." Klosowski begins to beat Maud. Also begins to photograph Maud as he slowly kills her as a collection.
December 1901	Klosowski tries to burn down the Monument for insurance claim.
Before Dec 25, 1901	Klosowski moves into the Crown public house at 213 Borough High Street with Maud Marsh. He is one mile from Whitechapel.
April 17, 1902	Ameer Ben Ali is pardoned for the Carrie Brown murder, and declared innocent by the Governor. He returns to Algiers.
June 1902	Klosowski hires Florence Rayner as a barmaid. He asks her to go to America with him. He is preparing to leave the country and continues to poison Maud Marsh. Keeps his money at the Crown.
June 1902	Klosowski falsely accuses Alfred Clark & Matilda Gilmor of conspiracy to defraud him of £700. Clark is convicted but later released. Gilmor is freed with no sentence given.
June 7/8, 1902	**Salamanca Place Torso murder.** Fifth and final Torso murder.
October 22, 1902	**Maud Marsh is murdered by poison.** The final murder by serial killer Severin Klosowski is completed.
October 23, 1902	Klosowski asks Maud's sister to be his new barmaid.
October 25, 1902	Klosowski is arrested for Maud Marsh's murder by Inspector George Godley at the Crown public house.
January 17, 1903	Newspaper reports on possible ship Klosowski took to America in 1891. Klosowski still claims to be an American.
March 16, 1903	Klosowski's trial begins.
March 20, 1903	Klosowski is convicted of Maud Marsh's murder. Jury takes eleven minutes to convict. Klosowski is sentenced to death.
March 24, 1903	Inspector Abberline names Severin Klosowski as Jack the Ripper.
April 7, 1903	Severin Antoniovich Klosowski goes to the scaffold at Wandsworth Prison. Given a drop of 6 feet 6 inches and the mystery of Jack the Ripper continues.

Bibliography

British Press Reports

London Times
    August 10, 1888 — "The Murder in Whitechapel"
    August 24, 1888 — "Inquests"
    September 1, 1888 — "Another Murder in Whitechapel"
    November 10, 1888 — "Another Whitechapel Murder"
    April 8, 1903 — "Execution — Severin Klosowski"
    August 19, 1988 — "Ripper Papers Unveiled, 100 Years On"

East London Advertiser
    August 11, 1888
    August 18, 1888
    September 8, 1888

Weekly Herald
    August 17, 1888 — "A Mysterious Murder"
    September 7, 1888 — "Horrible Murder of a Woman"
    September 28, 1888 — "A Terrible Murder at Gateshead"
    October 5, 1888 — "London's Horrors"
    November 16, 1888 — "A Woman Fiendishly Mutilated"
    December 7, 1888 — "The Whitechapel Fiend"

Daily Telegraph
    October 4, 1888 — "The Whitehall Murder"
    October 5, 1888 — "Whitehall Tragedy"
    November 10, 1888 — "Locality of the Seven Undiscovered Murders"
    November 12, 1888
    April 16, 1966 — "Letters by Jack the Ripper Published, Skill Theory Rejected"
    April 20, 2001 — "Lost Jack the Ripper Letter Remains a Riddle"

Illustrated Police News
    November 24, 1888 — "Is He the Murderer?"

London Observer
    October 9, 1888

The *Star*
    August 7, 1888 — "A Whitechapel Horror"
    August 31, 1888 — "A Revolting Murder"
    September 8, 1888 — Horror upon Horror"
    October 19, 1888

South London Observer
  November 1, 1902 — "Southwark Poisoning Mystery"
  November 2, 1902 — "Publican Charged with Murder"

South London Press
  June 14, 1902 — "Gruesome Discovery"
  March 20, 1903 — "The Southwark Poisonings"
  March 21, 1903 — "Southwark Murder"
  April 11, 1903 — "The Final Scenes"

Pall Mall Gazette
  October 19, 1888
  December 31, 1888 — "The Search for the Whitechapel Murderer"
  March 24, 1903 — "The Chapman — Ripper Theory"
  March 31, 1903 — "The Chapman — Ripper Theory"

Daily Chronicle
  March 23, 1903

Southwark and Bermondsey Recorder and *South London Gazette*
  November 1, 1902
  November 8, 1902 — "The Borough Mystery"
  November 15, 1902 — "Southwark Poisoning Mystery"
  November 22, 1902 — "Southwark Poisoning Mystery"
  November 29, 1902 — "Southwark Poisoning Case"
  December 20, 1902 — "Coroner's Inquest — Verdict"
  January 17, 1903 — "Southwark Poisoning Charge"
  January 31, 1903 — "The Charges against Chapman"

Police Review and Parade Gossip
  April 24, 1903
  May 15, 1908 — "Chief Inspector Godley Retires"

The News of the World
  October 7, 1888

Maclean's
  September 21, 1988 — "A Grisly Allure, Jack the Ripper's Mystery Defies Explanation"

Sunday Magazine
  July 16, 1995 — "Was This Jack the Ripper?"

County of Middlesex Independent
  January 7, 1889 — "Found in the River"

American Press reports

New York Times
  June 10, 1865 — Letter to the Editor — Dr. F. Tumblety
  September 1, 1888 — "A Terribly Brutal Murder in Whitechapel"
  September 9, 1888 — "Whitechapel Startled by a Fourth Murder"
  October 1, 1888 — "Dismay in Whitechapel"
  October 2, 1888 — "London's Awful Mystery"
  October 3, 1888 — "London's Record of Crime"
  October 5, 1888 — "The Whitechapel Murder Mysteries"
  November 10, 1888 — "Exciting London Events"
  December 11, 1888 — "Is This Jack the Ripper?"
  July 18, 1889 — "The Whitechapel Crime"
  July 21, 1889 — "Gossip of the Day Abroad"
  September 11, 1889 — "Another London Murder"

February 13, 1891—"Jack the Ripper Again"
February 14, 1891—"The Whitechapel Mystery"
April 25, 1891—"Choked, Then Mutilated"
April 26, 1891—"Byrnes Says He Had a Clue"
April 28, 1891—"The Murderer Still at Large"
April 29, 1891—"Byrnes Quite Mystified"
June 27, 1891—"Jury Ready for 'Frenchy' No. 1<in>
July 1, 1891—"'Frenchys' Varied Stories"
July 2, 1891—"Experts against 'Frenchy'"
July 3, 1891—"'Frenchy's' Trial Nearly Over
July 4, 1891—"'Frenchy' Found Guilty"
August 3, 1891—"A Long Island Mystery"
August 4, 1891—"It Was Matilda Haber"
August 5, 1891—"No Clue to the Murderer"
August 6, 1891—"The Glendale Mystery"
August 7, 1891—"She Was Hannah Robinson"
August 8, 1891—"It Is Still a Mystery"
August 9, 1891—"Hannah Robinson Buried"
August 10, 1891—"Hannah Robinson's Murder"
February 1, 1892 —"A Brutal New Jersey Murder"
February 4, 1892 —"The Murder of Mrs. Senior"
February 7, 1892 —"The Senior Murder"
February 18, 1892 —"The Murder of Mrs. Senior"
June 9, 1892 —"Found with Her Throat Cut"
June 10, 1892 —"He Eluded Observation"
June 11, 1892 —"At Loss for a Clue"
April 26, 1892 —"An Elizabeth Officer's Encounter with an Unknown Man"
April 17, 1902 —"'Frenchy' Is Pardoned"
June 13, 1892 —"Mary Anderson's Funeral"
June 14, 1892 —"Peterson's Friend Arrested"
June 17, 1892 —"Still Think Schliph Guilty"
June 18, 1892 —"Believe Schliph to Be Innocent"
July 21, 1892 —"Thinks His Mind Is Affected"
September 29, 1892 —"Did He Kill Hannah Robinson?"

Atlanta Constitution
March 24, 1903 —"Original Jack the Ripper"
April 5, 1903 —"Jack the Ripper to Die on the Gallows"

Elyria (Ohio) Daily Chronicle
October 7, 1903 —"Was He Jack the Ripper?"

Washington Post
October 26, 1913

Fort Wayne (Indiana) News
March 23, 1903 —"He Is 'Jack the Ripper'"

Los Angeles Times
October 1, 1888 —"London Alarmed — The Whitechapel Fiend Again at Work"
November 10, 1888 —"The Whitechapel Fiend"
November 11, 1888 —"Latest Device to Trap the Whitechapel Murderer"

New York World
December 3, 1888 —"Tumblety Is in the City"
December 6, 1888

Books

Adam, Hargrave L., ed. *Trial of George Chapman.* Toronto: Canada Law Book Company, 1930.
Anderson, Robert. *The Lighter Side of My Official Life.* London: Hodder & Stoughton, 1910.
Beggs, Paul, Martin Fido, and Keith Skinner. *The Jack the Ripper A to Z.* London: Headline Book Publishing, 1994.
Evans, Stewart P., and Keith Skinner. *The Ultimate Jack the Ripper Companion.* New York: Carroll & Graf, 2000.
Fido, Martin. *The Crimes, Detection and Death of Jack the Ripper.* London: George Weidenfeld and Nicolson, 1987.
Glyn Jones, Richard. *Unsolved Classic True Murder Mysteries.* New York: Peter Bedrick Books, 1987.
Gordon, R. Michael. *Alias Jack the Ripper: Beyond the Usual Whitechapel Suspects.* Jefferson, NC: McFarland, 2001.
_____. *The Thames Torso Murders of Victorian London.* Jefferson, NC: McFarland, 2002.
_____. *The American Murders of Jack the Ripper.* Westport, CT: Praeger, 2003.
London, Jack, *The People of the Abyss.* Sonoma, CA: Sonoma State University, 1903. Reprint. Joseph Simon, 1980.
Smith, Henry. *From Constable to Commissioner: The Story of My Sixty Years, Most of Them Misspent.* London: Chatto & Windus, 1910.
Sugden, Philip. *The Complete History of Jack the Ripper.* New York: Carroll & Graf, 1995.

Radio

The Black Museum — January 1, 1952–December 30, 1952, Mutual Network "The Straight Razor," episode number 44, staring Orson Welles, produced by Harry Alan Towers, scripts by Ira Marion, music by Sidney Torch.

Documents

Macnaughten's Memoranda
Melville Macnaughten, February 23, 1894

Littlechild Letter — Subject: Ripper suspects
Letter written by John G. Littlechild — September 23, 1913

Dr. Thomas Bond's Medical letter
Report on the Whitechapel murders, November 10, 1888

Personal Documents held by Severin Antoniovich Klosowski
- Birth Certificate, December 15, 1865
- Primary School Report, December 7–19, 1880
- Society of Surgeons Receipt, October 23–November 5, 1882
- Magistrate Conduct Certificate, November 16, 1882
- Surgical Pupil Registry Receipt, November 22–December 3, 1882
- Apprentice Certificate, June 1, 1885
- Instruction Certificate, April 29, 1886
- Employment Certificate, November 15, 1886
- Employment Certificate, November 24–December 6, 1886
- Klosowski Personal Biography, November 15, 1886
- Passport, November 24, 1886
- Junior Surgeon Degree Petition, December 1886
- Junior Surgeon Degree Acceptance, December 5, 1886
- Hospital Fees Receipt, February 28, 1887
- Death Certificate: Wohystaro Klosowski — March 3, 1891

Official Files

Public Record Office, Kew

Metropolitan Police:
- MEPO 3/140 — Whitechapel Murder Files
- MEPO 3/142 — "Jack the Ripper" letters
- MEPO 3/153 — Post Mortem — Mary Kelly, "Dear Boss" letter, Pinchin Street News report, Murder pardon — Kelly murder
- MEPO 3/155 — Whitechapel Murder Victims — Photos

(Material in the Public Record Office is the copyright of the Metropolitan Police and is reproduced by permission of the Commissioner of Police of the Metropolis.)

Home Office:
- HO 144/221/A49301 F — Mary Kelly murder
- HO 144/221/A49301 H — Rose Mylett murder
- HO 144/221/A49301 I — Alice McKenzie murder
- HO 144/221/A49301 K — Pinchin Street Torso murder
- HO 144/680/101992 — George Chapman Poison Case

Public Record Office, Chancery Lane
- CRIM 1/84 — George Chapman Poison Case, Depositions
- CRIM 4/1215 — George Chapman Poison Case, Indictments

Charge Sheet — Southwark Police Court, January 7, 1903

The National Archives of the United States

New York Passenger List Arrivals, Call number SL 1,027,611, Micro Copy number M237, Roll number 565 for April 13, 1891— April 24, 1891

Index

Names in **bold** indicate victims. Numbers in ***bold italic*** indicate illustrations.

Abberline, Chief Inspector George Frederick 5, 12, 33, 34, 37, 39, 50, **55**, 113, 141, 183, 184, 185; note on "Reminiscences" ***186–7***
Adam, Hargrave L. 34, 73, 128, 133, 145, 154, 188, 189
Albert Embankment 111
Albion Mansions 59, 64
Albion Public House 59
Alderney Street 18
Ali, Ameer Ben "Frenchy" 40, 41, 80, 90
All Hallow's Mission Church 79
Almy, Clarence 43
America 33, 34, 39, 42, 44, 46, 47, 50, 52, 58, 87, 94, 107, 109, 126, 144, 184, 185, 187, 188, 189, 190
The American Murders of Jack the Ripper 196
Anderson, Herta Mary 45, 46, 47, 48, 74
Anderson, Isabella Fraser 54
Anderson, Sir Robert 15, 24, 33, 80, 128
Andrews, Police Constable Walter 28
Antimony poison 64, 75, 76, 77, 91, 127, 149
Arizona 89
Arsenic 98, 103, 107, 116, 125
Arsten, George A. 36, 42
Atlanta Constitution press reports 185–7, 188
"Autumn of Terror" 10, 31, 193, 199

Baderski, Stanislaus 49; Police Court testimony 142; trial testimony 158
Barrett, Reverend Samuel Augustus 21
Barnard's Home, Dr. 70, 71
Barnett, Joseph 24
Bartholomew Square 65
Battersea Park 56
Baxter, Wynne Edwin (Coroner) 29

Beggs, Paul 196
Berner Street (No. 40) 13
Berry, James "Hangman" 107, 126
Bethoral Green 67
Betrikowski, Joseph: Police Court testimony 145
Biggs & Company 94
Bird, William: Police Court testimony 136
Birton, Police Constable 112
Bishops, Stortford 73, 74
Bishopsgate 121
Black Museum 95, 107, 119, 137, 139, 143, 191, 193, 194–6
The Black Museum (radio) 191–3
Blackwell, Dr. Frederick William 14
Blind Beggar gang 6
Bodkin, Archibald H. 133–4, ***134***, 139, 153
Bodmer, Dr. Richard 103; coroner's inquest testimony 127; trial testimony 171
Bond, Dr. Thomas 24, 27, 28; medical report 25
Bonnell's Hall 45
Bonner, Chief Inspector 118
Booth, William 3
Borough High Street (No. 213) 63, 82, 89, 105, 112, 113, 198, 199
Borough Poisoner 33, 64, 69, 70, 83, 86, 92, 100, 103, 105, 120, 123, 128, 135, 141, 144, 152, 154, 155, 177, 188, 191, 192, 193, 195
Borough Road (No. 81) 77
Bournemouth 26, 185
Bowyer, Thomas 22
Bray, William Lemain 51; trial testimony 159
Braund, Mr. 51
Bridge House Estates Committee 75
Britannia public house 22
British flag 89
Brixton Prison 117
Broad Street 111

Brooklyn Bridge 37
Brown, Carrie "Old Shakespeare" ***38***, 39, 40, 45, 47, 80, 90, 196; mortuary photos ***41***
Brown, James 35
Bruce Grove Railway Station 52, 53, 142
Buck's Row 8, 50
Bulling, Tom 11
Burke, Acting Chief of Police 46, 47
Burke, Detective Marshal 47
Burns, Elizabeth 12
Burridge, Mary 10
Bury, William Henry 107
Byrnes, Chief Inspector Thomas 37, 40, 41, 90

Cable Street (No. 123) 29, 52, 142, 199
Caledonian Gold Mining Company 110
Caledonian Road (No. 59) 101
"Call at the Monument ASAP" note 82
Callagher, Ellen 32
Calloway, Dr. 4
Camps, Prof. Francis 193
Canada Law Book Company 188
Carson, Edward 98, 151, 152, ***153***, 155, 178
"Casebook" 50
Casey, Michael 46
Castle Alley 28, 56
Catharine Street 90
Central Criminal Court 150, 152, 154
Central News Agency press report 11
Cerise Road (No. 2) 92
Chamber Street 32
Chandler, Inspector Joseph 10
Chapman, Annie 9, 10, 12, 13, 29, 34, 33, 51, 55, 83, 142, 189
Chapman, Annie "Georgina" 49, 50, 51, 52, 142; baby 53; trial testimony 168

209

Index

Chapman, Bessie: mourning card 80
Chapman, Cecil M. **133**, 135, 150
Chapman, George (alias) 33, 34, 54, 57, 59, 60, 62, 63, 65, 67, 70, 72, 73, 75, 76, 77, 79, 81, 82, 83, 84, 85, 87, 88, 89, 92, 94, 95, 96, 98, 99, 100, 101, 102, 104, 105, 106, 107, 108, 110, 111, 112, 113, 117, 120, 122, 123, 125, 126, 128, 134, 135, 137, 139, 143, 149, 151, 154, 184, 185, 187, 189, 193; arrest 109, 103; inquest 115, 136; Marsh 86; poison 64; publican 66; Spink 58; Taylor 74
Chapman I, Mrs. 139
Chapman II, Mrs. 139
Chapman III, Mrs. 92
Chapman IV, Mrs. 92
Cheshire 76, 79, 148
Chicago 46
Church Lane (No. 7) 58
City Road 65
Clark, Alfred 110, 111, 141
Clarke's Yard 26
Chelsea Embankment 56
Clerlenwell 142
Cleveland Street Scandal 50
Clinical Research Association 78, 102, 103, 125, 127
Clock Lane Police Station 17
Cobury Place (No. 1) 62
Cohen, Reverend Francis L. 17
Cole, Beatrice 94
Cole, Louisa B. 96, 123, 136
Coles, Frances 31–2, **32**, 33, 34, 56
Coller's Rents 135
Commercial Street 10, 22, 32, 142
Commercial Street Police Station 60
The Complete History of Jack the Ripper 196
Connally, Mary Ann 6
Correspondence of Jack the Ripper *see* Ripper correspondence
Cotter, Dr. P. G. 78, 101, 124, 125
Cox, John 112
Crickmen, Reverend J. H. 117
The Crime Museum 194
Crow, George 6
Crown Public House 2, 82, 86, 89–95, **93**, 97–8, 100–107, 109, 110, 111, 114, 115, 116, 118, 121, 122, 123, 124, 125, 126, 134, 135, 137, 139, 143, 145, 148, 161, 164, 165, 166, 167, 169, 174, 179, 180, 181, 195, 197–8; evidence list 108
Croydon Hospital 122
Cults 75
Cutbush, Thomas 54
Cypress Avenue 42

Dacre, Mr. Henry 59
Daily Chronicle press report 183
Daily Telegraph **23**; press reports 193, 194
Dakota Territory 47
Dance, George 151
Davidson, William Henry 63–4,
57, 110, 126; Police Court testimony 137; trial testimony 161
Davis, John 9
Dellow, John 194
Dickens, Charles 89
Diplock, Dr. Thomas Bramah 26
DNA 12, 193, 199
Documents: Note to Matthews 16; Official Police Notice 12; Pardon to murder accomplices 23–4; Police Notice to the Occupier 17; Victims Folder List 33; *see also* Biggs & Company note; Bond, Dr. Thomas: Medical report; "Call at the Monument ASAP" note; The East-End Murders letter; General Alarm!; Warren, Charles: Confidential Report; The Whitechapel Murder report
Dorset Street 22
Doubleday, Mrs. Martha 67, 68, 69, 70, 148; Police Court testimony 143–4; trial testimony 173–4
Doulton's Pottery Works 111, 112
Druitt, Montague John 26, 55, 196
Dutfield's Yard 14

East End 5, 9, 13, 15, 18, 22, 26, 27, 31, 37, 44, 53, 62, 64, 80, 141, 142, 151, 157, 193, 197; search 20
The East-End Murders letter 21
East London Advertiser press report 7
East River Hotel 37
Eddowes, Catherine 14, 15, 17, 18, 33, 34, 55, 189
Edward VII 105, 109
Elliott, George **152**, 154, 179
Evans, Stewart P. 194, 197

The Family Physician 107, 126
Farringdon Market 136
French, Dr. 101, 124, 125
Fido, Martin 196
Field, Jenny 86
Flower and Dean Street 12, 17, 28, 199
Forester's Tavern 94
Fort Wayne News press report 185
Forth Ward Hotel 90
Forty Years of Man-Hunting 190
Fouratt's Hat Shop 44
Freyberger, Dr. Emile Ludwig 101, 115, 118, 124, 126; coroner's inquest testimony 121

Gallagher, Police Constable John 13
General Alarm! 40
George Street 61, 59, 62, 64
George Yard 6, 14, 56, 157, 184, 187, 199
George Yard Dwellings 6
"George's American Bar" 66, 89, 105
Georgia 187
Georgian England 197
Gilbert, Frank L. 101; coroner's inquest testimony 123–4; trial testimony 172
Gilmor, Matilda 110
Glendale, Long Island 42
Glenmore Hotel 39, 40
Godley, Inspector George 12, 63, 82, 96, 103, **104**, 105, 106, 107, 108, 109, 110, 111, 113, 115, 120, 126, 128, 139, 141, 145, 148, 150, 159, 188, 190, 195; case testimony on his search 105–6; coroner's inquest testimony 126; Police Court testimony 113, 114, 148; trial testimony 159–60, 161, 174
Goulding, Police Constable Robert 26
Grainger, William Grant 53
Grantham, Justice **154**, 155; charges the jury 181
Grapel, Dr. Francis Gasper 98, 100, 125, 127; coroner's inquest testimony 125, 127; trial testimony 169
The Grapes Public House 73, 74, 75, 105, 106, 140
Great Eastern Railway Company 57
Green, Walter 185
Greenway, Harriet 62, 63; Police Court testimony 143
Gray's Inn Square 51
Gunner, Richard 197
Guy's Hospital 90, 104, 121, 122, 126, 128

Haberdasher Street (No. 8), Shoreditch 73
Haddin, Mr. 51
Hames, Margaret 5
Hanbury Street (No. 29) 9, 10, 12
Harris, Harry 18
Hastings 59, 60, 61, 62, 63, 64, 65, 126, 143
Hastings, Battle of 59
Healey, Mary 37
Helsdown, Mrs. Anna: case testimony 61; Police Court testimony 143; trial testimony 173
High Road (No. 518), Tottenham 51, 52
High Street (No. 66), Hastings 63
Hill Street (No. 10) 61
Hutchinson, George 22, 35
Hutton, Arthur 144, **145**, 149, 154
Huxton High Rips 6
H. W. Meyer's Cigar Factory 42

Ibbs, Sister Martha Elizabeth 77
Infant Jesus Hospital 147
Institute of Chemistry 103
International Workingman's Educational Club 13
Isllington 50

Jack the Ripper 3, 4, 5, 8, 11, 14, 15, 31, 37, 50, 52, 53, 54, 63, 80, 81, 83, 96, 106, 108, 109, 110, 128, 142, 150, 151, 155, 177, 185, 186, 187, 188, 189, 190, 191, 193, 194, 196, 198; American murders 139; Brown murder 40; Chapman 51; Coles murder 32; composite

Index

sketch *35*; computer composite *198*; letter 60; Lusk letter 20; New York 90; Robinson murder 42
The Jack the Ripper A to Z 196
Jackson, Elizabeth 27, 34
Jaquet, Dr. 105
Jersey City 42, 44, 54, 108, 185, 186, 187, 189
Jersey Railroad Police 46
Johnson, Florence Grace 54
Johnson, Police Constable John 12, 13

Kelly, Mary Jane 22, 23, 24, 26, 33, 34, 55, 189
Kelly, Mr. 36
Kelsall, William 177
Kemp, Detective Sergeant William 103, 104, 105, 106, 115, 118, 120, 126, 150
Kings Place (No. 9) 101
Klaiber, John 71
Klosowski, Lucy 29, 44, 48, 49, 50, 61, 110, 155, 190 Baderski
Klosowski, Severin Antoniovich 1–2, *2*, 6, 14, 17, 27, 29, 33, 34, 42, 44, 46, 48, 49, 50, 51, 52, 54, 57, 63, *72*, 73, *82*, 86, 99, 101, 103, 108, 110, 113, 115, 116, 117, 121, 122, 123, 124, 125, 126, 128, 137, 141, 142, 143, 144, 145, 151, 152, 155, *163*, 183, 187, 188, 189, 191, 192, 193; Anderson murder 47; arrest 109; Black Museum 195; execution 182, 185; inquest 136; name change 53; poison 64
Knaster, Ignatius: letter 147
Korminski, Aaron 196
Kosminski, Aaron 55
Kreuscher's Hotel 42

Lane, Long 123
Langham, Frederick George 59
Langton, Undersheriff 155
Latin Pharmacopieca 126
Lave, Joseph 14
Lawende, Joseph 35; case testimony on Eddowes Inquest 18
"Leather Apron" 10
Leck, Police Sergeant 105
"Letter from Hell" *21*, 199
Letters of Jack the Ripper *see* Ripper correspondence
Levisohn, Wolff 24, 49, 52, *53*, 141, 142; Police Court testimony 141–2; trial testimony 157
Levy, Joseph 18
Leytonstone, England 57
Limehouse Forty Thieves 6
Little Dorrit 89
Littlechild, Chief Inspector John 194
Liverpool, England 110
Llewellyn, Dr. Rees Ralph 9
Lloyd's Bank of London 145
London 3, 4, 18, 23, 26, 27, 42, 45, 47, 48, 50, 66, 80, 81, 82, 84, 90, 102, 103, 109, 110, 115, 118, 128, 139, 145, 184, 185, 186, 188, 193, 194, 197; ghetto 111; World War II 33
London, Jack 3, 109
London Bridge 82, 89
London Bridge Cloakroom 87
London County Council 10, 115, 126
London Hospital 6
London Road (No. 282) 98
London Times press report 185
Long, Elizabeth 9, 13, 35
Longfellow Road (No. 14) 81, 120, 135
Ludwig, Charles 12, 13
Lusk, George 9, 18, 19, 20, 21
Lymm Cemetery 123, 177
Lymm Churchyard 79, 148
Lynch, John 46
Lyntz, August: arrest for murder 45

Maclean's press report 194
Macnaghten, Chief Constable Melville Leslie 33, 54–7, 60, 128, 184
Macnaghten Memoranda 54–6
Maps: The American Murder Series, 1891–92 39; Spitalfields & Whitechapel Victims' Loggings, 1888 7
Marks, Joseph Henry 103
Marsh, Alfred 85
Marsh, Alice May 90, 97, 102, 122; Police Court testimony 137; trial testimony 166
Marsh, Daisy Harriet Helen 86, 87, 122; trial testimony 166
Marsh, Mrs. Eliza 82, 83, *84*, 85, 86, 91, 95, 96, 97, 98, 99, 100, 102, 105, 123; coroner's inquest testimony 119, 120, 126; Police Court testimony 135, 136; trial testimony 162–4
Marsh, Maud Elizabeth 81, *82*, 83, 84, 85, 86, 87, 88, 90, 91, 92, 93, 94, 95, 96, 97, 98, 99, 100, 101, 102, 103, 106, 107, 110, 111, 113, 115, 119, 121, 122, 124, 125, 126, 134, 139, 154, 155, 190; letter to "Dearest George" (July 31, 1902) 90; letter to mother (September 11, 1901) 84; letter to mother (September 12, 1901) 84–5; letter to "my Dearest Husband" 91; postmortem 128–30, 131–2
Marsh, Robert 82, 83, *84*, 85, 86, 97, 98, 117, 134, 135; coroner's inquest testimony 116, 118; Police Court testimony 135; trial testimony 164–5
Martin, Mrs. 64
Martin, William 36
Mattewan State Hospital 41, 90
Matthews, Charles 152, *153*
Matthews, Henry 16, 17, 30
Maurer's Hotel 46
McCarthy, Inspector 12
McCarthy, Police Sergeant 54
McKenna, Edward 12

McKenzie, Alice "Clay Pipe" 27, 28, 33, 34, 56, 189, 199
Men of Harleck 9
Metropolitan Police 19, 63, 109, 194, 195
Midland Bank 145
Milburn 44, 45
Miller's Court 22, 33, 55
Millwood, Annie 5, 34
Minter, Mary 35
Mission Hall, Collier Rents 115
Mitre Square 14, 15, 17, 18, 50, 55
Monro, James 30
Montagu, Samuel 24
Monument Tavern 75, 76, 77, 78, 79, 81–8, 89, 106, 113, 118, 119, 140, 141, 148, 156, 162, 163, 165, 166, 171, 175, 176
Moore, Chief Inspector Henry 12, 15, 60
Morris, Mrs. Louisa Sarah 86, 87, 95, 96, 120, 136; coroner's inquest testimony 121, 122, 123; case testimony on Marsh 95; Police Court testimony 136; trial testimony 165
Moshkovski, Dr. 1
Mosquito 62
Mount Olivet Cemetery 43
Mumford, Mrs. Jane: case testimony on Chapman 68; Police Court testimony 147–8
Muntzer, Robert William 111, 112
Murdering Tramp Theory 46
My Experience as an Executioner 107
Mylett, Rose 26, 33, 34, 189
Myrtle Avenue 42

Nagornack, Poland 1
Nearn, Inspector James William 12
Neil, Detective Sergeant Arthur 33, 73, 110, 150, 190–1; trial testimony 173
New Chambers Street 45
New Cut Market 136
New Jersey 43, 47, 48, 74, 184, 189
New Kent Road (No. 221) 77
New York City 37, 40, 43, 44, 47, 80, 90, 196
New York Times press reports 40, 42, 45, 46, 47, 90
Newman, E. H. A. 115
Nichols, Mary Ann "Polly" 8, 33, 34, 55, 70, 188; P.C. John Neil discovers body *8*
Nicoll, District Attorney 40
Nile Street, Horton 61
Normans 59
Notable British Trials 145

O'Connor, Martin 141
Odell, Governor Benjamin 41, 90
Old Bailey 103, 151, 152, 153, 154, 155
Old Hastings 59
Old Marshalsea Jail 89
Old Vestry Hall 101
Oliver, Detective 47
Openshaw, Dr. Thomas 54, 194

Ostrog, Michael 56, 196
Oxenford, Miss 110, 111

Paget, Susan: case testimony on Chapman 67
Painter, Elizabeth Ann 73, 74, 79; case testimony on Taylor 76; trial testimony 175–6
Park Lane (No. 52) 51
Parker, Matthew 35
Peace, Charlie 195
Pearce, Inspector 12
Peckham 74, 92, 94
Penfold, Alice 63, 64; case testimony on Chapman 65; Police Court testimony 143
Pennett, Police Constable William 29
Pentonville Road (No. 209) 50
People of the Abyss 109
Pepper Street 77
Perth Amboy 46, 47
Peterson, Axel 46, 47
Petticoat Lane 8
Pharmacopeia 126
Pharmacy Act 137
Phillips, Dr. 28
Phillips, Mortimer 43
Photography 66
Physical profile 198
Pierce, Henry Edward 70
Pinchin Street 29, 30, 52, 56, 111
Pincott, Mr. 51
Pistol, .32-caliber 46
Pizer, John 10
Poison label 64, 161
Poland 110, 141
The Police Gazette press report 21–2
The Police Review and Parade Gossip 109
Poplar 25–6
Poplar High Street 26
Poland 1, 2, 52, 189
Postmortems: **Marsh, Maud** 128–30, 131–2, **Spink, Mary** 131, **Taylor, Elizabeth** 130–1
Poycott, Dr. 101
A Practice of Physics 126
The Prince of Wales public house 65, 67, 68, 69–70, 71–3, 106, 140, 143, 156, 174
Psychological abuse 75
Public Houses (bars) *see* Albion Public House; Britannia; Crown Public House; Forester's Tavern; "George's American Bar"; The Grapes Public House; Monument Tavern; The Prince of Wales; Unicorn Tavern; White Hart Public House

Queen's Road, Hastings 64

Race, Inspector William 56
Radin, Mrs. Ethel: trial testimony 157–8
Rahway 45
Rainham 4, 111
Rainham Mystery 56

Rappaport, Senior Surgeon Moshko 1
Rauch, Mrs. Stanislaus 49, **91**, 110, 147; Police Court testimony 142; trial testimony 158–9
Rayner, Florence 92, 94; trial testimony 167–8
Reed, Mary 102
Reeves, John Saunders 7
Regent's Canal 4
Reid, Detective Inspector Edmund John 7, 12, 33
Renton, Joseph Smith 57, 59; Police Court testimony 142–3
Richards, Layra 198
Ridgewood 42
Ripper correspondence Dear Boss letter 11; Dear Friend letter 19; Juwes message 15; Letter from Hell 20, 21; Have not caught letter 28; October 14, 1896, letter 60; Openshaw letter **54**; postcard 11
"Ripper" letter **54**
Robinson, Hannah 42, 43, 47
Rogers, Dr. 67, 68, 69, 70, 143
Rombro, Jacob 14
Ross, John 193, 195
Ruggles-Brise, Sir Evelyn 16

Sadler, James Thomas 32, 56
St. George-in-the-East 52
St. George's Cathedral, Southwark 73
St. George's Church 101
St. George's Stair 27
St. James Place 14
St. John's Square 142
St. Leonard's Church 24, 65, 75
St. Pancras Station 79
St. Patrick's Cemetery 70
St. Savior's Church 117
Salamanca Place 111, 112
Sanders, J.S. 30
Scarborough Street (No. 26) 49
Schlipf, Harry 40
"Schloski" 51
Schumann, George: trial testimony 160
Scotland Yard 5, 12, 19, 28, 30, 53, 54, 56, 63, 89, 107, 109, 113, 119, 141, 143, 184, 185, 188, 191, 193, 194, 195, 196, 198, 199
Seaside Home 33
Secret black bag 63, 143, 198
Senior, Elizabeth 44, 45, 47
Senior, Joseph 44
Serial killer 1, 2, 4, 9, 21, 24, 29, 31, 34, 44, 50, 53, 59, 62, 66, 67, 71, 78, 79, 81, 85, 94, 96, 97, 100, 107, 109, 123, 126, 128, 134, 147, 151, 170, 183, 184, 196, 198
Shaw, George Bernard 17
Shelden, Neal 50
Sherman, George 61
Shivarty, Israel 35
Sibley, Ernest John 75
Simmonds, Mrs. Edith 62
Sims, Mr. George R. 153, 194
Skinner, Keith 196, 197

Smith, Detective 43
Smith, Emma Elizabeth 33
Smith, Lt. Col. Henry 17, 33
Smith, John 46
Smith, Recorder 40
Smith, Police Constable William 35
Smith's Undertaking 79, 101
Somerset House 73
South Bridge Road 101
South London 76, 92, 103
South London Fire Brigade 87
South London News press report 77
South London Observer press reports 114, 115
South London Press press reports 178, 182
South Tottenham 51, 58, 142
Southwark 83, 85, 110, 115, 135
Southwark and Bermonsey Recorder and South London Gazette press reports 59–60, 65, 67, 70, 144, 116–7, 108, 127, 137–8
Southwark Borough Council Medical Department 101
Southwark Bridge Road 78, 79
Southwark Coroner's Court 117, 120
Southwark Police Court 113
Southwark Police Station 107
Southwark Street (No. 1) 102
Spink, Mary Isabella 54, 57–8, 59, 61, 63, 64, 66, 67, 68, 69, 70, 71, 73, 75, 78, 109, 127, 134, 139, 142, 143, 144, 190; Mrs. Chapman I 65; postmortem 131
Spink, Shadrack 59
Spink, William "Willie" 57, 61, 70, 71, 73, 75, 143, 148
Spitalfields 9, 22, 25, 53
Springfield Avenue 44
Star press report 10
Stevens, Mrs. Martha 78, 79; case testimony on Taylor 77; trial testimony 176–7
Stevenson, Dr. Thomas 58, 106, 124, 125, 126–7, 128, 134; coroner's inquest testimony 127; Police Court testimony 149; trial testimony 172–3, 174–5, 178–9
Stoker, Dr. James Maurice 79, 92, 95, 97, 98, 101, 102, 103, 150; case testimony on Marsh 100; case testimony on Taylor 77–8; coroner's inquest testimony 124–5, 127; Police Court testimony 149; trial testimony 170–1
"Stones End" 105
The Straight Razor (radio show) 191–3
Stride, Elizabeth 13, 20, 29, 33, 34, 55, 189; coroner's inquest into murder **20**
Stringer, William Henry 71
Sugden, Philip 196
Sunday Magazine press report 194
Sunderland, Dr. 78
Sunderland, England 41
Suspect descriptions 6, 18, 21, 22, 25, 35–6, 38, 39, 40, 42, 184, 198

Index

Sutton, Mr. H. 153
Swallow Gardens 32, 38, 56
Swanson, Chief Inspector Donald 21, 33
Sydney, Thomas 52, 108, 113, 115, 118, 142, 144, 150, 154

Tabard Street 102
Tabram, Martha 6, 7, 27, 33, 34, 56, 157, 188
Targett, Dr. James Henry 90; coroner's inquest testimony 124, 127; trial testimony 167
Taylor, Elizabeth "Bessie" *72*, 73, 74, 75, 76, 77, 78, 80, 81, 95, 105, 109, 123, 125, 127, 134, 139, 148, 149, 177, 190; exhumation 138; Mrs. Chapman II 79; postmortem 130–1
Taylor, Dr. Michael 112, 113
Taylor, Mrs. 105
Taylor, Paul 102, 113, 133
Taylor, Thomas Parsonage 73
Taylor, William 75, 76, 79; Police Court testimony 148, 149; trial testimony 175
Testimony (Coroner's Inquest) Session 1 (October 28, 1902) 115–6; Session 2 (November 11, 1902) 117–120; Session 3 (November 18, 1902) 120–123; Session 4 (November 25, 1902) 123–125; Final Session (December 18, 1902) 126–7
Testimony (Police Court) October 27, 1902 113–116; November 12, 1902 134–35; November 28, 1902 135–37; December 17, 1902 137–38; December 31, 1902 139–40; January 7, 1903 140–143; January 14, 1903 143–44; January 21, 1903 144–48; February 4, 1903 148–9; February 11, 1903 150
Thames Embankment 112
Thames Magistrates Court 13
Thames River 111, 112

Thames Torso Murders 4, 19, 27, 29, 31, 51, 52, 80, 83, 111, 112, 113, 126
Thicke, Inspector William 12
Thomas, Dr. G. Danford 4
Thompson, Police Constable Ernest 32
Thorneycroft's Torpedo Works 26
Thorpe, Dr. 78
Times of London press report 194
Toon, Mrs. Jessie 83, 96, 97, 101, 122, 137; coroner's inquest testimony 123, 126; Police Court testimony 137; trial testimony 166–7
Toronto, Canada 188
Trial: jury charge 181; prosecution rebuttal 180–1; speech for the defense 179–80; speech for the prosecution 155–6; verdict and sentence 181–2
Trial of George Chapman 96, 128, 145, 173, 190
Trial testimony March 16, 1903 155–161; March 17, 1903 162–169; March 18, 1903 170–177; March 19, 1903 178–182
Trunk of a Female 33
Tull, Mr. William 79, 177
Tumblety, "Dr." Francis 194
"Tuppeny Tube" 86

The Ultimate Jack the Ripper Companion 197
Unicorn Tavern 5
United States 34, 35, 36, 37, 54, 74, 92, 100, 110
Unknown Torso 34, 35
Union Street 76, 82, 142

Victor, Prince Albert 50
Victoria, Queen 3, 50
Victoria Park 17
Victoria Street 195
Vigilance Committee 9, 18, 20

Waesland 37, 196

Waldo, Dr. F. J. 103, 115, 120, 123, 125; coroner's inquest testimony 127; Police Court testimony 134
Walters, Police Superintendent 118
Water Street 90
Ward, John 58, 142
Ward, Mrs. 58, 142
Ward, Queen Victoria 90, 91, 121
Ward, Susan 10
Warren, Sir Charles 16, 19, 21, 23, 128; Confidential Report 15–6
Warrinfton 73
Warsaw, Poland 1, 2, 53, 147
Watney's Brewery 89
Waymark, Mrs. Elizabeth 68, 69; case testimony on Spink 69; Police Court testimony 148; trial testimony 174
Welles, Orson 191, 192, 193
Wensley, Police Constable Frederick P. 32
Wentworth Street 32
Wenzel, William 58
Wenzel's 59
West Croydon 31, 82, 83, 85, 87, 95, 116, 117, 120, 122
West Green Road (No. 5) 51, 142
"White Duster" 89
White Hart Public House 61, 141, 157, 160
Whitechapel 4, 5, 6, 10, 19, 21, 22, 24, 25, 27, 31, 42, 48, 49, 53, 54, 58, 75, 89, 90, 141, 142, 143, 160, 184, 185, 187, 188, 189, 190, 194
Whitechapel High Street 13, 61
Whitechapel Killer 10, 14, 27, 30, 55, 60, 190
Whitechapel Murder report 30–1
Whitehall Mystery 56
Whiting, Charles 111, 112
Wicken, Alfred 51; trial testimony 159
Wilde, Oscar 152
William Hodge & Company 188
Wilson, Ada 5, 34, 35

Zagowski, Ludwig 52, 141, 142

www.ingramcontent.com/pod-product-compliance
Ingram Content Group UK Ltd.
Pitfield, Milton Keynes, MK11 3LW, UK
UKHW050528150426
5217IPUK00026B/1849